THE ART and SCIENCE of PSYCHOTHERAPY

THE ART and
SCIENCE of
PSYCHOTHERAPY

Edited by
Stefan G. Hofmann
Joel Weinberger

Routledge
Taylor & Francis Group
New York   London

Routledge is an imprint of the
Taylor & Francis Group, an informa business

Routledge
Taylor & Francis Group
270 Madison Avenue
New York, NY 10016

Routledge
Taylor & Francis Group
2 Park Square
Milton Park, Abingdon
Oxon OX14 4RN

Printed in the United States of America on acid-free paper
10 9 8 7 6 5 4 3 2 1

International Standard Book Number-10: 0-415-95215-8 (Hardcover)
International Standard Book Number-13: 978-0-415-95215-6 (Hardcover)

Library of Congress Cataloging-in-Publication Data

The art and science of psychotherapy / Stefan G. Hofmann, Joel Weinberger, editors.
    p. cm.
    ISBN 0-415-95215-8 (hb)
    1. Psychotherapy. 2. Psychotherapy--Philosophy. I. Hofmann, Stefan G. II. Weinberger, Joel L.

RC480.A78 2007
616.89'14--dc22
                                         2006027421

Visit the Taylor & Francis Web site at
http://www.taylorandfrancis.com

and the Routledge Web site at
http://www.routledge-ny.com

Contents

About the Editors   ix

Contributors   xi

The Art and Science of Psychotherapy: An Introduction   xvii

Stefan G. Hofmann and Joel Weinberger

SECTION I   *Theoretical Issues*

1   Discovering What Works in the Community:
Toward a Genuine Partnership of Clinicians and Researchers 3

Drew Westen

2   Methodcentric Reasoning and the Empirically Supported
Treatment Debates 31

Mark A. Blais and Mark J. Hilsenroth

3   An Integrative, Principle-Based Approach to Psychotherapy 49

John E. Pachankis and Marvin R. Goldfried

4   Efficacy, Effectiveness, and the Clinical Utility of
Psychotherapy Research 69

Peter E. Nathan

5   The Local Clinical Scientist 85

George Stricker

SECTION II   Nonspecific and Common Factors

6   Empirically Supported Common Factors................................... 103

         Joel Weinberger and Cristina Rasco

7   Toward the Integration of Technical Interventions,
         Relationship Factors, and Participants Variables....................... 131

         David Clinton, Elaine Gierlach, Sanno E. Zack,
         Larry E. Beutler, and Louis G. Castonguay

8   Alliance Ruptures: Theory, Research, and Practice 155

         Karyn D. Ruiz-Cordell and Jeremy D. Safran

9   Understanding and Working with Resistant Ambivalence in
         Psychotherapy: An Integrative Approach 171

         Hal Arkowitz and David Engle

SECTION III   Treatments of Axis I Disorders

10   General Principles for the Treatment of Emotional Disorders
         Across the Lifespan.. 191

         Jill T. Ehrenreich, Brian A. Buzzella, and David H. Barlow

11   The Art of Evidence-Based Treatment of Trauma Survivors 211

         Brett T. Litz and Kristalyn Salters-Pedneault

SECTION IV   Treatments of Axis II Disorders

12   Personality Diagnosis with the Shedler-Westen
         Assessment Procedure (SWAP): Bridging the Gulf Between
         Science and Practice.. 233

         Jonathan Shedler

13   The "Art" of Interpreting the "Science" and the "Science" of Interpreting the "Art" of the Treatment of Borderline Personality Disorder.. 269

Kenneth N. Levy and Lori N. Scott

Conclusions Let a Hundred Flowers Bloom; Let One Hundred Schools of Thought Contend... 301

Joel Weinberger and Stefan G. Hofmann

Index.. 307

About the Editors

Stefan G. Hofmann, Ph.D., is an associate professor at the Department of Clinical Psychology at Boston University and the director of the social anxiety program at the Center for Anxiety and Related Disorders. He received his Ph.D. (1993) from the University of Marburg, Germany. His main research interests are in the area of psychotherapy research, anxiety disorders, especially social phobia, and the psychophysiology of emotions. He is an Aaron T. Beck Scholar and the recipient of numerous awards, including a First Independent Research and Transition Award from the National Institute of Mental Health, two Young Investigator Awards by the Alliance for Research on Schizophrenia and Depression, and awards from the Anxiety Disorders Association of America and the Association for Clinical Psychosocial Research. He is editor of *Cognitive and Behavioral Practice*, associate editor of *Cognitive Behaviour Therapy* and the *International Journal of Psychology*, and is a member of the editorial board of various journals. He has published more than 100 books, book chapters, and articles, including the popular text (together with Dr. Martha Tompson) *Treating Chronic and Severe Mental Disorders: A Handbook of Empirically Supported Interventions*.

Joel Weinberger, Ph.D., received his doctorate in clinical psychology from the New School for Social Research and completed a postdoctoral fellowship in human motivation at Harvard University. He is currently professor of psychology at the Derner Institute of Advanced Psychological Studies at Adelphi University. He is author or co-author of more than 60 published articles and chapters. His interests include unconscious processes, personality, motivation, and effective components of psychotherapy. Dr. Weinberger has co-edited (with Dr. Todd Heatherton) a book on personality change. He received a First Award from NIMH. He was conferred the Ulf Kragh Award (University of Lundh, Sweden) for his work on unconscious processes. Dr. Weinberger is also a practicing clinical psychologist.

Contributors

Hal Arkowitz, Ph.D., is associate professor of psychology at the University of Arizona. He has published in the areas of anxiety, depression, psychotherapy, and psychotherapy integration. He is co-author of *Ambivalence in Psychotherapy: Facilitating Readiness to Change* and has co-edited *Psychoanalytic and Behavior Therapy: Toward an Integration,* and the *Comprehensive Handbook of Cognitive Therapy.* For 10 years, he served as editor of the *Journal of Psychotherapy Integration.* Since receiving his Ph.D., he has also maintained an active clinical practice and values the interplay between research and practice.

David H. Barlow, Ph.D., received his doctorate from the University of Vermont in 1969 and has published over 500 articles, chapters, and books mostly in the area of the nature and treatment of emotional disorders. He is the recipient of numerous awards, including the distinguished Scientific Award for Applications of Psychology from the American Psychological Association.

Larry E. Beutler, Ph.D., is distinguished professor and former chair, and director of training at the Pacific Graduate School of Psychology in Palo Alto, California. Dr. Beutler is the past editor of the *Journal of Clinical Psychology* and of the *Journal of Consulting and Clinical Psychology.* He is a fellow of the American Psychological Association and the American Psychological Society. He is the past-president of the Society for Clinical Psychology (Division 12 of APA), a past-president of the Division of Psychotherapy (APA), and a two-term past-president of the (International) Society for Psychotherapy Research (SPR). He is the recipient of the Distinguished Career Award from SPR and of a Presidential citation from the American Psychological Association. He is the author of approximately 300 scientific papers and chapters, and is the author, editor, or co-author of 14 books on psychotherapy and psychopathology. Dr. Beutler is the co-editor (with L. G. Castonguay) of a task force report, titled "Principles of Therapeutic Change that Work" that was co-sponsored by the Society of Clinical Psychology (Division 12) and the North American Society for Psychotherapy Research.

Mark A. Blais, Psy.D., graduated from Nova Southeastern University in 1990 where he specialized in psychodynamic psychology and psychological assessment.

He is currently associate chief of psychology at Massachusetts General Hospital and associate professor of psychology at Harvard Medical School. His professional activities include teaching and supervising psychology interns, providing psychological and neuropsychological assessment consultations, and conducting individual psychotherapy. His research interests include evaluating psychiatric treatment outcomes and studying personality development and its disorders.

Brian A. Buzzella is currently pursuing his doctorate in clinical psychology at Boston University. His research interests include the developmental progression and treatment of emotional disorders in childhood and adolescence. Currently, he is working on a parent-training manual for the treatment of children with Selective Mutism.

Louis Castonguay, Ph.D., completed his doctorate in clinical psychology at the State University of New York at Stony Brook and a postdoctorate at Stanford University. He is currently an associate professor at the Department of Psychology at The Pennsylvania State University. His empirical work focuses on the process of change in different forms of psychotherapy, the efficacy of integrative treatments, and the conduct of effectiveness studies (especially in the context of Practice Research Networks). He is former president of the North American Society for Psychotherapy Research and recipient of the Early Career Contribution Award from the Society of Psychotherapy Research, the David Shakow Early Career Award from the Division of Clinical Psychology of the American Psychological Association, the Jack D. Krasner Memorial Award and the Distinguished Psychologist Award from the Division of Psychotherapy of the American Psychological Association, as well as other research awards.

David Clinton is a Ph.D. student at Pacific Graduate School of Psychology in Palo Alto, California. He plans to be both a practitioner and a researcher of psychotherapy process and has co-authored several articles on prescriptive psychotherapy and systematic treatment selection.

Jill T. Ehrenreich, Ph.D., received her doctorate in 2002 from the University of Mississippi. She is research assistant professor of psychology and associate director of the Child Program in the Center for Anxiety and Related Disorders at Boston University, where her research focuses on the etiology and treatment of adolescent anxiety and depression.

David Engle, Ph.D., has been a practitioner and instructor of gestalt and experiential psychotherapy for many years. He is a co-author of *Focused Expressive Psychotherapy and Ambivalence in Psychotherapy: Facilitating Readiness to Change.* He is also author or co-author of numerous articles about the treatment effects of experiential approaches to therapy. He has been a summer faculty member at the University of Arizona. Dr. Engle was the coordinator of the

Arizona Psychotherapy Project at the University of Arizona College of Medicine for five years. He is currently in private practice in Tucson, Arizona and has a special interest in the psychosocial effects of chronic disease on patients.

Elaine Gierlach is working on a Ph.D. in clinical psychology at the Pacific Graduate School of Psychology in Palo Alto, California. She is a research assistant and program director of the Medical Reserve Corps program within the National Center for the Psychology of Terrorism.

Marvin R. Goldfried, Ph.D., is distinguished professor of psychology at Stony Brook University. He is a diplomate in clinical psychology and recipient of numerous awards from the American Psychological Association, and awards from the Association for Advancement of Behavior Therapy (AABT) and the Society for Psychotherapy Research (SPR). He is past president of SPR, founder of the journal *In Session: Psychotherapy in Practice*, and author of numerous articles and books. Dr. Goldfried is cofounder of the Society for the Exploration of Psychotherapy Integration (SEPI) and founder of AFFIRM: Psychologists Affirming Their Lesbian, Gay, Bisexual and Transgender Family (www.sunysb.edu/affirm).

Mark J. Hilsenroth, Ph.D., is an associate professor at the Derner Institute for Advanced Psychological Studies, Adelphi University. He is a diplomate of the American Board of Assessment Psychology (ABAP). He has published broadly in the areas of applied clinical practice, specifically psychological assessment and psychotherapy. Dr. Hilsenroth has served as an associate editor for the *Journal of Personality Assessment* and currently is on the editorial boards of *The Clinical Supervisor, Psychotherapy, Psychotherapy Research,* and *Stress, Trauma & Crisis: An International Journal.*

Kenneth N. Levy, Ph.D., is an assistant professor in the Department of Psychology at The Pennsylvania State University. Dr. Levy is also an adjunct assistant professor of psychology in psychiatry at the Joan and Sanford I. Weill Medical College of Cornell University. His primary interests are in attachment theory, social cognition, emotion regulation, borderline personality disorder, and mechanisms of change in psychotherapy.

Brett Litz, Ph.D., is a professor in the Department of Psychiatry at Boston University School of Medicine. Dr. Litz conducts research on the risk and resilience factors that affect mental health adaptation to trauma across the life span, various forms of early intervention for trauma, and emotional-regulation in trauma-linked disorders. In his capacity as associate director of the Behavioral Sciences Division of the National Center for PTSD at the VA Boston Health Care System, Dr. Litz is responsible for overseeing educational activities pertaining to clinical care and research.

Peter E. Nathan, Ph.D., is currently University of Iowa Foundation Distinguished Professor of Psychology and Public Health. After receiving his doctorate in clinical psychology from Washington University, he spent seven years on the faculty of Harvard Medical School. He then joined the faculty of Rutgers University in 1969 where, from 1983 until 1989, he was Henry and Anna Starr Professor and Director of the Center of Alcohol Studies. After two years at the MacArthur Foundation in Chicago, between 1987 and 1989, on leave from Rutgers, he spent six years at the University of Iowa as provost. Dr. Nathan has been president of the Division of Clinical Psychology of the APA and the recipient of the APA Award for Distinguished Professional Contributions to Knowledge.

John Pachankis is completing his Ph.D. in clinical psychology at the State University of New York at Stony Brook. His research interests include identifying the effective components of psychotherapy for individuals facing identity-related stress. He is currently conducting research that examines the mental health implications of possessing a concealable stigma.

Cristina Rasco is a second year doctoral candidate at Adelphi University in Clinical Psychology. Her interests in the field are in unconscious processes, psychotherapy research, and treating culturally diverse populations.

Karyn Ruiz-Cordell is an advanced Ph.D. candidate in clinical psychology at the New School for Social Research in New York City.

Jeremy D. Safran, Ph.D., is professor and director of clinical psychology at the New School for Social Research in New York City. He is also senior research scientist at Beth Israel Medical Center, and on faculty at the New York University Postdoctoral Program in Psychotherapy and Psychoanalysis. He has published several books including: *Emotion in Psychotherapy, Interpersonal Process in Cognitive Therapy, Widening the Scope of Cognitive Therapy, Negotiating the Therapeutic Alliance: A Relational Treatment Guide,* and *Psychoanalysis and Buddhism: An Unfolding Dialogue.*

Kristalyn Salters-Pedneault, Ph.D., is a postdoctoral fellow at the National Center for PTSD Behavioral Science Division, VA Boston Healthcare System. Her research focuses on operant and associative conditioning processes as they relate to the emotional disruption typical of chronic PTSD. She is also interested in how contemporary learning research may improve interventions for PTSD and other trauma-linked conditions.

Lori N. Scott is a doctoral student in clinical psychology at The Pennsylvania State University. She is interested in social cognition, mechanisms of change in psychotherapy, and borderline personality disorder.

Jonathan Shedler, Ph.D., is clinical associate professor at the University of Denver and associate clinical professor at the University of Colorado Health

Sciences Center. He has authored scientific papers on a wide range of topics in psychology and psychiatry and is co-author of the *Shedler-Westen Assessment Procedure* for personality diagnosis.

George Stricker, Ph.D., is professor of psychology at Argosy University, Washington, D.C. He received the American Psychological Association (APA) Award for Distinguished Contribution to Applied Psychology, the APA Award for Distinguished Career Contributions to Education and Training in Psychology, the Florence Halpern Award for Distinguished Professional Contributions in Clinical Psychology from the Society of Clinical Psychology (Division 12), and the Bruno Klopfer Lifetime Achievement Award from the Society for Personality Assessment. He has been president of the Division of Clinical Psychology of APA, the Society for Personality Assessment, and the National Council of Schools of Professional Psychology. His most recent books are *A Case Book of Psychotherapy Integration*, with Jerry Gold, and *The Scientific Practice of Professional Psychology*, with Steven Trierweiler.

Drew Westen, Ph.D., is professor, Departments of Psychology and Psychiatry and Behavioral Sciences, and director of the Clinical Psychology Program at Emory University. Prior to joining the faculty at Emory, he taught at the University of Michigan, Harvard Medical School, and Boston University. Professor Westen is both a clinician and an active researcher, who has written upwards of 100 scientific papers and 2 books, and has been funded on his work on the classification of personality pathology in adolescents and adults by the National Institutes of Mental Health. He is currently an investigator on an NIMH Center Grant on biological and psychosocial predictors of treatment response in first-episode major depression. His major areas of research are personality and personality disorders, adolescent psychopathology, psychotherapy, eating disorders, emotion regulation, emotional influences on political decision making, and the intersection of psychodynamics and cognitive neuroscience. He has been a commentator for *All Things Considered* on National Public Radio (NPR) and has performed as a stand-up comic. He is currently working on a book, tentatively titled, *The Political Brain: And What Happens When You Don't Use It.*

Sanno E. Zack is a doctoral candidate at The Pennsylvania State University, working with Louis Castonguay. She has life span clinical interests and conducts research related to adolescent psychotherapy process and outcome.

The Art and Science of Psychotherapy: An Introduction

STEFAN G. HOFMANN AND JOEL WEINBERGER

Psychotherapy is an *art* and a *science*. It is a *science* because therapeutic techniques should be empirically supported and rooted in falsifiable models of the psychological problem that is being treated. Psychotherapy is also an *art* because these techniques need to be applied flexibly and creatively to a specific person. Therefore, an effective therapist needs to be knowledgeable in the science of psychotherapy while at the same time being able to apply the techniques artfully to a specific client and problem.

Nevertheless, our discipline is divided. Some clinicians have developed specific and protocolized interventions to modify the problem behaviors and distress associated with a particular diagnosis. Some have conducted randomized controlled trials to examine the relative efficacy of a study treatment compared to a control condition. The treatments that follow this efficacy approach have been termed *empirically supported treatments* or ESTs, and have been held to represent the *science* aspect of psychotherapy.

The EST movement has been highly controversial. Opponents of this movement criticize it because they believe that a number of important variables are ignored that are considered central for conducting effective psychotherapy are ignored. These variables, which are often associated with what many see as the *art* of psychotherapy, include *common factors*, such as the client-therapist relationship and other aspects of treatment that cut across or are common to the different kinds of psychotherapy. Additionally, common factors such as the therapeutic relationship can be studied scientifically so that the EST movement does not have a monopoly on science. Similarly, ESTs need to be and usually are applied flexibly and creatively. They therefore have what can be considered an artistic component, as we have defined it. So what we have called science (ESTs) and art (relationship and common factors), in accordance with how they are often seen in the literature, actually contain aspects of both. This, we believe, has led to some of the acrimony between the two as EST supporters insist that they are not advocating rigid adherence to technique and common factor supporters resent their points being referred to as nonspecific and/or nonscientific.

An effective clinician, whether she supports the EST or common factor/therapeutic relationship approach, needs to be both an artist and a scientist. A good therapist needs to have knowledge about specific treatment strategies in order to treat a particular problem and also needs to be able to create the appropriate relationship with the patient and make use of common factors in order to treat a particular person. Although these two sets of skills are not in the least incompatible, the field of clinical psychology is split into researchers and scholars who approach psychological problems similar to medical conditions to develop disorder-specific treatment techniques in efficacy studies, or who focus on effectiveness, common factors, and the study of the process of psychotherapy.

Managed health care has further polarized these two groups, which has led to heated debates around the report by the APA Division 12 (Society of Clinical Psychology) Task Force on Promotion and Dissemination of Psychological Procedures. In an effort to identify problems in the dissemination of psychological interventions, this Task Force constructed a list of efficacious treatments (*empirically supported treatments*) for various mental disorders, including anxiety, depression, substance use problems, and personality disorder (e.g., Chambless & Hollon, 1998). In an effort to offer an alternative to the recommendations of this Task Force, Division 29 (Division of Psychotherapy) of the APA formed its own Task Force on Empirically Supported Therapy Relationships with the objective to identify effective elements of the therapy relationship (*empirically supported relationships, ESR*) and to determine effective means of tailoring them to the individual patient (e.g., Norcross, 2002).

Whereas previous books have sufficiently identified and summarized selected empirically supported treatments, including a recently published volume co-edited by one of us (Hofmann & Tompson, 2002), little attempt has been made to summarize so-called unspecific and common factors in psychotherapy. The goal of this book is to facilitate communications between these two schools of thought, to synthesize the two practice guidelines described by Divisions 12 and 29, and to provide clinicians with balanced training in specific treatment technique and general therapy skills.

The two editors of this book are associated with each of the two opposing camps: Stefan G. Hofmann has been trained as a clinical scientist, has been conducting clinical trials in anxiety disorders, and has been teaching a seminar entitled "Empirically Supported Treatments for Psychological Disorders at Boston University. Joel Weinberger is a psychodynamically oriented scholar, teacher, and clinician who believes that common factors are essential for effective psychotherapy. We believe that our differences are complementary, not incompatible. We hope we represent an example for future EST/ESR alliances.

The text consists of 13 chapters organized into four main sections: (I) Theoretical Issues, (II) Nonspecific and Common Factors, (III) Treatments of Axis I disorders, and (IV) Treatments of Axis II disorders. All chapters were written by experts in the respective fields with a clear emphasis on the practical relevance and *how to* aspect of therapy. In order to achieve this goal, we asked our contributors to include case examples and patient-client dialogues whenever feasible.

Our hope is that this text not only facilitates communications between these schools of thought, but also that the combined expertise from these two movements will benefit those who matter the most in this debate: our patients.

REFERENCES

Chambless, D. L., & Hollon, S. D. (1998). Defining empirically supported therapies. *Journal of Consulting and Clinical Psychology, 66,* 7–18.

Hofmann, S. G., & Tompson, M. C. (Eds.) (2002). *Treating chronic and severe mental disorders: A handbook of empirically supported interventions.* New York: Guilford Press.

Norcross, J. C. (2002). *Psychotherapy relationships that work: Therapist contributions and responsiveness to patients.* New York: Oxford University Press.

Section I
THEORETICAL ISSUES

1

Discovering What Works in the Community

Toward a Genuine Partnership of Clinicians and Researchers

DREW WESTEN

These may be the most acrimonious times between clinicians and researchers in the history of our field. The relationship has never been an easy one, generally characterized on both sides by feelings of superiority and occasional public snipes. But the present era represents the confluence of three forces that have changed the nature of the relationship.

The first is the near-ubiquity of managed care, which has been a disaster for mental health. Managed care has been problematic in many areas of medicine, but it has been especially damaging in psychology and psychiatry, given our culture's implicit attitudes toward mental health. We do not, for example, put patients with heart disease out on the street when we have difficulty treating their symptoms. Schizophrenia patients suffer a very different fate, simply by virtue of having chosen the wrong organ in which to develop a disease.

The second force that has changed the relation between clinicians and researchers is the capitalization of academia, reflecting the tremendous importance to universities of capturing indirect costs on research grants—typically on the order of 50 to 70 cents to the university for every dollar of grant money awarded to an investigator—which creates enormous (and understandable) incentives for universities to select faculty with strong grant records. This has shifted the priority of questions raised in tenure and hiring decisions from quality of thought and research to quantity of dollars. Research dollars are, of course, often a reasonable proxy measure for quality of research, with, perhaps, a moderate $r = .40$.[1] The existence of federal funding in the United States (and governmental grants in other countries) has no doubt vastly improved the methodological rigor of psychological and psychiatric research. At the same time, the shift from scholarship to grantsmanship as the primary index of prestige and accomplishment in our field has placed severe limits on creative thinking, dissenting views, and, most importantly, on *clinically* informed research, because academics no longer have time to "waste" on practice when they have grants to write, staff who need salaries and continuity without funding lapses (which requires constant attention to grant cycles), and so forth.[2]

The primacy of funding demands has also placed a premium on *doing* rather than *thinking* in clinical psychology (see Wachtel, 1973), minimizing the emphasis once placed on reflection implied by a Doctor of Philosophy (Ph.D.)—and particularly reflection on one's own assumptions and meta-assumptions. I suspect Kuhn's (1962) description of the stranglehold of paradigms on scientific progress would have been even more dire if he were writing a contemporary history of psychotherapy research. Today, getting an academic job, negotiating a salary (or receiving any salary at all, now that medical schools have virtually eliminated hard money, forcing researchers to study whatever their colleagues think is important), and virtually everything else important to an academic career all hinge on convincing committees of the value of one's ideas and methods.

Having served on many such committees as both a standing and ad hoc member, I can attest to the good will, integrity, and sound intellect and knowledge base of the overwhelming majority of reviewers. But I can also attest to the conservative biases that can inadvertently creep into the review process when innovative proposals are compared to business-as-usual proposals. Innovative proposals are, by definition, risky proposals. They employ less tried-and-true methods and present different payoff matrices—notably, large gains if they succeed and large losses (wasted time and funding) if they do not. Such payoff matrices are likely to raise the anxiety of at least one of the three to four reviewers who must unanimously agree on the merits of the proposal for it to have a reasonable chance of funding given scarcity of resources, leading to admonitions of caution, concerns about possible departures from standard methods, and the search for fatal flaws. The problem is amplified in psychotherapy research, where virtually all committee members tend to share the same methodological and theoretical assumptions—because they have all been funded by a system that selects for those assumptions—creating a state of affairs that violates all of the conditions that render scientific method more useful than clinical consensus or expert opinion.

The third force shaping the relationship between clinicians and researchers is the evidence based practice (EBP) movement in medicine, which has been an essential step forward in principle but a mixed blessing in reality. In psychology, until a recent policy statement by the American Psychological Association that

I hope will reshape the terms of the debate in positive ways (APA Task Force on Evidence Based Practice, 2006), EBP has been operationalized exclusively as the utilization of brief manualized therapies tested in randomized clinical trials (RCTs). As described below, although the use of clinical trials methodologies is an essential component of EBP, the assumption that empirically supported therapies (ESTs) of this sort provide the basis for practice not only discounts the ideas, trial and error (and hence operant conditioning of technical strategies), and procedural knowledge that may emerge from years of clinical practice but, as importantly, de facto relegates *basic* science (e.g., on cognition, emotion, interpersonal functioning, persuasion, implicit processes, etc.) to irrelevance for EBP.

The convergence of these forces has led to a state of affairs in our field in which many researchers not only devalue clinicians and clinical practice but also are attempting to prescribe and proscribe how clinicians should practice. Most of the leading journals in clinical psychology are edited by researchers who do not themselves practice, and regardless of their explicit attitudes, their implicit attitudes toward practice are manifest in invited articles and special sections on errors in clinical judgment (without corresponding articles on errors in research judgment, which in my experience are equally substantial) and on how clinicians should replace their foolish folk ways with researchers' empirically supported but clinically often naïve notions about how people who *do* practice should think about, assess, and treat patients (e.g., Garb, 2005; Widiger & Trull, 2005).

With a handful of exceptions,[3] clinical training is increasingly being routed out of the top programs in clinical psychology, which often place clear admonitions to applicants with primarily clinical interests not to apply. Indeed, I now advise our brightest, most socially skilled undergraduates (i.e., those who are, empirically, likely to be the best clinicians) at Emory (GPAs above 3.7, GREs in the 700s, a rigorous grounding in psychological science and methods) who value research but primarily want to *practice* clinical psychology to take the following strategy in identifying appropriate graduate programs: Obtain the *U.S. News and World Report* national rankings of clinical psychology programs, put a big *X* through the top 25, and start looking at the Web sites of the next 25. I also advise them to look at counseling programs with a good balance of research and practice and a range of theoretical perspectives offered and at Psy.D. programs with the highest faculty-to-student ratios and the lowest applicant acceptance rates.

This advice is borne of sad experience. I cannot count the number of times I have heard superbly bright students from some of the best clinical psychology programs in the country—including students who started out intending an academic career but came to prefer clinical work—describe how they had to "hide" their clinical interests or how they felt ashamed and alienated by professors who talked about how stupid clinicians are, how becoming a clinician is a bad outcome of graduate training, and so forth.[4] Ironically, the main effect of this "clinicism" (Westen & Weinberger, 2004)—the devalued view of clinicians and clinical practice—has been to send the most clinically talented students to clinical psychology programs that place the least emphasis on science, as they increasingly learn to avoid programs where their interests—including their interests in scientifically informed practice—may be unwelcome. To be sure, Boulder-model programs still exist. However, in my estimation, the correlation between national rankings (which largely reflect research and grant productivity, as they largely, but not exclusively, should) and the value placed on clinical experience is strongly negative, in part simply because of limits in the number of hours in the day (for both students and faculty) and in part because of a rising class of academic clinicians who hold (and implicitly convey, even when they explicitly deny them) strongly negative biases toward clinicians and clinical work.

I should perhaps declare my allegiance here from the start in this not-so-civil war. I am a full-time academic. Of the 60 hours or so a week I spend away from my family, roughly 20 are devoted to professional and administrative responsibilities (running a program, reviewing manuscripts and grant proposals, teaching, attending meetings, etc.), roughly 35 are devoted to research and writing, and roughly 5 are devoted to clinical practice. What is frightening is that this puts me in the upper percentiles among academic clinical psychologists in the number of clinical hours I maintain.

Let me add that I have no illusions about clinicians; nor am I longing for the "good old days," when only one or two faculty members at some of the most highly esteemed clinical psychology programs in the country (e.g., the University of Michigan, where I received my Ph.D.) even knew that regression was a statistical technique (and not just a psychoanalytic construct). Although the research evidence suggests that most clinicians in the community actually do quite well by their patients (see Wampold, 2001), I would not refer a patient to many of my colleagues in the community. And many clinicians do not keep abreast of scientific developments that might be helpful to their patients.

However, as academics, we do little to make our articles in scholarly journals, and particularly in the flagship journals of our field, either accessible or useful to clinicians, which I believe accounts for most of the variance in clinicians' failure to read what we have to say. One of the most important steps we could take to bring science to practice would be to do something akin to what the journal *Science* does, namely to hire a competent "bilingual" psychologist (i.e., one who understands how to read research but also practices—I know several such individuals) to write periodic articles, in language directed at clinicians who may not keep abreast of the latest developments in structural equation modeling, to introduce, tie together, and highlight the clinical implications of selected articles in each issue of the *Journal of Consulting and Clinical Psychology* and the *Journal of Abnormal Psychology*.[5]

Publishing review articles in prestigious journals about the silly errors clinicians make, referring in our literature to the work of overburdened paraprofessionals in community mental health centers as *treatment as usual* or *treatment in the community*, and studiously refusing to compare our academic treatments of choice to the treatments practiced by experienced professionals send a clear metamessage to clinicians about the academic clinical psychology community's attitude toward them and can only sabotage efforts at disseminating relevant research findings to practitioners (Westen, Novotny, & Thompson-Brenner, 2005). These practices also betray an assumption—and one I believe is seriously mistaken—that bottom-up innovations (from practice to science) have little place in knowledge development in clinical science (see Westen & Weinberger, 2005).

My experience presenting to clinical audiences suggests that most clinicians are actually hungry to hear about new data and new methods that might help them with their patients, particularly with patients who do not respond to their usual methods or who are difficult to treat—as long as I am respectful of their knowledge and of the problems they encounter with real patients. I have probably sold more copies of Dave Barlow's *Anxiety and Its Disorders* (2002) in talks and workshop presentations than anyone other than Dave Barlow, particularly when I speak to psychodynamic clinicians who may not otherwise have been exposed to the research on cognitive behavioral therapy (CBT) for panic.

As my colleagues and I have argued elsewhere (Westen, Novotny, & Thompson-Brenner, 2005), most clinicians would like to be partners with researchers in a bidirectional exchange of ideas to learn what would be most helpful to their patients. They do not, however, care to be disseminated at or disseminated on, particularly by backseat drivers who may not even have a license. I suspect researchers would not take kindly to being told how to practice *their* craft (which is equally an admixture of artful innovation and rigorous attention to scientific method and data) by clinicians who had not done a study since their dissertation but thought that the quality of research would be improved by requiring researchers to follow manuals directing them how to tackle complex research questions the clinicians had never themselves actually addressed empirically.

THE PRESENT CHAPTER

No sensible participant in the current debate about the value of ESTs denies the value of RCTs (Chambless & Ollendick, 2000; Norcross, Beutler, & Levant, 2006; Wampold, 2001; Westen, Novotny, & Thompson-Brenner, 2004b; Westen, Novotny, & Thompson-Brenner, 2004b). Just as there is nothing so practical as a good theory, there is nothing so causally decisive as a good experiment (or, more accurately, a meta-analytic aggregation of a body of such experiments). The major question is the extent to which RCTs as they have been conducted to date provide answers to the questions most important to everyday clinical practice. This chapter reflects the view that evidence based practice is as essential in psychotherapy as in all areas of medicine, and that the best way to learn about what works and for whom is to triangulate on conclusions using multiple designs, including traditional efficacy designs (RCTs), more naturalistic designs that differentially balance internal and external validity, and designs that allow identification and testing of intervention strategies that work in the community.

The first part of this chapter argues that clinically sensible, evidence based practice requires both a broader knowledge base in basic science and a greater emphasis on procedural knowledge obtained through clinical experience and trial and error than the application of empirically supported therapies—akin to the creative but nonarbitrary, scientifically grounded process of designing a research study. It suggests that RCTs could be used in far more effective ways if researchers attended to aspects of experimental design and credibility to experienced clinicians such as using scientifically appropriate control conditions (most importantly, clinicians in the community attempting to do their best work) and patient samples resembling those seen in the community seeking treatment for the kinds of problems that lead most patients to present for treatment. The remainder of the chapter describes a complementary methodology to the use of RCTs to test researcher-developed manualized treatments. This methodology brings researchers and clinicians together in a collaborative enterprise aimed at learning, first, whether manualized treatments in fact outperform the practices of experienced clinicians, something that we currently do not know; and second, whether experienced clinicians are doing anything in practice from which we as researchers might learn.

The hybrid designs I am proposing build on many advantages of both efficacy and effectiveness studies (i.e., studies that maximize internal validity, or experimental rigor, and those that maximize external validity, or generalizability to real patients in everyday practice).[6] Indeed, they make use of RCT methodology in the community, not only to test manualized therapies against established practice but also to see if there might be something to learn from the clinicians and interventions on the right tail of the distribution of clinical outcomes. The goal of such an alternative methodology is to see what might be learned if clinicians and researchers were to form a genuine partnership that did not assume that one or the other already knows the answers to the questions at the heart of clinical practice and optimal patient care. Throughout, I use examples from the literature on bulimia nervosa (BN), which in many respects presents prototypical problems faced by practitioners who must keep an eye on both overt (and often quite dangerous) symptoms and on the personality diatheses that render patients vulnerable to these symptoms and to symptomatic exacerbations (see Westen, Gabbard, & Blagov, 2006; Westen, Thompson-Brenner, & Peart, 2006).

EMPIRICALLY SUPPORTED COMPLEXITY

The prototypical efficacy study over the last 20 years has a number of characteristics (Goldfried & Wolfe, 1998): (1) Treatments are designed for a single disorder; (2) patients are screened not only for inclusion (i.e., having the disorder under consideration) but also to rule out patient characteristics (e.g., particular forms of comorbidity) that could render causal inference more difficult; (3) outcome assessment focuses primarily on the symptom or syndrome that is the focus of the study; (4) treatments are of brief and fixed duration; and (5) treatments are manualized.

In many respects these characteristics make good scientific sense, allowing researchers to discern cause and effect. Given the limited sample size attainable in most studies for pragmatic reasons, some degree of homogeneity is essential to minimize within-condition variation in outcome, which reduces power. The focus on a single disorder also makes sense in minimizing sample heterogeneity. If patients present with different symptoms, it is difficult to know which interventions account for change in particular symptoms, especially with samples of 20–50 per group. The reasons for fixed duration are equally compelling; if comparison conditions differ in length, length could be an important confound. The advantages of brevity lie in cost-containment and experimental control: Long treatments introduce substantial latitude for clinician variability in choice of interventions, targets, and so forth that can threaten standardization. Manualization similarly serves the functioning of standardizing the treatment delivered.

On the other hand, numerous researchers, including many leading psychotherapy researchers and methodologists (e.g., Borkovec & Castonguay, 1998; Kazdin, 1997), have noted limitations of the efficacy designs that have constituted the state of the art in psychotherapy research for two decades. Elsewhere (Westen & Morrison, 2001; Westen, Novotny, & Thompson-Brenner, 2004b; Westen, Novotny, & Thompson-Brenner, 2004b) my colleagues and I have argued that efficacy designs used to identify ESTs reflect a series of potentially problematic empirical assumptions that limit their applicability to patients in everyday practice. Although some commentators have questioned whether all of these assumptions are inherent in the designs used to identify ESTs (Crits-Christoph, Wilson, & Hollon, 2005; Weisz, Weersing, & Henggeler, 2005), I simply note here that, empirically, the vast majority of efficacy studies conducted over the last decade do in fact have the design features we identified. The assumptions of EST methodology, and some of their empirical limitations, include the following.

Psychological Processes Are Highly Malleable

The *malleability assumption* is implicit in the treatment lengths used in virtually all ESTs, which typically range from 6 to 20 sessions. For patients with BN, for example, the modal treatment tested in RCTs is 19 to 20 sessions (Thompson-Brenner, Glass, & Westen, 2003). Although researchers converged on such brief treatments for many reasons, brevity is necessitated by a simple fact of experimental method as applied to psychotherapy: The longer the treatment, the more within-group variability; the more variability, the less one can draw precise causal conclusions. We know of few experiments in the history of psychology in which a manipulation intended to constitute a single experimental condition (and partially dependent on the subject's ongoing responses) approached 20 hours.

The malleability assumption appears to be valid for some disorders and treatments, notably anxiety syndromes characterized by an association between an identifiable stimulus or small set of stimuli and a conditioned emotional response (e.g., simple phobia, uncomplicated specific phobias, uncomplicated panic, where the stimuli are interoceptive cues such as shortness of breath or identifiable situational cues such as those that often precipitate agoraphobia). For most disorders, however, studies of both naturalistic and treated samples find that relapse and residual impairment are the rule rather than the exception. The natural course of eating disorders (EDs), for example, involves exacerbations and remissions, residual symptoms, and crossover between bulimic to anorexic symptoms (see, e.g., Eddy et al., 2002). Naturalistic studies of psychotherapy for a range of disorders find that patients often show substantial initial symptom relief in the first five to six sessions, buoyed by a supportive relationship with a presumed expert who helps instill hope (Howard, Lueger, Maling, & Martinovich, 1993; Kopta, Howard, Lowry, & Beutler, 1994). These findings mirror the findings of many RCTs, including RCTs for BN, where patients who do not show improvement by the sixth session generally do not improve (Agras et al., 2000; see also Wilson, 1999).

Psychopathology Is Independent of Personality

The *independence assumption* is inherent in a methodology that places a premium on brevity, given that no theory or research of which we are aware has ever suggested that fundamental aspects of personality can be altered in six to twenty 50-minute sessions, particularly when many such personality processes are encoded in implicit networks that take time to identify and longer to change (see Westen, 1998, 2000). For example, the primary treatments tested in RCTs for BN to date (behavior therapy, CBT, and interpersonal therapy [IPT]) were never intended to effect personality change. The IPT manual is explicit in its focus on *current* rather than *re*current interpersonal patterns. Although the CBT manual targets personality-related processes such as perfectionism where appropriate, time constraints limit the extent to which clinicians can attend to the range of ways perfectionism may express itself in the patient's life or to other personality processes.

A welcome recent development in the BN literature is the development of an expanded, more integrative transdiagnostic CBT manual for EDs (Fairburn, Cooper, & Shafran, 2003), although the time frame remains very brief (4–5 months). The only EST for personality disorders, Linehan's (1993) dialectical behavior therapy (DBT) for borderline personality disorder (BPD), takes a year to complete the first of several stages not yet developed (Linehan, 2002, personal communication). This treatment is efficacious in reducing high-risk behaviors and is increasingly being applied to BN patients (Safer, Telch, & Agras, 2001), but has not yet been shown to produce enduring changes in personality variables such as feelings of emptiness (see Linehan, Heard, & Armstrong, 1993).

Paradoxically, the movement to codify a list of ESTs for specific disorders has emerged at the same time as basic scientists have come to the conclusion that vulnerabilities based in personality account for much of the variance in psychiatric symptoms (Brown, Chorpita, & Barlow, 1998; Krueger, 2002; Mineka, Watson, & Clark, 1998; Watson & Clark, 1992; Westen, Gabbard, & Blagov, 2006). Research using structural equation modeling consistently finds that personality variables such as negative affectivity underlie an internalizing spectrum of pathology that includes all of the mood and anxiety disorders on axis I of *DSM-IV*, with each disorder comprising a substantial common component as well as the specific variance that has been the target of RCTs to date. The comorbidity of EDs, including BN, with mood and anxiety disorders suggests that internalizing pathology may represent one of the diatheses for EDs as well. Several other studies now suggest that different personality constellations (e.g., a constricted, overcontrolled style or an emotionally dysregulated, impulsive, undercontrolled style) are also associated with EDs (Westen & Harnden-Fischer, 2001; Westen, Thompson-Brenner, & Peart, 2006).

Most Patients Have Only One Discrete Syndrome or Can Be Treated as if They Do

The *discreteness assumption*—that patients can be treated as if they have one primary syndrome, or that patients with multiple diagnoses can be treated using multiple manuals sequentially—is inherent in the attempt to identify treatment packages targeting specific disorders. Without this assumption, researchers would need to test—and clinicians would need to learn—dozens of manuals to address all the possible interaction terms for even a handful of disorders (e.g., BN x panic disorder, BN x substance abuse, BN x panic x substance abuse).

The available evidence does not, however, support this assumption. Single-disorder presentations are the exception in both clinical practice and research settings (e.g., Kendler, Prescott, Myers, & Neale, 2003; Kessler et al., 1996). Most clinical syndromes are comorbid with other syndromes or with personality disorders, and the presence of co-occurring conditions, like the presence of personality pathology, augurs poorly for therapy outcome in many (but by no means all) disorders (see Westen, Novotny, & Thompson-Brenner, 2004b). Unfortunately, most RCTs impose so many exclusion criteria that explicitly or de facto exclude patients with severe personality pathology (e.g., the near-universal exclusion of patients with substance abuse and suicidal ideation from treatment studies of depression and BN, which together excludes most patients with borderline pathology) that we know little about personality moderators of response to many treatments even where this is assessed because of restricted range.

EST advocates often suggest addressing co-occurring symptoms by applying manuals sequentially, beginning with the most distressing or debilitating disorder first and then working one's way through manuals for the other disorders (Crits-Christoph, Wilson, & Hollon, 2005; Wilson, 1998). This strategy is likely to be problematic, however, when seemingly distinct syndromes reflect common diatheses or when the presence of multiple syndromes has emergent properties not reducible to each alone. In fact, little is currently understood about symptomatic improvement patterns within the context of multiple other symptoms (Kopta, Howard, Lowry, & Beutler, 1994).

There could perhaps be no more important treatment study than one that compared one experimental condition that began with a structured interview, prioritized diagnoses, and addressed each syndrome sequentially; with a second condition, more closely approximating clinical practice, in which the clinician began with a systematic clinical diagnostic interview (see, e.g., Westen & Muderrisoglu, 2003, 2006), made a case formulation including both symptoms that require immediate attention and personality characteristics that will likely take years to address, and proceeded to treat the symptoms in the context of the person.

Equally problematic for the EST approach to evidence based practice is an emerging body of data suggesting that subthreshold and not-otherwise specified (NOS) conditions are as or more common in everyday practice as the syndromes for which manualized treatments are designed (e.g., Fairburn, Cooper, & Shafran, 2003; Zinbarg, Barlow, Liebowitz, & Street, 1994). To what extent syndromal and subsyndromal pathologies respond to the same interventions is unknown. Also unknown is the extent to which treatments designed for discrete disorders are efficacious for patients with NOS diagnoses. For example, many patients in clinical practice present with BN symptoms as well as symptoms of anorexia nervosa (AN) that fall below the DSM-IV threshold. These patients currently receive an ED-NOS diagnosis, for which no treatments have been tested.

As noted above, a promising recent trend is the development of treatments intended to apply to patients across a range of axis I diagnoses by leading anxiety and ED researchers, notably Barlow's treatment aimed at both mood and anxiety disorders (Barlow, Allen, & Choate, 2004) and Fairburn's treatment aimed at patients with a range of ED symptoms (e.g., Barlow, Allen, & Choate, 2004; Fairburn, Cooper, & Shafran, 2003). To what extent these treatments will prove efficacious or will be able to maintain their brevity is unknown. Also unclear is whether RCTs for these treatments will be able to maintain experimental control in the face of variation in patient presentation and therapist activity that follows from reduced patient homogeneity. Nevertheless, such manuals are essential in moving beyond the discreteness assumption in future RCTs.

The Interventions Specified in the Manual Are the Ones That Are Causally Related to Outcome

The *causation assumption* is central to the rationale for the experimental study of psychotherapy. A growing body of research, however, suggests limitations to this assumption, particularly when the goal of research is to provide support for treatment packages designed for "transportation" to the community rather than to test broad strategies or specific interventions (see Borkovec & Castonguay, 1998; Rosen & Davison, 2003; Westen, 2006a). In part sparked by the common factors literature, which consistently found factors common across therapies to account for much of the variance in outcome (Wampold, 2001; Weinberger, 1995), researchers began to question the extent to which the active ingredients formulated theoretically and prescribed in treatment manuals actually account for outcomes (see Castonguay, Goldfried, Wiser, Raue, & Hayes, 1996). Using the Psychotherapy Process Q-set (PQS), a Q-sort measure of psychotherapy process,

Ablon, Jones, and colleagues (Ablon & Jones, 2002; Jones & Pulos, 1993) have produced substantial evidence suggesting that outcomes of ESTs for a range of disorders, notably major depression (MDD), are only variably related to the processes hypothesized to produce change and emphasized by the manual.

Hypothesis Testing Is the Sine Qua Non of Science and of the Science of Psychotherapy

The *hypothesis testing assumption* reflects a viewpoint enunciated most clearly by the philosopher of science Karl Popper (1959), who equated scientific method with hypothesis testing. According to Popper, where we get our hypotheses is our own business, as long as we test them appropriately. I would argue, however, that the question of how we choose which hypotheses to test is of central scientific significance, particularly when methodological considerations (e.g., brevity) influence the kinds of treatments tested.

From a scientific standpoint, the current situation, in which researchers primarily test brief variants of CBT (and occasionally IPT) and then draw conclusions about treatment of choice, is scientifically untenable, akin to the practice of holding a "world series" of baseball in which only U.S. teams compete. The problem in psychotherapy research is heightened by the fact that most treatments for most disorders tend to work when tested by investigators and conducted by therapists who believe in them (Luborsky et al., 1999; Wampold, 2001). Wampold (personal communication) has recently found that 60% of therapists in an outpatient HMO sample actually obtain results comparable to those obtained in RCTs. We cannot make determinations of treatment of choice unless we compare laboratory-generated treatments to treatments in widespread use in the community.

Choice of Control Conditions Minimally Constrains Generalizations Drawn from RCTs

The *control condition assumption* can be seen in the control conditions researchers regularly use to bolster claims that ESTs should be preferred over other treatments used or taught in practice. The modal psychotherapy trial uses waitlist or no-treatment controls; controls labeled as "treatment as usual" (TAU) that typically represent treatment as usual for people who have no resources to obtain reasonable treatment (see Westen, 2006b); non-bona fide (Wampold et al., 1997) treatments that do not control for confounds essential for drawing causal inferences (e.g., therapist enthusiasm, patient expectancy, and common factors); and other intent-to-fail conditions (Westen, Novotny, & Thompson-Brenner, 2004a) carried out by the same graduate student therapists who are conducting the experimental (preferred) treatment, who know that their own success and that of their mentors depends on the failure of the control treatment they are conducting. Unlike placebo pills, placebo therapists *know* they are supposed to be inert, which renders control conditions in psychotherapy research very different from placebos in medication trials (see Wampold, 2001).

When researchers *do* compare two bona fide, intent-to-succeed conditions, the effects are generally small, with an average Cohen's *d* of around .20 (Luborsky et al., 2002; Wampold, 2001). When they compare ESTs to control conditions without obvious confounds that complicate causal inference (e.g., differing treatment durations, injunctions against talking about the symptom in the control condition), the average *d* = .15 (Baskin, Tierney, Minami, & Wampold, 2003). This is not an effect to be dismissed, but it is also not an effect one would want associated with a genuine treatment of choice, particularly when, for any given treatment, researchers typically only have tested one or two intent-to-succeed treatments.

In fact, the choice of a control group is intimately related to what one can generalize from the data. If researchers compare an experimental treatment they believe to be state of the art to any treatment *not* intended by competent clinicians administering it to be the best treatment *they* have to offer, the only inference they can draw is that a treatment intended to succeed is superior to a treatment that is not. If the goal is to convince experienced, doctoral-level clinicians in private practice to use a manualized treatment in lieu of their current practices, the only appropriate control group is treatment by experienced doctoral-level clinicians in private practice.

As suggested above, the normative research practice of comparing laboratory treatments to *everything but* the longer-term integrative, eclectic, and psychodynamic treatments that evolved over the last century is not only scientifically problematic but pragmatically inadvisable, because it leaves empirically minded clinicians without the most important piece of evidence they need to guide their practices and can only increase clinicians' resistance to data from psychotherapy research. I would argue, in fact, that using any control group other than experienced clinicians doing their best work is at this point no longer scientifically useful.

If our goal is to improve current practice, we have to show that our experimental treatments improve current practice. As an evidence-based practitioner, I pay little attention to evidence showing that an experimental condition outperforms control conditions intended to be inert unless I have found my own approach to be inert in similar circumstances (or unless I have tried my best with a patient to no avail or have not encountered a problem before, in which case I do in fact turn immediately to the experimental literature for guidance). For example, I have not switched to brief CBT for depression because my success rate is far higher than the success rates reported in the best studies of CBT for depression, in which 60–75% of patients either fail to recover or relapse within 2 years (e.g., Hollon et al., 2005; Westen & Morrison, 2001).

Evidence Based Practice Is Synonymous with Empirically Supported Therapies

The *EBP=EST assumption,* reflected in the widespread use of these terms as synonyms (e.g., Crits-Christoph, Wilson, & Hollon, 2005; Weisz, Weersing, & Henggeler, 2005), reflects what philosophers call a category error, confusing a part with a whole. The EST movement is the latest in a long line of empirical approaches to psychotherapy (Orlinsky, Ronnestad, & Willutzski, 2004). The RCTs conducted during the EST era are only a subset of relevant RCTs, let alone studies using other designs. Prior to the current era, researchers did not assume that *DSM* diagnoses provide the only useful way of grouping patients for psychotherapy trials and often included mixed patient groups. As noted above, EST researchers are beginning to return to this practice, based on evidence that comorbidity is neither incidental nor accidental.

Other designs of potential relevance include data collected in naturalistic settings, correlational studies on treatment variables associated with outcome (Ablon & Jones, 2002; Orlinsky, Ronnestad, & Willutzski, 2004), research on therapist and patient variables associated with outcome, basic science, and anthropological data relevant to cultural differences relevant to treatment response. For example, meta-analytic data have conclusively shown that the quality of the therapeutic relationship accounts for much of the variance in outcome in both RCTs and treatments in naturalistic settings (see Horvath, 2001; Norcross, 2001; Wampold, 2001), and that therapist effects, when appropriately tested (i.e., nested within treatments), tend to account for substantially more variance than treatment effects across studies, particularly if one holds constant investigator allegiance (Wampold, 2001). These data would suggest the importance of devoting considerably more resources to studying individual differences among clinicians and developing expert systems models of skilled practice. Developments in basic science, such as the neurosciences and psychopathology, also have tremendous implications for EBP (see Samoilov & Goldfried, 2000; Westen, 2000; Westen, 2005; Westen & Gabbard, 2002).

For example, we now know that various kinds of implicit processes (e.g., networks of association, procedural knowledge) are not only functionally but neuroanatomically distinct from explicit processes. In light of this, we should test, not assume, that technical strategies useful for altering explicit processes (e.g., most cognitive interventions) will alter implicit networks or implicit relational procedures that run people into trouble interpersonally and hence lead to relapse prevention as well as immediate symptomatic change. Similarly, we should not assume that strategies useful for identifying and altering implicit networks (e.g., many psychodynamic techniques) are efficacious for altering explicit processes (e.g., deficits in interpersonal problem-solving) or conditioned emotional responses (e.g., fear of fear in panic; see Barlow, 2002).

Summary and Implications

As should be clear, my argument is not that we should replace one limited methodology with another. Experimental methods, appropriately applied, allow more definitive causal conclusions than do other methods. My argument is that one methodology does not fit all questions and stages of the research enterprise; that tradeoffs between internal and external validity are inherent in psychotherapy research, and we should be careful not to err consistently on one side or the other;

and that we should be cautious not to assume the preferability of treatments that happen to be well suited to our preferred methods (RCTs) when the assumptions that render these treatments readily testable in brief manualized formats may be associated with substantial limitations for some disorders.

Lest readers interpret these arguments as an elaborate rationalization for clinicians to practice as they have for years (i.e., that I am simply trying to provide refuge for psychodynamic clinicians to continue doing what they have been doing), I hasten to add that we have no idea whether the longer-term dynamic, integrative, and eclectic treatments widely practiced are more, less, or equally effective as treatments widely designated as "treatment of choice," and that addressing that question should be the top priority of psychotherapy research. There was once a time when the fault for the absence of data on the effectiveness of psychodynamic and integrative treatments rested squarely on the shoulders of their advocates. Unfortunately, that is no longer primarily the case, and until such time as major funding agencies lift the embargo on studying what experienced clinicians do (or variants of what has already been done), statements about treatment of choice will have the scientific status of election results in one-party states.

DEVELOPING A COMPLEMENTARY METHODOLOGY

The concept of *effectiveness* studies has been widely interpreted to describe a final phase of hypothesis testing, in which treatment packages well tested in RCTs in the laboratory are then tested in more naturalistic settings. Elsewhere colleagues and I have proposed an alternative type of effectiveness design, intended as a *first* phase of hypothesis generation and testing in psychotherapy research (Westen & Morrison, 2001). This alternative approach starts with the assumption that we may not know which of the many interventions used by clinicians and researchers are the most important to test in the community, and that what we think are the active ingredients of the interventions we have tested may or may not be what leads to therapeutic change.

Thus, as a complement to RCTs testing investigator-initiated treatments, we propose a way of identifying best practice in the community, by observing the therapeutic strategies used by experienced clinicians; studying these interventions with a wide range of patients with a broadly defined symptom pattern (e.g., BN-spectrum pathology) who may or may not have substantial comorbidities; examining the correlations between specific intervention strategies and outcome; and *then* experimentally studying interventions or constellations of interventions associated with positive outcomes, including matching treatment approaches with empirically defined subsets of patients defined by variables such as personality constellations (Thompson-Brenner & Westen, 2005c).

I would argue that the choice of hypotheses to test—in this case, therapeutic interventions we believe are worthy of time and resources to study—should be just as systematic as the procedures we use to test them. In Popperian terms, the use of scientific method in the context of discovery is likely to lead to the testing of more useful hypotheses in the context of justification.[7] Thus, I would propose using clinical practice as a natural laboratory, making use of the wide variation that exists in what clinicians who practice using the major approaches to treatment do in practice, to see what intervention strategies appear to work with what kinds of patients. Instead of requiring individual investigators to choose *a priori* which treatments they believe are most likely to work (the pitfalls of which were well described by Meehl's (1954) description of "clinical judgment," of which this is an example), the approach I am suggesting would allow us to determine empirically which interventions are associated with outcome and for which kinds of patients. We could then focus our experiments on these interventions as well as on laboratory-derived interventions we have good reason to believe are likely to be particularly useful (or are currently believed to be the treatment of choice but without benefit of comparison with treatments as practiced by experienced private practitioners).

Indeed, one could develop a hybrid strategy that uses RCT methodology to test hypotheses in community samples in a way that does not assume that we already know what the best treatment strategies are for a given kind of patient.[8] Once again using BN-spectrum pathology as an example, consider a study designed to compare manualized CBT taken into the community (the way effectiveness research is now widely understood) with two alternative treatments: CBT as practiced in the community (which prior naturalistic research suggests strongly resembles the manualized variant but is much more flexible; Thompson-Brenner & Westen, 2005a, 2005b, 2005c) and psychodynamic therapy as practiced in the community, which has never been studied. Researchers could invite experienced CBT-spectrum and dynamic-spectrum clinicians in the community (i.e., including the majority of clinicians, who integrate other approaches into a primarily dynamic or CBT framework) to join a practice network; the goal of including "impure" clinicians— who are, empirically, the majority (Norcross, Karpiak, & Lister, 2005)—would be to maximize variance within conditions, rather than, as in current RCTs, to minimize variance it, so we could empirically identify characteristics of successful treatments within as well as across conditions. The researchers would then advertise for BN or BN-spectrum patients (again, to maximize generalizability to patients with BN symptomatology who, by virtue of arbitrary cutoffs, fall into the ED-NOS category in *DSM-IV*) and randomize patients to one of the three conditions: manualized CBT, CBT as practiced in the community, and psychodynamic therapy as practiced in the community.

With a large enough N (e.g., 90 per condition), such a study would have the statistical power to determine whether one or another treatment produces better outcomes as defined multiple ways, including symptomatic improvement, length of time to remission, relapse rates and length of time to relapse, quality of life, adaptive functioning in domains such as romantic relationships and work and personality change. With three conditions and an N of 270, such a study could also examine variation within and across conditions. Using correlational methods applied to audiotaped samples of hours coded using instruments such as the Psychotherapy Process Q-set or the Comparative Psychotherapy Process Scale (CPPS) (see Hilsenroth, DeFife, Blagys, & Ackerman, in press; Thompson-Brenner & Westen, 2005b), such a study could identify interventions associated with each kind of outcome at multiple clinically relevant follow-up intervals (e.g., 3 months, 1 year, 2 years, 5 years). These correlational findings could then be used to identify treatment strategies, or *constellations* of strategies, that are, empirically, the most effective (or the most effective with particular kinds of patients, e.g., those who are high-functioning and perfectionistic versus those who are emotionally dys-regulated; see Thompson-Brenner & Westen, 2005c). These constellations could then be used to create *empirically derived treatments*. Thus, in the *next* study, clinicians could be randomized to an active control condition, in which they prac-tice their treatment as usual (including consultation/supervision with an expert in their theoretical approach, to maximize similarity across conditions); or to an experimental condition, in which they are supervised to match an empirically derived prototype of what worked in the prior, correlational stage of research.

In this methodology, we have reversed the "natural order of things." Currently, researchers start with a manual, test it in the laboratory with generally unrepre-sentative samples against generally unrepresentative control conditions, almost inevitably find that it outperforms intent-to-fail conditions, and then, after years of such efforts, may test it in a community mental health center against treatments conducted by paraprofessionals. In the alternative I am proposing, we would first see whether manualized treatments outperform treatments as currently delivered by experienced clinicians in private practice, derive best practice empirically using correlational methods, and then test these empirically derived treatments experimentally in the community. Doing so eliminates the stage of manual devel-opment, currently required for all psychotherapy research, which requires an omniscient researcher to predict a priori, largely based on his or her theoretical and clinical biases and predilections, which of several hundred combinations of possible interventions should be tested.

Why Bother, Part I: The Limits of ESTs

This may seem like a radical proposal, particularly in light of the successes of psychotherapy research in identifying potentially useful treatments (what others have called treatment of choice). But a more careful look behind the curtain suggests both reasons for optimism about what we have accomplished thus far and reasons for developing complementary methodologies—including radically different ones such as the ones I am proposing. In psychotherapy research, several metrics provide nonredundant indicators of outcome that can be aggregated meta-analytically to provide a more comprehensive portrait of treatment efficacy and generalizability than has often been the case in the EST literature (what we have called a multidimensional meta-analysis; Westen & Morrison, 2001). The first and most familiar, *effect size*, provides crucial information on the impact of the treatment on the average patient. A treatment could obtain a moderate effect, how-ever, by producing a very large effect for a small subset of patients or a moderate reduction in symptoms for many. Thus, two other useful metrics are *percent recovered* and *percent improved*. Another measure of outcome is *residual post-treatment symptomatology*. A treatment could lead to substantial improvement in most patients and hence yield a large effect size but nevertheless leave them highly symptomatic. Another important metric is *sustained efficacy* over time. A treatment that produces an initial response, or a response that holds up to a year after termination, may or may not be an efficacious treatment for a disorder that is often longstanding or recurrent. A final set of variables provide indices of generalizability. Because of the small sample sizes in most RCTs (reflecting the cost of obtaining large samples), researchers generally screen carefully to maximize the sample homogeneity. To index generalizability, one can aggregate modal *inclusion/exclusion criteria* and calculate the *percent of patients excluded of screened*.

Thus far we have completed multidimensional meta-analyses of six widely common disorders: MDD, panic disorder, GAD, OCD, BN, and PTSD (Bradley, Greene, Russ, Dutra, & Westen, 2005; Eddy, Dutra, Bradley, & Westen, 2004; Thompson-Brenner, Glass, & Westen, 2003; Westen & Morrison, 2001). We focus here again on treatments of BN, which have been some of the most efficacious reported in the EST literature.

Mean effect sizes in the RCTs we meta-analyzed were substantial and very promising (.88 and 1.01 for binge eating and purging, respectively). However, these effect sizes are within the range of the effects obtained by virtually every therapy intended to succeed that has been studied over the last 30 years (Wampold, 2001). More problematic, however, was that most patients treated with ESTs for BN continued to be symptomatic at the end of treatment. Of those who completed, 40% recovered; of those who entered treatment, 33% recovered. The average patient continued to binge 1.7 times per week and purge 2.3 times per week at the end of treatment. Although this still comes close to the diagnostic threshold for bulimia nervosa in *DSM-IV*, it nevertheless represents a very substantial improvement from baseline. The findings were somewhat better for individual CBT (which tended to fare slightly better than other treatments, particularly group CBT), with an impressive 48.0% of completers recovering by the end of treatment but only 38.0% of intent-to-treat samples recovering. Findings at one-year follow-up, though hard to come by, were similar to post-treatment data, with the average patient across treatments showing substantial improvement over pretreatment baseline but also substantial residual symptomatology. However, only one-third of patients showed sustained recovery at one year (that is, recovered at termination and remained recovered at 1 year).

With respect to exclusion rates and criteria, the average study excluded 40% of the patients screened, which is substantially lower than the exclusion rate for many other disorders. However, approximately half the studies excluded patients for either low or high weight (excluding patients with both anorexic symptoms and obesity) and suicide risk, and an additional one-third excluded patients for substance abuse or dependence (31%). A large number of studies also excluded patients who had "major psychiatric illness," "serious comorbidity," or similar nonspecific exclusion criteria.

Taken together, the data suggest a glass that is simultaneously half empty and half full: Brief treatments for BN reduce symptoms dramatically for the average patient and lead to recovery for a substantial minority of those who enter treatment. However, roughly half of completers, and almost two-thirds of intent-to-treat samples, do not respond even to the treatment with the best track record in RCTs, individual CBT. Many patients show residual symptomatology, and still others are excluded from RCTs, including many with ED-NOS who have mixed BN and AN features. The data on BN, which are among the best in the EST literature, provide strong empirical support for humility—and a strong rationale for continuing to search for additional interventions and methodologies that may prove useful to patients with the disorder.

Why Bother, Part II: Glimpses from Naturalistic Studies

We have recently embarked on a series of naturalistic pilot studies of treatments in the community for anxiety, mood, and EDs, and the results provide glimpses of what we might learn from rigorous multi-observer prospective studies using samples of patients and clinicians from the community (Morrison, Bradley, & Westen, 2003). Consider the following study. We asked a random national sample of clinicians to describe their most recently terminated patient with bulimia spectrum pathology (Thompson-Brenner & Westen, 2005a, 2005b, 2005c). Respondents were evenly distributed by theoretical orientation, with 37.3% describing their theoretical orientation as CBT or primarily CBT, 33.8% psychodynamic or primarily psychodynamic, and 28.9% identifying themselves as purely eclectic or primarily subscribing to some other orientation. Patients averaged 28 years of age, and were, like the population from which they were drawn (women with eating disorders), primarily middle class and Caucasian. We focus here on the findings most relevant to the present argument.

First, although most clinicians described their patients as improved at the end of treatment, only 53% reported that their patients completely recovered. Interestingly, clinicians were not shy about admitting treatment failures, and equal numbers did so across theoretical orientations. Second, as in our naturalistic studies of mood and anxiety spectrum disorders, clinicians of all theoretical orientations reported treating patients for much longer than the 12 to 20 sessions prescribed in the most widely tested and disseminated treatment manuals. Although CBT treatments were of shorter duration than eclectic/integrative and psychodynamic treatments for BN, the average CBT treatment lasted 69 sessions—roughly a year and a half. Third, comorbidity was the rule rather than the exception, and both axis I and axis II comorbidity were negatively associated with treatment outcome. Over 90% of the sample met criteria for at least one comorbid Axis I diagnosis other than an ED. Axis II comorbidity was also high: One-third met criteria for at least one Cluster B (dramatic, erratic) diagnosis, and the same proportion met criteria for at least one Cluster C (anxious) diagnosis. Several comorbid axis I disorders (notably MDD, PTSD, and Substance Use Disorders) and Axis II disorders (Borderline, Dependent, and Avoidant) were positively correlated with treatment length and negatively correlated with outcome. When we applied four common exclusion criteria from RCTs to the naturalistic sample (substance use disorder; weight 15% or more over ideal; weight 15% or more below ideal; and bipolar disorder), we found that approximately 40% of the naturalistic sample would have been excluded (the same percent excluded in the average RCT). Two-thirds of the patients with borderline personality disorder (BPD) would have been excluded, and the 40% of patients who would have been excluded (whether or not they had BPD) showed worse treatment outcome across a number of indices.

As part of this study, we measured intervention strategies by asking clinicians to complete an interventions questionnaire adapted from the CPPS, developed by Hilsenroth and colleagues to assess therapeutic strategies and process variables that empirically distinguish CBT and PT (Blagys, Ackerman, Bonge, & Hilsenroth, 2000, 2003). Factor analysis of the CPPS yields two factors, a CBT and a PT interventions factor. Previous research has demonstrated adequate interrater reliability for independent judges using the CPPS (Ackerman, Hilsenroth, & Knowles, 2005; Hilsenroth, Ackerman, Blagys, Baity, & Mooney, 2003; Hilsenroth, DeFife, Blagys, & Ackerman, in press; Hilsenroth, Ackerman, & Blagys, 2001). To be maximally relevant to the treatment of BN, we modified the CPPS by adding (1) items specific to the treatment of BN adapted from CBT manual (Fairburn, Marcus, & Wilson, 1993); (2) items assessing psychodynamic interventions not addressed in the original item set (e.g., interpretation of conflict, focus on sexuality); and (3) items assessing interventions commonly employed for personality problems of relevance to ED patients (e.g., interventions addressing emotional dysregulation; Linehan, 1993). The adapted questionnaire, the CPPS-BN, has 41 items, which can be self-reported by clinicians or rated from audiotapes of psychotherapy hours. We instructed clinicians to rate the extent to which each item was characteristic of their work with their patient, where "1 = not at all characteristic" and "5 = very characteristic." Factor analysis of the CPPS-BN yielded three factors: psychodynamic, cognitive-behavioral, and adjunctive interventions (e.g., pharmacotherapy, hospitalization).

Several findings are of note. First, validity checks found highly significant differences on the CBT and PT factors between self-identified CBT and PT clinicians, with eclectic and other clinicians falling in between. Although there is no PT manual with which to compare the PT treatments in practice, CBT clinicians reported using a constellation of interventions that strongly resembled the CBT manual, even though few reported using the manual directly. As in research by Ablon and colleagues using the Psychotherapy Process Q-set (Ablon & Jones, 2002), however, clinicians of both orientations reported using a number of items from the other orientation, suggesting both that clinicians in practice tend to be integrative in working with BN spectrum patient and that response biases did not prevent them from endorsing items associated with their nonpreferred orientation.

Second, across the entire sample, greater use of CBT interventions was associated with more rapid remission of eating symptoms, whereas greater use of
psychodynamic interventions was associated with larger changes in global outcome.
These findings were obtained across orientations and hence are not readily attributable to clinician biases (e.g., the more self-identified PT clinicians reported using
CBT interventions, the more rapidly their patients' symptoms remitted). In many
respects these findings make sense: Clinicians who target symptoms help patients
with their symptoms; clinicians who target broader aspects of functioning help
patients with their broader functioning.

Third, clinicians appear to alter their interventions depending on characteristics
of patients other than ED diagnosis, such as axis I and II comorbidity. Clinicians
of all theoretical backgrounds reported using more psychodynamic interventions
when treating patients with comorbid pathology. Of particular interest, personality
subtype showed a systematic relation to the way clinicians reported intervening.
Psychodynamic clinicians tended to use more structured CBT interventions
when working with constricted patients, whereas CBT clinicians tended to use
more psychodynamic interventions when working with emotionally dysregulated
patients. For clinicians who reported a psychodynamic orientation, the extent to
which the patient showed a constricted style correlated approximately $r = .30$ with
the extent to which they reported that they "Taught the patient specific techniques
for coping with her symptoms" and "Actively initiated the topics of discussion and
other therapeutic activities"; and correlated $r = -.30$ with the item, "Preferred that
the patient, rather than the therapist, initiate the discussion of significant issues."
For CBT clinicians, the extent to which the patient showed evidence of dysregulation correlated approximately $r = .50$ with their endorsement of statements such
the following: "Helped the patient come to terms with her relationships with and
feelings about significant others from the past (e.g., mother, father)"; "Focused on
similarities between the patient's relationships (and perceptions of relationships)
repeated over time, settings, or people"; "Addressed the patient's avoidance of
important topics and shifts in mood"; "Focused on the relationship between the
therapist and patient"; and "Focused on the influence of unconscious processes
on behavior, emotions, beliefs." These findings are particularly striking given the
response biases one would expect to lead clinicians not to endorse items prototypical of the "other" theoretical orientation.

The data from this study are clearly very preliminary. The exclusive reliance on
clinicians as respondents, the retrospective design, the use of a brief therapy process measure completed by the treating clinician without independent assessment
by external observers, and the lack of follow-up data impose severe constraints
on conclusions. We also do not know whether patients in this study fared better or
worse than patients RCTs, except by clinicians' own report (slightly greater than
50% recovery at termination, very close to the percentage of those who recover in
RCTs). That question can only be answered by comparing outcome in a prospective naturalistic study with outcome in RCTs using shared outcome measures.

CONCLUSIONS

I conclude with the words of the immortal philosopher, Rodney King: "Why can't we all just get along?" The reality is that I have met few clinicians who do not care about their patients, and I have met few researchers who do not have the same goal squarely in mind. The problem arises when clinicians do not read the available science and when researchers do not consider the possibility that part of the reason clinicians are ignoring their work is that the science they are generating is not addressing the questions clinicians need answered.

The best way to solve this problem is for clinicians and researchers to engage in a genuinely collaboratively enterprise, with clinicians doing what they do best— treating patients —and researchers doing what they do best—testing hypotheses— not just the hypotheses they favor a priori but also those generated by seasoned clinicians and those identified empirically, which I suspect, on simple statistical grounds (i.e., they have been identified empirically), have at least as high a probability of being valuable. I suspect researchers would also test better treatments at the front end, and have less difficulty "selling" them to clinicians at the back end (dissemination), if they would assemble focus groups of experienced private practitioners of more than one theoretical orientation (paid as consultants at an appropriate rate) to review their manuals and inclusion/exclusion criteria, *prior* to ever undertaking a study. This would maximize the likelihood of applicability to everyday practice and likely "catch" problems (e.g., inadequate duration, failure to address typical comorbidities, failure to address personality diatheses) that competent clinicians who see patients on a daily basis would likely recognize.

The *worst* way to address the problem is the way we are addressing it now, with clinicians often assuming the validity of their current practices and researchers often assuming that they have demonstrated something of value when they compare one treatment on which they have prematurely bet their (and the taxpayers') money with *everything but* the right control group: *experienced private practitioners attempting to do their best work.* Particularly in light of the enormous impact of clinician effects (effects attributable to whomever the particular clinician happens to be) in even RCTs (Wampold, 2001), at this point, we might do well to call a moratorium on experimenter-generated treatments and see how the ones we have fare against best practice as identified empirically in the community—that is, clinicians and interventions that empirically obtain the best results.

REFERENCES

Ablon, J. S., & Jones, E. E. (2002). Validity of controlled clinical trials of psychotherapy: Findings from the NIMH Treatment of Depression Collaborative Research Program. *American Journal of Psychiatry, 159,* 775–783.

Ackerman, S., Hilsenroth, M., & Knowles, E. (2005). Ratings of therapist dynamic activities and alliance early and late in psychotherapy. *Psychotherapy: Theory, Research, Practice, Training, 42*(2), 225–231.

Agras, W. S., Crow, S. J., Halmi, K. A., Mitchell, J. E., Wilson, G. T., & Kraemer, H. C. (2000). Outcome predictors for the cognitive behavior treatment of bulimia nervosa: Data from a multisite study. *American Journal of Psychiatry, 157,* 1302–1308.

APA Task Force on Evidence Based Practice. (2006). Evidence-based practice in psychology. *American Psychologist, 61,* 271–285.

Barlow, D. (2002). *Anxiety and its disorders* (2nd ed.). New York: Guilford Press.

Barlow, D. H., Allen, L. B., & Choate, M. L. (2004). Toward a unified treatment for emotional disorders. *Behavior Therapy, 35,* 205–230.

Baskin, T. W., Tierney, S. C., Minami, T., & Wampold, B. E. (2003). Establishing specificity in psychotherapy: A meta-analysis of structural equivalence of placebo controls. *Journal of Consulting & Clinical Psychology, 71*(6), 973–979.

Blagys, M., Ackerman, S., Bonge, D., & Hilsenroth, M. (2000). *The development, reliability, and validity of a measure of therapist activity in psychodynamic-interpersonal and cognitive-behavioral psychotherapy.* Society for Psychotherapy Research, Chicago, IL.

Blagys, M., Ackerman, S., Bonge, D., & Hilsenroth, M. (2003). Measuring psycho-dynamic-interpersonal and cognitive-behavioral therapist activity: Development of the comparative psychotherapy process scale. Unpublished manuscript.

Borkovec, T. D., & Castonguay, L. G. (1998). What is the scientific meaning of empirically supported therapy? *Journal of Consulting & Clinical Psychology, 66,* 136–142.

Bradley, R., Greene, J., Russ, E., Dutra, L., & Westen, D. (2005). A multidimensional meta-analysis of psychotherapy for PTSD. *American Journal of Psychiatry, 162,* 214–227.

Brown, T. A., Chorpita, B. F., & Barlow, D. H. (1998). Structural relationships among dimensions of the DSM-IV anxiety and mood disorders and dimensions of negative affect, positive affect, and autonomic arousal. *Journal of Abnormal Psychology, 107,* 179–192.

Castonguay, L. G., Goldfried, M. R., Wiser, S., Raue, P. J., & Hayes, A. M. (1996). Predicting the effect of cognitive therapy for depression: A study of unique and common factors. *Journal of Consulting & Clinical Psychology, 64*(3), 497–504.

Chambless, D., & Ollendick, T. (2000). Empirically supported psychological interventions: Controversies and evidence. *Annual Review of Psychology, 52,* 685–716.

Crits-Christoph, P., Wilson, G., & Hollon, S. D. (2005). Empirically supported psycho-therapies: Comment on Westen, Novotny, and Thompson-Brenner (2004). *Psycho-logical Bulletin, 131,* 412–417.

Eddy, K. T., Dutra, L., Bradley, R., & Westen, D. (2004). A multidimensional meta-analysis of pharmacotherapy for obsessive-compulsive disorder. *Clinical Psychology Review, 24,* 1011–1030.

Eddy, K. T., Keel, P. K., Dorer, D. J., Delinsky, S. S., Franko, D. L., & Herzog, D. B. (2002). A longitudinal comparison of anorexia nervosa subtypes. *International Journal of Eating Disorders, 31,* 191–201.

Fairburn, C., Cooper, Z., & Shafran, R. (2003). Cognitive behaviour therapy for eating disorders: A "transdiagnostic" theory and treatment. *Behaviour and Research Therapy, 41,* 509–528.

Fairburn, C. G., Marcus, M. D., & Wilson, G. T. (1993). Cognitive-behavioral therapy for binge eating and bulimia nervosa: A comprehensive treatment manual. In C. G. Fairburn & G. T. Wilson (Eds.), *Binge eating: Nature, assessment, and treatment* (pp. 361–404). New York: Guilford Press.

Garb, H. N. (2005). Clinical judgment and decision making. *Annual Review of Clinical Psychology, 1*, 67–89.

Goldfried, M. R., & Wolfe, B. E. (1998). Toward a more clinically valid approach to therapy research. *Journal of Consulting and Clinical Psychology, 66*, 143–150.

Hilsenroth, M., Ackerman, S., Blagys, M., Baity, M., & Mooney, M. (2003). Short-term psychodynamic psychotherapy for depression: An evaluation of statistical, clinically significant, and technique specific change. *Journal of Nervous and Mental Disease, 191*, 349–357.

Hilsenroth, M., DeFife, J., Blagys, M., & Ackerman, S. (in press). Effects of training in short-term psychodynamic psychotherapy: Changes in graduate clinician technique. *Psychotherapy Research.*

Hilsenroth, M. J., Ackerman, S. J., & Blagys, M. D. (2001). Evaluating the phase model of change during short-term psychodynamic psychotherapy. *Psychotherapy Research, 11*, 29–47.

Hollon, S., DeRubeis, R. J., Shelton, R. C., Amsterdam, J. D., Salomon, R. M., O'Reardon, J. P., et al. (2005). Prevention of relapse following cognitive therapy versus medications in moderate to severe depression. *Archives of General Psychiatry, 62*, 417–422.

Horvath, A. O. (2001). The therapeutic alliance: Concepts, research and training. *Australian Psychologist, 36*, 170–176.

Howard, K. I., Lueger, R., Maling, M., & Martinovich, Z. (1993). A phase model of psychotherapy: Causal mediation of outcome. *Journal of Consulting and Clinical Psychology, 54*, 106–110.

Jones, E. E., & Pulos, S. M. (1993). Comparing the process in psychodynamic and cognitive-behavioral therapies. *Journal of Consulting and Clinical Psychology, 61*(2), 306–316.

Kazdin, A. E. (1997). A model for developing effective treatments: Progression and interplay of theory, research, and practice. *Journal of Clinical Child Psychiatry, 26*(2), 114–129.

Kendler, K. S., Prescott, C. A., Myers, J., & Neale, M. C. (2003). The structure of genetic and environmental risk factors for common psychiatric and substance use disorders in men and women. *Archives of General Psychiatry, 60*, 929–937.

Kessler, R. C., Nelson, C. B., McGonagle, K. A., Liu, J., Swartz, M., & Blazer, D. G. (1996). Comorbidity of DSM-III-R major depressive disorder in the general population: Results from the US National Comorbidity Survey. *British Journal of Psychiatry, 168*(Suppl. 30), 17–30.

Kopta, S., Howard, K., Lowry, J., & Beutler, L. (1994). Patterns of symptomatic recovery in psychotherapy. *Journal of Consulting and Clinical Psychology, 62*, 1009–1016.

Krueger, R. F. (2002). The structure of common mental disorders. *Archives of General Psychiatry, 59*, 570–571.

Kuhn, T. (1962). *The structure of scientific revolutions.* Chicago: University of Chicago Press.

Linehan, M. M. (1993). *Cognitive-behavioral treatment of borderline personality disorder.* New York: Guilford.

Linehan, M. M., Heard, H. L., & Armstrong, H. E. (1993). Naturalistic follow-up of a behavioral treatment for chronically parasuicidal borderline patients. *Archives of General Psychiatry, 50*(12), 971–974.

Luborsky, L., Diguer, L., Seligman, D. A., Rosenthal, R., Krause, E. D., Johnson, S., et al. (1999). The researcher's own therapy allegiances: A "wild card" in comparisons of treatment efficacy. *Clinical Psychology: Science and Practice, 6*, 95–106.

Luborsky, L., Rosenthal, R., Diguer, L., Andrusyna, T. P., Berman, J. S., Levitt, J. T., et al. (2002). The dodo bird verdict is alive and well—mostly. *Clinical Psychology: Science and Practice, 9,* 2–12.

Meehl, P. E. (1954). *Clinical vs. statistical prediction.* Minneapolis: University of Minnesota Press.

Mineka, S., Watson, D., & Clark, L. A. (1998). Comorbidity of anxiety and unipolar mood disorders. *Annual Review of Psychology, 49,* 377–412.

Morrison, C., Bradley, R., & Westen, D. (2003). The external validity of efficacy trials for depression and anxiety: A naturalistic study. *Psychology and Psychotherapy: Theory, Research and Practice, 76,* 109–132.

Norcross, J., Karpiak, C., & Lister, K. (2005). What's an integrationist? A study of self-identified integrative and (occasionally) eclectic psychologists. *Journal of Clinical Psychology, 61*(12), 1587–1594.

Norcross, J. C. (2001). Purposes, processes and products of the task force on empirically supported therapy relationships. *Psychotherapy: Theory, Research, Practice, Training, 38,* 345–356.

Norcross, J. C., Beutler, L. E., & Levant, R. F. (2006). *Evidence-based practices in mental health: Debate and dialogue on the fundamental questions.* Washington, DC: American Psychological Association.

Orlinsky, D. E., Ronnestad, M. H., & Willutzski, U. (2004). Fifty years of psychotherapy process-outcome research: Continuity and change. In M. Lambert (Ed.), *Bergin and Garfield's handbook of psychotherapy and behavior change* (5th ed., pp. 307–389). New York: Wiley.

Popper, K. (1959). *The logic of scientific discovery.* London, England: Hutchinson & Co.

Rosen, G. M., & Davison, G. C. (2003). Psychology should list empirically supported principles of change (ESPs) and not credential trademarked therapies or other treatment packages. *Behavior Modification. 27,* 300–312.

Safer, D., Telch, C., & Agras, W. (2001). Dialectical behavior therapy for bulimia nervosa. *American Journal of Psychiatry, 158,* 632–634.

Samoilov, A., & Goldfried, M. R. (2000). Role of emotion in cognitive-behavior therapy. *Clinical Psychology: Science and Practice, 7,* 373–385.

Thompson-Brenner, H., Glass, S., & Westen, D. (2003). A multidimensional meta-analysis of psychotherapy for bulimia nervosa. *Clinical Psychology: Science and Practice, 10,* 269–287.

Thompson-Brenner, H., & Westen, D. (2005a). A naturalistic study of psychotherapy for bulimia nervosa, Part 1: Comorbidity and therapeutic outcome. *Journal of Nervous and Mental Disease, 193*(9), 573–574.

Thompson-Brenner, H., & Westen, D. (2005b). A naturalistic study of psychotherapy for bulimia nervosa, Part 2: Therapeutic interventions in the community. *Journal of Nervous and Mental Disease, 193*(9), 585–595.

Thompson-Brenner, H., & Westen, D. (2005c). Personality subtypes in eating disorders: Validation of a classification in a naturalistic sample. *British Journal of Psychiatry, 186,* 516–524.

Wachtel, P. L. (1973). Psychodynamics, behavior therapy, and the implacable experimenter: An inquiry into the consistency of personality. *Journal of Abnormal Psychology, 82*(2), 324–334.

Wampold, B. E. (2001). *The great psychotherapy debate: Models, methods, and findings.* Mahwah, NJ: Lawrence Erlbaum Associates.

Wampold, B. E., Mondin, G., Moody, M., Stich, F., Benson, K., & Ahn, H. (1997). A meta-analysis of outcome studies comparing bona fide psychotherapies: Empirically, "all must have prizes." *Psychological Bulletin, 112*, 203–215.

Watson, D., & Clark, L. A. (1992). Affects separable and inseparable: On the hierarchical arrangement of the negative affects. *Journal of Personality and Social Psychology, 62*, 489–505.

Weinberger, J. (1995). Common factors aren't so common: The common factors dilemma. *Clinical Psychology: Science & Practice, 2*(1), 45–69.

Weisz, J. R., Weersing, V., & Henggeler, S. W. (2005). Jousting with straw men: Comment on Westen, Novotny, and Thompson-Brenner (2004). *Psychological Bulletin, 131*, 418–426.

Westen, D. (1998). The scientific legacy of Sigmund Freud: Toward a psychodynamically informed psychological science. *Psychological Bulletin, 124*, 333–371.

Westen, D. (2000). Integrative psychotherapy: Integrating psychodynamic and cognitive-behavioral theory and technique. In C. R. Snyder & R. Ingram (Eds.), *Handbook of psychological change: Psychotherapy processes and practices for the 21st century* (pp. 217–242). New York: Wiley.

Westen, D. (2005). Implications of research in cognitive neuroscience for psychodynamic psychotherapy. In G. Gabbard, J. Beck & J. Holmes (Eds.), *Oxford concise textbook of psychotherapy* (pp. 443–448). Oxford, England: Oxford University Press.

Westen, D. (2006a). Lost in transportation: On the transportability of empirically supported therapies. In J. C. Norcross, L. Beutler & R. F. Levant (Eds.), *Evidence-based practices in mental health: Debate and dialogue on the fundamental questions*. Washington, DC: American Psychological Association.

Westen, D. (2006b). Patients and treatments in clinical trials are not adequately representative of clinical practice. In J. C. Norcross, L. Beutler & R. F. Levant (Eds.), *Evidence-based practices in mental health: Debate and dialogue on the fundamental questions*. Washington, DC: American Psychological Association.

Westen, D., Gabbard, G., & Blagov, P. (2006). Back to the future: Personality structure as a context for psychopathology. In R. F. Krueger & J. L. Tackett (Eds.), *Personality and psychopathology: Building bridges* (pp. 335–384). New York: Guilford.

Westen, D., & Gabbard, G. O. (2002). Developments in cognitive neuroscience: II. Implications for theories of transference. *Journal of the American Psychoanalytic Association, 50*, 99–134.

Westen, D., & Harnden-Fischer, J. (2001). Personality profiles in eating disorders: Rethinking the distinction between Axis I and Axis II. *American Journal of Psychiatry, 165*, 547–562.

Westen, D., & Morrison, K. (2001). A multidimensional meta-analysis of treatments for depression, panic, and generalized anxiety disorder: An empirical examination of the status of empirically supported therapies. *Journal of Consulting and Clinical Psychology, 69*, 875–899.

Westen, D., & Muderrisoglu, S. (2003). Reliability and validity of personality disorder assessment using a systematic clinical interview: Evaluating an alternative to structured interviews. *Journal of Personality Disorders, 17*, 350–368.

Westen, D., & Muderrisoglu, S. (2006). Clinical assessment of pathological personality traits. *American Journal of Psychiatry, 163*, 1285–1297.

Westen, D., Novotny, C., & Thompson-Brenner, H. (2004a). The next generation of psychotherapy research. *Psychological Bulletin, 130*, 677–683.

Westen, D., Novotny, C., & Thompson-Brenner, H. (2004b). The next generation of psychotherapy research: Reply to Ablon and Marci (2004), Goldfried and Eubanks-Carter (2004), and Haaga (2004). *Psychological Bulletin, 130,* 677–683.

Westen, D., Novotny, C. M., & Thompson-Brenner, H. (2004b). The empirical status of empirically supported psychotherapies: Assumptions, findings, and reporting in controlled clinical trials. *Psychological Bulletin, 130,* 631–663.

Westen, D., Novotny, C. M., & Thompson-Brenner, H. (2005). EBP not-equal-to EST: Reply to Crits-Christoph et al. (2005) and Weisz et al. (2005). *Psychological Bulletin, 131,* 427–433.

Westen, D., Thompson-Brenner, H., & Peart, J. (2006). Personality and eating disorders. *Annual Review of Eating Disorders, 2,* 97–112.

Westen, D., & Weinberger, J. (2004). When clinical description becomes statistical prediction. *American Psychologist, 59,* 595–613.

Westen, D., & Weinberger, J. (2005). In praise of clinical judgment: Meehl's forgotten legacy. *Journal of Clinical Psychology, 61,* 1257–1276.

Widiger, T. A., & Trull, T. J. (2005). A simplistic understanding of the five-factor model. *American Journal of Psychiatry. 162*(8), 1550–1551.

Wilson, G. (1998). Manual-based treatment and clinical practice. *Clinical Psychology: Science & Practice, 5,* 363–375.

Wilson, G. T. (1999). Rapid response to cognitive behavior therapy. *Clinical Psychology: Science and Practice, 6,* 289–292.

Zinbarg, R. E., Barlow, D. H., Liebowitz, M., & Street, L. (1994). The DSM-IV field trial for mixed anxiety-depression. *American Journal of Psychiatry, 151,* 1153–1162.

ENDNOTES

Preparation of this manuscript was supported by NIMH grants MH62377 and MH62378.

1. I say this as a former study section member at the National Institutes of Mental Health (NIMH), where the correlation was reasonably high between research quality and consensus scores. Where the process tended to fail was in the fate of creative proposals, which often fell prey to unanswerable questions about the validity of measures and designs whose ultimate success could not be determined a priori, and in a conservative bias toward "business as usual" proposals whose strengths lay in the tried-and-true methods that are the natural consequence of minimally innovative designs.

2. I understand that treadmill well but had the good fortune of being an assistant professor in a prior era, when I could clock 10–15 hours a week in practice, following a two-year clinical post-doc.

3. Penn State and Boston University come to mind, but there are others.

4. Readers who are shaking their heads or writing in the margins that they have never heard faculty utter phrases such as "lost to practice" (to describe a student who chose to abandon the academy for the clinic) should consider their recall deficits an empirical demonstration of repressed memories.

5. My guess is that most clinicians can read *Psychological Assessment* without much additional guidance, although I am not sure we have done everything we could to make doing so a productive use of their time.

6. Parts of this chapter draw on material published elsewhere, notably Westen, Novotny, & Thompson-Brenner, 2004, 2005; Westen & Bradley, 2005.

7. Popper did distinguish between better and worse hypotheses, and argued for the importance of risky, falsifiable hypotheses. However, he did not address the problem, later elaborated by Kuhn (1962), of shared biases in the choice of hypotheses to test, or (as he could not have foreseen, as in psychotherapy research) of the enforcement of such biases by funding decisions.

8. Steve Hollon (personal communication) was instrumental in suggesting how one might introduce randomization into a naturalistic design aimed at comparing treatments as practiced in the community with each other.

2

Methodcentric Reasoning and the Empirically Supported Treatment Debates

MARK A. BLAIS AND MARK J. HILSENROTH

In his 1957 American Psychological Association Presidential address, entitled *The Two Disciplines of Scientific Psychology*, Lee Cronbach warned of a growing division within the field that threatened to pit groups of psychologists against one another (Cronbach, 1957). This division resulted from psychologists identifying primarily with a research methodology rather than with the broader field and it reflected the continuing influence of the two primary traditions of modern psychology, experimental and individual difference methodologies. Spearman (1930/1961) had also noted the tendency for psychologists to group themselves according to research methods and considered it irrational and potentially disastrous. Cronbach was especially concerned about the destructive effect that such a method-based division could have within the field of applied psychology (Cronbach, 1957). "In applied psychology, the two disciplines are in active conflict; and unless they bring their efforts into harmony, they can hold each other to a standstill" (Cronbach, 1957, p. 678). In this chapter, we argue that the tendency for psychologists to identify themselves with a preferred research methodology and the resulting division such identification produces remains a powerful but under-recognized force in psychology. This division also gives rise to what we term *methodcentric reasoning*. Methodcentric reasoning is a form of cognitive myopia that leads psychologists to judge their preferred research methodology superior to all others. We believe that methodcentric reasoning is exerting a powerful although insidious influence in the ongoing debates about Empirically Supported Therapies (EST).

In 1995, a Task Force commissioned by Division 12 (now the Society of Clinical Psychology, American Psychological Association) published, *Training in and Dissemination of Empirically-Validity Psychological Treatments: Report and Recommendations* (Chambless et al., 1995). The task force justified the actions recommended in their report as necessary to keep professional psychology on par with biological psychiatry. Among the distinguishing features of the report were a preliminary list of treatments judged to be empirically validated and a hierarchical set of criteria intended to assess the quality of psychotherapy research. Although the list of Empirically Validated Therapies (EVT; later changed to "supported" therapies, EST) was to be updated "as new evidence is provided" (p. 5), the criteria for evaluating psychotherapy research were presented as complete. The randomized controlled trial (RCT) method, a methodology developed for psychopharmacology research, was selected as the primary method and apparent "gold standard" for evaluating the scientific stature of psychotherapy. We suspect that methodcentric reasoning played a significant role in the selection process given that the appropriateness of the criteria was never seriously questioned despite some recognition that they were limited and somewhat arbitrary (Nathan & Gorman, 1998).

Assessing the quality of scientific evidence is inherently a subjective activity (Berger and Luckmann, 1966). The EST debates have been substantially influenced by strongly held beliefs about the nature of science and are as ideological in nature as they are empirical. And although establishing criteria implies objectivity, it does not insure that the process by which the criteria were selected was unbiased. As a result of the committee's actions, the definition of what constitutes acceptable scientific inquiry and evidence has become the fault line for a significant methodcentric division in the field of psychotherapy research (cf. Lambert, 1998). In our view, the Task Force's endorsement of the RCT method as the principal standard for evaluating psychotherapies was, at the very least, premature given the current state of the psychotherapy knowledge base.

In hindsight, the divisive affects of the committee's actions might have been minimized had they recognized the subjective nature of this activity and adopted a more pluralistic approach for selecting their criteria. In psychiatry, for example, where a potential division exists between practitioners and academic researchers, the polarizing affects of methodcentric actions has for the most part been avoided even in the contentious area of treatment guidelines. In developing their treatment guidelines, the American Psychiatric Association (APA, 1993, 1994a, 1995) adopted a liberal view of what constitutes adequate "proof" of validity (Nathan & Gorman, 1998). Their guidelines allowed expert clinical judgment (see Westen & Weinberger, 2004) to be considered along with empirical data, thereby providing a voice for both traditions. As a result, the American Psychiatric Association's list of endorsed treatments surpasses that of the Division 12 Task Force in both volume and diversity (Nathan & Gorman, 1998) and has generally been well received. Why the Division 12 committee did not adopt a similar measured and inclusive approach of seeking input from a broad sample of psychologists is unknown.

The recently released APA Task Force report on Evidence-Based Practices (EBP) employed a process similar to the American Psychiatric Association reviewed above (APA, 2006). The Task Force defined evidenced-based practice as integrating the best available research with clinical expertise in the context of patient variables. Furthermore the task forces explicitly recognized the importance of integrating data from multiple types of research.

RECONSIDERING THE ROLE OF RCT METHODOLOGY

We recognize the important role that the RCT design can play in identifying effective psychological treatments. But exclusive reliance upon it can be problematic. One limitation of relying exclusively upon RCT data for determining the validity of a treatment is that the validation process essentially stops once EST status is obtained. However, consistent with the views of many other psychologists (Blatt & Zuroff, 2005; Westen, Novotny, & Thompson-Brenner, 2004), we see the treatment validation process as a multiphased operation that extends well beyond determining whether an intervention demonstrates significant differences in relation to a randomized control group of patients. We would argue that in addition to RCT data, psychotherapy validation requires evidence of effectiveness in trials with high external validity. This would establish the appropriateness of the treatment for patients under actual clinical conditions and facilitate the adoption of these treatments by practicing clinicians (cf. Gonzales, Ringeisen, & Chambers, 2002). Adoption of these research intervention protocols by practicing clinicians is a problem for treatments validated solely though the RCT design. A recent survey of doctoral training programs and predoctoral internship sites found that, by some measures, training in EST procedures has actually declined nationwide since 1993 (Woody, Weisz, & McLean, 2005). These surprising findings clearly indicate the need for additional research evidence beyond that obtained from RCTs is needed to move ESTs into real world clinical practice.

To facilitate the transportation of treatments from research to practice we must view treatment validation as an interconnected multiphase process that utilizes a variety of research designs to fully evaluate *both* the efficacy and effectiveness of a specific treatment. Furthermore, we must be objective in our appraisal of the *strengths and weaknesses* of all research methods, including the RCT methodology. A brief review of the psychopharmacology literature highlights other RCT methodology limitations.

LIMITATIONS OF THE RCT METHODOLOGY

The RCT method has been the "gold standard" for evaluating pharmacotherapies for over 40 years and has been credited with making "clinical psychopharmacology … a rigorous science" (Coyle, 1992, p. v). However, although the RCT method has been fairly successful in advancing pharmacotherapy, it is not without its limitations and criticisms even in this setting. "The RCT is a beautiful technique … but as with everything else there are snags" (Cochrane, 1989, p. 22). One of the primary "snags" in applying the RCT method is that all participants (researchers and subjects) *must* be blind to which treatment (active treatment or placebo) the patient has been randomized. However, when the RCT method is operationalized, even in psychopharmacology studies, the blinding of the active treatment is rarely if ever completely achieved (Fisher & Greenberg, 1993). In fact, when placebo treatments are made physiologically active to improve blinding the treatment, effect sizes drop considerably (Greenberg, Bornstein, Greenberg, & Fisher, 1992). This holds true for the newer antidepressants (the SSRIs) as well as the older ones (Greenberg, Bornstein, Zborowski, Fisher, & Greenberg, 1994). Similarly, side-effect profiles are highly correlated with the improvement ratings of both patients and researchers (Greenberg et al., 1992). These findings suggest that improvement rates obtained from RCTs are significantly influenced by nontreatment-related factors. Further evidence of the powerful influence of nontreatment factors comes from a recent analysis of 52 RCT antidepressant clinical trails contained in the U.S. Food and Drug Administration (FDA) database (Khan, Detke, Khan, & Mallinckrodt, 2003). This meta-analysis revealed that manipulations and alterations in study designs (selection criteria, measures employed, drug, dose and nature of the placebo) had a significant effect on the response magnitudes of both placebos and antidepressants. Consistent with the studies above, the magnitude of placebo response was significantly correlated with the antidepressant response ($r = .40$). The authors concluded that study design (i.e., method) features alone accounted for up to a "twofold change in the magnitude of symptom reduction" (Khan, Detke, Khan, & Mallinckrodt, 2003, p. 217) and that "a successful trial does not imply that the antidepressant is effective for the majority of depressed patients in clinical practice" (p. 218). Together, these findings raise doubts as to the adequacy of blinding achieved in medication studies. Inadequate blinding strikes a blow to the very methodological heart of the RCT design. If both patients and researchers are not completely blind to which arm of the study a subject is in, the method is logically flawed. If achieving adequate blinding is suspect in medication studies, it is impossible in psychotherapy studies. A research therapist will always know who is in the experimental group and who is in the control group so a true double blind will never be achieved. Inferences drawn from such studies will therefore be of questionable validity (Westen, Novotny, & Thompson-Brenner, 2005). Given that such limitations are apparent in the pharmacotherapy RCT literature, it seems unwarranted for this methodology to have received uncritical endorsement by the Division 12 committee as *the* methodology for evaluating psychotherapy.

RCT AS A METHOD FOR STUDYING PSYCHOTHERAPY

The appropriateness of the RCT methodology for evaluating psychotherapies has not been adequately established. Westen and colleagues have pointed out that the logical assumptions inherent to the RCT methodology have never been fully explored in relationship to its adaptation for psychotherapy research (Westen, Novotny, & Thompson-Brenner, 2004). These authors have argued that a number of the RCT assumptions (or methodological requirements) are not as valid in psychotherapy research as they are in medication research. We will briefly explore the impact of four interrelated assumptions of RCT methodology: the use of treatment manuals, employing a fixed duration of treatment, applying extensive exclusion criteria for selecting study participants, and the lack of realistic comparison treatments (also see Blatt & Zuroff, 2005; Wampold, 2001; Westen, Novotny, & Thompson-Brenner, 2004).

The use of manualized treatments has been a requirement for RCT methodology, specifically endorsed in the committee's report. This requirement is consistent with the experimentalist tradition. In the experimental model, manipulations are standardized to reduce error variance and maximize internal validity (Campbell & Standley, 1967). In psychotherapy research, this means that the treatment being studied must be standardized, as the treatment is the manipulation. The assumption that a treatment can be adequately standardized would, on the surface, appear more reasonable for medication than for psychotherapy. Psychotherapy is a complex interpersonal treatment composed of multiple techniques and activities. Standardizing such a treatment without losing its complexity would be a substantial feat. Some have argued that, in order to align the complexity of psychotherapy with the requirements of the RCT model, researchers have had to either overly simplify the treatments they study or create manuals that are prescriptive, rigid, and inflexible (Beutler & Harwood, 2000; Westen, Novotny, & Thompson-Brenner, 2004). As a result of these efforts to standardize psychotherapy for research purposes, the external validity of RCT trials has been questioned. This may be one reason that practitioners often reject RCT findings as being irrelevant to clinical practice (Parloff, 1998). Successful psychotherapists rely upon interpersonal and therapeutic flexibility to match their interventions with the patient's needs (Beutler & Harwood, 2000; Strupp, 1996). As Seligman (1995, 1996, 1998) has observed, self-correction is one of the hallmarks of therapy in actual clinical conditions. Therefore the findings from any research method that does not reflect the flexible and self-correcting nature of psychotherapy as practiced in applied clinical settings, at least to some degree, are unlikely to influence practicing clinicians.

Another assumption required for the implementation of the RCT method is the use of fixed duration treatments. This unusual modification of therapy is due mainly to cost and feasibility issues (research studies cannot run indefinitely) and is *not* specifically a requirement of the RCT model. Interestingly, the use of fixed duration treatments actually runs counter to a body of empirical data supporting the Phase Model response of psychotherapy (Howard et al., 1986, 1996), a model of therapy response showing that different outcome dimensions change at different points in treatment. The typical RCT trial employs a standardized (manualized) therapy applied for a fixed duration, usually between 11 to 20 sessions. This modification of therapy raises an important external validity question, namely how representative is this range (11 to 20 sessions) relative to the natural course of therapy? Westen and colleagues have presented data from a naturalistic study of psychotherapy showing that under actual applied conditions, therapies tended to be considerably longer (Morrison, Bradley, & Westen, 2003). In this survey study, the median number of sessions for patients being treated for panic disorder was 52; it was 75 for patients treated for depression. In addition, Thompson-Brenner and Westen (2005a) also note longer-term treatments (i.e., >5 months) for both CBT and psychodynamic (PD) clinicians treating eating disorder patients in the community. Especially noteworthy was that CBT clinicians in the community treated patients over three times longer than the length prescribed in treatment manuals for this disorder (69 vs. 19 sessions), despite otherwise implementing procedures outlined in CBT manuals for these disorders (Fairburn, Jones, Peveler, Hope, & O'Connor, 1993; Fairburn, Marcus, & Wilson, 1993). These data are consistent with the findings from other naturalistic studies showing that longer-term therapies are undertaken by practicing clinicians, and raise the hypothesis that longer treatments may lead to more improvement (Howard et al., 1996; Lueger, Lutz, & Howard, 2000; Seligman, 1995). Despite the limitations of such naturalistic studies, they do provide an important perspective on actual clinical practice patterns of a substantial group of therapists. During actual clinical practice, many therapists appear to deliver their treatments for a much longer period than that studied by RCT trials. Therefore, it is little surprise that practitioners are unlikely to be affected by RCT findings employing these brief, fixed duration, treatments. Conversely, Olfson, Marcus, Druss, and Pincus (2004) report on trends in outpatient psychotherapy utilization in a nationally representative sample. This study found that 35% of patients only attended 1 or 2 sessions of psychotherapy and almost 40% attended between 3 and 10 sessions. Results from this study show that 75% of patients attended 10 or fewer psychotherapy sessions. Together, these data suggest that the duration of psychotherapy in actual clinical practice is highly variable and lacks the consistency or predictability designed into RCT studies. In sum, a fixed duration treatment does not match the clinical reality that actual treatment duration is highly variable and that, for many patients, longer treatments (i.e., > 20 sessions) seem to produce greater benefit. Individuals seeking treatment in the community seem to either terminate prior to the minimal time period for most RCT trials (i.e., <10 sessions) or those who successfully complete treatment most often do so in a manner beyond the maximal time period found in RCT trials (i.e., > 20 sessions). The lack of consistency between RCT studies and therapy durations in actual clinical practice further weaken the external validity of such studies.

The strict application of the RCT experimental model also has an impact on the nature or representativness of the subjects or samples studied. In order to minimize error variance due to heterogeneity within the samples, RCT studies often artificially restrict eligible participants to diagnostically "pure" cases. This means that subjects with comorbid or subclinical conditions, as well as conditions that do not neatly fit into the *DSM-IV* (APA, 1994b) categories are routinely excluded from efficacy study samples. Again, although this limitation increases internal validity and the ability to draw cause and affect inferences, it jeopardizes external validity. Patients seen in standard clinical practice (in community clinics or private offices) typically have comorbid conditions. In fact, it has been estimated that between 50 and 90% of psychotherapy patients suffer from either a comorbid Axis I or Axis II condition (Kessler, Stang, Wittchen, Stein, & Walters, 1999; Morrison, Bradley, & Westen, 2003; Zimmerman, McDermut, & Mattia, 2000). Furthermore, Stirman, DeRubeis, Crits-Christoph, and Brody (2003) found that two thirds of HMO patients would not meet the diagnostic screening criteria for inclusion in any RCT study.

Another factor that affects the representativeness of RCT samples is the rapid increase in combined psychotherapy and medication treatment in standard clinical practice. Olfson, Marcus, Bruss, and Pincus (2002) reported that the percent of patients receiving outpatient psychotherapy and psychoactive medications had significantly increased from 31% in 1987 to 61% in 1997. The percentage of patients receiving combined psychotherapy and medications is likely to continue to grow in real world samples and will serve to further stretch the credibility of RCT treatment findings as clinicians will treat more patients receiving medication and psychotherapy whereas RCTs typically study therapy-only subjects. Again, the exclusion of all but noncomplex (i.e., simple) disorders (i.e., limited or no comorbidity) in previous research has negative implications for generalizability and may have led to an overestimate of treatment effects.

Another problematic issue in current RCT research is the general lack of "bona fide" treatment comparison groups. That is, in current EST studies, outcomes are not compared with naturalistically occurring treatments that are equivalent in therapist experience, skill, and overall credibility. Baskin, Tierney, Minami, and Wampold (2003), Luborsky et al. (2002), Wampold (2001), Wampold et al. (1997), and Westen, Novotny, and Thompson-Brenner (2005) all review several instances in the manualized treatment research literature wherein the active treatment is compared to nonequivalent and inferior treatment (i.e., designed to fail). The lack of bona fide treatment comparison groups in the manualized RCT research literature has probably led to the overestimate of treatment effects. Specifically, when the outcome effects of two equivalent (i.e., bona-fide, intent-to-succeed) treatments are compared, the average differences are quite small (Cohen's d .15–.20; Baskin, Tierney, Minami, & Wampold, 2003; Luborsky et al., 2002; Wampold, 2001). Therefore, if the goal of the EST movement is to be preferable to independent practice, it would seem that the most appropriate comparison group for an RCT is treatment performed by experienced doctoral level clinicians in private practice doing their best work with an unconstrained time limit.

Because of the limitations of RCT methodology with regard to the use of treatment manuals, fixed durations of treatment, exclusion criteria for study participants and the lack of realistic comparison treatments (also see Blatt &

Zuroff, 2005; Wampold, 2001; Westen, Novotny, & Thompson-Brenner, 2004), we believe it necessary to complement current RCT models with research designs that focus more on ecological validity. Such an approach is needed to reduce a methodcentric approach to psychotherapy research. We believe that this kind of complementary research evidence would also increase the translation of the EST to clinical practice. We therefore briefly present descriptions of some alternative research models that address these issues.

A HYBRID MODEL OF PSYCHOTHERAPY RESEARCH

The hybrid model of psychotherapy research outlined here attempts to combine the rigor of the efficacy method with the external validity of effectiveness designs to examine interrelated issues regarding psychological assessment, clinical process, and treatment outcomes (e.g., Table 2.1; Adelphi University Psychotherapy Project, Hilsenroth, 2002, in press). Specifically, this treatment method applies the assessment and training in technique of an efficacy model, to a naturalistic setting (Seligman, 1995, 1996). The incorporation of these efficacy features in an otherwise naturalistic treatment delivery setting allows for the measurement of treatment fidelity in a more flexible treatment procedure. In this way, the model is closer to the real world of service delivery, and provides important information regarding treatment intervention that is not often evaluated in naturalistic psychotherapy effectiveness studies.

In this research method, treatment manuals are utilized for intensive training in technique. These manuals are used to aid, inform, and guide the treatment rather than to prescribe it. Therapists are encouraged to provide the interventions in an accurate (Crits-Christoph, Cooper, & Luborsky, 1988), congruent (Caspar et al., 2000; Connolly et al., 1999; Piper, Joyce, McCallum, & Azim, 1993; Silberschatz, Fretter, & Curtis, 1986), competent (Barber, Crits-Christoph, & Luborsky, 1996), and optimally responsive (Stiles, Honos-Webb, & Surko, 1998) manner. This flexible approach is emphasized over producing a high volume of certain techniques within a predetermined session framework. Another difference between the findings from the application of this method and those from the strict RCT model is the inclusion of all patients, regardless of comorbidity (i.e., Axis II), as well as not setting an arbitrary time limit on the provision of treatment. As such, this research model more closely approximates a naturalistic examination of patient change during psychotherapy as delivered in the community.

Another unique feature of this hybrid research model is that it takes on a broader view of outcome than the traditional RCT, which emphasizes symptom change. In the hybrid model, patients are seen as multidimensional beings who vary not only from one another (the nomothetic dimension), but also in the way they view themselves (self perception), and the way that others view them (social perception). This broad approach to outcomes assessment strives for a comprehensive understanding of an individual and allows for the exploration of comorbidity, severity levels, and change in relation to therapeutic intervention. To achieve this multidimensional perspective, outcomes in this program are evaluated from three perspectives (Strupp, 1996) including: patient self-report, therapist ratings, and external raters via videotape. Pre- and post-measures include well-normed questionnaires evaluating psychiatric symptoms, social functioning (work, family, leisure), interpersonal functioning, dynamic personality characteristics, well-operationalized behavioral criteria, and survey material. This array of measures is designed to assess changes across a broad range of functioning, including productivity at work, quality of interpersonal relations, improvement on the presenting problem, satisfaction with treatment and global improvement.

As shown in Table 2.1, these measures are administered longitudinally: prior to beginning treatment, at standardized points during the treatment, and at termination of treatment. Videotaped psychotherapy sessions are viewed and coded on a number of different process dimensions. At the end of treatment, patients complete an exit evaluation. Thus, measures of clinical assessment and psychotherapy process can be evaluated in relation to the outcome of treatment. Additionally, this type of program is distinctive in that one can examine the effects of a psychological assessment process itself on the ensuing treatment.

PRACTICE NETWORK MODEL OF PSYCHOTHERAPY RESEARCH

Another alternative to the efficacy RCT research model is a practice network approach, in which randomly (or in some cases nonrandom) selected, experienced clinicians provide data on patients that can be aggregated across large samples (Bradley, Greene, Russ, Dutra, & Westen, 2005; Borkovec, Echemendia, Ragusea, & Ruiz, 2001; Morey, 1988; Shedler & Westen, 2004a, 2004b; Stricker & Trierweiler, 1995; Thompson-Brenner & Westen, 2005a, 2005b; West, Zarin, & Pincus, 1997; Westen & Shedler, 1999a, 1999b; Westen, Shedler, Durrett, Glass, & Martens, 2003). This model allows for naturalistic data from clinicians in the community to provide information on patients from everyday practice and to identify variables they predict to influence treatment outcomes in real-world settings. Seligman (1995) and others (e.g., Goldfried & Wolfe, 1998) have argued that most treatment outcome studies are not clinically representative; that is, they do not possess characteristics that are routinely present in applied clinical practice. Clinicians are unlikely to use the same exclusionary criteria (e.g., no current substance abuse or comorbidity, or no concurrent treatment with psychotropic medications) and clinical procedures (e.g., random assignment of clients, manualized treatment, or a fixed number of sessions) commonly used in treatment studies. As a result, differences between efficacy RCT and clinically representative studies have produced mixed results and important differences (Thompson-Brenner & Westen, 2005; Weisz, Weersing, & Henggeler, 2005; Westen & Morrison, 2001; Westen et al., 2004a, 2004b, 2005; Woody et al., 2005).

Table 2.1 Example of a Hybrid Model of Psychotherapy Research: Adelphi University Psychotherapy Project-Assessment Schedule

	Assessment	3rd	9th/15th/27th/36th/64th	21st/52nd/76th/Final
Patient	Self-report Rorschach Early Memory Protocol[a] Process Alliance	Process Alliance	Self-report Process Alliance	Self-report Process Alliance
Therapist	Semistructured Clinical Interview DSM-IV-Multiaxial Process Alliance	Psychodynamic Q-Sort & Ratings DSM-IV-Multiaxial Process Alliance	DSM-IV-Multiaxial Process Alliance	Psychodynamic Q-Sort & Ratings DSM-IV-Multiaxial Process Alliance
External rater (videotape)	DSM-IV-Multiaxial Process Alliance	Psychodynamic Q-Sort & Ratings DSM-IV-Multiaxial Therapist activity Process Alliance	DSM-IV-Multiaxial Therapist activity Process Alliance	Psychodynamic Q-Sort & Ratings DSM-IV-Multiaxial Therapist activity Process Alliance

[a] See Hilsenroth, M. J. (2002) for a detailed description of this assessment process and the instruments and procedures employed.

EFFECTIVENESS-RCT MODEL OF PSYCHOTHERAPY RESEARCH

Westen and colleagues (2001, 2003, 2004, 2005) have recently proposed an alternative to the efficacy-RCT model that extends the Practice Network Model through the use of multi-observer (patient, clinician, independent observers via audio/video) assessment of both interventions and outcomes, random assignment of patients to experienced clinicians in the community as well as longitudinal follow-up using a prospective design. Their Effectiveness-RCT model of psychotherapy research begins by identifying effective practice in the community, by observing the therapeutic techniques used by experienced clinicians, studying these interventions with a wide range of patients with clinical and subclinical symptomatology and not excluding patients with comorbid conditions. By measuring rather than prescribing interventions, one may better discern what works for whom under naturalistic conditions, within as well as across treatments. This model uses applied clinical practice as a natural laboratory for identifying interventions associated with success irrespective of theoretical orientation, captures the natural variation that exists among clinicians as well as patients and, in the analysis of intervention-outcome relationships, creates prototypes of successful treatments which can then guide empirically derived treatment manuals based on actual practice. The major advantage afforded by this complementary RCT model is that treatments constructed around empirically supported change processes practiced by experienced clinicians would likely encounter much less resistance than many laboratory-derived treatment manuals. Such an alternative approach to treatment development and training may be said to be even *"more"* empirically based than current approaches to manual construction. It also makes a great deal of conceptual sense. That is, the identification of what techniques are empirically related to patient outcomes in applied practice *"before"* organizing a treatment manual.

CONCLUSIONS

In this chapter, we have suggested that some aspects of the debate regarding ESTs reflect a tendency for psychologists to define themselves by a preferred research method rather than to identify professionally with the broader field of psychology. In this context, many of the heated debates concerning RCT methodology are seen as resulting, in part, from methodcentric reasoning and as reflecting an ideological position rather than being a dispassionate evaluation of science. We have reviewed some of the limitations of the RCT methodology as it is applied in psychopharmacology studies. We went on to raise additional concerns regarding the RCT model's appropriateness for psychotherapy research including; inadequate blinding, restrictive or inflexible treatment packages, fixed treatment durations, restrictive inclusion criteria, and the lack of realistic treatment comparison groups. Together, these limitations combine to reduce the external validity of the RCT models of psychotherapy research. The limitation in external validity likely plays a role in the slow translation and adoption of ESTs in actual clinical practice. Finally, we presented alternative research designs that could be used in conjunction with current efficacy-RCT models to increase external validity as well as to facilitate the exploration of other promising areas of psychotherapy research such as the therapeutic alliance, specific therapist interventions, and patient-therapist interactions. By acknowledging the value of these additional research designs and alternative areas of research focus, we believe that the goals expressed by Division 12 would likely achieve greater support and ultimately wider adoption in applied practice.

We fully support the need for evidence-based psychotherapy practice but believe that this evidence must flow from a variety of avenues. We feel that the nature of psychotherapy is too complex for a single research method or model to be the exclusive means for demonstrating a treatment's validity. In our opinion, understanding *how* and *why* psychotherapy works in an applied setting is just as important as understanding if it works in an experimental setting. Additionally, in the current healthcare environment, methodcentric actions, even if well intentioned, are likely to produce little more than internal conflict and ideological battles. This is not the time for psychotherapy researchers (or the broader field of psychology) to be divided along methodological lines. Rather, it is a time for us to work together in a manner that draws on the best of our diverse research perspectives, professional allegiances, and practice environments. Efforts to shape the practice of psychology that avoid methodcentric reasoning and reflect the diversity of our profession will, in our opinion, have the best chance of succeeding. We also support the value of having psychologists, researchers and clinicians, learn to practice (when appropriate) time-sensitive and symptom-effective treatments for the more common (and uncomplicated) psychiatric disorders like depression and anxiety. However, we recognize that much of the therapy that takes place in applied clinical practice does not match this scenario. In applied clinical practice, patients do not always have a clear or specific psychiatric condition; treatments require adjustment and modification due to the interaction of patient and therapists variables, the length of treatment is unpredictable, and benefits are desired across a wide range of important outcome dimensions.

Toward the close of his Presidential address, Cronbach (1957) stated, "Psychology requires combined, not parallel labors from our two historic disciplines. In this common labor they will almost certainly become one, with a common theory, a common method, and common recommendations for social betterment" (p. 680). While we wait on the developments of a common theory and method, a common message we should be sending is that psychotherapy has much to offer both as a means of reducing human suffering and improving individual functioning. Here we are fortunate, because there is overwhelming scientific evidence supporting the general effectiveness of psychotherapy (Howard et al., 1986, 1996; Lambert and Bergin, 1994; Lipsey & Wilson, 1993; Lueger et al., 2000). However, as with all complex human activities, there is still much to learn about *how and why* psychotherapy is effective and this is not the time to limit the methodological options available for achieving this desired understanding.

REFERENCES

American Psychiatric Association. (1993). Practice guidelines for major depressive disorder in adults. *American Psychiatric Association, 150* (4, Suppl.), v, 1–26.

American Psychiatric Association. (1994a). Practice Guidelines for the Treatment of Patients with Bipolar Disorder. *American Psychiatric Association, 151*(12, Suppl.), iv, 1–36.

American Psychiatric Association. (1994b). *Diagnostic and statistical manual of mental disorders* (4th ed.). Washington, DC: Author.

American Psychiatric Association. (1995). Practice guidelines for the treatment of patients with substance use disorders: Alcohol, cocaine, opioids. *American Psychiatric Association, 152*(11, Suppl.), 1–59.

American Psychological Association. (2006). Evidence-based practice in psychology: APA Presidential Task Force on evidence-based practice. *American Psychologist, 61*, 271–285.

Barber, J., Crits-Christoph, P., & Luborsky, L. (1996). Effects of therapist adherence and competence on patient outcome in brief dynamic therapy. *Journal of Consulting and Clinical Psychology, 64*, 619–622.

Baskin, T., Tierney, S., Minami, T., & Wampold, B. (2003). Establishing specificity in psychotherapy: A meta-analysis of structural equivalence of placebo controls. *Journal of Consulting and Clinical Psychology, 71*, 973–979.

Berger, P. L., & Luckmann, T. (1966). *The social construction of reality: A treatise in the sociology of knowledge.* Harmondsworth, England: Penguin Books.

Blatt, S. J. (1995). The destructiveness of perfectionism: Implications for the treatment of depression. *American Psychologist, 50*, 1003–1020.

Blatt, S. J., & Zuroff, D. C. (2005). Empirical evaluation of the assumptions in identifying evidenced based treatments in mental health, *Clinical Psychology Review, 25*, 459–486.

Beutler, L. E., & Harwood, T. M. (2000). *Prescriptive psychotherapy: A practical guide to systematic treatment selection.* New York: Oxford Press.

Borkovec, T. D., Echemendia, R. J., Ragusea, S. A., & Ruiz, M. (2001). The Pennsylvania Practice Research Network and future possibilities for clinically meaningful and scientifically rigorous psychotherapy effectiveness research. *Clinical Psychology: Science and Practice, 8*, 155–167.

Bradley, R., Greene, J., Russ, E., Dutra, L., & Westen, D. (2005). A multidimensional meta-analysis of psychotherapy for PTSD. *American Journal of Psychiatry, 162*, 1–14.

Campbell, D. T., & Stanley, J. C. (1967). *Experimental and quasi-experimental designs for Research.* Chicago: Rand McNally Publishing Company.

Caspar, F., Pessier, J., Stuart, J., Safran, J., Samstag, L., & Guirguis, M. (2000). One step further in assessing how interpretations influence the process of psychotherapy. *Psychotherapy Research, 10*, 309–320.

Chambless, M. (1995). Training in and dissemination of empirically-validated psychological treatments: Report and recommendations. *The Clinical Psychologist, 48*, 3–24.

Cochrane, A. (1989). *Effectiveness and efficacy.* Cambridge, England: Royal Society of Medicine.

Connolly, M., Crits-Christoph, P., Shappell, S., Barber, J., Luborsky, L., & Shaffer, C. (1999). Relation of transference interpretations to outcome in early sessions of brief supportive-expressive psychotherapy. *Psychotherapy Research, 9*, 485–495.

Coyle, J. T. (1992). Forward. In F. Fava & J. F. Rosenbaum (Eds.), *Research designs and methods in psychiatry.* New York: Elsevier, v.

Crits-Christoph, P. (1992). The efficacy of brief dynamic psychotherapies: A meta-analysis. *American Journal of Psychiatry, 149,* 151–158.

Crits-Christoph, P., Cooper, A., & Luborsky, L. (1988). The accuracy of therapists' interpretations and the outcome of dynamic psychotherapy. *Journal of Consulting and Clinical Psychology, 56,* 490–495.

Cronbach, L. J. (1957). The two disciplines of scientific psychology. *American Psychologist, 12,* 671–684.

Fairburn, C., Jones, R., Peveler, R., Hope, R., & O'Connor, M. (1993). Psychotherapy and bulimia nervosa. *Archives of General Psychiatry, 50,* 419–428.

Fairburn, C., Marcus, M., & Wilson, G. (1993). Cognitive-behavioral therapy for binge eating and bulimia nervosa: A comprehensive treatment manual. In C. Fairburn & G. Wilson (Eds.), *Binge eating: Nature, assessment, and treatment* (12th ed., pp. 317–360). New York: Guilford.

Fisher, S. & Greenberg, R. (1993). How sound is the double-blind design of evaluating psychotropic drugs? *The Journal of Nervous and Mental Disease, 181,* 345–350.

Frank, J. (1979). *Persuasion and healing.* Baltimore, MD: The Johns Hopkins University Press.

Goldfried, M., & Wolfe, B. (1998). Toward a more clinically valid approach to therapy research. *Journal of Consulting and Clinical Psychology, 66,* 143–150.

Gonzales, J. J., Ringeisen, H. L., & Chambers, D. A. (2002). The tangled and thorny path of science to practice: Tensions in interpreting and applying "evidence." *Clinical Psychology: Science and Practice, 9,* 204–209.

Greenberg, R., Bornstein, R., Greenberg, M., & Fisher, S. (1992). A meta-analysis of anti-depressant outcome under "blinder" conditions. *Journal of Consulting and Clinical Psychology, 60,* 664–669.

Greenberg, R., Bornstein, R., Zborowski, M., Fisher, S., & Greenberg, M. (1994). A meta-analysis of fluoxetine in the treatment of depression. *The Journal of Nervous and Mental Disease, 182,* 547–551.

Hilsenroth, M. J. (2002). Adelphi University: Psychotherapy Process and Outcome Research Team. In P. Fonagy, J. Clarkin, A. Gerber, H. Kachele, R. Krause, E. Jones, R. Perron, & E. Allison (Eds.), *An open door review of outcome studies in psychoanalysis* (2nd ed, pp. 241–247). London: International Psychoanalytic Association.

Hilsenroth, M. (In Press). A Programmatic Study of Short-Term Psychodynamic Psychotherapy: Assessment, Process, Outcome and Training. *Psychotherapy Research.*

Howard, K. I., Kopta, S. M., Krause, M. S., & Orlinsky, D. E. (1986). The dose-effect relationship in psychotherapy. *American Psychologist, 41,* 159–164.

Howard, K., Moras, K., Brill, P., Martinovich, Z., & Lutz, W. (1996). Evaluation of psychotherapy: Efficacy, effectiveness, and patient progress. *American Psychologist, 51,* 1059–1064.

Kessler, R. C., Stang, P., Wittchen, H. U., Stein, M., & Alters, E. E. (1999). Lifetime comorbidities between social phobia and mood disorders in the US national comorbidity survey. *Psychological Medicine, 29,* 555–567.

Khan, A., Detke, M., Khan, S. R., & Mallinckrodt, C. (2003). Placebo response and anti-depressant clinical trial outcome. *The Journal of Nervous and Mental Disease, 191,* 211–218.

Lambert, J. L. (1998). Manual-based treatment and clinical practice: Hangman of life or promising development. *Clinical Psychology: Science and Practice, 5*, 391–395.

Lambert, J. L., & Bergin, A. E. (1994). The effectiveness of psychotherapy. In A. E. Bergin & S. L. Garfield (Eds.), *Handbook of psychotherapy and behavior change* (4th ed., pp. 143–189). New York: Wiley.

Lipsey M., & Wilson, D. (1993). The efficacy of psychological, educational, and behavioral treatment: Confirmation from meta-analysis. *American Psychologist, 48*, 1181–1209.

Luborsky, L., Diguer, L., Seligman, D. A., Rosenthal, R., Johnson, S., Halperin, G., Bishop, M., & Schweizer, E. (1999). The researcher's own therapeutic allegiance: A "wild card" in comparisons of treatment efficacy. *Clinical Psychology: Science and Practice, 6*, 95–132.

Luborsky, L., Rosenthal, R., Diguer, L., Andrusyna, T. P., Levitt, J., Seligman, D. A., & Krause, E. D. (2002). The dodo bird verdict is alive and well—mostly. *Clinical Psychology: Science and Practice, 9*, 2–12.

Lueger, R., Lutz, W., & Howard, K. (2000). The predicted and observed course of psychotherapy for anxiety and mood disorders. *Journal Nervous Mental Disease, 188*, 127–134.

Morey, L. (1988). Personality disorders in DSM-III and DSM-III-R: Convergence, coverage, and internal consistency. *American Journal of Psychiatry, 145*, 573–577.

Morrison, C., Bradley, R., & Westen, D. (2003). The external validity of efficacy trails for depression and anxiety: A naturalistic study. *Psychology and Psychotherapy: Theory, Research and Practice, 76*, 109–132.

Nathan, P. E., & Gorman, J. M. (1998). Treatments that work—and what convinces us they do. In P. Nathan & J. Gorman (Eds.), *A guide to treatments that work* (pp. 3–26). New York: Oxford University Press.

Olfson, M., Marcus, S. C., Bruss, B., & Harold, P. A. (2002). National trends in use of outpatient psychotherapy. *American Journal of Psychiatry, 159*, 1914–1920.

Parloff, M. B. (1998). Is psychotherapy more than manual labor? *Clinical Psychology: Science and Practice, 5*, 376–381.

Piper, W., Joyce, A., McCallum, M., & Azim, H. (1993). Concentration and correspondence of transference interpretations in short-term therapy. *Journal of Consulting and Clinical Psychology, 61*, 586–595.

Seligman, M., (1995). The effectiveness of psychotherapy: The consumer reports study. *American Psychologist, 50*, 965–974.

Seligman, M. (1996). Science as an ally of practice. *American Psychologist, 51*, 1072–1079.

Seligman, M. E. (1998). Afterward—A plea. In P. Nathan & J. Gorman (Eds.), *A guide to treatments that work* (pp. 568–571). New York: Oxford University Press.

Shedler, J., & Westen, D. (2004a). Dimensions of personality pathology: An alternative to the Five Factor Model. *American Journal of Psychiatry, 161*, 1743–1754.

Shedler, J., & Westen, D. (2004b). Refining personality disorder diagnoses: Integrating science and practice. *American Journal of Psychiatry, 161*, 1350–1365.

Silberschatz, G., Fretter, P., & Curtis, J. (1986). How do interpretations influence the process of psychotherapy? *Journal of Consulting and Clinical Psychology, 54*, 646–652.

Smith, M., & Glass, G. (1977). Meta-analysis of psychotherapy outcome studies. *American Psychologist, 32*, 752–760.

Spearman, C. (1961). In C. Murchison (Ed.), *A history of psychology in autobiography* (Vol. 1, pp. 200–333). New York: Russell and Russell (original work published in 1930).

Stiles, W., Honos-Webb, L., & Surko, M. (1998). Responsiveness in psychotherapy. *Clinical Psychology: Science and Practice, 5,* 439–458.

Stricker, G., & Trierweiler, S. (1995). The local clinical scientist: A bridge between science and practice. *American Psychologist, 50,* 995–1002.

Stirman, S. W., DeRubeis, R. J., Crits-Christoph, P., & Brody, P. E. (2003). Are samples in randomized controlled trails of psychotherapy representative of community outpatients? A new methodology and initial findings. *Journal of Consulting and Clinical Psychology, 71,* 963–972.

Strupp, H. (1996). The Tripartite Model and the *Consumer Reports* study. *American Psychologist, 51,* 1017–1024.

Thompson-Brenner, H., & Westen, D. (2005a). A naturalistic study of psychotherapy for bulimia nervosa, Part 1: Comorbidity and Therapeutic Outcome. *Journal of Nervous and Mental Disease, 193,* 573–584.

Thompson-Brenner, H., & Westen, D. (2005b). A naturalistic study of psychotherapy for bulimia nervosa, Part 2: Therapeutic interventions and outcome in the community. *Journal of Nervous and Mental Disease, 193,* 585–595.

Thompson-Brenner, H., & Westen, D. (2005). Personality subtypes in eating disorders: Validation of a classification in a naturalistic sample. *British Journal of Psychiatry, 186,* 516–24.

Wampold, B. (2001). *The great psychotherapy debate: Models, methods, and findings.* Mahwah, NJ: Erlbaum.

Wampold, B., Mondin, G., Moody, M., Stich, F., Benson, K., & Ahn, H. (1997). Methodological problems in identifying efficacious psychotherapies. *Psychotherapy Research, 7,* 21–43.

Weisz, J., Weersing, V., & Henggeler, S. (2005). Jousting with straw men: Comment on Westen, Novotny, and Thompson-Brenner (2004). *Psychological Bulletin, 131,* 418–426.

West, J., Zarin, D., & Pincus, H. (1997). Clinical and psychopharmacologic practice patterns of psychiatrists in routine practice. *Psychopharmacology Bulletin, 33,* 79–85.

Westen, D., & Morrison, K. (2001). A multidimensional meta-analysis of treatments for depression, panic, and generalized anxiety disorder: An empirical examination of the status of empirically supported therapies. *Journal of Consulting and Clinical Psychology, 69,* 875–899.

Westen, D., Novotny, C., M., & Thompson-Brenner, H. (2004a). The empirical status of empirically supported psychotherapies: Assumptions, findings, and reporting in controlled clinical trails. *Psychological Bulletin, 130,* 631–663.

Westen, D., Novotny, C., M., & Thompson-Brenner, H. (2004b). The next generation of psychotherapy research: Reply to Ablon and Marci (2004), Goldfried and Eubanks-Carter (2004), and Haaga (2004). *Psychological Bulletin, 130,* 677–683.

Westen, D., Novotny, C. M., & Thompson-Brenner, H. (2005). EBP does not equal EST: Reply to Crits-Christoph et al. (2005) and Weisz et al. (2005). *Psychological Bulletin, 131,* 427–433.

Westen, D., & Shedler, J. (1999a). Revising and assessing axis II, part I: Developing a clinically and empirically valid assessment method. *American Journal of Psychiatry, 156,* 258–272.

Westen, D., & Shedler, L. (1999b). Revising and Assessing Axis II, Part II: Toward an Empirically Based and Clinically Useful Classification of Personality Disorders. *American Journal of Psychiatry, 156,* 273–285.

Westen, D., Shedler, L., Durrett, C., Glass, S., & Martens, A. (2003). Personality diagnosis in adolescence: DSM-IV diagnoses and an empirically derived alternative. *American Journal of Psychiatry, 160,* 952–966.

Westen, D., & Weinberger, J. (2004). When clinical description becomes statistical prediction. *American Psychologist, 59,* 595–613.

Woody, S. R., Weisz, J., & McLean, C. (2005). Empirically supported treatments: 10 years later. The *Clinical Psychologist, 58*(4), 5–11.

Zimmerman, M., McDermut, W., & Mattia, J. (2000). Frequency of anxiety disorders in psychiatric outpatients with major depressive disorder. *American Journal of Psychiatry, 157,* 1337–1340.

3

An Integrative, Principle-Based Approach to Psychotherapy

JOHN E. PACHANKIS AND MARVIN R. GOLDFRIED

INTRODUCTION

To this day, professionals with an interest in therapy continue to bemoan the fragmented approach to treatment that has characterized their field. This fragmentation takes many forms. Therapists trained in various approaches to treatment often seem reluctant to approach clinical issues from the point of view of practitioners trained in theoretical orientations other than their own. Psychotherapy researchers produce manuals that many practitioners lament do not address the real-world clinical realities that they face. Thumbing through current psychotherapy-related conference program bulletins, one is just as likely to find presentations touting the unique strengths of any one of hundreds of empirically supported treatments as he or she is likely to find presentations pointing out the common factors—such as the therapy relationship—shared by all treatments. Potential clients often call asking for expert treatment in the latest brand-name therapies. Potential students choose training programs based on preconceived biases about the relative good and evil inherent in the various orientations upon which the programs are based.

Over a quarter-century ago, one of us noted the crisis that the field of psychotherapy was facing as a result of this fragmentation, as well as potential solutions that could allay the then-current state of affairs (Goldfried, 1980). Here, we revisit that discussion, noting both the increasing proliferation of disjointed approaches to treatment as well as the innovative movements toward unifying approaches to treatment. Both trends are closely tied to research paradigms, which, ultimately, are influenced by external forces.

This chapter begins by addressing the external forces that influence the shape of psychological approaches to treatment. The increase in empirically validated, manual-based treatments, resulting largely from the application of controlled clinical trials to psychotherapy research, has done little to advance a unified approach to psychotherapy. Clinicians are realistically skeptical of the empirically supported treatments that emerge from such research, as it fails to examine the effectiveness of therapy as it is practiced in the real world. We argue that psychotherapy process research, on the other hand, is better suited to determining the process of change associated with our interventions. Unfortunately, such research has been in decline with the increasing presumption by funding agencies that randomized clinical trials offer a "gold standard" by which all psychotherapy treatment research should be judged. However, process research could reasonably make a comeback, given the recent increase in collaborative efforts that delineate broad-based principles of change. These principles are in need of empirical support of the type that process research methodology is suitable for determining. Principles of change include hypotheses about the core ingredients necessary for client change. Because such principles lie at a level of abstraction between technique and theory, they lend themselves to investigation and utilization by researchers and clinicians from all theoretical backgrounds. Our chapter concludes by addressing the merits of training therapists to think in terms of principles of change. Although it does not preclude the effective implementation of treatment manuals, such an approach, it is argued, far exceeds training that focuses on manual-based treatments and may, in fact, lead to even more effective use of manuals than traditional training affords.

CURRENT APPROACH TO OUTCOME RESEARCH

Therapists increasingly receive the message that to be optimally therapeutic with clients, they need to implement a treatment that has empirical support for its effectiveness. This message often takes the form of: "When data exist supporting the effectiveness of treatment X for problem A, it is wrong-headed to implement anything but treatment X when working with a client with problem A." Yet, the context in which data regarding the effectiveness of a treatment emerges is often quite different than the context in which these treatments might ultimately be put to use. For that reason, clinicians do not use data-supported treatments as frequently as they could (Cohen, Sargent, & Sechrest, 1986). This situation results from the inherent limitations of the current psychotherapy research paradigm and compounds (and likewise, is compounded by) the gap between psychotherapy researchers and clinicians.

The limitations of the current psychotherapy research paradigm are closely intertwined with the broader context from which this paradigm has emerged. Early research simply attempted to determine if psychotherapy produced changes in personality. Before the 1950s, researchers paid little attention to the nature of the treatments being employed or the problems being targeted. However, with the rise of behavior therapy in the 1960s, researchers began comparing different approaches to treating specific clinical issues, giving rise to therapy manuals, randomized assignment to treatment conditions, and other methodological advances. Beginning in the 1980s, psychotherapy research increasingly came to resemble the clinical trial methodology used in drug trial research (Goldfried & Wolfe, 1996).

As psychotherapists came under increased pressure from Congress and third-party payers to demonstrate that their interventions were effective, indeed as effective as proliferating psychiatric drug treatments, therapy researchers increasingly adopted the methodology used in drug trials to demonstrate the effectiveness of their work. The NIMH Treatment of Depression Collaborative Research Program (Elkin, Parloff, Hadley, & Autry, 1985) set the methodological standard for the evaluation of the effectiveness of psychosocial treatments. This standard, which continues to exist today, requires that NIMH-funded treatment research include manualized therapies for *DSM* disorders. The resulting research has successfully reached its aims. Today, practitioners can draw on lists, practice-guidelines, and textbooks of empirically supported treatments that rival the resources used by psychiatrists when determining their approach to treating a particular client problem. However, because of the problematic assumptions underlying the methodology used to test the efficacy of psychotherapy, the resulting treatments that are currently touted as best-practice have a number of limitations (Westen, Novotny, & Thompson-Brenner, 2004).

One such limitation is the proliferation of treatment manuals. Some have pointed out that manuals, originally designed as research tools to ensure high internal validity, are now often regarded as a necessary protection against fallible clinical judgment (Goldfried & Eubanks-Carter, 2004; Westen et al., 2004). However, as Safran and Muran (2000) note, learning to do therapy is similar to learning any complex skill, and the didactic presentation of declarative knowledge through manuals is unlikely to convey the largely tacit, procedural tasks required to be an effective therapist. Westen et al. (2004) note a number of limitations inherent in the current assumptions underlying manuals. Specifically, they describe the constraining nature of presenting manuals as whole packages, the deviation from which renders one's treatment approach invalid. They also note a shift from manuals-as-descriptive (documenting what therapists in treatment studies implement) to manuals-as-prescriptive (specifying exactly what therapist behaviors ought to be employed when). Further, they point out that manuals often preclude the active client-therapist collaboration that is essential to optimal therapeutic outcomes but detrimental to experimental control.

Limitations such as these widen the divide between clinician and researcher. The use of a medical model approach to research that randomly assigns single-diagnosis patients to treatment groups, including a time-limited, theoretically pure treatment group, does not provide very clinically useful information (Goldfried & Wolfe, 1996). Whereas psychotherapy researchers are concerned with maximizing the internal validity of their studies, clinicians are concerned with treating clients with comorbid disorders, addressing the underlying inter-personal and intrapersonal issues maintaining clients' problems, and responding to therapy ruptures and impasses (Goldfried & Wolfe, 1996).

The recent report of the American Psychological Association (APA) Presidential Task Force on Evidence-Based Practice (APA, 2005) emerged in a context in which the gap between clinician and researcher was becoming increasingly apparent. In this context, third-party payers (e.g., state Medicaid programs) paid greater attention to empirically supported treatments with the goal of improving the cost-effectiveness and accountability of mental health service provision. At the same time, many were raising concerns about the clinical utility of empirically-supported treatments. As a result of these simultaneous developments, the Task Force report explicitly addresses the increasing disconnect between clinicians and researchers. It defines evidence-based practice as "the integration of the best available research with clinical expertise" (p. 5). The report emphasizes two dimensions—treatment efficacy and clinical utility—adopted from the Criteria for Evaluating Treatment Guidelines (APA, 2002), which must be considered in evaluating research that seeks to determine if a given treatment works.

Clinically efficacious treatments are those that have been empirically shown to be more effective than a control condition in a randomized controlled trial (Seligman, 1995), whereas clinical utility refers to the usefulness of a particular treatment approach given the generalizability and feasibility of implementing that treatment for a particular case at hand (APA, 2005). The recommendations of the task force simultaneously consider these two dimensions that seem promising in their ability to promote the type of approach to research, practice, and training that we advocate here. For example, the report calls for greater use of multiple sources of research evidence, including clinical observations, process-outcome research, and interventions as they are delivered in naturalistic settings. Further, it explicitly notes the necessity of studying the skills of clinicians who obtain optimal outcomes in the community, as well as the establishment of practice-research networks, in which clinicians from the community generate data suitable for empirical examination from the clients that they see in their practices. Recommendations such as these encourage clinician-researcher collaboration to determine the components of effective therapy as it is practiced outside of controlled research trials.

The empirical identification of treatments that work is certainly laudable. In recent years, given the external pressures under which providers of psychosocial treatments have found themselves, it has become crucial to demonstrate the effectiveness of psychosocial treatments for mental health disorders (Barlow, 1994). Additionally, such research represents an attempt to offer clinicians an alternative to the fallibility of clinical decision-making (Meehl, 1997). As noted above, however, the treatments that emerge from controlled clinical trials are limited in their clinical utility, as this methodology precludes a focus on the complexities of therapy as clinicians in the community practice it. Instead, the resulting research findings simply demonstrate that treatment X works as well as or better than treatment Y. Many therapists working in the community are likely to disregard such findings as overly simplistic and not based in the complex realities that they face in their practices. In fact, some therapists may believe that the way that therapy is practiced in the real world is simply too complex to be studied. Those therapists who are most inclined to believe that therapy is an art, enhanced by interpersonal skills unique to individual clinicians and refined only after years of training and practice are probably the least likely to believe that they can benefit from psychotherapy research. Therapy is indeed a highly complex, dynamic process for which some research designs, such as the randomized clinical trial, are poorly suited to addressing. As is the case with drug effectiveness studies, little attention is given to understanding the mechanisms underlying the effectiveness of psychotherapy in randomized controlled psychotherapy studies. Attention is only paid to whether or not the treatment is efficacious. However, unlike research that simply considers outcomes across treatment groups, process research methodology, although challenging to conduct, can determine the complex mechanisms that lead to successful outcomes.

PSYCHOTHERAPY PROCESS RESEARCH

Beginning attempts to study the process of change focused on assessing what actually occurred in therapy sessions. Kiesler's (1973) *The Process of Psychotherapy: Empirical Foundations and Systems of Analysis,* the first book entirely devoted to the topic of process research, mostly described specific instruments and approaches to examining what occurred in therapy sessions and the measurement of the immediate effects of particular in-session occurrences. Despite the strengths of measuring specific therapist-client communications and examining the subsequent therapeutic impact of those communications, endeavors in process research at the time lacked coherence. In the Preface to his book, Kiesler describes the then-current state of affairs noting that: "Psychotherapy process research has to rank near the forefront of research disciplines characterized as chaotic, prolific, unconnected, and disjointed, with researchers unaware of much of the work that has preceded and the individual investigator tending to start anew completely ignorant of closely-related previous work" (1973, p. xvii).

Over ten years later, Kiesler (1986) revisited this statement and noted that the state of process research had changed for the better. In particular, he noted that process research had become increasingly collaborative and programmatic. Around the same time, other trends in process research began to emerge. Instead of studying the therapy process, researchers began focusing on "process of change." That is, rather than simply describing what occurred in the session, process researchers were increasingly interested in studying those aspects of therapy that were likely to lead to client change, defined in a broader, more contextual way. Process researchers became more collaborative in their work and began examining a broader range of variables and considering their impact on eventual outcome. This shift in looking at the process of change resulted in a greater integration of process and outcome considerations (Greenberg, 1986; Greenberg & Pinsof, 1986; Kiesler, 1983). These trends heralded the promise that process research continues to hold today for elucidating the nature of therapeutic change and the role that therapist and client behaviors may play in facilitating that change.

Just as process researchers have come to realize the benefits of looking at the findings of their work in terms of client outcome, so have outcome researchers come to realize the importance of specifying the process that contributes to the outcomes they find. Thus, researchers from both process and outcome camps are more likely to appreciate the fact that effective process of change research requires an examination of the process of therapy as well as the change that occurs as a result of this process. The goal of process-outcome research therefore has become not only looking at what goes on in therapy nor only on comparing outcomes across treatment groups, but rather on "identifying, describing, explaining, and predicting the effects of the processes that bring about therapeutic change over the entire course of therapy" (Greenberg, 1986). Further, process-outcome research also began placing greater importance on identifying the context in which change occurs. Greenberg (1986) proposed a hierarchical system for establishing this context in process research. In an initial description of this system, he suggested three levels of analysis, in ascending order according to the hierarchy: speech act, episode, and therapeutic relationship. Embedding an examination of the impact of therapeutic occurrences in a context, whether it is a therapeutic episode or a specific therapeutic relationship, more accurately captures the process of change as clinicians are likely to experience it in their day-to-day work with clients.

In fact, many of the findings and methods of process research readily lend themselves to useful application by clinicians. For example, Benjamin's (1993) Structural Analysis of Social Behavior (SASB) offers a framework from which to consider therapeutic interactions in terms of control and affiliation. The work of Safran and Muran (1996; 2000) has resulted in guidelines for identifying potential ruptures in the therapeutic alliance. Elliott, Watson, Goldman, and Greenberg (2004) provide guidance in recognizing in-session markers that can serve as cues to intervene in a specific therapeutically optimal manner. In addition to determining important therapeutic occurrences, process researchers also attempt to address therapeutic interventions that will facilitate the process of change at these markers. Therefore, many of the findings of process research provide empirically supported guidelines for therapeutic tasks to be employed at important points in treatment, such as when a client confronts the therapist in a hostile manner as a result of a disagreement over therapeutic goals, or when a client responds in a way that indicates that he or she could potentially benefit from an intervention designed to facilitate the letting go of resentments or unmet needs in relation to others.

Instead of providing pre-post comparisons of criteria checklists, process research looks at the actual components of therapy (e.g., through coding therapy recordings for specific verbal exchanges or social transactions) and their subsequent effects on the change process. Whereas controlled clinical trials offer information regarding broad outcomes (i.e., by comparing whole-package treatments with whole-package controls), process research describes more fine-grained components of therapy and the effect of these components on client change. As noted above, process research also considers these components in the contexts in which they occur. Further, the clinically useful products of these two research approaches differ substantially. Whereas randomized clinical trials provide treatment manuals originally designed as research tools to document what occurs in therapy, process research provides guidelines regarding how to operate at specific junctures in therapy. It seems likely, then, that the type of clinical guidance that emerges from process research would influence practice more than would the findings of outcome research. As process research findings much more closely address the actual practice of therapy, they can help bridge the gap between clinician and researcher.

Unfortunately, around the time that the goals of process research became more coherent and clinically useful, process research also began to decline as a result of the increased focus on funding randomized controlled trials. In 1986, NIMH awarded 16 grants to process research; in 1990, only six such grants were awarded (Wolfe, 1993). However, in recent years many important occurrences have paved the way for increased interest in process research. One of the most relevant of these changes has been greater interest in identifying principles of therapeutic change, including qualities of the treatment, therapist, or client that cannot be randomly assigned to groups. Process research that examines correlates, mediators, and moderators of change, is well suited to the study of these principles (Castonguay & Beutler, 2006).

PRINCIPLES OF CHANGE

Despite increasing awareness of the promise of psychotherapy integration, many therapists continue to operate from circumscribed theoretical orientations. Theoretical orientations, whether psychoanalytic, cognitive-behavioral, experiential, or any other, offer a framework from which to consider the origin and maintenance of problematic behavior. The means through which such behavior is reduced take the form of clinical procedures or techniques. Techniques, such as analysis of transference, between session homework, or two-chair interventions for experiential splits, are usually unique to each orientation. However, somewhere between the abstract level of theory and the more concrete level of technique are common principles of change that account for the effectiveness of therapeutic techniques (Goldfried, 1980).

These principles of change are shared by all theoretical orientations. Principles include, for example, (1) promoting client belief in the notion that therapy will help, (2) establishing an optimal therapeutic alliance, (3) facilitating client awareness of the factors that maintain his or her difficulties, (4) encouraging the client to engage in corrective experiences, and (5) emphasizing ongoing reality testing in the client's life. These general principles underlie the effectiveness of the many different techniques that vary largely as a function of therapist theoretical orientation.

The first principle listed before, promoting client belief in the fact that *therapy can help*, is essential to all approaches to therapy and can be implemented using a variety of approaches. Prochaska and DiClemente (2005) have demonstrated that clients who have not yet contemplated the necessity of change are unlikely to respond well to therapy. Thus, successful therapists of all orientations, using a variety of techniques, recognize the importance of first increasing precontemplative clients' motivation for change and, later, offering therapy as one of the means to such change (Miller & Rollnick, 2002).

Likewise, a strong *therapeutic alliance* is essential for optimal change to occur across orientations. A strong alliance can be encouraged by focusing on a variety of factors, many of which are outlined by Safran and Muran (2000). Such factors include attending to a client's own experience of interventions, accepting one's contributions to therapeutic interactions, and identifying markers of problematic interpersonal functioning. Bordin (1979) has suggested that a successful alliance adequately addresses three factors: (1) the establishment of a personal bond between therapist and client in which the client accepts the therapist as competent and understanding, (2) an agreement on the goals of the therapeutic work, and (3) an agreement on the tasks or methods in which the client-therapist dyad will engage in order to reach their goals. The presence of these factors is essential to all therapeutic approaches, regardless of the theory from which a particular therapist works or the techniques that one subsequently employs.

The *facilitation of client awareness* is also a principle of change common to all theoretical orientations, even though the actual therapeutic technique used to encourage such insight likely differs across therapists from various theoretical backgrounds. For example, providing feedback regarding the interpersonal effectiveness of a role-play performance *and* making an interpretation about the cyclical themes that guide a client's relationships *both* facilitate client awareness of possible factors that may be maintaining his or her problematic relationships, despite the fact that each technique is informed by a distinct theory.

Alexander and French (1946) first suggested the importance of facilitating "corrective emotional experiences," those therapeutic experiences that serve to disconfirm previously held negative expectations. Therapists can facilitate a *corrective experience*, for example, by encouraging clients to behave more assertively in situations that clients have heretofore perceived as risky, or by therapists, themselves, responding to an instance of assertive in-session behavior in a manner that serves to disconfirm clients' previous expectations of others' reactions to that behavior. Both techniques promote a corrective experience in that they can update clients' original expectations that have prevented them from behaving in ways that are more conducive to adaptive functioning. Because one such experience is unlikely to lead to long-lasting change, therapists can encourage clients to engage in *ongoing reality testing* until a critical mass of corrective experiences is encountered to allow for more stable and long-lasting changes in expectations, feelings, and behavior.

INCREASED INTEREST IN PRINCIPLES

Recent attempts to delineate effective therapy approaches are impressive yet limiting. The first of these attempts was the ambitious process of identifying treatments for which enough empirical support exists to support their effectiveness. This task was carried out by the Society for Clinical Psychology (Division 12) of the American Psychological Association (Chambless, Baker et al., 1998) and resulted in the publication of *A Guide to Treatments that Work* (Nathan & Gorman, 1998; 2002), a voluminous work outlining efficacious treatments and the empirical evidence supporting them. As a result of the criticisms of this endeavor, such as dissatisfaction with the over-emphasis on cognitive-behavioral treatments and other treatments that are most able to meet the assumptions of RCT methodology, the Division of Psychotherapy (Division 29) convened another task force to identify client, therapist, and client-therapist relationship factors that have been shown to influence client change. The resulting compendium, *Psychotherapy Relationships that Work* (Norcross, 2002), was also inherently limited in that it focused on relationship factors at the expense of not considering other factors that have been shown to lead to client change, such as other treatment approaches and models.

The dissatisfaction that resulted from these related attempts to delineate effective treatment approaches to client problems led to the formation of yet another task force sponsored jointly by the Society for Clinical Psychology and the North American Society for Psychotherapy Research. This taskforce set out to identify therapeutic principles that have been shown to lead to client change (Castonguay & Beutler, 2006). The members of the task force, as well as others (e.g., Goldfried and Davila, 2005) noted that pitting technique and relationship factors against each other in the quest to account for the "best" agents of therapeutic change seemed a less-than-ideal approach to identifying therapeutic agents of change. The technique vs. relationship dialogue also seems unlikely to provide the most clinician-friendly information. Instead, some have pointed out that the client-therapist relationship and therapy techniques can *both* produce change, and, in fact, at times the provision of a supportive, corrective relationship *is* the technique accounting for this change (Arkowitz, 1992; Castonguay & Beutler, 2006; Gelso & Hayes, 1998; Goldfried & Davila, 2005). Instead of focusing, then, on either the relationship or technique offered to clients, a more fruitful endeavor would focus on the higher-order principles of change, such as encouraging client expectations that therapy will help, which both the relationship and technique can facilitate. These principles, in turn, can flexibly guide therapists working from a variety of modalities with a range of client characteristics and clinical issues.

Westen et al. (2004) note the limitations of the randomized clinical trial approach that produces potentially constraining manuals that attempt to outline exactly what needs to be done in treating a client with a particular problem. They suggest that a superior alternative would be for researchers to attempt to identify principle-based intervention strategies that can be incorporated into therapists' overall approach to treating clients. Such principle-driven interventions would attempt to identify what treatment techniques provided to whom under which conditions work best. This endeavor is clearly consistent with the definition of principles that has been agreed upon over the years (e.g., Castonguay & Beutler, 2006; Goldfried, 1980; Paul, 1967). The definition of principles that guided the recent task force on that topic—"general statements that identify participant characteristics, relationship conditions, therapist behaviors, and classes of intervention that are likely to lead to change in psychotherapy" (Castonguay & Beutler, 2006, p. 5)—clearly calls for researchers to identify the correlates, mediators, and moderators of change that are facilitated by principles such as those noted earlier (e.g., increasing client expectation that therapy can help).

Castonguay and Beutler (2006) summarize the attempts of the Task Force to identify additional principles that guide client change. They categorize these principles using three variable domains (i.e., relationship, treatment, and participant characteristics). Principles involving at least two of the four disorders covered in their book (i.e., dysphoric disorders, anxiety disorders, personality disorders, and substance abuse disorders) include, for example, that clients who experienced significant interpersonal problems during early childhood may have difficulty responding to therapy. Other examples include the principle that the provision of a structured treatment and clear focus throughout therapy is associated with beneficial change, as is addressing clinically-relevant interpersonal issues, facilitating changes in clients' cognitions, and helping clients to accept, tolerate, and, at times, fully experience their emotions. Clearly, keeping factors such as these in mind can greatly inform therapist's work with clients. Additionally, familiarity with so-called "matching" principles (e.g., the principle that therapist directiveness should inversely match client level of resistance) can guide therapists in implementing a particular intervention strategy when working with a client with particular personality characteristics with a particular clinical disorder (Castonguay & Beutler, 2006).

A program of principle-focused research could take many forms; however, ideally, any attempt would attend to what takes place in actual clinical practice and would identify client, therapist, and relationship factors associated with therapeutic change. For example, researchers could identify optimal ways of handling alliance ruptures by asking therapists to provide audiotapes of therapy sessions demonstrating how they handled a rupture with a particular client. At the same time, they could examine client and therapist historical, demographic, and personality factors in addition to eventual outcome data for the client on the audiotape. From an analysis of these tapes, the researchers can propose optimal responses to alliance ruptures and can later compare the relative effectiveness of these particular responses for various rupture types. Such an approach would lead to the identification of approaches associated with the most therapeutic benefit for a particular combination of participant and relationship factors. As noted above, psychotherapy process research is particularly suited to identifying principles of change, as it looks at what goes on in therapy in the context of other important variables such as therapist and client variables as well as the interaction of these variables in the therapy relationship. As will be discussed next, the increasing identification of therapeutic change principles bodes well for the future of the psychotherapy integration movement.

PSYCHOTHERAPY INTEGRATION

Over the past two decades, clinicians have increasingly recognized psychotherapy integration as an established and respected movement. In fact, close to one-third of American clinicians now prefer the label "integrative" or "eclectic" (Norcross, 2005). Castonguay and Goldfried (1994) outline the factors that have contributed to increased movement toward psychotherapy integration, such as the continuing discontent with prevailing models of change and questions regarding the effectiveness of the different schools of therapy. They highlight the fact that many voices from within traditional approaches to therapy have noted the limitations of their own approaches. Mahoney (1979), for one, speaking from within the cognitive-behavioral approach, has noted the limitations of this particular approach, and points to the benefit of attending to client unconscious processes and emotional experiencing. Similarly, psychodynamic therapists have questioned some fundamental assumptions of their approach, such as the value, and even possibility, of a neutral therapist (Strupp & Binder, 1984; Wachtel, 1977). Further, an examination of therapy sessions reveals that what therapists do often differs from what they say they do and, in fact, often extends beyond the dictates of the specific theoretical approach from which they operate (Castonguay & Goldfried, 1994). For example, therapists operating from a cognitive-behavioral model often attend to emotional experiencing, insight, and transference-countertransference (Arnkoff, 1981; Goldfried & Davison, 1994; Marmor & Woods, 1980); whereas psychodynamic and psychoanalytic therapists have recognized the utility of learning theory for understanding client-therapist interactions (Alexander, 1963; Wachtel, 1977).

The future of the psychotherapy integration movement is likely to be heavily influenced by the increasing search for common principles of change. The common factors approach to integration, in fact, focuses on a shift away from identifying the unique characteristics of each therapy approach toward identifying the variables that different orientations share that lead to client change. As therapists and researchers have increasingly come to realize that no one approach to treatment is consistently superior to any other (e.g., Luborsky, Singer, & Luborsky, 1975; Stiles, Shapiro, & Elliot, 1986), there has been a shift toward identifying the commonalities shared by all approaches. Until recently, most integrationists described the commonalities inherent in all approaches as "nonspecific factors," implying that these factors were unable to be identified or studied, and establishing their existence as mere background noise. With increased interest in common factors, however, these variables became regarded as important ingredients not only capable of being addressed, but essential to address. Thinking along these lines, some authors have argued for the elimination of the term "nonspecifics" (e.g., Kazdin, 1986). For example, researchers have strongly established that one such variable, the therapeutic alliance, accounts for much client change (Orlinsky & Howard, 1986). In fact, some writers have challenged researchers to establish that anything but the alliance accounts for client change with certain clinical problems, such as depression (e.g., Arkowitz, 1992). However, several researchers have identified many commonalities that contribute to client change (summarized in Greencavage & Norcross, 1990). These commonalities, such as client characteristics, treatment characteristics, qualities of the therapeutic relationship, and the interaction of these factors closely resemble the principles of therapeutic change outlined by Castonguay and Beutler (2006).

It should be noted that the common factors/converging themes approach to psychotherapy integration is somewhat distinct from the route to integration known as eclecticism. Eclecticism, or technical eclecticism as it is often known, systematically draws techniques from diverse systems without necessarily being concerned about their theoretical or epistemological compatibility (Lazarus, 1967; Norcross, 2005). Eclectic integrationists are not particularly concerned with the original theoretical base of various approaches to treatment. Still, eclecticism should not be equated with a whimsical, haphazard combination of various techniques without concern for their efficacy. Instead, eclectic integrationists search for techniques based on data regarding what has worked in the past for which clients.

The search for principles of change is closely in line with the goals of the psychotherapy integration movement, including both the common factors/ converging themes and eclectic approaches. Principles of change are, by definition, atheoretical. As noted earlier, principles lie at a level of abstraction below theory and above technique. As a result of their transcendent nature, the identification of principles of change holds promise for the advancement of a more integrative approach to therapy. The identification of principles is similar to the common factors approach to integration as both seek to specify common ingredients underlying the effective techniques of all approaches. The search for principles is also directly in line with the eclectic approach to integration as both establish instructions for optimally matching client, therapist, relationship, and treatment variables. Moreover, we can view the variety of techniques that therapists use as reflecting the different ways in which they implement principles of change.

Attempts at integration are becoming increasingly common (Goldfried, Pachankis, & Bell, 2005). The growing recognition of common principles of change shared by all traditional approaches offers a framework to further guide integration efforts (Davison, 1998; Rosen & Davison, 2003; Weinberger, 1993). As suggested earlier, psychotherapy process research particularly lends itself to advancing integrative trends in psychotherapy (Goldfried & Safran, 1986). Examining the in-session microprocesses that yield therapeutic benefit is likely to reveal components, or *principles*, shared by all theoretical approaches, which can then serve as the building blocks for a more integrative approach to psychotherapy (Wolfe & Goldfried, 1988). Moreover, continuing research into the identification of these principles can help address some of the integration movement's own challenges, such as the lack of an action plan that challenges the current research paradigm (Eubanks-Carter, Burckell, & Goldfried, 2005).

AN INTEGRATIVE, PRINCIPLE-BASED APPROACH TO TRAINING

Training beginning therapists to think conceptually in terms of the integrative principles of change noted above would be an improvement over training that emphasizes manual-based treatments. Manuals, developed to specify therapy approaches as implemented in research that places one theory-based treatment in competition with another, have now become the primary tools by which some professionals encourage all beginning therapists to be trained (e.g., Calhoun, Moras, Pilkonis, & Rehm, 1998; APA, 1996). However, it seems that the implementation of such training may not be as widespread in training programs as many supporters of empirically supported therapy believe to be ideal (Crits-Christoph, Frank, Chambless, Brody, & Karp, 1995). The resistance on the part of many training programs may be due to the fact that faculty members in these programs see more benefit in training beginning therapists to focus on understanding and implementing treatment approaches that facilitate principles of change such as those mentioned above than in training them to implement any of the hundreds of manuals that currently exist. Principle-based training encourages clinicians to think at a more abstract and effective level about what treatment approach would most likely lead to client change given the contextual factors relevant to the case at hand. As will be seen, training beginning therapists to think in terms of these principles does not preclude the ability to effectively implement manuals and instead may foster better use of manuals. However, the type of therapist training advocated here eschews rigid adherence to the dictates of manuals that are not at least accompanied by conceptual thinking in terms of principles of change.

Process research has revealed that strict adherence to therapy manuals may contribute to poorer outcome than might occur when greater flexibility is encouraged. For instance, in a study of the efficacy of cognitive therapy techniques in reducing depressive symptoms, Castonguay, Goldfried, Wiser, Raue, & Hayes, (1996) unexpectedly found that therapists' focus on clients' cognitive distortions was negatively correlated with client outcome. Upon further inspection of therapy transcripts, the researchers found that in sessions where the alliance was rated as low, therapists persisted in encouraging skeptical clients to appreciate the benefit of focusing on their cognitions. It seems that if therapists in this study were afforded more flexibility, especially in focusing on and addressing the strength of the therapeutic alliance, less-than-optimal outcomes may have been avoided. The Vanderbilt II study (Henry, Strupp, Butler, Schacht, & Binder, 1993) trained therapists in brief, psychodynamic therapy. Surprisingly, certain therapist interpersonal and interaction skills examined in this study seemed to deteriorate as a result of the training that was, in part, designed to address these very same therapist behaviors. The researchers in this study hypothesized that "attempts at changing or dictating specific therapist behaviors may alter other therapeutic variables in unexpected and even counterproductive ways" (Henry et al., 1993, p. 438). Revisiting their work a few years later, the researchers note that manuals should not be expected to be of much help except as a "useful beginning or a reference" (Strupp & Anderson, 1997, p. 80).

In light of findings such as these that warn against strict conformity to manualized therapy instructions, some have pointed out that therapy manuals afford greater flexibility than is often assumed (e.g., Kendall, 1998; Wilson, 1998). Others have noted that self-correcting features can be built into manualized therapies in response to patient progress (e.g., Jacobson & Christensen, 1996). Still others note that manual developers can strengthen the effectiveness of their manuals by providing a greater focus on the common factors that have been proposed to account for client change (e.g., Addis, 1997). Such built-in flexibility certainly seems reasonable. Still, it seems unlikely that training that overlooks the principles that underlie client change—such as a focus on establishing a strong therapeutic alliance or the provision of corrective experiences—will prepare therapists to effectively implement such flexibility, self-correction, and attention to common factors, as this ultimately requires thinking broadly about potential factors that may lead to or impede progress. Thus, learning how to effectively use manuals first requires a strong grounding in principles of change. However, once such skills and knowledge have been instilled, therapists will be well prepared to implement manuals flexibly. For example, therapists implementing cognitive therapy of the type examined by Castonguay et al. (1996), instead of continuing to persist with an examination of maladaptive cognitions despite client resistance, will be able to recognize the importance of establishing and maintaining a strong therapeutic alliance and the promotion of a positive expectation that therapy can help.

With that said, strict adherence to manuals has been shown to produce substantial benefit for some *DSM* disorders (Barlow, 2002; Roth & Fonagy, 1996; Westen et al., 2004). These disorders tend to be those that are relatively clear-cut, involving a link between a stimulus and a problematic cognitive, affective, or behavioral response. Examples of such disorders include simple phobia, specific social phobia, obsessive-compulsive disorder, panic, and uncomplicated PTSD (Westen et al., 2004). Manualized treatment for these disorders is likely to be most effective when the disorder occurs in isolation and is not closely linked with problematic personality traits. To the extent that a client's difficulties are not so focal, however, prescriptive manualized treatments are not so effective in alleviating clients' problems, especially in the long term (e.g., Judd, 1997). Many clients present with multiple concerns and *DSM* disorders, often intertwined with complicating contextual issues; in fact, single-diagnosis clinical presentations may be the exception rather than the rule (Howard et al., 1996). These complex presentations would seem to require equally complex clinical thinking, which controlled clinical trials and therapy manuals are unlikely to sufficiently capture. Training programs that have the primary goal of training students to effectively implement empirically supported therapy manuals, then, are at risk of sacrificing the goal of instilling effective clinical judgment of the type that can be quite useful for more difficult client concerns.

Integrative, principle-based approaches to training can take a variety of forms. Essential to any approach, however, is a broad background in theories of psychopathology and intervention strategies. Whether or not this background should be grounded in one primary theory is subject to debate (e.g., Norcross & Halgin, 2005). However, faculty should at least systematically and nonjudgmentally expose students to the existing approaches to human behavior (e.g., psychodynamic, experiential, cognitive-behavioral). Here, students may become frustrated with the lack of one, solid approach to conceptualizing human behavior. However, as integrative thinking is subsequently approached, students will be able to appreciate the overarching, unifying nature of principles of change.

At this point, intervention courses can introduce and explicate core principles of change. Specifically, therapeutic principles—such as a strong therapeutic alliance, an expectation that therapy can help, the facilitation of insight, the provision of corrective experiences, and ongoing reality testing—can be introduced alongside approaches that ensure their effective implementation. Trainers can emphasize how each of these principles cuts across all theoretical orientations, albeit through a variety of techniques (e.g., corrective experiences often occur in the context of the therapy relationship in psychodynamic therapy, whereas it often occurs in between-session homework in cognitive-behavior therapy). In this way, the training proposal advocated here seeks to blend various theoretical approaches by focusing on a framework at a mid-level of abstraction (i.e., between theory and technique). This unifies the various approaches at a conceptual level.

Student readings should encourage thinking in terms of these principles. The work of Safran and Muran (2000) is a good example in that it provides a framework from which to address ruptures and strains in the therapeutic alliance while offering suggestions for using these occurrences in an optimally therapeutic manner. Likewise, the work of Miller and Rollnick (2002) can demonstrate how to activate clients' expectations that therapy can help with their problems. Such readings can occur alongside readings of the research literature that demonstrate the effectiveness of specific therapy techniques and interventions, with a particular focus on the research that address principles related to client, therapist, and relationship factors. These principles are of the type outlined in Castonguay and Beutler's (2006) volume on effective principles of therapeutic change.

Fostering therapist thinking in terms of principles can also occur during practica and supervision. Supervisors may wish to have students bring in therapy tapes from particular sessions while encouraging students to determine principles of change that may have been relevant in that session. Further, supervisors can spend separate sessions of group supervision for each principle, having every student present a case in which each of the core principles noted here may have been applicable. For example, students may each present a case in which the alliance was key or in which a corrective experience occurred. Fellow students can subsequently offer feedback on each others' attempts to guide treatment according to the particular principle illustrated in that session. Such a principle-guided approach to supervision allows students to witness, first hand, the manner in which principles of change guide specific technical and theoretical approaches to treatment. By this point, with a clearer conceptual understanding of change, the frustration of beginning therapists might subside somewhat. Still, beginning therapists should be supported as they accept the limits of the current knowledge in the field and begin to acknowledge, humbly, the realities of working clinically from a novel approach that still needs more data to support its effectiveness.

CONCLUSION

As it begins its second century of offering therapy interventions, the field continues to be disjointed. However, unlike in years past, this fragmentation is not so much due to the blindness of clinicians to theoretical frameworks other than their own, but rather to the limitations of current research paradigms, the proliferation of therapy manuals, and the seemingly continuing, if not growing, gap between clinician and researcher. Similar to years past, however, external forces continue to influence the shape of the field and the work of its professionals. Whereas two or three decades ago, the differing schools of therapy were attempting to establish their superiority over one another; today, professionals from all schools of therapy have become concerned with demonstrating the efficacy of their work in the face of economic threats from third-party payers. Although this could potentially lead to greater unification in the field, it seems that this has not been the case thus far. Instead, researchers have applied drug trial methodology to the study of psychotherapy's effectiveness. This has led to the proliferation of whole-package, brand-name therapies and accompanying manuals that are of limited use for the day-to-day practical experiences of established clinicians and the training experiences of beginning therapists.

However, attempts at psychotherapy integration have become increasingly common, and the renewed interest in identifying principles of change has the potential to further strengthen the integration movement. In fact, this growing trend is coming closer to producing the types of changes for which Goldfried (1980) expressed hope over a quarter-century ago, when he described a "textbook of the future" that would not be divided into separate sections for each theoretical approach, with a final chapter offering an attempt at integrative therapy. Instead, this textbook would present various agreed-upon principles of therapeutic change and an outline of the effectiveness of various techniques as used in the context of various client, therapist, and relationship factors. The attempts of the recent Task Force charged with identifying principles of change as summarized by Castonguay and Beutler (2006) has produced a volume that comes close to resembling this textbook of the future. With more process-outcome research to back up the existence of these principles, subsequent editions of this book will come even closer to looking like the clinician-friendly, empirically informed text described years ago.

REFERENCES

Addis, M. E. (1997). Evaluating the treatment manual as a means of disseminating empirically validated psychotherapies. *Clinical Psychology: Science and Practice, 4,* 1–11.

Alexander, F. (1963). The dynamics of psychotherapy in light of learning theory. *American Journal of Psychiatry, 120,* 440–448.

Alexander, F. & French, T. (1946) *Psychoanalytic therapy: Principles and applications.* New York: Ronald Press.

American Psychological Association. (1996). *Guidelines and principles for accreditation of programs in professional psychology.* Washington, DC: Author.

American Psychological Association. (2002). Criteria for evaluating treatment guidelines. *American Psychologist, 57,* 1052–1059.

American Psychological Association. (2005). *Report of the 2005 Presidential Task Force on Evidence-Based Practice.* Washington, DC: Author.

Arkowitz H. (1992). Common factors therapy for depression. In J. C. Norcross & M. R. Goldfried (Eds.), *Handbook of psychotherapy integration* (pp. 402–433). New York: Basic Books.

Arnkoff, D. B. (1981). Flexibility in practicing cognitive therapy. In G. Emery, S. D. Hollon, & R. Bedrosian (Eds.), *New directions in cognitive therapy: A casebook* (pp. 203–222). New York: Guilford.

Barlow, D. H. (1994). Psychological interventions in the era of managed competition. *Clinical Psychology: Science and Practice, 1,* 109–122.

Barlow, D. (2002). *Anxiety and its disorders* (2nd ed.). New York: Guilford.

Benjamin, L. S. (1993). *Interpersonal diagnosis and treatment of personality disorders.* New York: Guilford.

Bordin, E. (1979). The generalizability of the psychoanalytic concept of the working alliance. *Psychotherapy: Theory, Research and Practice, 16,* 252–260.

Calhoun, K. S., Moras, K., Pilkonis, P. A., & Rehm, L. P. (1998). Empirically supported treatments: Implications for training. *Journal of Consulting and Clinical Psychology, 66,* 151–162.

Castonguay, L. G., & Beutler, L. E. (Eds.). (2006). *Principles of therapeutic change that work.* New York: Oxford University Press.

Castonguay, L. G., Goldfried, M. R., Wiser, S., Raue, P. J., & Hayes, A. H. (1996). Predicting outcome in cognitive therapy for depression: A comparison of unique and common factors. *Journal of Consulting and Clinical Psychology, 64,* 497–504.

Castonguay, L. G., & Goldfried, M. R. (1994). Psychotherapy integration: An idea whose time has come. *Applied and Preventive Psychology, 3,* 159–172.

Chambless, D. L., Baker, M. J., Baucom, D. H., Beutler, L. E., Calhoun, K. S., Crits-Christoph, P., Daiuto, A., DeRubeis, R., Detweiler, J., Haaga, D.A.F., Johnson, S. B., McCurry, S., Mueser, K. T., Pope, K. S., Sanderson, W. C., Shoham, V., Stickle, T., Williams, D. A., & Woody, S. R. (1998). Update on empirically validated therapies, II. *The Clinical Psychologist, 51,* 3–13.

Cohen, L. H., Sargent, M., & Sechrest, L. (1986). Use of psychotherapy research by professional psychologists. *American Psychologist, 41,* 198–206.

Crits-Christoph, P., Frank, E., Chambless, D. L., Brody, C., & Karp, J. F. (1995). Training in empirically validated treatments: What are clinical psychology students learning? *Professional Psychology: Research and Practice, 26,* 514–522.

Davison, G. C. (1998). Being bolder with the Boulder Model: The challenge of education and training in empirically supported treatments. *Journal of Consulting and Clinical Psychology, 66,* 163–167.

Elkin, I., Parloff, M., Hadley, S., & Autry, J. (1985). NIMH Treatment of Depression Collaborative Research Program: Background and research plan. *Archives of General Psychiatry, 42,* 305–316.

Elliott, R., Watson, J., Goldman, R., & Greenberg, L.S. (2004). *Learning emotional focused therapy: The process-experiential approach to change.* Washington, DC: APA.

Eubanks-Carter, C., Burckell, L. A., & Goldfried, M. R. (2005). Future directions in psychotherapy integration (pp. 503–521). In J. C. Norcross and M. R. Goldfried (Eds.), *Handbook of psychotherapy integration* (2nd ed.). New York: Oxford University Press.

Gelso, C. J., & Hayes, J. A. (1998). *The psychotherapy relationship: Theory, research, and practice.* New York: Wiley.

Goldfried, M. R. (1980). Toward the delineation of therapeutic change principles. *American Psychologist, 35,* 991–999.

Goldfried, M. R., & Davila, J. (2005). The role of relationship and technique in therapeutic change. *Psychotherapy: Theory, Research, Practice, and Training, 42,* 421–430.

Goldfried, M. R., & Davison, G. C. (1994). *Clinical behavior therapy* (2nd ed.). New York: Wiley.

Goldfried, M. R., & Eubanks-Carter, C. (2004). On the need for a new psychotherapy research paradigm: A comment on Westen, Morrison and Thompson-Brenner (2004). *Psychological Bulletin, 130,* 669–673.

Goldfried, M. R., Pachankis, J. E., & Bell, A. C. (2005). A history of psychotherapy integration (pp. 24–60). In J. C. Norcross and M. R. Goldfried (Eds.), *Handbook of psychotherapy integration* (2nd ed.). New York: Oxford University Press.

Goldfried, M. R. & Safran, J. D. (1986). Future directions in psychotherapy integration. In J. C. Norcross (Ed.), *Handbook of eclectic psychotherapy* (pp. 463–483). New York: Brunner/ Mazel.

Goldfried M. R., & Wolfe B. E. (1996). Psychotherapy practice and research: Repairing a strained alliance. *American Psychologist, 51,* 1007–1017.

Greenberg, L. S. (1986). Change process research. *Journal of Consulting and Clinical Psychology, 54,* 4–9.

Greenberg, L. S., & Pinsof, W. M. (1986). *The psychotherapeutic process: A research handbook.* New York: Guilford.

Greencavage, L. M., & Norcross, J. C. (1990). What are the commonalities among the therapeutic factors? *Professional Psychology, 21,* 372–378.

Henry, W. P., Strupp, H. H., Butler, S. F., Schacht, T. E., & Binder, J. L. (1993). Effects of training in time-limited dynamic psychotherapy: Changes in therapist behavior. *Journal of Consulting and Clinical Psychology, 61,* 434–440.

Howard, K. I., Cornille, T. A., Lyons, J. S., Vessey, J. T., Lueger, R. J., & Saunders, S. M. (1996). Patterns of mental health service utilization. *Archives of General Psychiatry, 53,* 696–703.

Jacobson, N. S., & Christensen, A. (1996). *Acceptance and change in couple therapy: A therapist's guide for transforming relationships.* New York: Norton.

Judd, L. (1997). The clinical course of unipolar major depressive disorders. *Archives of General Psychiatry, 54,* 989–991.

Kazdin, A. E. (1986). Comparative outcome studies of psychotherapy: Methodological issues and strategies. *Journal of Consulting and Clinical Psychology, 54*, 95–105.

Kendall, P. C. (1998). Empirically supported psychological therapies. *Journal of Consulting and Clinical Psychology, 66*, 3–6.

Kiesler, D. J. (1973). *The process of psychotherapy: Empirical foundations and systems of analysis.* Chicago: Aldine.

Kiesler, D. J. (1983). *The paradigm shift in psychotherapy process research.* Summary Discussant Paper, NIMH Workshop on Psychotherapy Process Research, Bethesda, MD.

Kiesler, D. J. (1986). Foreword. In L. S. Greenberg & W. M. Pinsof (Eds.), *The psychotherapeutic process: A research handbook* (pp. vii–xi). New York: Guilford.

Lazarus, A. A. (1967). In support of technical eclecticism. *Psychological Reports, 21*, 415–416.

Luborsky, L., Singer, B., & Luborsky, L. (1975). Comparative studies of psychotherapies. *Archives of General Psychiatry, 32*, 995–1008.

Mahoney, M. J. (1979). Cognitive and non-cognitive views in behavior modification. In P. O. Sjoden, S. Bates, & S. Dockens (Eds.), *Trends in behavior therapy* (pp. 39–54). New York: Plenum Press.

Marmor, J., & Woods, S. M. (Eds.). (1980). *The interface between psychodynamic and behavioral therapies.* New York: Plenum Press.

Meehl, P. E. (1997). Credentialed persons, credentialed knowledge. *Clinical Psychology: Science and Practice, 4*, 91–98.

Miller, W. R., & Rollnick, S. (2002). *Motivational interviewing* (2nd ed.). New York: Guilford.

Nathan, P. E., & Gorman, J. M. (Eds.). (1998). *A guide to treatments that work.* New York: Oxford University Press.

Nathan, P. E., & Gorman, J. M. (2002). *A guide to treatments that work* (2nd ed.). New York: Oxford University Press.

Norcross, J. C. (Ed.). (2002). *Psychotherapy relationships that work.* New York: Oxford University Press.

Norcross, J. C. (2005). A primer on psychotherapy integration. In J. C. Norcross and M. R. Goldfried (Eds.), *Handbook of psychotherapy integration* (2nd ed.), (pp. 3–23). New York: Oxford University Press.

Norcross, J. C., & Halgin, R. P. (2005). Training in psychotherapy integration. In J. C. Norcross & M. R. Goldfried (Eds.), *Handbook of psychotherapy integration* (2nd ed.) (pp. 439–458). New York: Oxford University Press.

Orlinsky, D. E., & Howard, K. I. (1986). Process and outcome in psychotherapy. In S. L. Garfield & A. E. Bergin (Eds.), *Handbook of psychotherapy and behavior change* (pp. 311–385). New York: Wiley.

Paul, G. L. (1967). Strategy of outcome research in psychotherapy. *Journal of Consulting and Clinical Psychology, 31*, 109–119.

Prochaska, J. O., & DiClemente, C. C. (2005). The transtheoretical approach. In J. C. Norcross & M. R. Goldfried (Eds.), *Handbook of psychotherapy integration* (pp. 147–171). New York: Basic Books.

Rosen, G. M., & Davison, G. C. (2003). Psychotherapy should identify empirically supported principles of change (ESPs) and not credential trademarked therapies or other treatment packages. *Behavior Modification, 27*, 300–312.

Roth, A., & Fonagy, P. (1996). *What works for whom? A critical review of psychotherapy research.* New York: Guilford.

Safran, J. D., & Muran, J. C. (1996). The resolution of ruptures in the therapeutic alliance. *Journal of Consulting and Clinical Psychology, 64*, 447–458.

Safran, J. D., & Muran, J. C. (2000). *Negotiating the therapeutic alliance: A relational treatment guide.* New York: Guilford.

Seligman, M. E. P. (1995). The effectiveness of psychotherapy: The Consumer Reports study. *American Psychologist, 50*, 965–974.

Stiles, W. B., Shapiro, D. A., & Elliott, R. (1986). Are all psychotherapies equivalent? *American Psychologist, 41*, 165–180.

Strupp, H. H., & Anderson, T. (1997). On the limitations of therapy manuals. *Clinical Psychology: Science and Practice, 4*, 76–82.

Strupp, H. H., & Binder, J. L. (1984). *Psychotherapy in a new key: A guide to time-limited dynamic psychotherapy.* New York: Basic Books.

Wachtel, P. L. (1977). *Psychoanalysis and behavior therapy: Toward an integration.* New York: Basic Books.

Weinberger, J. (1993). Common factors in psychotherapy. In G. Stricker & J. R. Gold (Eds.), *Comprehensive handbook of psychotherapy integration* (pp. 43–56). New York: Plenum Press.

Westen, D., Novotny, C. M., & Thompson-Brenner, H. (2004). The empirical status of empirically supported psychotherapies: Assumptions, findings, and reporting in controlled clinical trials. *Psychological Bulletin, 130*, 631–663.

Wilson G. T. (1998). Manual-based treatment and clinical practice. *Clinical Psychology: Science and Practice, 5*, 363–375.

Wolfe, B. E. (1993). Psychotherapy research funding for fiscal years 1986–1990. *Psychotherapy & Rehabilitation Research Bulletin, 1*, 7–9.

Wolfe, B. E., & Goldfried, M. R. (1988). Research on psychotherapy integration: Recommendations and conclusions from an NIMH workshop. *Journal of Consulting and Clinical Psychology, 56*, 448–451.

4

Efficacy, Effectiveness, and the Clinical Utility of Psychotherapy Research

PETER E. NATHAN

Many psychologists have observed that the practice of psychotherapy remains surprisingly unaffected by the spate of psychotherapy research during the past half century by psychologists (including Barlow, 1981; Castonguay & Beutler, 2006; Kopta, Lueger, Saunders, & Howard, 1999; and Nathan, Stuart, & Dolan, 2000). Of the several explanations that have been offered, the continuing controversy among researchers on the relative worth of the efficacy and effectiveness models of psychotherapy research bulks large. If psychotherapy researchers, after more than 50 years of trying, cannot agree on how best to assess the worth of a given therapeutic strategy, the logic of this explanation goes, is it any wonder that clinicians do not put much faith in therapy research outcomes and many question the concept of evidence-based treatments? This chapter looks carefully at the data on this issue, past and present, in the effort to understand both why practitioners to date have largely ignored therapy research findings and whether and how they might be induced not to do so in the future.

THE EFFICACY AND EFFECTIVENESS MODELS

Recognition of the worth of the concept of empirically supported or evidence-based treatments depends in part on ultimate resolution of the continuing controversy over which of two research models best captures the most salient differences among psychotherapy techniques and procedures. The two are the efficacy model and the effectiveness model. These two research models take quite different views of the best way to study behavior change. Historically, if you endorsed the efficacy model and used it to identify empirically-supported treatments, you were unlikely to value the efforts of effectiveness model researchers to validate evidence-based treatments. Similarly, if you thought that only by means of effectiveness research could appropriate empirical support be marshaled to validate a behavior change technique, you would almost certainly be unimpressed by data on outcomes generated by efficacy researchers. In truth, as what follows in this chapter suggests, neither model by itself captures all—or perhaps even most—of what makes a therapy approach work. As a consequence, as we observe later in the chapter, researchers are now trying to capitalize on the most important elements of each approach to integrate them in a new research model that might yield a broader base of empirical support for the treatments it evaluates.

Efficacy research is concerned above all with *replication* because replicated psychotherapy outcome findings are more likely to be valid. Efficacy studies contain a number of research elements that, historically, have not often been included in effectiveness studies. Prominent among them is *inclusion of an appropriate control or comparison condition with which the experimental treatments can be compared*; the control or comparison condition helps document the impact of the experimental treatments. Whenever possible, efficacy research promotes *random assignment of subjects either to experimental or comparison/control treatments*, in order to ensure to the extent possible the absence of systematic, subject-based bias. Efficacy studies also *carefully describe the components of the treatment,* so that it can be accurately replicated in follow-up studies. This quest for replication of treatment conditions, both within a study and between studies, has led to the widespread—and controversial—use of *treatment manuals*; manuals help ensure that therapists conducting the intervention will do so with fidelity. Finally, priority is given in efficacy studies to *diagnostically homogeneous groups of patients whose psychopathology is well defined by reliable and valid measures of psychopathology*, so the diagnostic groups that respond to the experimental treatment can be clearly specified.

Above all, *effectiveness research* is concerned with the *feasibility of treatments in real-world settings*. Individuals in need of treatment, regardless of diagnosis, comorbid psychopathology, or duration of illness, participate in effectiveness studies. Therapists in effectiveness studies are not usually specially trained to deliver the experimental treatment with the fidelity that is a hallmark of efficacy studies. Clinical considerations rather than the demands of the research design typically dictate choice of treatment method, as well as its frequency, duration, and assessment in effectiveness studies. Although assignment of patients to treatments in these studies may be randomized, disguising the treatment to which the patient has been assigned is rarely feasible. Outcome assessments are often broadly defined, and may include "soft" indices of change like changes in degree of disability, quality of life, or personality rather than targeted evaluations of symptoms by structured interviews.

Barlow (1996) succinctly differentiated efficacy and effectiveness methods as follows: Efficacy studies yield "a systematic evaluation of the intervention in a controlled clinical research context. Considerations relevant to the internal validity of these conclusions arc usually highlighted" (1996, p. 1051); effectiveness studies explore "the applicability and feasibility of the intervention in the local setting where the treatment is delivered" and are designed to "determine the generalizability of an intervention with established efficacy" (1996, p. 1055).

Psychotherapy and behavior therapy are an important part of what clinical psychologists do; they also play a significant role in the work of other professionals. In the early pages of the initial chapter of *Evidence-Based Practices for Social Workers*, for example, O'Hare (2005) distinguishes between "efficacious practice," which involves "selecting and implementing interventions that have been shown to be efficacious in controlled practice research" (p. 4), and effectiveness practice, in which "practitioners incorporate evaluation methods into practice and, based on feedback from the client, make incremental changes to the intervention in the hopes of achieving optimal client outcomes" (p. 4). O'Hare's emphasis on the primary roles of efficacy and effectiveness in determining effective social work practice contrasts with psychology's principal use of them as methods for assessing therapeutic outcomes. Reflecting a parallel view in psychology, though, O'Hare goes on to observe that, "in reality, the distinction between efficacy and effectiveness is far from absolute, and both concepts are essential to implementing EBPSW" (Evidence-Based Practice in Social Work) (2005, p. 5).

To this time, most research designed to establish evidence-based treatments has followed the efficacy model although, as what follows later in this chapter suggests, that preference may be undergoing change.

A BRIEF HISTORY

Long-time psychotherapy researcher David Barlow was one of the first to call attention to the problem of the clinical utility of psychotherapy research when, in 1981, he observed that, "At present, clinical research has little or no influence on clinical practice," and continued: "This state of affairs should be particularly distressing to a discipline whose goal over the last 30 years has been to produce professionals who would integrate the methods of science with clinical practice to produce new knowledge" (1981, p. 147). These concerns continued to be expressed through the 1980s.

In 1991, acknowledging the limited value of most psychotherapy outcome research for clinicians, Persons reemphasized questions about the external validity of efficacy research in claiming that the designs of many psychotherapy outcome studies are not compatible with the models of psychotherapy those studies set out to evaluate. Persons assigned principal responsibility for this situation to the tradition that efficacy research assigns patients to treatments by diagnosis rather than after a theory-driven psychological assessment of each individual. Persons would solve this long-standing problem by adopting a "case formulation approach to psychotherapy research" and consequent development of an "assessment-plus-treatment protocol" based directly on the psychotherapeutic model.

Three years later, in 1994, 180,000 subscribers to *Consumer Reports* were asked a series of questions about their experiences with mental health professionals, physicians, medications, and self-help groups, in the largest survey to date of mental health treatment outcomes. The survey's principal finding included the following:

- Almost half of the respondents whose emotional state was "very poor" or "fairly poor" reported significant improvement following therapy.
- The longer psychotherapy lasted, the more it helped.
- Psychotherapy alone worked as well as combined psychotherapy and pharmacotherapy.

Psychologist Martin Seligman, a consultant to the survey, reviewed its findings a year later, detailed its "methodological virtues and drawbacks," and proposed eight characteristics of efficacy studies that he thought differentiated them from effectiveness studies. He concluded that the *Consumer Reports* survey "complements the (more traditional) efficacy method, (so that) the best features of these two methods can be combined into a more ideal method that will best provide empirical validation of psychotherapy" (1995, p. 965).

A year later, several commentaries on Seligman's article appeared. Most took up the clinical significance of the distinction between efficacy and effectiveness research. Suggesting ways to heighten clinical utility, Goldfried and Wolfe (1996) proposed "a new outcome research paradigm that involves an active collaboration between researcher and practicing clinician" (p. 1007) which "individualizes the intervention on the basis of an initial assessment and case formulation" (1996, p. 1013), while Howard, Moras, Brill, Martinovich, and Lutz (1996) suggested eschewing treatment-focused research altogether in favor of "patient-focused research," which monitors therapeutic progress and provides feedback to the clinician over the course of treatment.

Rejecting Seligman's critique of efficacy research, Hollon (1996) admitted that efficacy studies "leave much to be desired," but added that effectiveness designs are not a panacea, in large part because they cannot substitute "for the randomized controlled clinical trial when it comes to drawing causal inferences about whether psychotherapy (or any other treatment) actually works" (1996, pp. 1029–1030). In the same vein, Jacobson and Christensen (1996) found the *Consumer Reports* study to be so seriously flawed that they could draw few conclusions from it and, like Hollon, they expressed the view that "the randomized clinical trial is as good a method for answering questions of effectiveness as it is for answering questions of efficacy (1996, p. 1031).

Seligman (1996) acknowledged the validity of the criticisms of the *Consumer Reports* study but maintained that the study had nonetheless had significant value:

Both the experimental method (efficacy) and the observational method (effectiveness) answer complementary questions ... (although) efficacy studies ... cannot test long-term psychotherapy because long-term manuals cannot be written and patients cannot be randomized into two-year-long placebo controls, so the "empirical validation" of long-term therapy will likely come from effectiveness studies. (Seligman, 1996, p. 1072)

The decade of the 1990s also witnessed further advances in psychotherapy outcome research methodology, as well as several large-scale randomized clinical trials of behavioral and cognitive behavioral treatments for alcoholism, the mood disorders, and the anxiety disorders (Nathan & Gorman, 1998, 2002). Publication of practice guidelines for the treatment of a wide range of psychopathological conditions by the American Psychiatric Association, the Division of Clinical Psychology of the American Psychological Association, a few federal agencies, including the Veterans Administration, and several health maintenance organizations accompanied—and, in part, reflected—these developments. Most of the practice guidelines depended heavily on the results of research according to the efficacy model. As a consequence, the appearance of the guidelines generated predictably strong negative reactions from persons who questioned the clinical utility of the psychotherapy outcome research on which the guidelines were based (Nathan, 1998).

Sol Garfield, a well-known psychotherapy researcher, took especially strong exception to the initial list of "empirically validated treatments" published in 1995 by the Task Force of the Division of Clinical Psychology (1996). His concerns prominently included questions of the worth of the efficacy model, especially the distortion to the psychotherapy process he believed manuals typically used in efficacy studies cause, as well as the lack of comparability between psychotherapy patients in efficacy studies and those in real-world psychotherapy settings.

Kopta, Lueger, Saunders, and Howard (1999) expressed similar sentiments in a comprehensive review of contemporary psychotherapy research that emphasized the continuing gap between clinical research and clinical practice. Concluding that part of the problem might lie in the preference for randomized clinical trials (RCTs), they proposed instead "that this approach should be replaced by naturalistic designs, which can provide results more applicable to real clinical practice, therefore strengthening external validity" (1999, p. 449). Effectiveness studies, of course, epitomize "naturalistic designs."

RECENT EFFORTS TO INTEGRATE THE EFFICACY AND EFFECTIVENESS MODELS

The efforts to integrate the efficacy and effectiveness models reviewed in this section of the chapter reflect both awareness of the limited impact of psychotherapy research findings on clinical practice to this time and recognition that responsibility for this problem stems in substantial part from the failure to extend the results of efficacy research to community settings.

NIMH Initiative: Intervention Research Centers

Norquist, Lebowitz, and Hyman proposed in 1999 that the National Institute of Mental Health (NIMH), which Hyman directed at the time, in collaboration with basic scientists, advocates, and other federal agencies, endeavor to bridge the gap between the efficacy and effectiveness models (NAMHC Workgroup, 1999; Niederehe, Street, & Lebowitz, 1999; Norquist, Lebowitz, & Hyman, 1999). In so doing, they relabeled the models in "administratese," terming the efficacy model the "regulatory" model and the effectiveness model the "public health" model. The regulatory model derives from the detailed steps the U.S. Food and Drug Administration requires drug manufacturers to take to demonstrate the safety and efficacy of new products; the public health model reflects the research public health workers undertake to evaluate the effectiveness of clinical interventions delivered in the community.

The NIMH Initiative envisioned a new research paradigm that would combine "the designs of traditional clinical and services research studies" to achieve a more useful balance between the strict randomized designs of traditional clinical research and the more flexible observational designs of services research. To do so, NIMH administrators would "bring together methodologists with expertise across these fields to delineate what we currently know and what we don't (because it is) quite likely that new methods and statistical analytic approaches will need to be developed to address studies in the mental health area" (1999, p. 6). Beyond the new methods and new statistical approaches required to achieve these ambitious goals, new methods for grant review and a new research infrastructure at NIMH to facilitate grant submission, review, and funding would be required. While capable of supporting exciting new developments, which could include a quantum leap in the clinical utility of psychotherapy research, the NIMH Initiative will nonetheless founder unless the promised new methods and statistical procedures, which have yet to be developed, can in fact be brought about.

Frank, Rush, Biehar, Essock, and Hargreaves on the NIMH Clinical Trials and Translation Work Group, part of the NIMH Initiative, reported on an initial planning effort to achieve some of the ambitious NIMH goals for mood disorder treatments in 2002. Pointing out that the "disparity between treatments selected and carried out in clinical trials and those selected and carried out in 'real world' (i.e., primary care and specialty practice) settings has led to considerable tension between clinical researchers and practitioners and between clinical trials or 'efficacy' and 'effectiveness' researchers" (2002, p. 632), Frank and her associates set out an ambitious research agenda that is distinctly more tightly focused than that of the original NIMH Initiative. Their goal is to plan clinical trials and translate research findings in order to achieve three specific goals, all designed to heighten the clinical utility of research on treatments. The first is the most relevant to the topic of this chapter: "How do we maximize the effectiveness and cost-effectiveness of initial (acute) treatments for mood disorder already known to be efficacious in selected populations and settings when they are applied across all populations and care settings" (2002, p. 633)? While, like the NIMH Initiative itself, the research agenda spelled out by Frank and her colleagues is long on promise, a bit short on content, it is nonetheless substantially more specific than the Initiative, promises less, and hence may ultimately be more successful.

Efficacy/Effectiveness Clinics

Also in 1999, Klein and Smith urged creation of "dedicated, multi-site efficacy/ effectiveness clinics" as a means of confronting the conflicting demands and capabilities of efficacy and effectiveness studies. The clinics would presumably facilitate studies of process and outcome and help accumulate outcome norms for "well-defined populations" on such variables as diagnosis, economic status, psychiatric history, and comorbidity. The proximal goal of the clinics would be to attract and serve "a large volume of well-delineated patients who could be treated and studied and may have high comorbidity with medical, psychiatric, and substance abuse conditions" (1999, p. 5). Distal goals include development of outcome benchmarks for these distinct groups of patients by means of normative sampling, as well as generation of hypotheses the clinics would be in an excellent position to test. As with the NIMH Initiative, however, the proposal for efficacy/effectiveness clinics is long on enthusiasm, problem identification, and aspirations for change, short on concrete design, methodology, and details of statistical analyses. This lack of detail leaves the individual who appreciates the problems of integrating efficacy and effectiveness studies uncertain whether the integration these authors propose can actually be brought about by the method they propose.

Practice Research Network

In articles published in 2001 (Borkovec, Echemendia, Ragusea, & Ruiz) and 2002 (Borkovec), Borkovec and his colleagues propose the establishment of a network of research practice clinics, initially in Pennsylvania (2001), then throughout the country in conjunction with clinical psychology training clinics (2002). Their goals would be similar to the clinics proposed by Klein and his colleagues, although they would go about their work somewhat differently. Borkovec's plan would "foster the true integration of science and practice, wherein large numbers of practicing clinicians and clinical scientists would be brought together in collaborative research on clinically meaningful questions" (2002, p. 98). Unlike Klein's Efficacy/Effectiveness Clinics, which would put into practice a set of research goals centrally mandated, the Practice Research Network (PRN) would invite collaboration between clinicians and clinical scientists that would extend to both efficacy and effectiveness trials, with the eventual goal of identifying the most appropriate models for testing promising treatments in community/clinical settings. The methods and goals of Borkovec's PRN are strikingly similar to the case-based research methods Edwards initially proposed in 1996 and Edwards, Dattilio, and Bromley extended in 2004.

Longtime psychotherapy researcher Gordon Paul has most recently endorsed the PRN as a means of developing "studies of psychosocial procedures that are explicitly designed and executed in the 'real-world' to maximize both internal and external validity as well as to elucidate the basic principles underlying change" (2006, p. 13).

Stage/Hybrid Model of Behavioral Therapies Research

Rounsaville, Carroll, and Onken's Stage Model of Behavioral Therapies Research (2001a) was initially outlined by Onken, Blaine, and Battjes in 1997. It incorporates three sequential steps leading from an initial innovative clinical procedure through efficacy and then effectiveness testing. Thus,

> Stage I consists of pilot/feasibility testing, manual writing, training program development, and adherence/competence measure development for new and untested treatments. ... Stage II initially consists of randomized clinical trials (RCTs) to evaluate efficacy of manualized and pilot-tested treatments which have shown promise or efficacy in earlier studies. Stage II research can also address mechanisms of action or effective components of treatment for those approaches with evidence of efficacy derived from RCTs. Stage III consists of studies to evaluate transportability of treatments for which efficacy has been demonstrated in at least two RCTs. Key Stage III research issues revolve around generalizability; implementation issues; cost effectiveness issues; and consumer/marketing issues. (Rounsaville, Carroll, & Onken, 2001a, pp. 133–134)

Asked to critique the model, Kazdin (2001) first acknowledged the "critically important goal" of developing treatments that can be used effectively by practitioners. He then emphasized his view of the importance as well of addressing— and answering—crucial questions about "why and how new treatments work." In Kazdin's view, the Stage Model as Rounsaville and his colleagues (2001a) detailed it, did not address these questions.

Responding to Kazdin's critique, Rounsaville, Carroll, and Onken (2001b) reconceptualized his concerns as follows: "(a) Lack of emphasis on theory-driven components to stage model research; (b) Failure to address the need for research on 'what are the mechanisms through which therapy operates and under what conditions is therapy likely to be effective and why,' and (c) Exclusive reliance on randomized clinical trials as the basis for evidence of efficacy/effectiveness of a treatment under study" (2001b, p. 152). Rounsaville and his colleagues then proceeded to refer to several previous publications demonstrating their own concerns about these matters, making clear they also wanted these issues addressed in this effort, and concluding as well that "implicit in Kazdin's characterization and reaction to the stage model is a cut-and-dried, assembly line view of the process." By contrast, they conceptualized it as "a tree, which has a directional, upward course, but a course that branches to catch the most light and to bear more than one fruit" (2001b, p. 154).

A year later, Carroll and Nuro (2002) detailed the processes by which manuals for empirically supported treatments might be developed according to the stage model process. Then, in 2003, Carroll and Rounsaville elaborated on how what they now referred to as a "hybrid" model could link findings from efficacy and effectiveness research for substance abuse treatments, noting that "The hybrid model retains essential features of efficacy research (randomization, use of control conditions, independent assessment of outcome, and monitoring of treatment delivery) while expanding the research questions to also address issues of importance in effectiveness studies (including) diversity in settings, clinicians, and patients, cost-effectiveness of treatment, training issues, and patient and clinician satisfaction" (pp. 333–334).

Most recently, August et al. (2004) and Nash, McCrory, Nicholson, and Andrasik (2005) have used variants of this model to validate behavioral interventions for youthful drug use and primary headache. Calling their approach a "modified (hybrid) model for program development and evaluation," August and his colleagues used it to "examine the challenges faced by developers of youth drug abuse prevention programs in transporting scientifically proven or evidence-based programs into natural community practice systems" (2004, p. 2017). Nash, McCrory, Nicholson, and Andrasik employed "a three-phase linear progression model" (2005, p. 507) to evaluate methods for developing, evaluating, and implementing behavioral treatments for primary headache in a variety of settings.

META-ANALYSES OF PSYCHOTHERAPY OUTCOMES

Shadish and his colleagues (1996, 1997, 2000, 2005) have undertaken a series of meta-analyses of the psychotherapy outcome literature that offer an important perspective on whether and how efficacy and effectiveness trials of psychotherapy can be integrated. In some cases secondary analyses of earlier meta-analyses were done, in others, analyses of fresh sets of treatment outcome studies were completed. In both instances, the aim was to determine whether therapy outcome studies ranging from less to more "clinically representative" differed in effectiveness as judged by an impressive array of outcome variables. Using sophisticated random effects regression analyses, Shadish and his coauthors explored the question that is at the core of this chapter: Do psychological treatments tested by the efficacy research model and psychological treatments assessed by the effectiveness research model differ in outcome? Their studies revealed that in no instance did a meta-analysis reveal differences in therapeutic outcome as a function of where on the efficacy/effectiveness ("clinically representative") continuum a group of studies fell. The meaning of this finding, presumably, when extended beyond the research to the clinical setting, is that the outcomes of efficacy and effectiveness studies were independent of where on a hypothetical efficacy-effectiveness continuum the study lay. While these findings should certainly not be used to convince us of the possibility of converting the real methodological differences between the efficacy and effectiveness research models into semantic ones, they do suggest that, in terms of one very important factor, clinical usefulness, the distinction may be more apparent than real.

EFFICACY, EFFECTIVENESS, AND THE CLINICAL UTILITY OF EVIDENCE-BASED PRACTICE: A REPRISE

The past three decades have witnessed clear, evidence-based gains in the effectiveness of psychological treatments for both mental and physical disorders.

Advocates for behavioral and cognitive-behavioral treatments can now assert their documented effectiveness as treatments of choice for the anxiety and mood disorders (Chambless & Ollendick, 2001; Roth & Fonagy, 1996), while cognitive-behavioral treatments for alcohol abuse, eating disorders, and several other common psychopathologic conditions are also widely studied and well-accepted (Nathan & Gorman, 2002). More recently, the efficacy of psychological treatments for certain physical disorders has also been established empirically (e.g., Barlow, 2004). Marked advances in outcome research methodologies, including intensive efforts to integrate the effectiveness and efficacy research models, have energized efforts to promote empirically supported treatments.

Regretfully, despite these clear advances, many of the theories and therapeutic approaches used by clinicians today remain unsupported empirically (Beutler, Williams, Wakefield, & Entwistle, 1995; Castonguay & Beutler, 2006; Plante, Andersen, & Boccaccini, 1999). In provocative recent articles that raised questions about the empirical basis for empirically-supported treatments, Westen and his colleagues (2001, 2004) argued that "the attempt to identify empirically supported therapies imposes particular assumptions on the use of randomized controlled trial (RCT) methodology that appear to be valid for some disorders and treatments ... but substantially violated for others" (2004, p. 631). Accordingly, they suggested that the field "shift from validating treatment packages to testing intervention strategies and theories of change that clinicians can integrate into *empirically informed therapies*" (2004, p. 631). Of relevance to the focus of this chapter, Westen and his colleagues clearly believe that psychotherapy researchers' reliance on RCTs as the "gold standard" of efforts to identify empirically supported treatments unduly restricts the kinds of settings and patients in such studies to those more characteristic of efficacy trials than of effectiveness studies.

Crits-Christoph, Wilson, and Hollon (2005) and Weisz, Weersing, and Henggeler (2005) took issue with this position, arguing that Westen and his colleagues selected only research findings that supported their position and ignored voluminous data attesting to the heterogeneity of research participants, settings, and procedures incorporated into contemporary effectiveness studies using randomized clinical trials. Of relevance to this matter as well, Stirman, DeRubeis, Crits-Christoph, and Rothman (2005) recently tested the validity of Westen and Morrison's claim (2001) that the exclusion criteria for the disorders studied in RCTs "often eliminated more troubled and difficult-to-treat patients" (2001, p. 880), reporting instead that "most of the patients in the sample who had primary diagnoses represented in the RCT literature were judged eligible for at least 1 RCT" (2005, p. 127).

There is also widespread, growing support for the view that research on empirically supported treatments ought to be augmented by studies of other factors affecting therapeutic outcomes, primarily including therapist variables and common factors (Wampold & Bhati, 2004). Most recently, Castonguay and Beutler (2006) have proposed an additional factor they think influences therapeutic outcome, principles of therapeutic change, which they believe transcend techniques and treatments.

FUTURE PROSPECTS

Our field's intense preoccupation over the past decade and more with heightening the clinical utility of psychotherapy research by resolving the efficacy/effectiveness paradox, however frustrating it may have been, may nonetheless ultimately prove to have been a success. A number of solutions to the paradox posed by internal and external validity have been proposed, although none has yet proven ideal (Addis, 2002; McCabe, 2004). We believe, however, that, within a shorter rather than a longer time, a solution will be found and the evidence base underlying psychological treatments for a number of disorders will become more widely accepted. Exclusive endorsement of either the efficacy or the effectiveness research models alone will likely not be sufficient; efforts to date along those lines haven't yielded much encouragement. Similarly, tinkering with both models simultaneously to achieve some more optimal balance of the two does not seem to be the answer either; experience does not suggest it will be.

Serious doubts must also be expressed about whether it will be possible to develop new conceptual and statistical methods to permit integration of the two models that NIMH and others envision. Instead, the most likely solution seems to be to take findings from the best efficacy studies and use them to design the most robust effectiveness studies. Then, in bootstrap fashion, alternating between the two, meaningful and clinically relevant findings might well emerge. This back-and-forth variant of the Onken Stage/Hybrid Model of Behavioral Therapies Research makes the most sense to us and seems to have generated the most productive research to date. That this approach has recently been endorsed by NIDA, NIAAA, and NIMH (Gotham, 2004) to guide their efforts to diffuse technological innovations to the field attests to the attractiveness of this model.

Resolution of the efficacy/effectiveness controversy would nonetheless be but the first step, albeit a substantial one, toward solution of the fundamental unresolved issue of when and how psychotherapy researchers and clinicians will feel comfortable enough with each other to benefit from each others' contributions. Perhaps this will occur when research on therapy outcomes comes close enough to actual clinical practice to enable practitioners to recognize themselves and their patients in the research settings in which effectiveness research takes place.

There are encouraging signs of progress. In particular, as we have already observed, the Stage/Hybrid Model of Behavioral Therapies Research has generated more and more research that subjects efficacy findings to effectiveness trials. Moreover, recent reports suggest that clinicians and researchers have been able to come together to make decisions about empirically supported treatments that bridge the efficacy/effectiveness gap (including Chorpita et al., 2002; and Zapka, Goins, Pbert, & Ockene, 2004). Notable in this regard is the report by Chorpita and his colleagues (2002) describing the large-scale, successful implementation of empirically supported treatments for children by the Hawaii Empirical Basis to Services Task Force. Chorpita and his colleagues describe the process by which a broad-based group of administrators, providers, consumers, and researchers—"health administrators, parents of challenged children, clinical service providers, and academicians from the areas of psychology, psychiatry, nursing, and social work" (2002, p. 167)—reviewed findings on treatment efficacy "... through a systematic cataloguing of effectiveness parameters across more than one hundred treatment outcome studies" (2002, p. 165) and ultimately agreed on a set of treatments meeting efficacy and effectiveness standards that were then recommended to providers throughout an entire state. What accounts for the apparent success of this effort? Three factors: (1) most of the work was done by dedicated, committed volunteers who cared enough to do much of the work on their own time; (2) the effort was open to anyone with a stake in the system, so a diverse group of interested persons came together to develop the standards; (3) once the State of Hawaii recognized what the group had achieved, it decided to invest funds in the initiative, thereby making its dissemination and implementation possible.

It seems clear that this effort presages more such efforts in the future.

REFERENCES

Addis, M. E. (2002). Methods for disseminating research products and increasing evidence-based practice: Promises, obstacles, and future directions. *Clinical Psychology: Science and Practice, 9,* 367–378.

August, G. J., Winters, K. C., Realmuto, G. M., Tarter, R., Perry, C., & Hektner, J. M. (2004). Moving evidence-based drug abuse prevention programs from basic science to practice: "Bridging the efficacy-effectiveness interface." *Substance Use & Misuse, 39,* 2017–2053.

Barlow, D. H. (1981). On the relation of clinical research to clinical practice: Current issues. *Journal of Consulting and Clinical Psychology, 49,* 147–155.

Barlow, D. H. (1996). Health care policy, psychotherapy research, and the future of psychotherapy. *American Psychologist, 51,* 1050–1058.

Barlow, D. H. (2004). Psychological treatments. *American Psychologist, 59,* 869–878.

Beutler, L. E., Williams, R. E., Wakefield, P. J., & Entwistle, S. R. (1995). Bridging scientist and practitioner perspectives in clinical psychology. *American Psychologist, 50,* 984–994.

Borkovec, T. D. (2002). Training clinic research and the possibility of a National Training Clinics Practice Research Network. *Behavior Therapist, 25,* 98–103.

Borkovec, T. D., Echemendia, R. J., Ragusea, S. A., & Ruiz, M. (2001). The Pennsylvania Practice Research Network and future possibilities for clinically meaningful and scientifically rigorous psychotherapy effectiveness research. *Clinical Psychology: Science and Practice, 8,* 155–167.

Carroll, K. M., & Nuro, K. F. (2002). One size cannot fit all: A stage model for psychotherapy manual development. *Clinical Psychology: Science and Practice, 9,* 396–406.

Carroll, K. M., & Rounsaville, B. J. (2003). Bridging the gap: A hybrid model to link efficacy and effectiveness research in substance abuse treatment. *Psychiatric Services, 54,* 333–339.

Castonguay, L. G., & Beutler, L. E. (2006). Common and unique principles of therapeutic change: What do we know and what do we need to know? In L. G. Castonguay & L. E. Beutler (Eds.), *Principles of therapeutic change that work* (pp. 353–370). New York: Oxford University Press.

Chambless, D. L., & Ollendick, T. H. (2001). Empirically supported psychological interventions: Controversies and evidence. In S. T. Fiske, D. L. Schacter, & C. Zahn-Waxler (Eds.), *Annual review of psychology*, vol. 52 (pp. 685–716). Palo Alto, CA: Annual Review.

Chorpita, B. F., Yim, L. M., Donkervoet, J. C., Arensdorf, A., Amundsen, M. J., McGee, C., Serrano, A., Yates, A., Burns, J. A., & Morelli, P. (2002). Toward large-scale implementation of empirically supported treatments for children: A review and observation by the Hawaii Empirical Basis to Service Task Force. *Clinical Psychology: Science and Practice, 9*, 165–190.

Crits-Christoph, P., Wilson, G. T., & Hollon, S. D. (2005). Empirically supported psychotherapies: Comment on Westen, Novotny, and Thompson-Brenner (2004). *Psychological Bulletin, 131*, 412–417.

Edwards, D. J. A. (1996). Case study research: The cornerstone of theory and practice. In M. Reinecke, F. M. Datillio, & A. Freeman (Eds.), *Cognitive therapy with children and adolescents: A casebook for clinical practice* (pp. 10–37). New York: Guilford.

Edwards, D. J. A., Dattilio, F. M., & Bromley, D. B. (2004). Developing evidence-based practice: The role of case-based research. *Professional Psychology: Research and Practice, 35*, 589–597.

Frank, E., Rush, A. J., Biehar, M., Essock, S., & Hargreaves, W. (2002). Skating to where the puck is going to be: A plan for clinical trials and translation research in mood disorders. *Biological Psychiatry, 52*, 631–654.

Garfield, S. L. (1996). Some problems associated with "validated" forms of psychotherapy. *Clinical Psychology: Science and Practice, 3*, 218–229.

Goldfried, M. R., & Wolfe, B. E. (1996). Psychotherapy practice and research: Repairing a strained alliance. *American Psychologist, 51*, 1007–1016.

Gotham, H. J. (2004). Diffusion of mental health and substance abuse treatments: Development, dissemination, and implementation. *Clinical Psychology: Science and Practice, 11*, 160–176.

Hollon, S. D. (1996). The efficacy and effectiveness of psychotherapy relative to medications. *American Psychologist, 51*, 1025–1030.

Howard, K. I., Moras, K., Brill, P. L., Martinovich, Z., & Lutz, W. (1996). Evaluation of psychotherapy: Efficacy, effectiveness, and patient progress. *American Psychologist, 51*, 1059–1064.

Jacobson, N. S., & Christensen, A. (1996). Studying the effectiveness of psychotherapy: How well can clinical trials do the job? *American Psychologist, 51*, 1031–1039.

Kazdin, A. E. (2001). Progression of therapy research and clinical application of treatment require better understanding of the change process. *Clinical Psychology: Science and Practice, 8*, 143–151.

Klein, D. F., & Smith, L. B. (1999). Organizational requirements for effective clinical effectiveness studies. *Prevention & Treatment, 2*, Article 0002a.

Kopta, S. M., Lueger, R. J., Saunders, S. M., & Howard, K. I. (1999). Individual psychotherapy outcome and process research: Challenges leading to greater turmoil or a positive transition? In J. T. Spence, J. M. Darley, & D. J. Foss (Eds.), *Annual review of psychology*, vol. 50 (pp. 441–470). Palo Alto, CA: Annual Reviews, Inc.

McCabe, O. L. (2004). Crossing the quality chasm in behavioral health care: The role of evidence-based practice. *Professional Psychology: Research and Practice, 35,* 571–579.

Nash, J. M., McCrory, D., Nicholson, R. A., & Andrasik, F. (2005). Efficacy and effectiveness approaches in behavioral treatment trials. *The Journal of Head and Face Pain, 45,* 507–512.

Nathan, P. E. (1998). Practice guidelines: Not yet ideal. *American Psychologist, 3,* 290–299.

Nathan, P. E., & Gorman, J. M. (1998). *A guide to treatments that work.* New York: Oxford University Press.

Nathan, P. E., & Gorman, J. M. (2002). *A guide to treatments that work* (2nd ed.). New York: Oxford University Press.

Nathan, P. E., Stuart, S. P., & Dolan, S. L. (2000). Research on psychotherapy efficacy and effectiveness: Between Scylla and Charybdis? *Psychological Bulletin, 126,* 964–981.

National Advisory Mental Health Council (NAMHC) Workgroup. (1999). *Bridging science and service.* Washington, DC: National Institute of Mental Health.

Niederehe, G., Street, L. L., & Lebowitz, B. D. (1999). NIMH support for psychotherapy research: Opportunities and questions. *Prevention & Treatment, 2,* Article 0003a.

Norquist, G., Lebowitz, B., & Hyman, S. (1999). Expanding the frontier of treatment research. *Prevention & Treatment, 2,* Article 0001a.

O'Hare, T. (2005). *Evidence-based practices for social workers.* Chicago: Lyceum Books, Inc.

Onken, L. S., Blaine, J. D., & Battjes, R. (1997). Behavior therapy research: A conceptualization of a process. In S. W. Henngler & R. Amentos (Eds.), *Innovative approaches from difficult to treat populations* (pp. 477–485). Washington, DC: American Psychiatric Press.

Paul, G. L. (2006). Psychotherapy outcome can be studied scientifically. In S. O. Lilienfeld & W. O'Donohue (Eds.), *The great ideas of clinical science: The 18 concepts every mental health researcher and practitioner should understand.* New York: Brunner-Routledge.

Persons, J. B. (1991). Psychotherapy outcome studies do not accurately represent current models of psychotherapy: A proposed remedy. *American Psychologist, 46,* 99–106.

Plante, T. G., Andersen, E. N., & Boccaccini, M. T. (1999). Empirically supported treatments and related contemporary changes in psychotherapy practice: What do clinical ABPPs think? *The Clinical Psychologist, 52,* 23–31.

Roth, A. D., & Fonagy, P. (1996). *What works for whom? A critical review of psychotherapy research.* New York: Guilford.

Rounsaville, B. J., Carroll, K. M., & Onken, L. S. (2001a). A stage model of behavioral therapies research: Getting started and moving on from stage 1. *Clinical Psychology: Research and Practice, 8,* 133–142.

Rounsaville, B. J., Carroll, K. M., & Onken, L. S. (2001b). Methodological diversity and theory in the stage model: Reply to Kazdin. *Clinical Psychology: Science and Practice, 8,* 152–154.

Seligman, M. E. P. (1995). The effectiveness of psychotherapy: The *Consumer Reports* study. *American Psychologist, 50,* 965–974.

Seligman, M. E. P. (1996). Science as an ally of practice. *American Psychologist, 51,* 1072–1079.

Shadish, W. R., & Baldwin, S. A. (2005). Effects of behavioral marital therapy: A meta-analysis of randomized controlled trials. *Journal of Consulting and Clinical Psychology, 73,* 6–14.

Shadish, W. R., Matt, G. E., Navarro, A. M., & Phillips, G. (2000). The effects of psychological therapies in clinically representative conditions: A meta-analysis. *Psychological Bulletin, 126,* 512–529.

Shadish, W. R., Matt, G. E., Navarro, A. M., Siegle, G., & Crist-Christoph, P. (1997). Evidence that therapy works in clinically representative conditions. *Journal of Consulting and Clinical Psychology, 65,* 355–365.

Shadish, W. R., & Ragsdale, K. (1996). Random versus nonrandom assignment in controlled experiments: Do you get the same answer? *Journal of Consulting and Clinical Psychology, 64,* 1290–1305.

Stirman, S. W., DeRubeis, R. J., Crits-Christoph, P., & Rothman, A. (2005). Can the randomized controlled trial literature generalize to nonrandomized patients? *Journal of Consulting and Clinical Psychology, 73,* 127–135.

Wampold, B. E., & Bhati, K. S. (2004). Attending to the omissions: A historical examination of evidence-based practice movement. *Professional Psychology: Research and Practice, 35,* 563–570.

Weisz, J. R., Weersing, V. R., & Henggeler, S. W. (2005). Jousting with straw men: Comment on Westen, Novotny, and Thompson-Brenner (2004). *Psychological Bulletin, 131,* 418–426.

Westen, D., & Morrison, K. (2001). A multidimensional meta-analysis of treatments for depression, panic, and generalized anxiety disorder: An empirical examination of the status of empirically-supported therapies. *Journal of Consulting and Clinical Psychology, 69,* 875–899.

Westen, D., Novotny, C. M., & Thompson-Brenner, H. (2004). The empirical status of empirically-supported psychotherapies: Assumptions, findings, and reporting in controlled clinical trials. *Psychological Bulletin, 130,* 631–663.

Zapka, J., Goins, K. V., Pbert, L., & Ockene, J. K. (2004). Translating efficacy research to effectiveness studies in practice: Lessons from research to promote smoking cessation in community health centers. *Health Promotion Practice, 5,* 245–255.

5

The Local Clinical Scientist

GEORGE STRICKER

The Local Clinical Scientist (LCS) model initially was presented (Stricker & Trierweiler, 1995; Trierweiler & Stricker, 1998) as a bridge between science and practice. As such, it was conceptualized as an instantiation of the scientist-practitioner model (Raimy, 1950), the most influential and least applied (Stricker, 2000) approach to training in clinical psychology. Ironically, the LCS model has been widely adopted by professional schools of psychology (R. L. Peterson, Peterson, Abrams, & Stricker, 1997) that emphasize training for practice, but has not been accepted by schools more focused on the training of scientists. The much-lauded intention to train psychologists in both practice and science, in a way that takes both missions seriously, occurs less frequently, and is the vision of the LCS approach. This chapter will describe the LCS model, look at some contributions to the application of science from social psychology, recognize some drawbacks to the implementation of the model, and describe a successful approach to such implementation.

THE LOCAL CLINICAL SCIENTIST MODEL

Each of the three words in the term "Local Clinical Scientist" is crucial to an understanding of the overall meaning. The central word, "Clinical," describes the context in which LCSs operate. They are clinicians and they are functioning in the role of a clinician trying to be helpful to patients. The patients they are helping are immediately there before them, not abstract conglomerates of diagnostic terms. The immediacy of this contact represents the "Local" aspect of the construct. Finally, and perhaps most novel, even though they are operating clinically in a local context, nonetheless they are functioning as scientists, treating each patient contact as an experiment to which much previous knowledge is brought and from which much is to be learned. This model initially was applied to psychotherapy (Stricker & Trierweiler, 1995; Trierweiler & Stricker, 1998), but has been expanded to apply to personality assessment (Stricker, 2006) as well.

The LCS model begins with the assumption that science is defined by attitudes, not by activities or generalizations. The variability of activities and generalizations, accompanied by the stability of attitudes, is crucial to the functioning of the scientist, and it also is crucial to the functioning of the clinician. The activities of the scientist vary depending upon the area of study under investigation. The generalizations that are drawn may differ in validity as new knowledge replaces old, only to be replaced itself at a future time. Thus, practice based solely on scientific conclusions today can be hopelessly dated by tomorrow. Attitudes, however, are similar for the scientist in every area of inquiry. All scientists, regardless of specific discipline, should be keen observers who are characterized by disciplined inquiry, critical thinking, imagination, rigor, skepticism, and openness to change in the face of evidence. The LCS carries these attitudes into the practice setting, raising hypotheses in the consulting room and seeking confirmatory or disconfirmatory evidence in the immediate response of the patient.

Formal data may be collected, but it often is not. Nevertheless, LCSs approach the patient using the appropriate literature from both psychotherapy and general psychology insofar as it is applicable, applying it whenever it seems potentially helpful to do so, but also supplementing it by an intuitive grasp of the situation, based on prior experience with similar situations. However, as no two patients are exactly alike, the similarity may not point to an effective intervention. Therefore, it is crucial for LCSs to observe the effects of the intervention, and to add it to their personal data bank so that what they learn can be applied, tentatively, to the next patient/research project for whom it may appear to be applicable. The only way experience can accumulate in a meaningful way is if this process is systematic, and LCSs strive to improve their functioning on the basis of past experience. Because of the problems inherent in memory, this process of systematic learning is facilitated if careful records are kept. Thus, as a clinician, the LCS always is learning and using the product of the learning to apply to new situations. So it is with the scientist as well, as no single research project is definitive, and science proceeds with the accretion of knowledge.

To summarize this portrait to this point, LCSs may be expected to engage in the following activities:

1. the display of a questioning attitude and search for confirmatory or disconfirmatory evidence;
2. the application of relevant research findings to the clinical case immediately at hand;
3. the documentation of each individual clinical contact; and
4. the production of research, either collaboratively or more traditionally.

Not every activity is performed in every instance by the LCS. Rather, these activities have been presented in descending order of frequency, with the questioning attitude the most pervasive and critical feature of the LCS, and the conduct of formal research activity the least likely to occur, although it is highly desirable, and has happened on many occasions. The LCS can be described as

A person who, on the basis of systematic knowledge about persons obtained primarily in real-life situations, has integrated this knowledge with psychological theory, and has then consistently regarded it with the questioning attitude of the scientist. In this image, clinical psychologists see themselves combining the idiographic and nomothetic approaches, both of which appear to them significant. (Shakow, 1976, p. 554)

In this statement, Shakow was not describing a LCS, a term that had not yet been coined, but a scientist-practitioner. The similarity between the two descriptions (a LCS and a scientist-practitioner) is striking, and raises the question as to the relationship between the two concepts. My guess is that Shakow would have been very comfortable with the notion of a LCS, and might have seen it, as it was intended, as an instantiation of his influential recommendation. Unfortunately, the more common implementation of the scientist-practitioner recommendation is heavily tilted toward science as it is practiced in the academy, which is the locus of clinical training programs. It is not as much concerned with science as it may be practiced in the community, which is the site of employment of most graduates of clinical training programs. In many cases, the scientist-practitioner model is implemented in a sequential fashion, with science being taught in graduate school and practice occurring during the career of the psychologist (Kanfer, 1990).

There is an important distinction between idiographic and nomothetic, terms used quite appropriately by Shakow. The scientist, working in a laboratory, seeks nomothetic data, which characterize large groups; the clinician, working with one individual at a time, generates idiographic data. A major problem confronting all clinicians is how to apply nomothetic conclusions to local, idiographic presentations, or, more simply, how to apply group findings to individuals. Shakow, of course, did not force a choice between the two, but instead understood that both are legitimate, and he challenged the scientist-practitioner to combine the two. The clinician, faced with the need to respond to a single individual, should apply whatever nomothetic generalizations are relevant, but also must recognize that there will be gaps in knowledge and the nomothetic conclusions cannot be applied blindly. Patients expect clinicians to integrate their professional experience with the nomothetic data to reach an informed and local idiographic intervention.

It should be clear at this point that the LCS model is most focused on the implementation of a scientific attitude and should not be taken as an alternative to scientific activity. LCS activity may not lead to a firmly established set of conclusions and generalizations, but it does seek to develop a loosely determined set of hypotheses. The LCS differs from the ordinary clinician by engaging in the systematic study of the clinical work, a process that will reduce the extent to which the LCS's observations are subject to the distortions of the cognitive heuristics (Tversky & Kahneman, 1974) that are common to all thinking. It is foolish to ignore the results of research, but it also is foolish to apply those results without consideration of the local circumstances that generated the findings, and the inevitable difficulties with generalization. Instead, LCSs will consider whether and how these research findings can be incorporated in their local activity. It must be reiterated that the LCS model does not provide the clinician with an excuse to ignore research. Rather, the model requires LCSs to attend to research done by others, to apply it where applicable, but also to systematically study prior clinical activities so that local hypotheses can be raised a step closer to generalizations. This leads to a continuing process rather than a firm product, and the result should be a closer and closer approximation to choosing appropriate and helpful local interventions.

SIMILAR APPROACHES

It would be foolish to think that the LCS model (or any other psychological construct, regardless of the imaginativeness of the nomenclature) arose *sui generis*. I already noted that the scientist-practitioner model bears considerable resemblance to the LCS model, although many proponents of the former might disavow connection with the latter. A much closer and more readily acknowledged resemblance is with the concept of disciplined inquiry (D. R. Peterson, 1991).

Disciplined inquiry is an approach that flows from a consideration of the relationship between research and practice, carefully avows that professional education never should suggest the rejection of research, but states that the training and goals of researchers and practitioners are quite different. Peterson applauded the scientist-practitioner model but criticized the application of that model as it had been implemented, leading him to suggest a new approach to training practitioners. I agree with his criticism of the implementation of the scientist-practitioner model (Stricker, 2000), agree that a different approach than has been taken is required for adequate training of practitioners, but feel that it can be done within a true scientist-practitioner framework, and the necessary approach is the LCS model. In fact, in light of the recent concerns he has expressed about professional schools (D. R. Peterson, 2003), I wonder if Peterson might be more inclined to agree with the wisdom of adhering more closely to a scientist-practitioner model, assuming it was implemented as originally proposed and not as more typically distorted. Nonetheless, Peterson's suggested approach (disciplined inquiry) has a good deal to recommend it.

In analyzing differences between science and practice, Peterson stated:

The simplifications and controls that are essential to science cannot be imposed in practice. Each problem must be addressed as it occurs in nature, as an open, living process in all its complexity, often in a political context that requires certain forms of action and prohibits others. All functionally important influences on the process under study must be considered. At its best, practice runs ahead of research. Each case is unique. The pattern of conditions the client presents has never occurred in exactly this form before, and the most beneficial pattern of professional action cannot rest only on scientifically established procedures, although any contingencies established in prior research must not be ignored. The measure of effect goes beyond statistical significance to functional importance. It is not enough to determine whether a difference is random or replicable. The difference has to matter to the client. (D. R. Peterson, 1991, p. 426)

Peterson's emphasis on local conditions, along with the recognition of some of the limitations of research precedents without discarding the contributory value of those findings, is consistent with the LCS approach.

Peterson then went on to describe his approach to disciplined inquiry. He advocated that we "start with the client and apply all the useful knowledge we can find" (D. R. Peterson, 1991, p. 426), a procedure quite different than starting with science. In doing so, careful assessment leads to a formulation that results in an action, the effects of which must be evaluated carefully. Depending on the evaluation, either the action can be continued or a reformulation and alternative action is required, with additional analyses and possible reformulation following until the problem is resolved. Finally, it is noted that the results of this sequence become part of the knowledge base of the practitioner, leading to more adequate formulations in similar future cases.

The resemblance of this approach to the LCS model is striking. In both, science is drawn upon when relevant, local conditions are taken into account, and the prior experience of the practitioner is a source of hypotheses that feed into the clinical formulation. There is a need to systematically record the experience so as to benefit future interventions and not start over at the beginning each time. Perhaps the major differences (and these are comparatively minor) are the emphasis on the scientific thought process in the LCS model and the conviction in that model that a scientist-practitioner framework need not be discarded.

It also should be noted that Kanfer (1990) has a slightly different approach, although one that also is quite consistent with the meaningful relationship between science and practice. For Kanfer, as with Peterson, the practitioner is best advised to begin with the patient, not the science, and then seek information in the scientific corpus that will assist with the theory driven hypotheses that have been developed. Here, too, the science is applied where relevant, but the entry into science begins with a formulation about the patient.

THE PRESIDENTIAL TASK FORCE

When Ronald Levant assumed the presidency of the American Psychological Association, he constituted a task force that was charged with studying evidence-based practice. The final report of that group (American Psychological Association, 2005) is particularly instructive. Evidence-based-practice, if it is interpreted literally, and in a manner that can present a straight jacket rather than a set of permissive guidelines (Chambless & Ollendick, 2001), would hamper the activities recommended for the LCS.

The Task Force was constituted of a heterogeneous group of psychologists, some of whom had clear allegiances to the strict and sole application of evidence-based practices and others who were more aligned with practice as usual (as well as many in between these alternatives). The conclusions they drew were consistent with the LCS model, and mentioned that model favorably.

The Task Force began by adopting the definition of evidence-based practice from the important report of the Institute of Medicine: "Evidence-based practice is the integration of best research evidence with clinical expertise and patient values" (Institute of Medicine, 2001, p. 147). This definition presages their conclusions and is consistent with an LCS approach. That is, the report attends to research evidence but also incorporates clinical expertise (patient values can be considered part of the local component of the LCS). This led to their definition of evidence-based practice in psychology as "the integration of the best available research with clinical expertise in the context of patient characteristics, culture, and preferences" (American Psychological Association, 2005, p. 5).

The Task Force went on to endorse the consideration of multiple sources of evidence, recognizing the need to appraise the strengths and weaknesses of each source of information. Its approach to evidence follows from that of the Template for Developing Guidelines (American Psychological Association Task Force on Psychological Intervention Guidelines, 1995; Stricker et al., 1999). This was a document that proposed a dual axis approach to evidence, thereby giving credibility to both efficacy and effectiveness approaches to psychotherapy research, and recognizing the inherent tradeoff between internal and external validity.

In the consideration given to clinical expertise, an important aspect of the LCS model (as is acknowledged in the report), there is explicit recognition that the clinician is responsible for integrating the best of research data and clinical data, keeping in mind the patient's characteristics and the goals of treatment. Thus, recognition is given to the local aspects of the clinical situation and potential problems with the generalizability of some efficacy data based on controlled trials. It is this aspect of the report, the recognition that different patients require different treatment in different circumstances, that is characterized as patient preferences and this represents an emphasis on local conditions.

The report concludes with a summary statement that clearly supports the crux of the LCS model: "What this document reflects, however, is a reassertion of what psychologists have known for a century: that the scientific method is a way of thinking and observing systematically and is the best tool we have for learning about what works for whom" (American Psychological Association, 2005, p. 18).

In an interesting complement to the report, and an additional endorsement of multiple sources of evidence, the philosopher Cranor (2005), writing within a legal context summarized his article by stating that:

If the *Daubert* trilogy of decisions tried to ensure that the law better comports with the relevant science, this will happen only if courts recognize the complexity of scientific evidence, how scientists draw inferences from such evidence and the fact of reasonable disagreements between respectable scientific experts. With the help of the public health community, judges might rectify overreactions to the initial *Daubert* teaching and help ensure that the courts use in the courtroom the kinds of inferences that public health scientists use in their research. (Cranor, 2005, p. S127)

If we read this as referring to the need to ensure that practice comports with the relevant science, and that the psychological community, particularly its practitioners, use the same inferences from research that scientists use in their research, we have a sound statement about the problems with, and solutions to, current statements about research. The LCS certainly should recognize all of the value that research has to contribute to clinical practice, but also should have a keen awareness of the limitations of that research.

SOME LESSONS FROM SOCIAL PSYCHOLOGY

About 40 years ago I had a conversation with Paul Rozin, an old friend from college days. At the time, I was engaged in research in some clinical areas and Rozin was identified as a physiological psychologist with a particular interest in taste. He was astonished by my concern with significance levels, preferring to subject findings to an interocular test (did the results hit you between the eyes). He felt that science, in general, proceeded by the presence of striking findings rather than simply probabilistic ones. In fact, Rozin's formulation anticipated Peterson's (1991) concern about placing statistical significance above functional importance. I did not agree with him then about the lack of value of significance testing, and I do not thoroughly agree with him now, but it is an issue worth considering.

It was in that context that I saw a familiar article addressing this topic in a recent journal in social psychology (Rozin, 2001), Rozin's newest interest. He took his cue from Solomon Asch, an old colleague of his and certainly a respected social psychologist. Rozin introduced the article with a quotation from Asch's work:

In their anxiety to be scientific, students of psychology have often imitated the latest forms of sciences with a long history, while ignoring the steps these sciences took when they were young. They have, for example, striven to emulate the quantitative exactness of natural sciences without asking whether their own subject matter is always ripe for such treatment, failing to realize that one does not advance time by moving the hands of the clock. Because physicists cannot speak with stars or electric currents, psychologists have often been hesitant to speak to their human participants. (Asch 1952/1987, pp. xiv–xv; from Rozin, 2001, p. 2)

The LCS model is concerned with the practice of clinical psychology rather than research in social psychology, but the ideas Rozin expressed are relevant. In an attempt to be scientific, clinicians often can become overly scientistic and trade narratives for statistics in an attempt to understand and treat their patients. We probably are at a point of development where description remains a valuable activity and definitive conclusions are beyond our grasp.

Rozin indicated that "There are many possible methods, including examination of historical materials or literature, observation, participant observation, laboratory experiment, natural experiment, questionnaire/survey, and interview" (Rozin, 2001, p. 4). He went on to note that "It is as if the experiments in question transcend time, location, culture, race, religion, and social class" (Rozin, 2001, p. 4). He was discussing social psychology, but the same observation pertains to clinical psychology and describes the approach and methods of the LCS. Notice that traditional research, whether in a laboratory or in the field, was not denigrated, but the available and appropriate methodology was extended to include theoretical and observational work. The local aspects of the research were noted, and the problems with generalizability were emphasized.

Although Rozin understood the power of a well-controlled experiment, he also recognized its limitations. In the course of instituting appropriate controls in an experiment, there are two risks that we must attend to: "(a) they allow for the possibility that the results will not bear on real social situations and (b) they may generalize to only a very narrow range of apparently similar experimental situations" (Rozin, 2001, p. 9). Again, the potential failure of generalizability forces us to turn to the local aspects of the clinical situation, and all clinical work, like all politics, is local.

The lesson from social psychology is that we should recognize the stage of scientific endeavor we have reached and not discard methodology appropriate to that stage by engaging in physics envy (physics, being more advanced, has progressed beyond simple and exclusive reliance on experimental methods). The LCS has learned this lesson and attends to research data as appropriate, while remaining cognizant of limitations of generalizability and local considerations that impact the interpretation of those findings.

A WORD OF CAUTION

The LCS model places great reliance on the skill of the individual clinician, acting with the curiosity and skepticism of a scientist. However, as the presidential task force report notes:

> experts are not infallible. All humans are prone to errors and biases. Some of these stem from cognitive strategies and heuristics that are generally adaptive and efficient. Others stem from emotional reactions, which generally guide adaptive behavior as well but can also lead to biased or motivated reasoning (e.g., Ditto & Lopez, 1992; Ditto et al., 2003; Kunda, 1990). Whenever psychologists involved

in research or practice move from observations to inferences and generalizations, there is inherent risk for idiosyncratic interpretations, overgeneralizations, confirmatory biases, and similar errors in judgment (Dawes, Faust, & Meehl, 2002; Grove et al., 2000; Meehl, 1954; Westen & Weinberger, 2004). Integral to clinical expertise is an awareness of the limits of one's knowledge and skills and attention to the heuristics and biases-both cognitive and affective-that can affect clinical judgment. Mechanisms such as consultation and systematic feedback from the patient can mitigate some of these biases. (American Psychological Association, 2005, p. 10)

This introduces a class of potential errors that generally can be considered as cognitive heuristics (Tversky & Kahneman, 1974). Cognitive heuristics are mental shortcuts that allow us to make judgments quickly but sometimes erroneously because the shortcut disregards some of the available information. These heuristics characterize a good deal of cognitive activity, often have much functional value, but occasionally can lead to significant error. Among the most frequently used heuristics by clinicians are the availability heuristic, the representativeness heuristic, and the anchoring heuristic.

The availability heuristic refers to the tendency to reach solutions that come to mind most easily, so that a dramatic instance of a previous case will be remembered more readily than frequent but unremarkable exceptions. A clinician can draw upon past experiences, use the availability heuristic, and be certain that a particular intervention is warranted because it "always" has worked in the past. Of course it has not, and the only relevant counter to this heuristic is careful record keeping, so that a probabilistic rather than absolute conclusion can be reached, and the probability can be determined by actual occurrence rather than faulty memory processes. It should be noted that the availability heuristic probably underlies the phenomenon of the illusory correlation (Chapman, 1967), another frequent error that a clinician may demonstrate. An illusory correlation consists of the impression that two variables are correlated when, in fact, they are not. This can result from faulty recollection of the co-occurrence of the two variables, a recollection based on the availability heuristic. A LCS will be skeptical about presumed probability statements unless there are supportive data available.

The representativeness heuristic links judgments to signs that are representative of the group in general, so that it is assumed, once it is determined that a patient is a member of a particular diagnostic group (or has a particular set of psychodynamics), that the patient has all of the characteristics of that group. This is the object of the diagnostic procedure, but it is not always an accurate basis for individual judgment, as not all patients with borderline personality disorder, for example, have all of the characteristics of borderline personality disorder (e.g., not all cut themselves). It is also important to recognize that the representativeness heuristic is the source of much stereotyping and subsequent bias. The assumption, for example, that all members of a particular racial group, gender, or religious persuasion are characterized by specific features are examples of the representativeness heuristic at work, and must be guarded against.

In fact, the representativeness heuristic can be seen as a failure in generalizability, and is a source of potential difficulty for the universal adoption of interventions that are empirically supported. This strange connection between the scientific inclinations of proponents of empirically supported techniques and the pitfalls of the representativeness heuristic rarely is noted, and represents a danger to the "scientific" practitioner as well as to the clinician in the field. However, the LCS, maintaining scientific objectivity and skepticism, should be better prepared than the ordinary clinician to deal with the problem (although no one is immune).

The anchoring heuristic is a process by means of which the clinician (actually, all human beings) draws conclusions early in the therapeutic process, and then is more likely to respond to confirmatory evidence afterwards, unwittingly failing to be as responsive to evidence contrary to the early conclusion. This also can be seen as a confirmation bias.

The approach of forming hypotheses and then seeking confirmatory or disconfirmatory evidence is an important aspect of clinical functioning, but it is prone to the danger of sorting of evidence so that only the confirmatory is considered seriously. Awareness of this tendency is one way of guarding against it, but as with all heuristics, it is easier said than done. We should note that it is not only "consultation and systematic feedback from the patient [that] can mitigate some of these biases (American Psychological Association, 2005, p. 10)," but also careful attention to the existence and problems created by them, and systematic record keeping that can mitigate the natural errors created by cognitive heuristics and other biases. The LCS, being aware of the tendency of the heuristics to mislead, and having systematic data available, can reduce the likelihood of error, but no human being can avoid it entirely, regardless of the approach taken to clinical practice.

In addition to cognitive heuristics, errors also can be made simply because of faulty memory and the limitations created by theoretical and social expectations. There is a need to keep these possible problems in mind when considering the use of clinical judgment and expertise.

THE LOCAL CLINICAL SCIENTIST IN ACTION

The LCS model cannot be implemented by means of a manual. It is more a model of a mind set and process than it is of a series of carefully crafted interventions. Nonetheless, there are some good examples of approaches, both in the clinical and in the research literature, that embody this approach.

Before looking at specific examples, it must be noted that a general approach to patients that cuts across theoretical lines is entirely consistent with the LCS model. The model consists of an informed sequence of hypothesis formation, testing, and revision on the part of the therapist. This process has been presented most clearly, for psychodynamic therapists, by Sullivan (1954). He explicitly stated that "the interviewer obtains impressions which on scrutiny may or may not be justifiable. More or less specific testing operations should be applied to those impressions with the idea of getting them more nearly correct" (Sullivan,

1954, p. 122). In order to get them more nearly correct, "the testing of hypotheses cannot safely bc lcft wholly to relatively unformulated referential operations. Instead it is well for the interviewer now and then to think about the impressions that he has obtained. The very act of beginning to formulate them throws them into two rough groups: *those about which one has no reasonable doubt* and *those which, when noted, are open to question*. The latter, of course, need further testing" (Sullivan, 1954, p. 122, italics in original). Finally, the "way of testing hypotheses is by *clearly purposed exploratory activity* of some kind. The interviewer asks critical questions—that is, questions so designed that the response will indicate whether the hypothesis is reasonably correct or quite definitely not adequate" (Sullivan, 1954, p. 122). Of course, to guard against the anchoring heuristic, the interviewer must be open to the evidence provided by the carefully crafted exploratory questions. This explicit description of the process of hypothesis testing is precisely what is required of the LCS, and the Sullivanian statement is echoed, in a more classical vein, by Greenson (1967), who refers to interpretations as alternative hypotheses. Greenson also wrote about the specific link between empathy and theory, so that the impressions that lead to hypotheses are based on a solid grounding in theoretical knowledge.

The method described above is not restricted to psychodynamic approaches. Beck's (Beck, Rush, Shaw, & Emery, 1979) cognitive behavioral approach relies on a method he calls collaborative empiricism. In this approach, the thoughts, attitudes, beliefs, and behaviors of the patient are tested through methods such as Socratic Questioning in order to determine their validity and usefulness. If these thoughts, attitudes, beliefs, and behaviors are not found to be valid or productive, a search for more functional substitutes is undertaken. Here, too, the process of explicit testing is undertaken, with an eye toward confirming or disconfirming the validity of the therapist's formulations and the patient's approach. Again, the expectations are informed by theoretical and research grounding, so that the approach to the patient is not based solely on empathic connection, and again, the anchoring heuristic remains a danger.

Finally, in describing the characteristics of a culturally competent psychotherapist, Sue (1998) lists scientific mindedness as the first of three cross-cultural skills. By scientific mindedness, he is thinking of "therapists who form hypotheses rather than make premature conclusions about the status of culturally different clients, who develop creative ways to test hypotheses, and who act on the basis of acquired data" (Sue, 1998, p. 445). He notes that "culturally competent therapists will try to devise means of testing hypotheses about their clients. This scientific mindedness may also help to free therapists from ethnocentric biases or theories" (Sue, 1998, p. 446). This skepticism guards against inappropriate generalizations from one culture to another. This scientific approach also will guard against the inappropriate stereotyping of a member of a different cultural group, a second characteristic of the culturally competent therapist, and one Sue refers to as dynamic sizing. Finally, the third characteristic is culture-specific expertise. The culturally competent therapist must have knowledge about the culture of the patient and the knowledge and skill to translate this expertise into culturally effective means of intervention. Each of these characteristics, a skeptical and scientific attitude, the ability to deal effectively with cognitive heuristics (the primary danger here is the representativeness heuristic), and knowledge of the culture of the patient, are part of the expected functioning of the LCS, who combines knowledge with experience to function in an effective manner.

The research community also has had much to contribute to the functioning of the LCS. Although research has not produced a manual that can be implemented without thought or regard to local conditions, it has contributed to a general fund of generalizable knowledge upon which the LCS can draw. The LCS, drawing upon experience to supplement extant data, relies on memory to recall like instances and to implement previously successful interventions. One difficulty with this is that memory is subject to distortions, predictably in the form of the cognitive heuristics, particularly the availability heuristic, that have been described. This leads to the necessity to document findings rather than to rely solely on memory. However, clinicians still are limited to their own experience, and this often is insufficient for new cases. By aggregating data across clinicians with similar local experiences, it is possible to construct a data base that is systematically derived and can be applied more readily to individual cases.

There are two specific examples of this type of research contribution that I would like to cite. The first of these is the practice research network (PRN; Wolf, 2005). A PRN consists of a group of clinicians in the community who collaborate on data collection for the purpose of research. This shifts the laboratory into the community and, just as the LCS views each patient as an experiment and the consulting room as a laboratory, the PRN aggregates data across these individual laboratories and creates a larger and more veridical data base than either the individual clinician or the individual scientist can do. PRNs have been constructed by national professional organizations (e.g., American Psychological Association, American Psychiatric Association), local professional organizations (e.g., Pennsylvania Psychological Association), and local clinical centers (e.g., Anna Freud Center). Perhaps the most developed of these PRNs is the one sponsored by the Pennsylvania Psychological Association. The work of that group has been described (Borkovec, Echemendia, Ragusea, & Ruiz, 2001) and several findings from the project have also been presented in the literature (e.g., Ruiz et al., 2004).

The second is an elaborate project known as patient-focused research (Lambert, Hansen, & Finch, 2001). Recent reports from this exciting project (Harmon, Lambert, Slade, Hawkins, & Whipple, 2005; Lambert, Harmon, Slade, Whipple, & Hawkins, 2005) show the value of aggregating data across many clinicians and then providing feedback to individual clinicians concerning the progress being made by their patients. In this project, patients regularly provide ratings of their progress in therapy; these are compared to normative ratings, and the therapist is advised if the ratings fall below a prescribed cutoff score. In some variations, the therapist also can be given some advice about possible alterations in treatment that might be helpful. The difference in outcome for patients whose therapists were provided with feedback and those who were not was striking, and clearly supported the value of the feedback. Actual therapist ratings, in contrast to the normative data base, were so overly optimistic that the value of pure clinical judgment must be questioned, and the need for systematic data collection as a source of information to supplement the clinician is underlined. It is also possible, within this design, to provide feedback in comparison to the therapist's own patients, or to patients from a particular diagnostic category. The general thrust of patient-focused research is to show the potential of actually using group findings as a guide for individual actions, which is the crux of the problem of the applicability of research findings.

CONCLUSION

Every clinician engages in evidence-based practice. Indeed, it would be both foolish and professionally irresponsible to knowingly ignore any available evidence. The key lies both in what evidence is available to each clinician, and how that evidence is weighed. In weighing evidence, it is critical to consider both internal and external validity. To speak in the vernacular, clinicians who rely exclusively on internal validity know more and more about less and less. Clinicians who rely exclusively on external validity know less and less about more and more. Clinicians who rely exclusively on internal validity are absolutely certain of something that may not apply to the patient in front of them. Clinicians who rely exclusively on external validity are absolutely certain about something that probably does apply to the patient, but it may not be true. Of course these are caricatures, and there is much room between absolute reliance on one type or another of validity. The LCS occupies this ground, seeks out relevant evidence, weighs it in a balanced, critical, and skeptical manner, and applies it as best as can be done. The LCS then systematically records this new experience so that it can be consulted the next time it may become relevant, not as a guiding principle but as one more piece of relevant evidence. By doing this, the LCS is functioning as a scientist-practitioner.

REFERENCES

American Psychological Association. (2005). *Report of the 2005 Presidential Task Force on Evidence-Based Practice*. Washington, DC: American Psychological Association.

American Psychological Association Task Force on Psychological Intervention Guidelines. (1995). *Template for developing guidelines: Interventions for mental disorders and psychosocial aspects of physical disorders* (Vol. 47). Washington, DC: Author.

Beck, A. T., Rush, A. J., Shaw, B. F., & Emery, G. (1979). *Cognitive therapy of depression*. New York: Guilford.

Borkovec, T. D., Echemendia, R. J., Ragusea, S. A., & Ruiz, M. (2001). The Pennsylvania practice research network and future possibilities for clinically meaningful and scientifically rigorous psychotherapy effectiveness research. *Clinical Psychology: Science and Practice, 8*, 155–167.

Chambless, D. C., & Ollendick, T. H. (2001). Empirically supported psychological interventions: Controversies and evidence. *Annual Review of Psychology, 52*, 685–716.

Chapman, L. J. (1967). Illusory correlation in observational report. *Journal of Verbal Learning and Verbal Behavior, 5*, 151–155.

Cranor, C. (2005). Scientific inferences in the laboratory and the law. *American Journal of Public Health, 95*, S121–S128.

Greenson, R. R. (1967). *The technique and practice of psychoanalysis* (Vol. I). New York: International Universities Press.

Harmon, C., Lambert, M. J., Slade, K., Hawkins, E. J., & Whipple, J. S. (2005). Improving outcomes for poorly responding clients: The use of clinical support tools and feedback to clients. *Journal of Clinical Psychology/In Session, 61*, 175–185.

Institute of Medicine (2001). *Crossing the quality chasm: A new health system for the 21st century*. Washington, DC: National Academy Press.

Kanfer, F. H. (1990). The scientist–practitioner connection: A bridge in need of constant attention. *Professional Psychology: Research and Practice, 21*, 264–270.

Lambert, M. J., Hansen, N. B., & Finch, A. E. (2001). Patient-focused research: Using patient outcome data to enhance treatment effects. *Journal of Consulting and Clinical Psychology, 69*, 159–172.

Lambert, M. J., Harmon, C., Slade, K., Whipple, J. L., & Hawkins, E. J. (2005). Providing feedback to psychotherapists on their patients' progress: Clinical results and practice suggestions. *Journal of Clinical Psychology, 61*, 165–174.

Peterson, D. R. (1991). Connection and disconnection of research and practice in the education of professional psychologists. *American Psychologist, 46*, 422–29.

Peterson, D. R. (2003). Unintended consequences: Ventures and misadventures in the education of professional psychologists. *American Psychologist, 58*, 791–800.

Peterson, R. L., Peterson, D. R., Abrams, J. C., & Stricker, G. (1997). The National Council of Schools and Programs of Professional Psychology educational model. *Professional Psychology: Research and Practice, 28*, 373–386.

Raimy, V. (Ed.). (1950). *Training in clinical psychology*. New York: Prentice-Hall.

Rozin, P. (2001). Social psychology and science: Some lessons from Solomon Asch. *Personality and Social Psychology Review, 5*, 2–14.

Ruiz, M. A., Pincus, A. L., Borkovec, T. D., Echemendia, R. J., Castonguay, L. G., & Ragusea, S. A. (2004). Validity of the Inventory of Interpersonal Problems for predicting treatment outcome: An investigation with the Pennsylvania Practice Research Network. *Journal of Personality Assessment, 83*, 213–222.

Shakow, D. (1976). What is clinical psychology? *American Psychologist, 31*, 553–560.

Stricker, G. (2000). The scientist-practitioner model: Gandhi was right again. *American Psychologist, 55*, 253–254.

Stricker, G. (2006). The local clinical scientist, evidence-based practice, and personality assessment. *Journal of Personality Assessment, 86*, 4–9.

Stricker, G., Abrahamson, D. J., Bologna, N. C., Hollon, S. D., Robinson, E. A., & Reed, G. M. (1999). Treatment guidelines: The good, the bad, and the ugly. *Psychotherapy: Theory, Research/Practice/Training, 36*, 69–79.

Stricker, G., & Trierweiler, S. J. (1995). The local clinical scientist: A bridge between science and practice. *American Psychologist, 50*, 995–1002.

Sue, S. (1998). In search of cultural competence in psychotherapy and counseling. *American Psychologist, 53*, 440–448.

Sullivan, H. S. (1954). *The psychiatric interview*. New York: W.W. Norton.

Trierweiler, S. J., & Stricker, G. (1998). *The scientific practice of professional psychology.* New York: Plenum Press.

Tversky, A., & Kahneman, D. (1974). Judgment under uncertainty: Heuristics and biases. *Science, 185,* 1124–131.

Wolf, A. W. (2005). Practice research networks in psychology. *Psychotherapy Bulletin, 40*(4), 39–42.

Section *II*
NONSPECIFIC AND COMMON FACTORS

6

Empirically Supported Common Factors

JOEL WEINBERGER AND CRISTINA RASCO

This chapter takes the position that scientific inquiry is the optimal way to determine what approach to psychotherapy works best.[1] Recently, the Empirically Supported Treatment (EST) movement (e.g., Chambless, Baker, Baucom, Beutler, Calhoun, Crits-Christoph et al., 1998; Chambless, Sanderson, Shoham, Johnson, Pope, Crits-Christoph et al., 1996) has taken primacy of place in this endeavor. The name itself carries with it the imprimatur of science. But the EST approach, in our opinion, is not the sole scientific line of inquiry possible or available. It has its strengths and, like any approach, it has its weaknesses. Moreover, as do other systems of scientific investigation, it carries with it certain assumptions that may be challenged. We believe that these assumptions are themselves open to empirical inquiry, although for the most part they have not yet been tested. We will examine a couple of these assumptions and then offer an alternative, common factors. In the end, we believe that the marketplace of competing ideas that should constitute much of science will determine which methodology is best. In all probability, it will be some combination or even a third, heretofore unthought of approach.

THE EST APPROACH

Empirically Supported Treatments (ESTs) has become a term rather than a description. ESTs are determined by a particular method of investigation termed efficacy research (e.g., Barlow, 1996; Nathan & Gorman, 2002). First, the empirical literature is examined so as to create a treatment for a particular disorder, say depression or anxiety. Alternatively, a treatment already in existence is chosen for investigation. This treatment is explicitly described, in detail, in the form of a treatment manual. Practitioners of the treatment are enjoined to follow the manual when delivering the treatment. Next, the treatment is compared to an alternative treatment. This can be an already existing treatment, often dubbed treatment as usual (TAU) or an ersatz treatment (placebo, wait list control, etc.). The idea is that the EST candidate must outperform the alternative treatment or be better than no treatment at all. Assignment of patients to the EST candidate treatment or the alternative (TAU or nontreatment) must be random. If the EST candidate turns out to be superior to either of the above two alternatives in two or more efficacy studies, it is considered empirically supported and is designated an EST. A great deal of data support the EST model (Barlow, 2004; Ollendick & King, 2006) but there are also credible and pointed critiques of the approach (Westen, Novotny, & Thompson-Brenner, 2004). The details of the EST debate are beyond the scope of this chapter except insofar as they contrast with the assumptions of the common factors model to be presented below. The interested reader will, no doubt, find all he or she needs to know about the pros and cons of ESTs in other chapters of this book.

There are many assumptions inherent in the EST model. One is that random assignment of patients to treatments is neutral as to outcome and therefore provides the least biased results. This is not necessarily the case (see Blatt & Zuroff, 2005). Another assumption is that if an EST works, it does so because of the specific interventions detailed in the treatment manual. This also does not necessarily follow and we will have more to say about this later in this chapter. The assumption most relevant to the approach that we wish to consider as an alternative to ESTs (i.e., common factors) is that treatments need to be specifically tailored to the disorder under investigation. This leads to a myriad of ESTs, at least one for each disorder. That is, there would be an EST for depression, another for anxiety, a third for Borderline Personality Disorder, and so on. There are currently more ESTs than any one clinician could possibly learn, at latest count over 150 (Beutler & Johannsen, 2006). Presumably, they would differ in important ways from each other. Dual diagnosis disorders would employ two or more ESTs as modules, with each module targeting a specific aspect of the problem. It is the universality of this assumption that we most wish to challenge. We believe that the data do not clearly support it and that the common factors approach offers an alternative based on a different assumption in accord with data. (As we detail below, at least one EST paper now argues for common underlying treatment techniques for the emotional disorders (Barlow, Allen, & Choate, 2004) so this may be changing.)

THE COMMON FACTORS APPROACH

The common factors approach basically states that all therapies work because of what they all have in common, rather than because of what differentiates them from one another. That is, different kinds of psychotherapy do not necessarily achieve their effects through the principles they espouse. Instead their effectiveness is due to often unacknowledged factors that they share, termed common factors. The conceptual task is to determine what psychotherapeutic treatments all have in common. These are the common factors. The empirical task is to test these factors in order to determine whether they contribute to successful outcome and do so in a variety of treatment contexts and approaches.

The common factors approach has a decades-long history probably beginning with Rosenzweig (1936) who posited that all therapies have four factors in common. He identified these as: (1) the therapeutic relationship, (2) a systematic rationale that helps explain the patient's issues and a means of addressing them, (3) integration of personality systems, and (4) the personality of the therapist. The first two have led to a great deal of scholarly work, both theoretical and empirical. The latter two have been relatively neglected (Weinberger, 2002). Many other thinkers have offered their views of common factors. The most systematic of these was Frank (1973, 1978, 1982) who, like Rosenzweig, posited four common factors: (1) the therapeutic relationship, (2) a healing setting, (3) a rationale that provides an explanation for the patient's difficulties as well as a means for relieving them, and (4) actual provision of prescribed treatments for alleviating suffering. Frank believed that these common factors worked by providing hope to demoralized patients. Many other thinkers have written about common factors. Goldfried (1982) has reprinted many of these contributions. Arkowitz (1992), Kleinke (1994), and Weinberger (1993) offer histories of these efforts.

If common factors are a genuine phenomenon, then different treatments ought to be equally effective, whatever their apparent differences. Rosenzweig (1936) predicted this as well and offered a quote from *Alice in Wonderland* to capture this prediction: "At last the Dodo said, 'Everybody has won, and all must have prizes'" (p. 412). This was later termed the Dodo verdict by Stiles, Shapiro, and Elliot (1986). The "Dodo verdict" has come to stand for the concept of outcome equivalence in psychotherapy research. The data seem to support the Dodo verdict. Meta-analyses beginning with the classic work of Smith, Glass, and Miller (1980) almost routinely find no differences between apparently diverse treatments. Thus Lipsey and Wilson (1993), Wampold, Mondin, Moody, Stich, Benson, and Ahn (1997) and Luborsky, Rosenthal, Diguer, Andrusyna, Berman, Levitt, and Krause (2002) all have replicated the results of Smith et al. Well-designed individual outcome studies report the same results. The sophisticated, multi-site collaborative depression study (Elkin, Shea, Watkins, Imber, Sotsky, Collins, Glass, et al., 1989), which is the prototype for efficacy research, reported virtually no differences between cognitive and interpersonal treatments for depression. Blatt and Zuroff (2005) recently reanalyzed these data, using different outcome measures, and came to the same conclusion (and by the way, supported a common factors understanding of the results). Sloane, Staples, Cristol, Yorkston, and Whipple (1975) compared renowned experts in their form of psychotherapy. The outcomes were equivalent despite radical differences in how these luminaries conducted treatment. Further, when the patients themselves were asked what was effective, they reported common factors like the relationship. When meta-analyses and individual studies do not seem to support the Dodo verdict, Luborsky, Diguer, Seligman, Rosenthal, Johnson, Halperin, Bishop, and Schweizer (1999) have shown that this can probably be attributed to allegiance effects. That is, the treatment identified with the researchers seemed, inevitably, to "win." This allegiance effect can probably be attributed to greater enthusiasm of practitioners, greater care in delivering the treatment of choice, and so on. In other words, the effects may be due to common factors. Not everyone has accepted the above understanding of the literature. EST advocates have especially been critical of this interpretation of the findings (e.g., Chambless, 2002; DeRubeis, Brotman, & Gibbons, 2005). We deal with these critiques after we present our common factors approach.

A SLIGHTLY DIFFERENT VIEW OF COMMON FACTORS

Most common factors approaches seem to be arguing that all forms of treatment employ the common factors equally. This then accounts for outcome equivalence or the Dodo verdict. Following Weinberger (1995) and Weinberger and Eig (1998), we have a somewhat different point of view. We take the schools at their word in terms of what they emphasize. That means that the different schools of therapy differ in their instantiation of the various common factors. Each school emphasizes one or two of the important common factors while relatively neglecting the others. These are then addressed in a haphazard way in the treatment. As a result, the different kinds of treatment are equally effective because they are equally deficient (cf., Weinberger, 1995).

The Factors

We would like to propose five common factors. We do not claim this to be an exhaustive or final list. We chose these because they seemed to us to be central to some schools of psychotherapy but not to others (one factor is not emphasized by any school) and, just as importantly, because empirical data seem to support them. The five factors are:

1. The therapeutic relationship. This is central to psychodynamic and humanistic/experiential approaches. It is relatively neglected, sometimes purposefully, by the behavioral and cognitive schools.
2. Expectations of treatment effectiveness. No psychotherapy school emphasizes this factor. It is often treated as error variance, as placebo, in accord with the medical model of identifying active ingredients of drugs and procedures. The efficacy approach, for example, tries to rule out the effects of this factor through its comparison of treatment with "placebo" controls. Frank (1973, 1982) and more recently, Kirsch (1999) emphasized its importance but neither is identified with any school.

3. Confronting or facing the problem (exposure). This factor is central to learning-based-behavioral approaches in the form of exposure. Since behavioral and cognitive approaches have generally combined into the cognitive-behavioral school, it is treated as important by cognitivists as well. Psychodynamic and humanistic/experiential thinkers tend to neglect this factor. Sometimes, they abjure it.

4. Mastery or control experiences. This factor is absolutely central to the cognitive school. To the extent that cognitive and behavioral approaches have combined into cognitive-behavioral therapy, it is treated as important by behaviorally oriented thinkers as well. It is relatively neglected by psychodynamic and humanistic/experiential thinkers.

5. Attribution of therapeutic outcome. This is a form of expectation but applied to the patient's understanding of outcome at the end of treatment (as opposed to expectations prior to or early in treatment). Cognitive therapy pays serious attention to it but it is not central to its tenets. Academic cognitive social psychologists have done the most work here but they tend not to be therapy minded. The other schools tend to neglect this factor.

The Therapeutic Relationship

The therapeutic relationship is, by far, the most written about common factor. Wolfe and Goldfried (1988) termed it the quintessential integrative psychotherapeutic factor. Probably the first theorist to write meaningfully of the place of the therapeutic relationship in psychotherapy was Freud (1910) who described a bond between therapist and patient. Many psychoanalytic theorists since have expanded on this concept (Gitelson, 1962; Menninger, 1958; Sterba, 1934; Zetzel, 1956). Most active in this regard was Greenson (1967) who coined the term working alliance. The therapeutic relationship is therefore central to psychodynamic notions of therapy.

Rogers (1951, 1957) brought the idea of the relationship to the center of humanistic/experiential psychotherapy. He argued that the necessary and sufficient conditions for successful psychotherapeutic treatment were therapist-offered unconditional positive regard, accurate empathy, and genuineness. In Rogerian therapy, the relationship is all. (Also see Barrett-Lennard, 1962; Bozarth, 1990; Brodley, 1990; and Meador and Rogers, 1984.) The relationship, although critically important in non-Rogerian humanistic/experiential treatments, is not all. It is necessary but not sufficient. The emphasis in these models is on deepening experience (e.g., Greenberg, Elliott, & Lietaer, 1994). The relationship provides the context for this therapeutic task (Gendlin, 1990; Greenberg et al. 1994).

Bordin (1979) generalized the concept of the therapeutic relationship to other kinds of therapy as did Gelso and Carter (1985) and Gaston (1990). The other schools did not embrace the centrality of the therapeutic relationship with the enthusiasm of the psychodynamic and humanistic schools however (Emmelkamp,

1986; Hollon & Beck, 1994; Lambert, 1989; Lambert & Bergin, 1994; Safran & Segal, 1990; Whisman, 1993). Beck, Rush, Shaw, and Emery (1979) in their classic manual for conducting cognitive therapy for depression devoted a chapter to the therapeutic relationship but argued that it was a facilitator of cognitive techniques rather than ameliorative in its own right. In line with this lesser emphasis, Whisman (1993) reported that there were only five studies in the cognitive literature, at the time of his writing, which dealt with the alliance. In contrast, research on technical variables was voluminous. Emmelkamp (1994) described a similar situation for behavioral treatments. This picture has not changed much in the intervening years. Some theorists have gone so far as to explicitly downgrade the importance of the therapeutic relationship. Thus, Ellis and Dryden (1987) have warned therapists not to overvalue the alliance. Kazdin (2005) has wondered whether the therapeutic relationship is a cause or a product of successful outcome.

Is the therapeutic relationship, in and of itself or perhaps in combination with other factors, an effective aspect of psychotherapy? Alternatively, is the relationship more a product rather than a cause of successful treatment, as Kazdin suggests? The answer seems to be that the therapeutic relationship does have causal relevance to psychotherapy outcome. Beutler (1989) and Lambert (1992) reported that the therapeutic alliance accounted for more of the variance in outcome than did technical interventions. Gaston, Marmar, Gallagher, and Thompson (1991) reported that the alliance accounted for more than 35% of the variance in outcome after controlling for initial symptom levels and symptom change. Blatt and Zuroff (2005) obtained highly significant effects for the therapeutic relationship when they controlled for contemporaneous clinical improvement. Hovarth and Symonds (1991) conducted a meta-analysis and found a small but reliable effect of the working alliance on therapeutic outcome. Additionally, the effect was similar in size across the various schools of therapy examined (psychodynamic, cognitive, eclectic/mixed) and across a wide variety of diagnoses. A more recent meta-analysis (Martin, Garke, & Davis, 2000) reported the same results. Finally, a task force commissioned by Division 29 (Psychotherapy) of the American Psychological Association concluded that the relationship was a critical factor in psychotherapy. They enumerated many studies and a host of data to support this conclusion (Norcross, 2002).

When one of us (Weinberger, 1995) published his paper on common factors, he reported a plethora of theoretical explanations for the efficacy of the relationship but bemoaned the lack of hard data. Further, there was virtually nothing empirical on how to best foster and improve the relationship. This is no longer the case. The data supportive of the efficacy of the therapeutic relationship are voluminous and there are also plenty of data on what aspects of it are ameliorative (Norcross, 2002; Wampold, 2001). The Division 29 task force (Norcross, 2002) concluded that the therapeutic alliance, empathy, goal consensus, and collaboration between therapist and patient, as well as a sense of cohesion between therapist and patient clearly contributed to therapeutic change. Positive regard, genuineness, and management of countertransference were believed to have empirical support as well but the data were not yet conclusive (Norcross, 2002). More specifically, Luborsky, McLellan, Diguer, Woody, and Seligman (1997) found that therapists who were helpful to their patients were better able to facilitate the therapeutic alliance. Safran and Muran (2000) found that a strong and therapeutically effective alliance could be encouraged by a few therapist factors. These included: attuning to the patient's experience of therapeutic interventions, therapist acceptance of her own contribution to therapeutic interactions, and therapist identification of problematic interpersonal issues between her and the patient. Beutler, Alomohamed, Moleiro, and Romanelli (2002) and Norcross and Lambert (2006) both reported that outcome was improved when patient and therapist were matched so as to maximize the therapeutic relationship. These data and more are reviewed in Norcross and Lambert (2006). At this point, even some strong advocates of ESTs agree that the therapeutic relationship is efficacious (Chambless & Crits-Cristoph, 2006).

Two compelling programs systematically examining the therapeutic relationship are being conducted under the leadership of Jeremy Safran (Safran & Muran, 2000) and Mark Hilsenroth (in press). Safran's group (Safran & Muran, 2000) focuses on what they term relationship ruptures. These are defined as moments of tension or breakdowns in communication between therapist and patient. There are two major forms of rupture: withdrawal and confrontation. Such ruptures can range from minor misunderstandings to breaks that threaten the entire therapeutic enterprise. Safran and Muran (1996) found that resolving ruptures in the therapeutic relationship can positively and importantly affect treatment process and outcome. Safran, Muran, Samstag, and Stevens (2002) review the relevant data.

Ackerman and Hilsenroth (2003) reviewed the extant literature and found that support, exploration, engagement, and attention to affective experience were positively related to the alliance. Highly structured and inflexible or completely unstructured management of therapy was detrimental to the alliance. Too much self-disclosure as well as too much or too little therapist verbalization were also negatively related to the alliance. In order to test whether a positive therapeutic relationship was beneficial to therapeutic process and outcome, the Hilsenroth group systematically examined the effects of the therapeutic relationship starting with initial assessment and continuing through several points in treatment. Ackerman, Hilsenroth, Baity, and Blagys (2000) examined the effects of their therapeutic model of assessment (TMA) with the more standard information gathering approach to initial assessment. In the TMA, the therapist explicitly tried to establish an empathic connection, work collaboratively, and discuss the assessment results. Ackerman et al. reported that patients in the TMA group had a stronger alliance and were more likely to begin treatment than were those in the standard information gathering group. These effects lasted, as alliance measured at initial assessment correlated with alliance early and late in treatment (Hilsenroth, Peters, & Ackerman, 2004).

The Hilsenroth group took these findings seriously and attempted to build them into therapeutic supervision. That is, they attempted to teach supervisees (clinical Ph.D. students) how best to foster a positive therapeutic relationship. Hilsenroth, Ackerman, Clemence, Strassle, and Handler (2002) compared a group receiving structured clinical training (1.5 hours of individual, 2 hours team) with a group receiving supervision as usual. The therapeutic bond as rated by both therapist and patient was greater in the structured group. The differences reflected the explicit goals of the training.

To summarize, the therapeutic relationship seems to be genuinely related to therapeutic success. The positive effects of the relationship hold across the various treatment modalities. It is not a product but rather a cause of treatment success. It can be operationalized. It can be measured. And, it can be taught. The therapeutic relationship is a genuine common factor. This factor is emphasized in the psychodynamic and humanistic schools of therapy but relatively neglected in cognitive behavioral treatments.

Expectancies of Treatment Effectiveness

The data attesting to the power of expectancies in medical treatments is so strong that medical clinical trials focus on demonstrating that treatments are superior to the power of expectancies. Medical clinical trials virtually always compare a supposedly active treatment to a purportedly inactive one, termed a placebo. The power of placebos is nothing short of astonishing (Wampold, Minami, Tierney, & Baskin, 2005). Volgyesi (1954) reported a 70% cure rate for placebo treatment of bleeding ventricular and duodenal ulcers. Boissel, Phillippon, Gauthier, Schbath, Destors, and the B. I. S. Research Group (1986) reported a 77% success rate for placebo treatment of angina pectoris. Thomsen, Bretlau, Tos, and Johnsen (1983) reported a 77% rate for placebo surgery for patients suffering from Meniere's disease. The comparison, so called active, surgery was only 70% effective. Kirsch (1985, 1990, 1999) reviews the literature. Wampold et al. provide a more recent review.

Expectancies are no less powerful in psychotherapeutic settings. In a series of studies, patients were assessed twice in a clinic prior to treatment, once well before and once immediately before treatment began. There was significant positive change during this time, despite the fact that no treatment had taken place (Frank, Nash, Stone, & Imber, 1963; Friedman, 1963; Kellner & Sheffield, 1971; Piper & Wogan, 1970; Shapiro, Struening, & Shapiro, 1980). Improvement was correlated with treatment expectations. Barker, Funk, and Houston (1988) conducted a meta-analysis on psychotherapy studies that used believable placebos as controls. Placebo effects were significant, although not as strong as treatment effects, and increased at follow-up. A more recent meta-analysis found even more powerful placebo effects in psychotherapy (Baskin, Tierney, Minami, & Wampold, 2003).

Howard, Kopta, Krause, and Orlinsky (1986) reported that expectancy effects hold across a variety of treatment modalities. In the behavioral tradition, Paul (1966) compared systematic desensitization with no treatment and a positive expectancy condition. The positive expectancy condition was superior to no treatment. Marcia, Rubin, and Efran (1969) and Leitenberg, Agras, Barlow, and Oliveau (1969) also reported that expectancies played a role in behavioral treatments. Some behavioral researchers found expectancies to be the equal of active behavioral treatments. Thus, Kazdin and Wilcoxin (1976) reported no difference between a systematic desensitization group and a positive expectancy group. Kirsch and Henry (1977) obtained similar results.

In the cognitive tradition, Hollon and Garber (1990) argued that negative expectancies of depressives lead to difficulties in initiating responses, which, in turn, account for some of their performance deficits. Catanzaro, Wasch, Kirsch, and Mearns (2000) reported that individuals who expected to be unable to regulate negative mood were more likely to evince symptoms of depression but not anxiety, and to cope through avoidance. These findings were independent of trait optimism and pessimism. Gaston, Marmar, Gallagher, and Thompson (1989) found that cognitive therapy patients who expected treatment to work obtained better outcomes than those who did not. A caveat is in order here. Positive expectations are not always salutary to outcome. Linehan, Cochran, Mar, Levensky, and Comtois (2000) reported that positive expectations of Borderlines had some association to therapy burnout.

Gomes-Schwartz, Hadley, and Strupp (1978) reviewed the psychodynamic literature and concluded that expectancy played a role in this type of treatment. Luborsky (1984) also came to this conclusion. Weinberger (1995), and Weinberger and Eig (1999) provide further examples of the power of expectancies in clinical and extra-clinical settings. By far the most prolific theorist addressing the issue of expectancies is Kirsch (1985, 1990, 1999) who has devoted his career to the study of expectancies. Wampold et al. (2005) and Baskin et al. (2003) provide more recent reviews.

Despite the obvious importance of expectancy, no school incorporates it into its systematic thinking. It seems to be more of an embarrassment. Freud (1917) took pains to argue that psychoanalysis was more than suggestion. ESTs explicitly try to control for expectancies through placebo treatment groups or TAUs. The problem, we believe, is two-fold. First, suggestion and expectancy seem trivial at best and disingenuous at worst. After all, most psychologists believe that faith healing is a product of expectancy. They do not want to be associated with that and they want to believe that they do a great deal more than that.

The second source of resistance to expectancy comes from the adoption of the medical model into psychotherapy research (cf., Weinberger, 1995; Weinberger & Eig, 1998). Medical treatments are meant to have a physical effect. Psychological effects are a nuisance or a danger. The medical community did not want to be seen advocating a procedure or medicine whose primary locus of effect was psychological. As a result, they devised the use of placebos in their clinical trials. Similarities between placebo and experimental groups were attributed to psychological factors and the treatment was deemed ineffective. Differences were attributed to physical factors and the treatment was deemed effective. Transposing this to psychotherapy research seems to us to be a mistake. After all, we are interested in psychological effects. We ought not to be systematically ignoring an important psychological variable. Instead, we should be investigating expectancies, exploiting them, and incorporating them into our treatments. Thus far, no school has engaged in this endeavor.

Confronting or Facing Problems (Exposure)

Kleinke (1994) argues that facing, rather than avoiding, anxiety is a goal in all schools of psychotherapy. Similarly, Seltzer (1986) says that all forms of therapy must encourage patients to face heretofore avoided fears. Frankl (1967) states that the therapist is obliged to help the patient engage in the very activities that he or she fears. Orlinsky and Howard (1986) reviewed the then extant literature and concluded that confrontation was an effective therapeutic technique.

Every school of therapy advocates helping patients to face their fears. The way this is done (technique) and the types of fears faced differ greatly. Psychodynamic treatments deal more than any other model with unconscious fears and anxieties. Therapists in this tradition try to lower resistance in order to bring conflict-laden, sometimes repressed wishes, beliefs, feelings, and fantasies to conscious awareness, where the patient can more adaptively deal with them (Alexander, 1963; Alexander & French, 1946; Rangell, 1989; Reich, 1933/1976; Weiss, Sampson, & the Mount Zion Psychotherapy Research Group, 1986). In order for this to happen, the therapist makes use of the therapeutic relationship and carries out an examination of associative networks. Dream analysis, analysis of slips, and analysis of the transference are also employed. Brenner (1982) provides a readable exposition of the classical psychoanalytic point of view on these issues.

Psychodynamic writers do not usually refer to this as exposure. It falls under the rubric of technique and is an area rife with controversy. Some theorists advocate a more directly confrontational form of what we are calling exposure (e.g., Kernberg, 1976; Reich, 1933/1976). And some insist upon a more supportive form of exposure to threatening issues (e.g., Kohut, 1984). This controversy has never been resolved in psychoanalysis (Josephs, 1995). One major reason, no doubt, is that no one conducts systematic research on it. This is one of the major criticisms of psychoanalysis generally (Grünbaum, 1984; Strupp, 1976) and, with a few notable exceptions (e.g., Roth & Fonagy, 2005; Levy, Clarkin, Yeomans, Scott, Wasserman, & Kernberg, 2006) it is a valid one.

There is a body of research that supports the psychodynamic view of exposure. Pennebaker (1997) has shown, in numerous studies, employing various populations, that writing or talking about upsetting or traumatic events has positive effects. His work was not conducted in the clinical setting. Rather, the group under study, typically college students, simply report to a lab and write of either a neutral or upsetting event. They do not do so to obtain relief in any way. They simply participate in a psychology experiment of unknown (until debriefing) purpose. Participants in the upsetting condition often felt worse immediately after the study but showed better emotional health and, perhaps even more remarkable, healthier immune functioning, and fewer health problems months later. (Pennebaker, 1997 summarized and discussed much of this.) Sloan and Marx (2004) conducted a study using undergraduates who obtained at least moderate scores on a scale of traumatic experiences and reported similar results. Liberman (1978) examined actual psychotherapy patients and obtained similar results for psychotherapy outcome measures one year after completion of his study. These findings suggest that the kind of confrontation or exposure practiced by psychodynamic clinicians is ameliorative.

Humanistic/experiential theorists (e.g., Greenberg, Elliott, & Lietaer, 1994) have also devoted attention to confrontation or facing problems (which we are identifying with exposure). Classical gestalt therapy (Perls, Hefferline, & Goodman, 1951) talks of little else in the form of focusing the treatment on making the patient aware of what he or she is doing and feeling in the here and now of the therapy room. There are some data that indicate that this type of confrontation is beneficial (Dierick & Lietaer, 1990). The most famous of these techniques is probably the empty chair technique. This involves expressing unresolved feelings toward a significant other in an intense and immediate way and role-playing how that person would respond (Daldrup, Beutler, Greenberg & Engle, 1988; Greenberg & Safran, 1987). There are no data pro or con on the efficacy of this emotionally powerful intervention (Greenberg et al., 1994).

Cognitive therapy explicitly makes use of a form of exposure. In Beck's (Beck et al., 1979) cognitive therapy, negatively toned cognitions, of which patients are relatively unaware (termed automatic thoughts), are recorded, examined, and thereby confronted in the therapeutic interaction. In Ellis' (1962) rational emotive therapy, the therapist forcefully confronts the patient with examples of his or her illogical thinking and/or self-defeating verbalizations. Additionally, patients are encouraged to expose themselves to problematic situations outside of the consulting room and report back on the outcome. Role-playing in the consulting room is also encouraged, often as a prelude to trying it out in the "real world" (Hollon & Garber, 1990). Thus exposure is clearly represented in the cognitive school. It is not central however. The purpose of such confrontation is to access and identify pathogenic cognitions and beliefs, which can then be altered (Beck et al., 1979; Hollon & Garber, 1990). In this model of therapy, confrontation is secondary to cognitive change. It is a way to get at the critical cognitions and is not necessarily ameliorative in its own right.

Behavior therapy has seen exposure as more central than any other school of treatment. It may be the most important therapeutic method used by behaviorists (Emmelkamp, 1994). They have therefore examined it in the most contexts. They have compared imaginal versus in vivo, versus modeled exposure to feared stimulation. They have exposed patients gradually to more and more frightening stimulation (systematic desensitization, Wolpe, 1958) and to the most frightening stimulus all at once (flooding, Stampfl & Levis, 1967). Interestingly, no one knows for sure why exposure works. The original formulations of counter conditioning (Davison, 1968) reciprocal inhibition (Wolpe, 1958), and extinction (Stampfl & Levis, 1967) do not seem to account for the phenomenon (Emmelkamp, 1982,

1994). More recent views make use of LeDoux's (1996) work on neurobiological underpinnings of anxiety that seem to rely on the amygdala. Thus, Phelps (2005) has presented data that suggest that the amygdala habituates to repeated stimulation. Whatever the cause, it seems clear that exposure works. Further, it is effective in its own right and not secondary to some other factor or factors.

To summarize, exposure or facing problematic issues is adaptation enhancing in psychotherapy. It is a legitimate common factor. The behavioral school is most advanced in employing this factor. Cognitive therapists, to the extent that they have combined forces with the behaviorists, also make systematic use of this factor. It has secondary and non-independent status in genuinely cognitive conceptions, however. Psychodynamic theorists allude to facing issues but do not devote much theoretical and virtually no empirical energy to understanding or systematically taking advantage of this factor. Experiential thinkers write about it but practically no empirical work has been conducted by this school. Surprisingly, no one, not even the behaviorists, are certain as to why and how exposure works (although numerous hypotheses exist).

Mastery

Evidence supporting the effectiveness of enhancing a sense of cognitive control or mastery is plentiful. Humanistic/experiential approaches have surprisingly little to say about it, however. In the Rogerian (e.g., Rogers, 1951) view, potential unfolds naturally and organically. There is thus no need for the therapist to encourage such a process explicitly or otherwise. It is more like she has to get out of the way and it will happen on its own. Experiential writers think that the process is not this automatic and there is some evidence that mastery experiences occurring within sessions generalize to the real world (Greenberg & Webster, 1982). Nevertheless, it is fair to say that the issue of mastery is relatively neglected in humanistic/experiential theorizing, research, and practice.

Psychodynamic schools believe that insight into patient desires, fears, and inhibitions will lead to mastery experiences. Once these usually unconscious processes and contents have been made public through interpretation and subsequent insight, their ability to produce maladaptive affective reactions and behaviors is reduced. The patient then has more resources available to him or her and is better able to adapt to the vagaries of life (cf. Rangell, 1989). Further, once these heretofore unconscious processes and contents are brought into consciousness, they can be dealt with rationally, intentionally and therefore effectively. There is an inner autonomous drive to develop the various ego functions that aids the patient in this endeavor (Hartmann, 1939/1958; Hendrik, 1943; Rapaport, 1960). White (1959) referred to this built-in drive as competence motivation and it is nothing less than an inherent desire to master life's challenges.

In psychodynamic thinking, attaining insight is not all there is to it. True mastery requires successfully applying the insight to life's challenges. In the jargon of psychoanalysis, this is called "working through" (Rado, 1925). The therapist does not assign any outside work to aid in the working through process. Instead she waits for the patient to spontaneously bring up examples of challenges from his or her life experiences and interprets them in terms of the relevant insights. The patient then presumably applies the insight to the relevant challenge. The sequence is then repeated for the next challenge until a large area of the patient's life has been covered. Control or mastery is thereby expanded over ever-increasing aspects of the patient's life. The process is long and painstaking. In traditional psycho-analysis, it can take years. Less writing is devoted to working through than to any other aspect of psychodynamic thinking, and there is virtually no empirical work concerning it. Mastery issues are the most seriously underdeveloped aspect of psychodynamic thinking, as far as common factors are concerned.

In the behavioral tradition, mastery and control are typically discussed in terms of skills training, or seen as an emergent quality of exposure. For example, Lewinsohn and Hoberman (1982) see depression as attributable to difficulties in obtaining gratification. Treatment involves teaching the patient the requisite need gratifying skills. The depression lifts once the patient is able to meet his needs. Exposure leads to greater control because the patient can go about his business no longer troubled by anxiety in important life situations.

A sense of mastery and cognitive control is central to cognitive conceptions. In Rational Emotive Therapy (Ellis, 1962, 1970; Ellis & Dryden, 1987), the patient is taught to rethink, challenge, contradict, and reverbalize assumptions until they become more logical and efficient. The therapist then helps the patient to develop more adaptive problem-solving techniques. Homework is assigned to aid in this endeavor. In the end, the patient learns that life circumstances and challenges may be unpleasant but they are not insurmountable. The patient gains a sense of mastery.

Beck's cognitive therapy (CT) very explicitly fosters mastery experiences. From its inception, Beck (1976) asserted that CT aims to help patients see them-selves as successful. To this end, CT provides its patients with structured tasks with well-defined goals. In this way, success is readily apparent. In order to ensure success or mastery experiences, Beck et al. (1979) recommended dividing such tasks into small, progressively more difficult steps. The first few such subtasks are conducted in the treatment room. When they prove successful, the remainder are assigned as homework. This is termed "graded task assignment" (also see Hollon & Garber, 1990) and is critical to CT. In order to track the patient's subjective sense of mastery and make his or her increasing sense of mastery as salient as possible to him or her, Beck et al. designed what they termed the "mastery and pleasure technique." Other mastery increasing techniques include logical analysis and hypothesis testing (Jarett & Nelson, 1987), role playing (Hollon & Garber, 1990), and reframing (Kleinke, 1994). All of these methods have strong empirical support (Hollon & Beck, 1994; Whisman, 1993).

It is clear that cognitive thinkers have made the most use of mastery tech-niques. By virtue of the merger between behavioral and cognitive therapy (see e.g., Hollon & Beck, 1994), behavioral clinicians have adopted these techniques.

Psychodynamic thinkers are far behind as they plod through the working through process. Humanistic/experiential theorists have devoted little attention to this factor.

Attributions of Therapeutic Outcome

Patients typically leave therapy much improved, but they do not always maintain this growth. Relapse is common. Freud (1937) recognized this long ago and the phenomenon is not unique to psychodynamic therapy. It has also been documented in behavioral (Bandura, 1989; Elkin, 1994; Lazarus, 1971), and cognitive therapy (Elkin, 1994; Evans, Hollon, DeRubeis, Piasecki, Grove, Garvey, & Tuason, 1992).

A large body of research suggests that how patients understand the outcome of their treatment affects the probability of relapse. Patients may attribute successful outcome to internal causes like their hard work in therapy, changes in their available coping skills, and/or altered personality styles. Alternatively, they can attribute change to external causes like the wonderful therapist they had and/or the powerful techniques therapy employed. Attributions of therapeutic failures can also be internal or external.

Treatment success is more likely to last when internal attributions are made because the patient believes that positive change lies within him or herself. He or she would therefore expect to be able to cope when new challenges arise. He or she would have a strong sense of efficacy (Bandura, 1989), which in turn predicts that therapy effects will last. The literature reviewed in the previous section on expectancy also supports this view. If the patient expects success, then success is more likely (with some possible exceptions). Conversely, relapse is more likely when external attributions are made because now the patient believes that the therapy worked due to the skills of the therapist or the power of the treatment techniques. Once these are removed, the perceived reasons for success are eliminated. The first challenge could be debilitating as the patient will not believe that he or she has the internal resources to meet it. The patient will have a sense of not being efficacious and will have negative expectancies.

The different schools of therapy have recognized the problem of relapse but they have done little more than pay lip service to it. Psychodynamic thinkers may discuss what Freud (1912) called "clearing away the transference" (whatever that means) and behaviorists look to generalize newly learned adaptive behaviors (Emmelkamp, 1994), but neither group has constructively discussed how to accomplish this feat. Cognitive theorists write of helping the patient to see him or herself as a "winner" (Beck, 1976) but no details are provided for maintaining this positive outlook. The solution provided thus far is that therapists from the varying orientations may provide booster sessions to reinvigorate gains (e.g., Freud 1937; Whisman, 1993), which essentially means that the patient must re-enter treatment. However, no school has offered a clear and systematic solution to this potential problem.

Research on attributions in the areas of personality and social psychology (e.g., Deci & Ryan, 1985; Peterson & Seligman, 1984; Weiner, 1986) may be useful. The self-efficacy work of Bandura (e.g., 1989) could also be of benefit. This research demonstrates that attributions of success or failure to internal factors have longer-lasting and farther-reaching effects than do attributions to external factors.

Summarizing the Common Factors

We have summarized five factors that we believe cut across the different forms of psychotherapeutic treatment. We have argued that all have empirical support. We have further argued that different schools of psychotherapy make differential use of these factors, and as a result, we believe that therapy is not as effective as it otherwise might be. Space prevents us from discussing the interaction and theoretical integration of these factors. The reader is referred to Weinberger (1995) and Weinberger and Eig (1999).

Is the Common Factors Approach Catching On?

Our list of common factors was not meant to be exhaustive or exclusive. We merely wanted to demonstrate the utility of a common factors approach. Recently, other writers have offered views that we believe complement and even support ours. We briefly mention some of these ideas.

Barlow, the original force behind ESTs, and his colleagues have proposed a common set of problems characterizing the various emotional disorders and a common set of techniques for treating them (Barlow, Allen, & Choate, 2004). These theorists aver that patients suffering from emotional disorders of any sort display similar maladaptive characteristics. The goal of treatment is to modify these maladaptive characteristics and help the person to develop new, adaptive responses to their affect. The technique is basically to provoke emotion through exposure-based procedures and/or to provoke an antagonistic emotion in the face of the usual emotion arousing stimulation. For example, a spider phobic would be encouraged to approach a spider or taught to smile or laugh in its presence. We are necessarily simplifying the method and leaving out a host of details. The interested reader is referred to the original paper cited above.

Although the term common factor is not used in the work of Barlow et al. (2004), they have targeted expectancies and employed exposure as a method. We do not mean to imply that this work is antagonistic to ESTs or a clear example of a common factors approach. Rather, we wish to emphasize that making use of commonalities in treatment is an effective way to arrive at treatment recommendations.

Goldfried (e.g., 1980) has long been an advocate of integrative approaches to treatment. Instead of using the term common factors, he prefers the term principles of change. Among the principles he identifies are: promoting belief that therapy will be effective, establishing a positive therapeutic relationship, helping the patient to realize the factors that maintain his or her problems, encouraging attempts to correct these difficulties, and emphasizing reality testing. Castonguay and Beutler (2006) also advocate the identification of principles of change. Their principles include provision of a structured treatment and clear therapy focus, addressing interpersonal issues, helping patients to change maladaptive cognitions, and helping patients to better tolerate difficult emotions.

Arguments Against the Common Factors Approach

Arguments against the common factors approach generally take one or more of three forms. First, the Dodo verdict is incorrect. If that is the case, the main justification for positing common factors disappears. Second, the Dodo verdict does not necessarily lead to the conclusion that common factors are responsible. Third, the factors presumed to underlie the Dodo effect cannot be or are not responsible for outcome equivalence.

The argument against the Dodo verdict can take several forms. The first to argue against it was Eysenck (1978) who declared that meta-analyses were uncritical amalgams of good and bad studies whose results are therefore meaningless. Essentially it is garbage in, garbage out. The number of meta-analyses conducted on psychotherapy as well as the increasing sophistication with which they are conducted, argue against this interpretation. In meta-analysis after meta-analysis, the results are the same, outcome equivalence. The Dodo verdict persists. There cannot be that much garbage, and if there is, we need to redo the whole field. Craighead, Sheets and Bjornsson (2005) argue that the sample sizes of the studies in meta-analyses are too small to capture treatment differences. They are arguing that the studies lack sufficient power and therefore a Type II error has been committed. There are two problems with this. First, meta-analyses aggregate studies so that sample sizes become quite large. That is one of the main purposes of a meta-analysis. Individual studies that demonstrate no effect, can, in combination, show a statistically significant effect. This has not happened for the most part. Even if this argument were valid, it is a weak one. It would suggest that treatment differences are so small that it would require huge samples to capture them. The clinical relevance of such small differences, say an effect size of $r = .05$ are questionable.

Beutler et al. (2002), Chambless (2002), Craighead, Sheets, and Bjornsson (2005) and DeRubeis, Brotman and Gibbons (2005) offer an argument that may have some merit. They point out that all therapies for all disorders are blended together in a meta-analysis. It is possible that a particular treatment for a particular disorder may be superior to other treatments for that disorder and that this will be lost in the overall meta-analysis. This masking could happen and it is precisely what EST advocates would predict. It is an empirical question. The best way to address it is to conduct a meta-analysis for the particular disorder in question. There are not yet enough studies to do this for many disorders so what Chambless and DeRubies et al. have done instead is resort to anecdote (Chambless) or citation of particular studies (DeRubeis et al.). This method is not satisfactory as individual studies are often open to interpretation and citations can be selective.

Wampold (2005) illustrates this when he disputes the DeRubeis et al. assertions about individual studies and questions their choices of studies to highlight. Meta-analyses were invented specifically to prevent this differential interpretation of individual studies. Until the relevant meta-analyses are conducted, this criticism cannot be proven one way or another. It also does not address the fact that many treatments for certain disorders (e.g., depression) seem to work equally well.

DeRubeis et al. (2005) and Kazdin (2005) argue that even if the Dodo bird verdict is correct, this does not necessarily support the case for common factors. Therapies can work equally well for a variety of reasons. There is more than one way to skin a cat, so to speak. This is possible but that does not mean it is true. Again, it is an empirical question and it could be answered by determining whether common factors exist and if they could account for effects in differ-ent treatments. Without such tests, this argument becomes a matter of taste and preference. As such, it currently has no ontological status. Incidentally, the same argument can be applied to ESTs in reverse. The fact that an EST works does not demonstrate that it does so because of the techniques specified in the manual. This is an empirical question that to our knowledge has not been addressed. It would require process rather then the kind of outcome research provided by an efficacy study. One could easily argue that the success of an EST is due to common factors and not to the variables the researchers have taken such pains to manualize. Again, this argument is a matter of taste until the requisite science has been conducted.

Finally, the common factors interpretation of the Dodo verdict is disputed by challenging the effectiveness of particular common factors. Usually, this is done through arguing against the power of the relationship. Critics posit that therapist and patient characteristics, as well as the role of early symptom improvement on the strength of the relationship, make it difficult to know whether the therapeutic relationship is really related to outcome equivalence (e.g., DeRubeis et al., 2005; Kazdin, 2005). First, this criticism leaves the question of outcome equivalence unanswered. The critic would have to offer an alternative explanation. Second, outcome equivalence is not necessarily completely dependent on one common factor. Other common factors like exposure and expectancies may also be implicated. Unless the critic is willing to see all of these as insignificant, the argument is weak. Third, the evidence for common factors, as we have tried to show, is strong. It seems to us that the burden is more on the theorist arguing in favor of treatment specific technique to make his or her case. As a side issue, we, like others (e.g., Castonguay, 1993; Weinberger, 1995), would like to see the term common factors used and the term "non-specific" (often used by critics of common factors) eliminated. It is counterproductive. It suggests that the factors studied are not specifiable and it tends to limit common factors to the relationship (see DeRubeis et al., 2005, for an example of this). In fact, these factors are quite specifiable and can be studied empirically. There are also other common factors besides the relationship, as we tried to show.

RESEARCH, TREATMENT, AND TRAINING IMPLICATIONS

If common factors exist and affect psychotherapy outcome across different treatments, certain implications follow. First, we need more research on these common factors. They need to be clearly operationalized, examined, and, when possible, manipulated. This is better done in process, than in outcome, research hence our first recommendation is a call for more systematic process research. Such research should be conducted in different kinds of treatment and across varying diagnostic categories. Only in this way will we be able to determine the exact loci, strengths, and generalizability of the various common factors. We also recommend bringing experienced therapists into this endeavor. Their insights can help us to determine where we should look. Perhaps we should examine the therapy of successful therapists naturalistically in an attempt to determine what they do and how they make use of common (or treatment specific) factors. We believe that practitioners are a wonderful resource for the discovery phase of science (cf., Westen & Weinberger, 2004, 2005). Therapists have been successfully employed in studies examining diagnostic categories (e.g., Shedler & Westen 1998). There is no reason that they could not be an invaluable resource in process and outcome research.

The call for more naturalistic and more process research does not indicate that outcome research (e.g., efficacy research) should cease. Rather it should be supplemented by process research focusing on the various common factors. After all, it behooves us to know how a treatment works if we are to design ever more effective ones. Simply knowing that a treatment is better than nothing or a TAU provides incomplete information at best. Once the common factors have been explicated, it makes more sense to design outcome studies to determine whether a treatment emphasizing them works better than currently existing treatment packages. We propose that as phase two of our research recommendations.

We believe that the common factors approach also has important implications for treatment, and that therapists, both practicing and budding, should take the common factors approach seriously. It behooves them to think about and work to develop the therapeutic relationship, the expectancies of their patients, and to develop exposure techniques that fit in to the type of treatment they are providing. It would also be useful for therapists to explicitly encourage mastery experiences, and to actively encourage their patients to see positive outcome as due to their own efforts and to changes in them. We think this is equally as important as learning a particular treatment package but even within such packages, we believe that practitioners would do well to keep the common factors in mind and try to make use of them. In this vein, we would like to advocate that clinicians collect data as described in Stricker's (Stricker & Trierweiler, 1995) view of the local clinical scientist. This would help in the collaboration that we envision between practitioners and researchers. The practitioners could share their findings with professional researchers who could test them formally. This collaboration may help heal the rift that has apparently formed between practicing clinicians and researchers (Goldfried & Wolfe, 1996; Howard, Moras, Brill, Martinovitch,

& Lutz, 1996; Kopta, Lueger, Saunders, & Howard, 1999) benefiting both and, most importantly, benefiting our patients.

Finally, we believe that the common factors approach has a contribution to make to the training of future clinicians. The task force of Division 12 that introduced ESTs (of which, parenthetically, one of us—J. W.—was a member) advocated training graduate students and interns in empirically supported treatments. We would like to advocate training them in the use of common factors as well. Such a skill can cut across treatment modalities and diagnostic categories. It also brings the art of psychotherapy to the fore. To this end, we again advocate collaboration with experienced clinicians. We further recommend the idea put forth by Stricker (Stricker & Trierweiler, 1995) concerning the local clinical scientist. We propose training in the collection of informal (formal would also be useful) data concerning therapy process, with a focus on common factors. These procedures may lead to important discoveries that can then be communicated to researchers who could then conduct more formal tests.

REFERENCES

Ackerman, S., & Hilsenroth, M. (2003). A review of therapist characteristics and techniques positively impacting the therapeutic alliance. *Clinical Psychology Review, 23,* 1–33.

Ackerman, S., Hilsenroth, M., Baity, M., & Blagys, M. (2000). Interaction of therapeutic process and alliance during psychological assessment. *Journal of Personality Assessment, 75,* 82–109.

Alexander, F. (1963). The dynamics of psychotherapy in the light of learning theory. *American Journal of Psychiatry, 120,* 440–448.

Alexander, F., & French, T. M. (1946). *Psychoanalytic psychotherapy: Principles and applications.* New York: Ronald Press.

Arkowitz, H. (1992). Integrative theories of therapy. In D. K. Freedheim (Ed.), *History of psychotherapy: A century of change* (pp. 261–303). Washington, DC: American Psychological Association.

Bandura, A. (1989). Human agency in social cognitive theory. *American Pyschologist, 44,* 1175–1181.

Barker, S. L., Funk, S. C., & Houston, B. K. (1988). Psychological treatment versus nonspecific factors: A meta-analysis of conditions that engender comparable expectations of improvement. *Clinical Psychology Review, 8,* 579–594.

Barlow, D. H. (1996). Health care policy, psychotherapy research, and the future of psychotherapy. *American Psychologist, 51,* 1050–1058.

Barlow, D. H. (2004). Psychological treatment. *American Psychologist, 59,* 869–878.

Barlow, D. H., Allen, D. H., & Choate, M. L. (2004). Toward a unified treatment for emotional disorders. *Behavior Therapy, 35,* 205–230.

Barrett-Lennard, G. T. (1962). Dimensions of therapist response as a causal factor in therapeutic change. *Psychological Monographs, 76,* 1–36.

Baskin, T. W., Tierney, S. C., Minami, T., & Wampold, B. E. (2003). Establishing specificity in psychotherapy: A meta-analysis of structural equivalence of placebo controls. *Journal of Consulting and Clinical Psychology, 71,* 973–979.

Beck, A. T. (1976). *Cognitive therapy and the emotional disorders*. New York: International Universities Press.

Beck, A. T., Rush, A. J., Shaw, F. B., & Emery, G. (1979). *The cognitive therapy of depression*. New York: Guilford.

Beutler, L. E. (1989). Differential treatment selection: The role of diagnosis in psychotherapy. *Psychotherapy, 26*, 271–281.

Beutler, L. E., Alomohamed, S., Moleiro, C., & Romanelli, R. (2002). Systemic treatment selection and prescriptive therapy. In F. W. Kaslow (Ed.), *Comprehensive handbook of psychotherapy: Integrative/eclectic*, vol. 4 (pp. 255–271). Hoboken, NJ: Wiley.

Beutler, L. E., & Johannsen, B. E. (2006). Principles of change. In J. C. Norcross, L. E. Beutler, & R. F. Levant (Eds.), *Evidence-based practices in mental health* (pp. 226–234). Washington, DC: American Psychological Association.

Blatt, S. J., & Zuroff, D. C. (2005). Empirical evaluation of the assumptions in identifying evidence based treatments in mental health. *Clinical Psychology Review, 25*, 459–486.

Boissel, J. P., Phillippon, A. M., Gauthier, E., Schbath, J., Destors, J. M., & the B. I. S. Research Group. (1986). Time course of long-term placebo therapy effects in angina pectoris. *European Heart Journal, 7*, 1030–1036.

Bordin, E. S. (1979). The generalizability of the psychoanalytic concept of the working alliance. *Psychotherapy, 16*, 252–260.

Bozarth, J. D. (1990). The essence of client-centered therapy. In G. Lietaer, J. Rombauts, & R. Van Balen (Eds.), Client-centered and experiential psychotherapy in the nineties (pp. 229–269). Leuven, Belgium: Leuven University Press.

Brenner, C. (1982). *The mind in conflict*. New York: International Universities Press.

Brodley, B. T. (1990). Client-centered and experiential: Two different therapies. In G. Lietaer, J. Rombauts, & R. Van Balen (Eds.), *Client-centered and experiential psychotherapy in the nineties* (pp. 87–107). Leuven, Belgium: Leuven University Press.

Castonguay, L. G. (1993). "Common factors" and "non-specific variables": Clarification of the two concepts and recommendations for research. *Journal of Psychotherapy Integration, 3*, 267–286.

Castonguay, L. G., & Beutler, L. E. (Eds.). (2006). *Principles of therapeutic change that Work*. Oxford University Press.

Catanzaro, S. J., Wasch, H. H., Kirsch, I., & Mearns, J. (2000). Coping related expectancies and dispositions as prospective predictors of coping responses and symptoms. *Journal of Personality, 68*, 757–788.

Chambless, D. L. (2002). Beware the Dodo bird: The dangers of overgeneralization. *Clinical Psychology: Science and Practice, 9*, 13–16.

Chambless, D. L., Baker, M. J., Baucom, D. H., Beutler, L. E., Calhoun, K. S., Crits-Christoph, P., et al. (1998). Update on empirically validated therapies, II. *The Clinical Psychologist, 51*, 3–16.

Chambless, D. L., & Crits-Christoph, P. (2006). The treatment method. In J. C. Norcross, L. E. Beutler, & R. F. Levant (Eds.), *Evidence based practices in mental health* (pp. 191–200). Washington, DC: American Psychological Association.

Chambless, D. L., Sanderson, W. C., Shoham, V., Johnson, S. B., Pope, K. S., Crits-Christoph, P., et al. (1996). An update on empirically validated therapies. *The Clinical Psychologist, 49*, 5–14.

Craighead, W. E., Sheets, E. S., & Bjornsson, A. S. (2005). Specificity and nonspecificity in psychotherapy. *Clinical Psychology: Science and Practice, 12*, 189–193.

Daldrup, R., Beutler, L., Greenberg, L., & Engle, D. (1988). *Focused expressive therapy: A treatment for constricted affect.* New York Guilford.

Davison, G. C. (1968). Systematic desensitization as a counterconditioning process. *Journal of Abnormal Psychology, 73,* 91.

DeRubeis, R. J., Brotman, M. A., & Gibbons, C. J. (2005). A conceptual and methodological analysis of the nonspecifics argument. *Clinical Psychology: Science and Practice, 12,* 174–183.

Deci, E. L., & Ryan, R. M. (1985). *Intrinsic motivation and self-determination in human behavior.* New York: Plenum.

Dierick, P., & Litaer, G. (1990). Member and therapist perceptions of therapeutic factors in therapy and growth groups: Comments on a category system. In G. Lietaer, J. Rombauts, & R. Van Balen (Eds.), *Client-centered and experiential psychotherapy in the nineties* (pp. 741–770). Leuven, Belgium: Leuven University Press.

Elkin, I., Shea, T., Watkins, J. T., Imber, S. D., Sotsky, S. M., Collins, J.F., Glass, D. R., Pilkonis, P. A., Leber, W. R., Docherty, J. P., Fister, S. J., & Parloff, M. B. (1989). National Institute of Mental Health Treatment of Depression Collaborative Research Program: General effectiveness of treatments. *Archives of General Psychiatry, 46,* 971–982.

Elkin, I. (1994). The NIMH Treatment of Depression Collaborative Research Program: Where we began and where we are. In A. E. Bergin & S. L. Garfield (Eds.), *Handbook of psychotherapy and behavior change* (4th ed., pp, 114–142). New York: Wiley.

Ellis, A. (1962). *Reason and emotion in psychotherapy.* New York: Lyle Stuart.

Ellis, A. (1970). *The essence of rational psychotherapy: A comprehensive approach to treatment.* New York: Institute for Rational Living.

Ellis, A., & Dryden, W. (1987). *The practice of rational-emotive therapy (RET).* New York: Springer.

Emmelkamp, P. M. G. (1982). *Phobic and obsessive-compulsive disorders: Theory, research and practice.* New York: Plenum.

Emmelkamp, P. M. G. (1986). Behavior therapy with adults. In S. L. Garfield & A. E. Bergin (Eds.), *Handbook of psychotherapy and behavior change* (3rd ed., pp. 385–442). New York: Wiley.

Emmelkamp, P. M. G. (1994). Behavior therapy with adults. In A. E. Bergin & S. L. Garfield (Eds.), *Handbook of psychotherapy and behavior change* (4th ed., pp. 379–427). New York: Wiley.

Evans, M. D., Hollon, S. D., DeRubeis, R. J., Piasecki, J. M., Grove, W. M., Garvey, M. J., & Tuason, V. B. (1992). Differential relapse following cognitive therapy and pharmacotherapy for depression. *Archives of General Pyschiatry, 49,* 802–808.

Eysenck, H. J. (1978). An exercise in mega-silliness. *American Psychologist, 33,* 517.

Frank, J. D. (1973). *Persuasion and healing.* Baltimore, MD: John Hopkins University Press.

Frank, J. D. (1978). Expectation and therapeutic outcome: the placebo effect and the role induction interview. In J. D. Frank, R. Hoehn-Saric, S. D. Imber, B. L. Liberman, & A. R. Stone (Eds.), *Effective ingredients of successful psychotherapy* (pp. 1–34). New York: Brunner/Mazel.

Frank, J. D. (1982). Therapeutic components shared by all psychotherapies. In J. H. Harvey & M. M. Parks (Eds.), *The Master Lecture Series: Vol. 1 Psychotherapy research and behavior change* (pp. 5–38). Washington, DC: American Psychological Association.

Frank, J. D., Nash, E. H., Stone, A. R., & Imber, S. D. (1963). Immediate and long-term symptomatic course of psychiatric outpatients. *American Journal of Psychiatry, 120,* 429–439.

Frankl, V. E. (1967). Logotherapy. *Israel Annals of Psychiatry and Related Disciplines, 5,* 142–155.

Freud, S. (1910). The future prospects of psychoanalytic therapy. In J. Strachey (Ed. and trans.), *The standard edition of the complete psychological work of Sigmund Freud* (Vol. 11, pp. 139–151). London: Hogarth Press.

Freud, S. (1912). Papers on technique. In J. Strachey (Ed. and trans.), *The standard edition of the complete psychological work of Sigmund Freud* (Vol. 12, pp. 85–174). London: Hogarth Press.

Freud, S. (1917). Introductory lectures on psychoanalysis: Lecture XXVIII: Analytic therapy. In J. Strachey (Ed. and trans.). *The standard edition of the complete psychological work of Sigmund Freud* (Vol. 16, pp. 448–477). London: Hogarth Press.

Freud, S. (1937). Analysis terminable and interminable. In J. Strachey (Ed. and trans.), *The standard edition of the complete psychological work of Sigmund Freud* (Vol. 23, pp. 216–254). London: Hogarth Press.

Friedman, H. J. (1963). Patient expectancy and symptom reduction. *Archives of General Psychiatry, 8,* 61–67.

Gaston, L., Marmar, C. R., Gallagher, D., & Thompson, L. W. (1989). Impact of confirming patient expectations of change processes in behavioral, cognitive, and brief dynamic psychotherapy. *Psychotherapy, 3,* 296–309.

Gaston, L., Marmar, C. R., Gallagher, D., & Thompson, L. W. (1991). Alliance prediction of outcome beyond in-treatment symptomatic change as psychotherapy processes. *Psychotherapy Research, 1,* 104–113.

Gaston, L. (1990). The concept of the alliance and its role in psychotherapy: Theoretical and empirical considerations. *Psychotherapy, 27,* 143–153.

Gelso, C. J., & Carter, J. A. (1985). The relationship in counseling and psychotherapy: Components, consequences, and theoretical antecedents. *The Counseling Psychologist, 13,* 155–243.

Gendlin, E. T. (1990). The small steps of the therapy process: How they come and how to help them come. In G. Lietaer, J. Rombauts, & R. Van Balen (Eds.), *Client-centered and experiential psychotherapy in the nineties* (pp. 205–224). Leuven, Belgium: Leuven University Press.

Gitelson, M. (1962). The curative factor in psycho-analysis. *International Journal of Psycho-Analysis, 43,* 194–234.

Goldfried, M. R. (1980). Toward the delineation of therapeutic change principles. *American Psychologist, 35,* 991–999.

Goldfried, M. R. (Ed.). (1982). *Converging themes in psychotherapy.* New York: Springer.

Goldfried, M. R., & Wolfe, B. E. (1996). Psychotherapy practice and research: Repairing a strained alliance. *American Psychologist, 51,* 1007–1016.

Gomes-Schwartz, B., Hadley, S. W., & Strupp, H. H. (1978). Individual psychotherapy and behavior therapy. *Annual Review of Psychology, 29,* 435–471.

Greenberg, L. S., Elliott, & Lietaer, G. (1994). Research on experiential psychotherapies. In A. E. Bergin & S. L. Garfield (Eds.), *Handbook of psychotherapy and behavior change* (4th ed., pp. 509–542). New York: Wiley.

Greenberg, L. S., & Safran, J. D. (1987). *Emotion in psychotherapy: Affect, cognition, and the process of change.* New York: Guilford.

Greenberg, L. S., & Webster, M. (1982). Resolving decisional conflict by means of two-chair dialogue and empathic reflection at a split in counseling. *Journal of Counseling Psychology, 29,* 468–477.

Greenson, R. R. (1967). *The technique and practice of psychoanalysis* (vol. 1). New York: International Universities Press.

Grünbaum, A. (1984). *The foundations of psychoanalysis: A philosophical critique.* Berkeley: University of California Press.

Hartmann, H. (1958). *Ego psychology and the problem of adaptation.* New York: International Universities Press. (Original work published in 1939)

Hendrick, I. (1943). The discussion of the "Instinct to Master." *Psychoanalytic Quarterly, 12,* 561–565.

Hilsenroth, M. J. (in press). A programmatic study of short-term psychodynamic psychotherapy: Assessment, process, outcome, and training. *Psychotherapy Research.*

Hilsenroth, M. J., Ackerman, S. J., Clemence, A. J., Strassle, C. G., & Handler, L. (2002). Effects of structured clinician training on patient and therapist perspectives of alliance early in psychotherapy. *Psychotherapy, 39,* 309–323.

Hilsenroth, M., Peters, E., & Ackerman, S., (2004). The development of therapeutic alliance during psychological assessment: Patient and therapist perspectives across treatment. *Journal of Personality Assessment, 83,* 332–344.

Hollon, S. D., & Garber, J. (1990). Cognitive therapy for depression: A social cognitive perspective. *Personality and Social Psychology Bulletin, 16,* 58–73.

Hollon, S. D., & Beck, A. T. (1994). Cognitive and cognitive-behavioral therapies. In A. E. Bergin & S. L. Garfield (Eds.), *Handbook of psychotherapy and behavior change* (4th ed., pp. 428–466). New York: Wiley.

Hovarth, A. O., & Symonds, B. D. (1991). Relation between working alliance and outcome in psychotherapy: A meta-analysis. *Journal of Counseling Psychology, 38,* 139–149.

Howard, K. I., Kopta, S. M. Krause, M. S., & Orlinsky, D. E. (1986). The dose-effect relationship in psychotherapy. *American Psychologist, 41,* 159–164.

Howard, K. I., Moras, K., Brill, P. L., Martinovich, Z., & Lutz, W. (1996). Evaluation of psychotherapy: Efficacy, effectiveness, and patient progress. *American Psychologist, 51,* 1059–1064.

Jarrett, R. B., & Nelson, R. O. (1987). Mechanisms of change in cognitive therapy of depression. *Behavior Therapy, 18,* 227–241.

Josephs, L. (1995). *Balancing empathy and interpretation: Relational character analysis.* Northvale, NJ: Jason Aronson.

Kazdin, A. E., & Wilcoxin, L. A. (1976). Systematic desensitization and nonspecific treatment effects: A methodological evaluation. *Psychological Bulletin, 83,* 729–758.

Kazdin, A. E. (2005). Treatment outcomes, common factors, and continued neglect of mechanisms of change. *Clinical Psychology: Science and Practice, 12,* 184–188.

Kellner, R., & Sheffield, B. F. (1971). The relief of distress following attendance at a clinic. *British Journal of Psychiatry, 118,* 195–198.

Kernberg, O. (1976). *Object relations theory and clinical psychoanalysis.* Northvale, NJ: Jason Aronson.

Kirsch, I., & Henry, D. (1977). Extinction vs. credibility in the desensitization of speech anxiety. *Journal of Consulting and Clinical Psychology, 45,* 1052–1059.

Kirsch, I. (1985). Response expectancy as a determinant of experience and behavior. *American Psychologist, 40,* 1189–1202.

Kirsch, I. (1990). *Changing expectations: A key to effective psychotherapy.* Pacific Grove, CA: Brooks/Cole.

Kirsch, I. (Ed.). (1999). *How expectancies shape experience.* Washington, DC: American Psychological Association.

Kleinke, C. L. (1994). *Common principles of psychotherapy.* Pacific Grove: CA: Brooks/Cole.

Kohut, H. (1984). *How does analysis cure?* Chicago: University of Chicago Press.

Kopta, S. M., Lueger, R. J., Saunders, S. M., & Howard, K. I. (1999). Individual psychotherapy outcome and process research: Challenges leading to greater turmoil or a positive transition? In J. T. Spence, J. M. Darley, & D. J. Foss (Eds.), *Annual review of psychology*, vol. 50 (pp. 441–470). Palo Alto, CA: Annual Reviews, Inc.

Lambert, M. J. (1989). The individual therapists' contribution to psychotherapy process and outcome. *Clinical Psychology Review, 9,* 469–486.

Lambert, M. J. (1992). Implications of outcome research for psychotherapy integration. In J. C. Norcross & M. R. Goldstein (Eds.), *Handbook of psychotherapy integration.* New York: Basic Books.

Lambert, M. J., & A. E. Bergin (1994). The effectiveness of psychotherapy. In A. E. Bergin & S. L. Garfield (Eds.), *Handbook of psychotherapy and behavior change* (4th ed., pp. 143–189). New York: Wiley.

Lazarus, A. A. (1971). *Behavior therapy and beyond.* New York: McGraw-Hill.

LeDoux, J. E. (1996). *The emotional brain: The mysterious underpinnings of emotional life.* New York: Simon & Schuster.

Leitenberg, H., Agras, W. S., Barlow, D. H., & Oliveau, D. C. (1969). Contribution of selective positive reinforcement and therapeutic instruction to systematic desensitization therapy. *Journal of Abnormal Psychology, 74,* 382–387.

Levy, K. N., Clarkin, J. F., Yeomans, F. E., Scott, L. N., Wasserman, R. H., & Kernberg, O. F. (2006). The mechanisms of change in the treatment of transference focused psychotherapy. *Journal of Clinical Psychology, 62,* 481–501.

Lewinsohn, P. M., & Hoberman, H. M. (1982). Depression. In A. S. Bellack, M. Hersen, & A. E. Kazdin (Eds.), *International handbook of behavior modification and therapy* (pp. 397–431). New York: Plenum.

Liberman, B. L. (1978). The role of mastery in psychotherapy: Maintenance of improvement and prescriptive change. In J. D. Frank, R. Hoehn-Saric, S. D. Imber, B. L. Liberman, & A. R. Stone (Eds.), *Effective ingredients of successful psychotherapy* (pp. 35–72). New York: Brunner/Mazel.

Linehan, M. M., Cochran, B. N., Mar, C. M., Levensky, E. R. & Comtois, K. A. (2000). Therapeutic burnout among borderline personality disordered clients and their therapists: Development and evaluation of two adaptations of the Maslach Burnout Inventory. *Cognitive and Behavioral Practice, 7,* 329–337.

Lipsey M., & Wilson, D. (1993). The efficacy of psychological, educational, and behavioral treatment: Confirmation from meta-analysis. *American Psychologist, 48,* 1181–1209.

Luborsky, L. (1984). *Principles of psychoanalytic psychotherapy: A manual for supportive-expressive (SE) methods.* New York: Basic.

Luborsky, L., Diguer, L., Seligman, D. A., Rosenthal, R., Johnson, S., Halperin, G., Bishop, M., & Schweizer, R. (1999). The researcher's own therapeutic allegiances: A "wild card" in the comparisons of treatment efficacy. *Clinical Psychology: Science and Practice, 6,* 95–132.

Luborsky, L., McLellan, A. T., Diguer, L., Woody, G., & Seligman, D. A. (1997). The psychotherapist matters: Comparison of outcomes across twenty-two therapists and seven patient samples. *Clinical Psychology: Science and Practice, 4,* 53–65.

Luborsky, L., Rosenthal, R., Diguer, L., Andrusyna, T. P., Berman, J. S., Levitt, J. T., Seligman, D. A., & Krause, E. D. (2002). The dodo verdict is alive and well—mostly. *Clinical Psychology: Science and Practice, 9,* 2–12.

Marcia, J. E., Rubin, B. M., & Efran, J. S. (1969). Systematic desensitization: Expectancy change or counterconditioning? *Journal of Abnormal Psychology, 74,* 382–387.

Martin, D. J., Garske, J. P., & Davis, M. K. (2000). Relation of the therapeutic alliance with outcome and other variables: A meta-analytic review. *Journal of Consulting and Clinical Psychology, 68,* 438–450.

Meador, B. D., & Rogers, C. R. (1984). Person-centered therapy. In R. J. Corsini (Ed.), *Current psychotherapies* (3rd ed., pp. 142–195). Itasca, IL: Peacock.

Menninger, K. A. (1958). *A theory of psychoanalytic technique.* New York: Basic Books.

Nathan, P. E., & Gorman, J. M. (2002). *A guide to treatments that work* (2nd ed.). New York: Oxford University Press.

Norcross, J. C. (Ed.). (2002). *Psychotherapy relationships that work.* New York: Oxford University Press.

Norcross, J. C., & Lambert, M. J. (2006). The therapy relationship. In J. C. Norcross, L. E. Beutler, & R. F. Levant (Eds.), *Evidence-Based Practices in Mental Health* (pp. 208–218). Washington, DC: American Psychological Association.

Ollendick, T. H., & King, N. J. (2006). Empirically supported treatments typically produce outcomes superior to non-empirically supported treatment therapies. In J. C. Norcross, L. E. Beutler, & R. F. Levant (Eds.), *Evidence-based practices in mental health* (pp. 308–317). Washington, DC: American Psychological Association.

Orlinsky, D. E., & Howard, K. I. (1986). Process and outcome in psychotherapy. In S. L. Garfield & A. E. Bergin (Eds.), *Handbook of psychotherapy and behavior change* (3rd ed., pp. 283–330). New York: Wiley.

Paul, G. L. (1966). *Insight vs. desensitization in psychotherapy.* Stanford, CA: Stanford University Press.

Pennebaker, J. W. (1997). *Opening up: The healing power of expressing emotions* (rev. ed.). New York: Guilford.

Perls, F. S., Hefferline, R. F., & Goodman, P. (1951). *Gestalt therapy.* New York: Julian Press.

Peterson, C., & Seligman, M. E. P. (1984). Causal explanations as a risk factor for depression: Theory and evidence. *Psychological Review, 91,* 347–374.

Phelps, E. A. (2005). The interaction of emotion and cognition: The relation between the human amygdala and cognitive awareness. In R. R. Hassin, J. S. Uleman, & J. A. Bargh (Eds.), *The new unconscious* (pp. 61–76). New York: Oxford University Press.

Piper, W. E., & Wogan, M. (1970). Placebo effect in psychotherapy: An extension of earlier findings. *Journal of Consulting and Clinical Psychology, 34,* 447.

Rado, S. (1925). The economic principle in psychoanalytic technique. *International Journal of Psychoanalysis, 6,* 35–44.

Rangell, L. (1989). Structural and interstructural change in psychoanalytic treatment. *Psychoanalytic Inquiry, 9,* 45–66.

Rapaport, D. (1960). The structure of psychoanalytic theory. *Psychological Issues, Monograph No. 6.* New York: International Universities Press.

Reich, W. (1976). *Character analysis.* New York: Pocket Books. (Original work published 1933).

Rogers, C. (1951). *Client-centered therapy.* Boston: Houghton Mifflin.

Rogers, C. (1957). The necessary and sufficient conditions of therapeutic personality change. *Journal of Consulting Psychology, 21,* 95–103.

Rosenzweig, S. (1936). Some implicit common factors in diverse methods of psychotherapy. *American Journal of Orthopsychiatry, 6,* 412–415.

Roth, A., & Fonagy, P. (2005). *What works for whom: A critical review of psychotherapy research* (2nd ed.). New York: Guilford.

Safran, J. D., & Muran, J. C. (1996). The resolution of ruptures in the therapeutic alliance. *Journal of Consulting & Clinical Psychology, 64,* 447–458.

Safran, J. D., & Muran, J. C. (2000). *Negotiating the therapeutic alliance: A relational treatment guide.* New York: Guilford Press.

Safran, J. D., Muran, J. C., Samstag, L. W., & Stevens, C. (2002). Repairing alliance ruptures. In J. C. Norcross (Ed.), *Psychotherapy relationships that work: Therapist contributions and responsiveness to patients* (pp. 235–254). New York: Oxford University Press.

Safran, J. D., & Segal, Z. V. (1990). *Interpersonal process in cognitive therapy.* New York: Basic Books.

Seltzer, L. F. (1986). *Paradoxical strategies in psychotherapy: A comprehensive overview and guidebook.* New York: Wiley.

Shapiro, A. K., Struening, E., & Shapiro, E. (1980). The reliability and validity of a placebo test. *Journal of Psychiatric Research, 15,* 253–290.

Shedler, J., & Westen, D. (1998). Refining the measurement of Axis II: A Q-sort procedure for assessing personality pathology. *Assessment, 5,* 333–353.

Sloane, D. M., & Marx, B. P. (2004). A closer examination of the structured written disclosure procedure. *Journal of Consulting and Clinical Psychology, 72,* 165–175.

Sloane, R. B., Staples, F. R., Cristol, A. H., Yorkston, N. J., & Whipple, K. (1975). *Psychotherapy vs. behavior therapy.* Cambridge, MA: Harvard University Press.

Smith, M. L., Glass, G. V., & Miller, F. I. (1980). *The benefits of psychotherapy.* Baltimore, MD: Johns Hopkins University Press.

Stampfl, T. G., & Levis, D. J. (1967). Essentials of implosive therapy: A learning-theory-based psychodynamic behavioral therapy. *Journal of Abnormal Psychology, 72,* 496–503.

Sterba, R. (1934). The fate of the ego in analytic therapy. *International Journal of Psychoanalysis, 38,* 140–157.

Stiles, W. B., Shapiro, D. A., & Elliott, R. (1986). Are all psychotherapies equivalent? *American Psychologist, 41,* 165–180.

Stricker, G., & Trierweiler, S. J. (1995). The local clinical scientist: A bridge between science and practice. *American Psychologist, 50,* 995–1002.

Strupp, H. H. (1976). Some critical comments on the future of psychoanalytic therapy. *Bulletin of the Menninger Clinic, 40,* 238–254.

Thomsen, J., Bretlau, P., Tos, M., & Johnsen, J. J. (1983). Placebo effect in surgery for Meniere's disease: Three year follow up. *Otolarungology-Head and Neck Surgery, 91,* 183–186.

Volgyesi, F. A. (1954). "School for patients," hypnosis therapy, and psychoprophylaxis. *British Journal of Medical Hypnotism, 5,* 8–17.

Wampold, B. E. (2001). *The great psychotherapy debate: Models, methods, and findings.* Mahwah, NJ: Erlbaum.

Wampold, B. E. (2005). Establishing specificity in psychotherapy scientifically: Design and evidence issues. *Clinical Psychology: Science and Practice, 12,* 194–197.

Wampold, B. E., Minami, T., Tierney, S. C., & Baskin, T. W. (2005). The placebo is powerful: Estimating placebo effects in medicine and psychotherapy from randomized clinical trials. *Journal of Clinical Psychology, 61,* 835–854.

Wampold, B. E., Mondin, G. W., Moody, M., Stich, F., Benson, K., & Ahn, H. (1997). A meta-analysis of outcome studies comparing bona fide psychotherapies: Empirically, "all must have prizes." *Psychological Bulletin, 122,* 203–215.

Weinberger, J. (1993). Common factors in psychotherapy. In J. Gold & G. Stricker (Eds.), *Handbook of psychotherapy integration* (pp. 43–56). New York: Plenum.

Weinberger, J. (1995). Common factors aren't so common: The common factors dilemma. *Clinical Psychology: Science and Practice, 2,* 45–69.

Weinberger, J. (2002). Short paper, large impact: Rosenzweig's influence on the common factors movement. *Journal of Psychotherapy Integration, 12,* 67–76.

Weinberger, J., & Eig, A. (1999) Expectancies: The ignored common factor in psychotherapy. In I. Kirsch (Ed.), *How expectancies shape experience.* Washington, DC: American Psychological Association.

Weiner, B. (1986). *An attributional theory of motivation and emotion.* New York: Springer-Verlag.

Weiss, J., Sampson, H., & the Mount Zion Psychotherapy Research Group. (1986). *The psychoanalytic process: Theory, clinical observation and empirical research.* New York: Guilford.

Westen, D., Novotny, C. M., & Thompson-Brenner, H. (2004). The empirical status of empirically-supported psychotherapies: Assumptions, findings, and reporting in controlled clinical trials. *Psychological Bulletin, 130,* 631–663.

Westen, D., & Weinberger, J. (2004). When clinical description becomes statistical prediction. *American Psychologist, 59,* 595–613.

Westen, D., & Weinberger, J. (2005). In praise of clinical judgment: Meehl's forgotten legacy. *Journal of Clinical Psychology, 61,* 1257–1276.

Whisman, M. A. (1993). Mediators and moderators of change in cognitive therapy of depression. *Psychological Bulletin, 114,* 248–264.

White, R. W. (1959). Motivation reconsidered: The concept of competence. *Psychological Review, 66,* 297–333.

Wolpe, J. (1958). *Psychotherapy and reciprocal inhibition.* Stanford, CA: Stanford University Press.

Wolfe, B. E., & Goldfried, M. R. (1988). Research on psychotherapy integration: Recommendations and conclusions from NIMH workshop. *Journal of Consulting and Clinical Psychology, 56,* 448–451.

Zetzel, E. R. (1956). Current concepts of transference. *International Journal of Psychoanalysis, 37,* 369–376.

ENDNOTE

1. This does not exclude regular consultation with practitioners in the field for both designing treatments and testing them. We believe that no one can contribute more to the discovery phase of the scientific enterprise than experienced clinicians. Similarly, the insights of those in the field as to how a treatment is working, would be invaluable.

7

Toward the Integration of Technical Interventions, Relationship Factors, and Participants Variables

DAVID CLINTON, ELAINE GIERLACH,
SANNO E. ZACK, LARRY E. BEUTLER,
AND LOUIS G. CASTONGUAY

INTRODUCTION

To a large extent the current state of psychotherapy research seems to be characterized by a schism with regard to the factors responsible for change. According to many influential researchers, the proper form of therapy must be implemented through a process of empirical validation to weed out those treatments whose effects cannot be demonstrated to have clinical significance over other forms of treatment (i.e., placebo or psychopharmacological interventions) (Chambless, Baker, et al., 1998; Chambless, Sanderson, et al., 1996; Nathan & Gorman, 2002; Task Force, 1995). From this argument, one can infer that theory-driven techniques (embedded in empirically supported treatments) are viewed as the primary key to facilitating positive outcomes. A contrasting viewpoint states that most forms of psychotherapy are essentially equivalent (Lambert, 1992; Luborsky, Rosenthal, et al., 2002; Wampold, 2001). Researchers who ascribe to this general perspective tend to believe that the therapeutic relationship and the participants (the therapist and client per se) are primarily responsible for growth and change (Bohart, 2006; Norcross, 2002; Wampold, 2001, 2006).

To date, prominent researchers and theorists representing each of these perspectives have contributed to a solid base of knowledge regarding factors that are important to positive client change. For the most part, however, they have done so independently of one another. Yet research indicates that no one element can sufficiently account for patient improvement, suggesting that an attempt at integration is both timely and necessary. In response to such findings, recent efforts have been geared toward developing an approach that allows for an integrated view of variables influencing the process of change in psychotherapy. The work done by the Task Force on Empirically Based Principles of Therapeutic Change (Castonguay & Beutler, 2006) and the work on Systematic Treatment Selection (Beutler, Clarkin, & Bongar, 2000; Beutler & Harwood, 2000) provide clinicians with a way of conceptualizing their patients through a process that integrates technical interventions, relationship factors, and participant variables, while developing a flexible and adaptive treatment plan.

Thus, the goal of this chapter is to review these recent efforts that offer clinicians an empirically based integrative approach to conceptualizing psychotherapy, drawing from meaningful contributions in the areas of technique, relationship, and participant factors. To this end, we will first summarize the current debate surrounding Empirically Supported Research and illuminate the schism between researchers in regards to psychotherapy outcomes. With this historical foundation in mind, the results of the Task Force on Empirically Based Principles of Therapeutic Change and the work on Systematic Treatment Selection will then be discussed. Finally, the integrative approach will be exemplified through the use of two clinical examples. As we explore these approaches, the interplays between science and practice will become clear.

THERAPY OUTCOME RESEARCH

Empirically Supported Treatments or Equality of Treatments

In 1952, Hans J. Eysenck caused an uproar in the field by declaring that psychotherapy was no more effective than the passing of time (Eysenck, 1952). In response to this claim, massive amounts of research on the impact of psychotherapy were generated, resulting in a general consensus that psychotherapy is, in fact, effective. The average effect size for these studies was .85, indicating that the average treated persons were better off than 80% of the untreated sample (Lambert & Ogles, 1988; Smith, Glass, & Miller, 1980). Despite agreement that therapy is effective, two fundamental but contrasting perspectives characterize the views of psychotherapists and psychotherapy investigators regarding the factors that are primarily responsible for psychotherapeutic change. The first of these views tends to emphasize the relative importance and efficacy of certain treatment procedures and models over others. In the last decade, this movement has resulted in a list of models and interventions, along with their associated manuals, that are frequently identified as being "empirically supported" treatments (Chambless et al., 1996; Chambless & Hollon, 1998) or ESTs. The identification of ESTs is the result of a Task Force of Division 12 (Clinical Psychology) of the American Psychological

Association (APA) (Chambless et al., 1998; Chambless et al., 1996; Hofmann & Tompson, 2002; Nathan & Gorman, 2002; Task Force, 1995).

A second major viewpoint asserts that common, rather than treatment-specific aspects of therapy, account for the preponderance of change. This latter viewpoint, classically termed the "Dodo Bird Effect," points to the fact that there are no statistical differences between the effectiveness of theoretical orientations as a whole, all having some successes, and suggests that "all have won and all must have prizes" (Luborsky, Singer, & Luborsky, 1975; p. 996) (e.g., Lambert, 1992; Luborsky et al., 2002; Wampold, 2001). Instead, it is suggested that there are factors that are common to all effective therapies regardless of theoretical orientation. These can include aspects related to the structure of treatment, the therapist, the client, or the therapeutic relationship. A list of empirically supported relationship factors has been identified by a Task Force constituted by the Division 29 (Psychotherapy) of APA (Norcross, 2002).

Proponents of the EST movement have emphasized the importance of determining which treatments are effective for a particular group of patients. Since no single therapy is effective for all patients, identifying an EST for a particular disorder allows therapists a place to start in determining an intervention. Treatment manuals associated with ESTs can thus be viewed as a "first line of attack" (Castonguay, Schut, Constantino, & Halperin, 1999). A clinician using an EST knows that the treatment has been tested and found to work for a particular disorder. This lessens the risk of utilizing a treatment that either provides no benefit or induces harm.

A major critique of ESTs is that, although they hold up well in randomized clinical trials, they may have limited applicability to clinical practice. This criticism has been countered by a limited number of effectiveness studies showing that when ESTs are compared to existing practices or treatment as usual, ESTs are more effective (see Chambless & Ollendick, 2001; Ollendick & King, 2006 for a review). However, the scope of the findings is arguably limited by the small number of effectiveness studies. Critics of ESTs also point to the process of defining what is "empirically supported," arguing that current definitions have borrowed heavily from a medical model (Wampold, 2001). As a result, they discriminate against certain treatments that are more difficult to test, such as those that have been expressly developed to meet the unique needs of a given minority group (e.g., Bernal & Scharrón-Del-Río, 2001; Sue & Zane, 2006). It is also conceivable that some of the criteria set forth by the Division 12 Task Force (e.g., emphasis on treatment manuals and randomized controlled studies) may explain, at least in part, the preponderance of cognitive and cognitive-behavioral approaches among ESTs (Wampold, 2001). Because behavior therapy has emerged from a scientific tradition that emphasizes the measure of observable and testable constructs, its proponents have taken great care to operationalize their interventions. As a natural outgrowth of such operationalizations, the construction of treatment manuals (which essentially represent definitions of independent variables to be tested) becomes a logical step in the development and refinement of cognitive-behavioral oriented treatments. As such, CBT protocols appear to be particularly amenable, almost de facto, to the kind of empirical investigation reflected in clinical trials, while other approaches may require greater transformations to be similarly tested. Thus, there is ambiguity as to whether cognitive-behavioral methods are superior to other treatments or if the nature of the treatment is simply more conducive to the Division 12 Task Force criteria. Exacerbating this issue is a tendency to assume that therapeutic approaches which are not part of the list of empirically supported treatment are not effective (Wampold, 2006), even though many treatments simply have not yet been studied using the guidelines proposed by the Division 12 Task Force. Interestingly, the Task Force did not study which treatments are *not* efficacious (Chambless & Ollendick, 2001). Consequently, though a treatment may not incur EST status, it does not mean that treatment is not effective.

Thus the utility of an *exclusive* focus on identifying ESTs is debatable. However, this is not to suggest that the empirical validation of technical aspects of psychotherapy is unimportant. Rather, we must distinguish between ESTs that focus on Treatment Models, entire treatment packages aligned with a given theoretical orientation, and empirically based therapy techniques. Interestingly this can lead to the recognition of techniques that are common to several approaches. For instance, CBT treatments for anxiety disorders frequently involve exposure as a main, and at times only, component of therapy (see Woody and Ollendick, 2006). However, exposure to fear situations has also been reported in psychodynamic treatments (see Goldfried, 1980; Wallerstein & Dewit, 1997). Furthermore, in as much as they prescribed the client's acknowledgement and deep experience of (staying with) painful emotions, humanistic treatments also include exposure. In other words, exposure is a technique or strategy of intervention that can occur across a variety of different treatment modalities and be constructed and labeled in a variety of different ways. Theoretically, any intervention utilizing any of these methods and following the common principle of exposure for anxiety (and perhaps for other clinical problems as well), should have a more favorable outcome than interventions that do not follow these principles and that do not expose the patient to the feared event or emotion, regardless of EST status. Common principles of change such as exposure to emotional experiences are at the core of integrative efforts described later in this chapter.

Entwined in this controversy surrounding the EST movement is the spectra of a larger and more fundamental debate in psychology—that of whether psychotherapy is most accurately conceptualized as an art or a science. To some extent the EST movement has been seen as representing the science based approach to psychotherapy whereas those in opposition to the movement, especially those who emphasize the role of relationships in healing, have been characterized as leaning more toward the view that the things that are really important in psychotherapy are more closely related to art than to science. However, we do not believe that the issue is as simple as choosing between art and science. We are among those who believe that *both* the art and the science of therapy are necessary for maximum success (Beutler, Clarkin, & Bongar, 2000; Beutler & Harwood, 2000). To some degree, the debate may be closer to one type of science or methodology that is favored by various scholars than it is to art versus science. Moreover, it is our view that even the most artistic of disciplines must rely on established principles. Even an artist as noted as Van Gough had to work within the scientifically established principles that governed the mixing of pigments—blue and yellow always yield green. As such, relationship factors in psychotherapy can and should be studied empirically. Despite the presence of such an integrative perspective among a large group of psychotherapy scholars, however, the debate about the process of change (whether or not it is framed as one of art versus science) appears to continue and seems to have been translated into the form of a specific controversy: whether it is the technique, the relationship, or the participant factors that have the largest influence on client outcome.

Technique, Relationship, and Participant Factors Debate

For many, a scientific/empirical approach of psychotherapy is based on the assumption that outcome is a predictable and manageable product of applying the right treatment to the right problem(s). Such a perspective is drawn from the under-pinning of contemporary health-related disciplines; namely, that effective clinical work is related to identifying treatments that are indicated and contra-indicated for different patients. Within the controversy that is most figural in psychotherapy in the twenty-first century, this perspective is closely associated with the EST movement, which has been used to provide support to the assumption that thera-peutic benefit is a direct (or at least a very close) function of identifying and using the correct and specific technical interventions for the problem presented. The sufficiency of this view for accounting for a meaningful portion of observed change, however, has been widely challenged. A factor that seems to undermine this perspective is the finding that relationship variables, including the working alliance between therapist and client, and participant factors (e.g., patient baseline levels of impairment and motivation for change) contribute at least as much to treatment outcomes as the model of treatment itself. Encouraging the separation of technical, relationship, and participant factors may lead to a distorted picture of the process of change in psychotherapy. Integration of these factors may prove the better strategy.

The effort to address this need for integration logically begins with a review of the contributions and limitations of each component that is involved in this debate about ESTs and about science: techniques, relationships, and participant factors.

Treatments That Work

Chambless & Crits-Christoph (2006) loosely define treatment as consisting of, "therapists' behaviors designed to foster therapeutic benefit" (p. 192). Treatment methods can include treatment principles, treatment techniques, and therapist behaviors that increase the therapeutic alliance. However, not all treatment methods are created equal. Advocates of the treatment method as the primary change agent in therapy emphasize that psychologists have an ethical obligation to base their treatment selection on what procedures have received empirically demonstrated support. The alternative, typically to utilize what might come from personal experience or clinical lore, opens the door to a number of potential problems (Chambless & Crits-Christoph).

Relying on empirical evidence to determine what is technically effective increases the likelihood that the therapist will not use a harmful intervention on a patient. The history of clinical intervention is sadly marked with examples of the damage that can occur when misguided approaches are applied such as facilitated communication with autistic children and insulin shock therapy for schizophrenia. Without a thorough investigation of the specific techniques used, it is impossible to know precisely which interventions are effective, which provide no benefit, and which may be harmful. As such, empirical studies of what therapists do with a client is essential. However, is it sufficient and at what level is it best accomplished?

Even the strongest advocates of the specific effects of treatments have come to acknowledge the importance of relationship factors in influencing outcomes (e.g., Chambless & Crits-Cristoph, 2006). Moreover, acknowledging the importance of empirically based technical factors in therapy outcome does not necessarily presume the need to focus on comprehensive models of treatment, as defined by ESTs. As discussed earlier, it is possible to delineate technical procedures (such as exposure) that are common to a number of effective treatment protocols. Conceivably, the important change agents might be best implemented when therapists are provided with general empirically based technical principles as opposed to entire treatment packages (Castonguay & Beutler, 2006). This may be more efficient and manageable for a variety of reasons, including the vast number of treatment packages that prohibit thorough training in all approaches, especially considering the time limitations of practicing clinicians (Beutler & Johannsen, 2006). In addition, while more than 150 different treatment manuals have been deemed effective, the differences among the effects of these various treatments, when compared head-to-head, appear to be negligible, raising questions regarding the equivalency of treatments. Moreover, therapists may feel pressured to pick a treatment method that may be too rigid and not generalize appropriately to the patient.

While honoring the importance of various treatment techniques, there are drawbacks to an over-emphasis on treatment packages, as has typified most EST research. The reliance on randomized clinical trials makes the study of participant and relationship factors difficult, as the variance they account for are mostly cancelled out as error (Wampold, 2001). By controlling for individual differences and other extraneous variables, relationship and participant factors are generally and easily overlooked. This is particularly problematic in light of the fact that meta-analyses have found that differences between most active treatments accounted for 10% or less of the variance in outcomes (e.g., Luborsky, Rosenthal, Diguer, Andrusyna, Berman, & Levitt, et al., 2002), leaving unaccounted for the vast majority of observed change. A reliance on randomized clinical trials alone potentially limits information that would be of applicable clinical significance since patients are not randomly assigned to treatments in clinical settings. In addition, Blatt and Zuroff (2005) found that random assignment is not a neutral intervention, as it is viewed negatively by some clients and may have negative consequences on therapeutic change. In sum, contemporary findings suggests that therapeutic techniques are an essential piece of the puzzle, but by themselves do not provide a nearly satisfactory explanation of psychotherapy outcomes.

Relationships That Work

The strongest reaction against the EST movement in psychotherapy was expressed by those who emphasized the importance of relationship variables, over technical aspects of treatment (cf., Norcross, 2002). Many of those who advocate the relationship as the primary change mechanism in therapy contend that virtually all of the relationship between "Empirically Supported Treatments" and outcomes, can be accounted for by the relationship itself. Meta-analyses, individual outcome studies, and client reports have provided evidence of the power of the therapeutic relationship (Norcross & Lambert, 2006). In fact, a substantial number of components of the therapeutic relationship have been identified as effective (e.g., alliance, empathy, goal consensus and collaboration, group cohesion) or promising (e.g., positive regard, genuineness, management of counter-transference) variables of change in the Division 29 Task Force (Norcross, 2002). As a group, these variables account for a substantially larger percentage of the outcome variance than specific technique, with some individual studies showing the alliance alone accounting for as much as 20% of the outcome variance (Wampold, 2001). Client reports on helpful aspects of therapy also demonstrate the centrality of the relationship, as clients tend to attribute the effectiveness of their treatment to the therapeutic relationship rather than to technical aspects of treatment.

Although few scholars dispute the importance of the therapeutic alliance, much of the evidence for its effectiveness and efficacy relies on correlational, naturalistic, and case-observational methods. These are useful methods in exploring relationships but they do not allow for cause and effect analyses, as do randomized designs. Teasing apart the relative contributions of different components of the therapeutic relationship has also proved to be difficult. Although the alliance generally, across studies, accounts for less than 10% of outcome variance, the effects of relationship factors as a whole may be significantly greater. However, it is difficult to determine how much so. Moreover, given the complexity of relationship effects, specifying relationship factors as the cardinal component in therapy outcome is difficult to translate into effective recommendations for therapist action.

PARTICIPANT FACTORS THAT WORK

In addition to delineating the contribution of general components of the therapeutic relationship, the Division 29 Task Force also reviewed evidence supporting the role of client characteristics as customizing variables—anchor points to determine how best to match therapist interventions to a particular client. For example, matching the patient's level of resistance with the therapist's level of directiveness has been found to be an effective way to tailor the relationship to best fit the patient (Beutler, Alomohamed, Moleiro, & Romanelli, 2002; Norcross & Lambert, 2006). The Division 29 effort to identify customizing variables is connected with the third prominent perspective in the current debate about what explains change. The primary factors responsible for therapeutic impact, according to some influential voices in the field (e.g., Bohart, 2006; Wampold, 2001), are the participants themselves. Patient characteristics are estimated to account for 25%–30% of the total variance in outcome studies (Norcross & Lambert, 2006), the largest identified contributor to outcome. As reviewed by (Clarkin & Levy, 2004), a considerable number of patient characteristics have been investigated, such as the degree of help seeking, diagnosis, symptom severity, demographic variables (e.g., age, race, gender, and socioeconomic status), personality variables (e.g., expectancies, motivation, and insight) and interpersonal factors (e.g., attachment). Categorizing these relevant patient characteristics serves a prognostic function, predicting how different people will do in therapy, as well as providing further information to aid clinicians in identifying which treatment methods may be effective.

As a major supporter of the perspective that participant factors are the main contributor to outcome, Bohart (2006) views the patient as an active agent in facilitating change in psychotherapy. Going beyond identifying certain patient characteristics that influence treatment outcome, he views psychotherapy as "a process of facilitating or releasing clients' natural self-healing tendencies," (Bohart, p. 219). Instead of placing emphasis on therapist skills or particular interventions, Bohart's perspective highlights the process of self-healing within the patient as primarily responsible for outcome. Bohart (2006) also argues that our current efforts to understand therapy outcomes are unfairly therapist-centric and do not give patients sufficient credit for their contribution to the change process.

Patient factors and characteristics undoubtedly contribute to therapy in a variety of ways. Not only do patients bring their own level of motivation and interactional style to the therapy, but, as noted by Frank (1973), patients often show improvement before they even attend their first session, suggesting the impact of an expectancy effect that could be considered to be located within the patient. In addition, the interventions of the therapist are filtered through the lens of the client, resulting in potentially altered meaning. In one study, patients questioned after therapy indicated that it was their interpretation of therapist interventions rather than the actual techniques that were useful (Kuhnlein, 1999 as cited by Bohart, 2006). Findings such as these support the notion that the client is not a blank slate that is molded by the therapist, but plays an active and important role in directing the course of therapy.

Studying the impact of the client, however, is challenging for a number of reasons. Like the therapeutic relationship, client factors are relatively neglected in efforts to establish ESTs. While most randomized trials carefully control for client diagnosis, they generally do not address equally important nondiagnostic factors such as attachment style or capacity for self-reflection. Moreover, as noted by Clarkin and Levy (2004), patient characteristics are not static traits, but represent dynamic and ever-changing influences, occurring in transaction with the therapist and the therapy over time. The meaning of a given client characteristic will not be uniform for every patient, as characteristics can act to moderate therapy and outcome in different ways. Thus, measuring client characteristics only at the outset of treatment, as is frequently done, is insufficient.

As part of the effort to recognize the role of participants, Wampold (2001) suggests that the therapist also has an important, if often overlooked, impact on treatment outcome. In addition to their role in developing and maintaining the therapeutic alliance, Wampold argues that therapists make a significant contribution in their own right. Supporting this view, randomized clinical trial designs produce considerable within-cell variability that is not accounted for by therapist adherence to a particular treatment protocol. In other words, therapists are not equally effective with clients, even when using the same theoretical approach and adhering to it equally well. Rather, a portion of the variance in treatment outcome can be attributed to therapist skill or competence, independently of what domain of procedures in which they may be skilled. Just how large this portion is, is unclear. Meta-analysis by Crits-Christoph and Mintz (1991) estimated that about 9% of the variance was accounted for by this factor. However, accurate estimates required re-analysis of original studies as the majority of them failed to consider variability of therapists. Some findings suggest that well-controlled studies may reduce this therapist variability through the use of therapist training, well-constructed manuals, and on-going supervision (e.g., Crits-Cristoph as cited in Wampold 2001). However, Blatt and colleagues, in a re-analysis of the well-controlled Treatment of Depresssion Collaborative Research Program supported by the National Institute of Mental Health in the 1970s and 1980s, found that therapist variability was substantial (Blatt, Sanislow, Zuroff, & Pilkonis, 1996). In addition to general competence, therapist variables have been categorized similarly to patient characteristics, with Beutler, Machado, and Neufeld (1994) describing characteristics along two dichotomous axes, objective—subjective and cross-situational—therapy specific. These dichotomies incorporated such therapist variables as age, sex, ethnicity, personality patterns, attitudes, and expectations.

Both therapist and patient characteristics are important contributors to effective treatments. Beutler and Johannesen (2006) argue, however, it is the *interaction* between patient and therapist characteristics and therapeutic interventions that is most strongly predictive of outcome. Another problem with much of the research on participant factors is the heavy reliance on correlational methods, which precludes definite conclusion about cause and effect relationships. Furthermore, in addition to minimizing the role of technical and relationship variables, the sole emphasis on one set of participant variables (associated either to the client or the therapist), makes it difficult to predict therapist-patient pairs that work.

AN INTEGRATIVE APPROACH

Logically, one must not only give due regard to the independent contributions of participants, relationships, and techniques, but to the ways that these domains of variables interact with one another, as well. It is here, at the interface of patient, therapist, treatment, and relationship, that a resolution of the struggle between art and science is likely to be achieved in psychotherapy.

Beutler and colleagues (Beutler, Moleiro, Malik, Harwood, Romanelli, Gallagher-Thompson, & Thompson, 2003), conducted a test of patient, treatment, relationship, and "goodness of treatment fit" among co-morbid, complex patients with chemical abuse disorders and mild to moderate depression. They separately tested the proportion of improvement associated with (1) patient prognostic factors, (2) interventions associated with different models of treatment, (3) the strength of the therapeutic alliance, and (4) the degree of fit between patient and treatment. With regard to depressive symptoms, results indicated that (1) each set of variables added independently of outcomes, and (2) end of treatment predictors favored the alliance, treatment, and patient variables, whereas long-term effects favored the fit of the treatment to the patient. Similar, albeit weaker, results were found using self-report measures; these results favored the role of treatment and intervention-patient matching over estimates of therapeutic alliance. Looking at changes in alcohol and drug use, (1) each set of variables added independent prediction to abstinence rates, (2) the pattern of prediction was similar at the end of treatment and at follow up, and (3) the total variance predicted and accounted for was substantially higher than models looking at one of the factors alone, achieving more than 70% accuracy of prediction.

Relative Contributions of Patient, Treatment, Relationship, and Fit

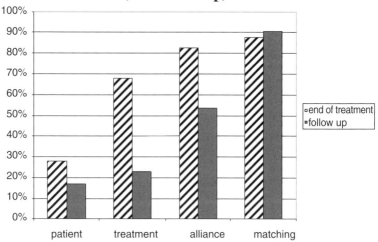

Figure 7.1 Percentage of Variance of HRSD Outcome

These results highlight the fact that the contributions of each factor, whether it is treatment, relationship, or participant, are not as significant individually as they are in combination. Such findings suggest the need to shift our focus beyond limited single-factor conceptualizations and to work toward an integrated approach. Efforts to discover the primary driving force behind psychotherapy has exposed an undeniable fact: treatment, relational, *and* participant factors are involved in determining therapeutic change for a patient. There is no doubt in our mind that focusing on one of these factors can lead to better refinement or understanding of their individual effects. In our view, however, the art of psychotherapy lies not in the ability of the therapist to individually focus on one part of her therapeutic skill, but instead on developing a base of research-derived principles that encourage the therapist to be aware of the contribution made by all of the major dimensions of the process of change. These process variables, focused upon singularly, tend not to explain a large proportion of the total variance in treatment (Beutler, Clarkin & Bongar, 2000). In contrast, the principles described above could allow the therapist to promote the strengths inherent in each facet of the therapeutic process in conjunction with each other. In accordance with this ideal, Division 12 of the American Psychological Association and the North American Society for Psychotherapy Research (NASPR) created a joint task force to identify empirically based principles of therapeutic change (Castonguay & Beutler, 2006).

Task Force on Empirically Supported Principles of Therapeutic Change

Born from the desire to establish broad principles of change derived from empirical research, the Task Force on Therapeutic Principles that Work sought the answers to several questions, primary among them were: (1) What is known about the nature of the participants, relationships, *and* procedures within treatment that induces positive effects across theoretical models? (2) How do factors related to these domains work together to enhance change? The specific goals of the task force comprised an attempt to integrate participant, relationship, and treatment factors while, at the same time, creating working principles that were supported by empirical research. These principles were to provide effective guidelines for planning and implementing treatment, while not being tied to any one particular therapeutic model.

The Task Force co-chairs specifically sought and selected Task Force members to represent a cross section of theoretical bases in order to reflect the current variety of opinion in the field of psychotherapy today. Members were chosen through a process of reviewing author lists in major reference volumes, nomination of names of renowned individuals, discussion among the editors and associates, and then discussing the project with the nominees. In this process, four criteria were targeted: (1) each participant must be an established scholar who had achieved visibility in the scientific community for their empirical research in a given problem area and variable domain, (2) each member must be willing and interested in working toward integration and synthesis of their research findings, (3) each must be willing to work with colleagues who did not share their own theoretical perspectives, and (4) each must be willing to work for little financial compensation (Castonguay & Beutler, 2006). Once a suitable set of candidates was found, they were paired together within a particular problem area and variable domain. The domains, as noted, included relationship factors, participant characteristics, and technical procedures, whereas the problem areas were represented by literature on depression, anxiety, personality disorder, and substance use. In these pairs, each author was (1) allowed to recruit additional colleagues to assist them and (2) given a set of primary readings coinciding with their domain to base their research upon. Their goal was to review these primary texts and extract from them broad principles of change that were likely to cut across theoretical orientations. These researchers also were armed with two basic definitions to guide their way (Castonguay & Beutler):

1. A principle defines the conditions under which a concept (participant, relationship quality, or intervention) will be effective. The concepts to be included should not be too general or theory-specific.
2. An empirically based principle is one that reflects the role of the participant characteristics, relationship qualities, or components of treatment that are found in the treatments defined by the Division 12 or Division 29 Task Force reports (see Chambless et al., 1998; Chambless et al., 1996; Task Force, 1995; Norcross, 2002), or that is supported by a preponderance of available evidence.

Ultimately, 24 senior scholars and 21 associated scholars were chosen. These authors were asked to review the empirical evidence and derive principles of change associated with one of three variable domains (participant factors, relationship factors, treatment/technique factors) and within one of four particular problem areas (dysphoric, anxiety, personality, and substance use disorders; see Figure 7.2). Once the individual set of principles had been derived, one author from each of the twelve groups was brought to a joint working group meeting, the objectives of which were to delineate a list of common principles across multiple problem areas, as well as to identify principles that were specific to a particular problem area.

	Dysphoric Disorders	Anxiety Disorders	Personality Disorders	Substance Use Disorders
Treatment Factors				
Relationship Factors				
Participant Factors				

Figure 7.2 A Schematic Outline of the Task Force Focus

When properly applied, these principles of change should allow clinicians to operate research-informed practices, to enhance their ability to serve a wider range of patients, and to use a broad array of empirically supported clinical methods. (A large number of these factors are presented in a later section of this chapter; for a complete list of the principles of change delineated by the Task Force, see Castonguay & Beutler, 2006.)

Applications of Principle-Based Treatments to Psychotherapy

There have been three systematic efforts to describe and apply a treatment based on principles of fundamental therapeutic change. The first two of these pre-date the findings of the Division 12/NASPR Task Force and the third is a direct application of the Task Force Findings.

Systematic Treatment Selection. Systematic Treatment Selection (STS; Beutler & Clarkin, 1990; Beutler, Clarkin, & Bongar, 2000) evolved from a series of comprehensive literature reviews from which the authors extracted 15 hypotheses about the conditions under which treatment effects would be optimized. These hypothesized relationships were re-framed as principles that described qualities of patients, qualities of treatment, and qualities of the therapeutic alliance. Other principles refer to interaction or fit between certain nondiagnostic patient variables and compatible classes of therapeutic intervention that were likely to enhance speed and maintenance of improvement. These principles were specifically framed to cut across theoretical models of treatment and different types of problems. Each hypothetical principle addressed either a factor that portended prognosis for treatment generally, a relationship quality that would enhance recovery and maintenance, or the best fit of patient and treatment.

To refine the principles, a list of patient qualities that were referenced in the research literature and had proven to be effective predictors of change was developed. To reduce this list of variables (many of which were quite esoteric), similar sounding concepts and those with similar behavioral correlates were clustered. This process was repeated until the resulting list contained only readily and reliably identified qualities that had been studied in at least five studies and had been observed to be positively related to treatment benefit in the preponderance of cases. Thus, concepts that were so esoteric that they could not be identified by simple descriptions of behavior patterns were excluded. The final list of patient variables included: patient demographic and cultural identifiers, level of impairment, complexity of problem (co-morbidity), chronicity of the problem (recurrence or length of time with disorder), coping style (internalizing/inhibited versus externalizing/impulsive), social support levels, level of resistance, traits expressed in history of relationships with others and with treatment resources, and level of current distress.

A rating system was then constructed from which clinicians could assess each of these patient qualities from standard intake materials. A similar procedure was undertaken for identifying reliable aspects of treatment that were represented in the reviews of literature, and that had been related to good outcomes in a preponderance of prior studies. Treatment qualities were also subjected to a process of eliminating esoteric and unreliably rated variables. The retained classes of treatment variables included intensity of treatment (length and frequency), mode (individual psychotherapy, group therapy, family therapy, pharmacotherapy, etc.), the focus (insight versus skill building and behavior change), level of therapist directiveness and skill, concentration on emotion and abreaction versus problem solving and control, and therapist activity level.

Once the principles were articulated and procedures were in place to measure patient, treatment, relationship, and outcome, a confirmatory study was undertaken on an archival group of 284 patient-therapist pairs who had participated in one of four previously completed randomized controlled trial studies of various forms of psychotherapy and pharmacotherapy for depression or chemical abuse. The samples of patients had all been carefully selected and evaluated at the beginning and end of treatment, as well as at a six-month follow-up. Audio and videotapes were obtained for the initial intake session on each patient, along with the results of various psychological tests and symptom change measures that had been completed at the time of entry to the study and at various points through follow-up.

Experienced clinicians first viewed the intake session and reviewed intake tests and materials that were available, which consisted of objective personality tests and various symptom and diagnostic measures. From these materials, the clinicians rated each of the patient qualities that had been identified by the literature review. Independently trained raters then viewed videotapes of early and late therapy sessions and made ratings of the degree to which various classes of intervention had been used. Finally, a new group of experienced clinicians reviewed outcome data and end of treatment tapes to derive both end of treatment and follow-up measures of depression, well-being, and chemical abuse.

The results confirmed the validity of 13 of the original 15 principles tested and to this list, were added 5 principles that had been independently identified by a consensus panel of experienced clinicians to pertain to low frequency events that bear upon matters of confidentiality and management of risk. The principles that were predictive of efficacy, are reported in Table 7.1. Basic principles are those that pertain to variables and dimensions that can be easily identified from patient treatment records and used for assessing compliance and fidelity of treatment (e.g., length and intensity of treatment, mode of treatment, format of treatment, etc.), whereas Optimal principles reflect dimensions that must be directly observed in the treatment itself.

The goal of the STS approach is to provide a method by which an individual clinician, regardless of theoretical orientation, can tailor a treatment plan in order to maximize outcomes for a particular patient. Many of the principles delineated in 2000 by Beutler and his colleagues were subsequently reviewed and adopted within the empirically-based clinical guidelines developed by the Division 12/NASPR Task Force. However, unlike the later work done by this Task Force, Systematic

Table 7.1 Principles for Systematic Treatment Selection

Reasonable and Basic Principles

Prognosis

1. The likelihood of improvement (prognosis) is a positive function of social support level and a negative function of functional impairment.

2. Prognosis is attenuated by patient complexity/chronicity, and by an absence of patient distress. Facilitating social support enhances the likelihood of good outcome among patients with complex/chronic problems.

Level and Intensity of Care

3. Psychoactive medication exerts its best effects among those patients with high functional impairment and high complexity/chronicity.

4. Likelihood and magnitude of improvement is increased among patients with complex/chronic problems by the application of multiperson therapy.

5. Benefits correspond to treatment intensity among functionally impaired patients.

Risk Reduction

6. Risk is reduced by careful assessment of risk situations in the course of establishing a diagnosis and history.

7. Risk is reduced and patient compliance is increased when the treatment includes family intervention.

8. Risk and retention are optimized if the patient is realistically informed about the probable length and effectiveness of the treatment and has a clear understanding of the roles and activities that are expected of him or her during the course of the treatment.

9. Risk is reduced if the clinician routinely questions patients about suicidal feelings, intent, and plans.

10. Ethical and legal principles suggest that documentation and consultation are advisable.

Optimal Principles

Note: The original order of the principles has been rearranged to reflect some commonalities.

Relationship Principles

1. Therapeutic change is greatest when the therapist is skillful and provides trust, acceptance, acknowledgment, collaboration, and respect for the patient within an environment that both supports risk and provides maximal safety

2. Therapeutic change is most likely when the therapeutic procedures do not evoke patient resistance.

Principle of Exposure and Extinction

3. Therapeutic change is most likely when the patient is exposed to objects or targets of behavioral and emotional avoidance.

4. Therapeutic change is greatest when a patient is stimulated to emotional arousal in a safe environment until problematic responses diminish or extinguish.

Principle of Treatment Sequencing

5. Therapeutic change is most likely if the initial focus of change efforts is to build new skills and alter disruptive symptoms.

Differential Treatment Principles

6. Therapeutic change is greatest when the relative balance of interventions either favors the use of skill building and symptom-removal procedures among patients who externalize or favors the use of insight and relationship-focused procedures among patients who internalize.

7. Therapeutic change is greatest when the directiveness of the intervention is either inversely correspondent with the patient's current level of resistance or authoritatively prescribes a continuation of the symptomatic behavior.

8. The likelihood of therapeutic change is greatest when the patient's level of emotional stress is moderate, neither being excessively high nor excessively low.

Treatment Selection provides clinicians tools through which to conceptualize a client, identify what treatment procedures are actually being delivered, and modify the treatment in a step-by-step fashion as their case develops.

Prescriptive Psychotherapy

Prescriptive Therapy (Beutler & Harwood, 2000) is a manualized version of Beutler et al.'s (2000) Systematic Treatment Selection for the special case of individual psychotherapy in the treatment of depression and substance abuse. Whereas the 18 principles of STS are applied broadly to treatment, including psychopharmacological and hospital recommendations, Prescriptive Therapy extracts the 10 principles that are applicable to individual treatment relationships and outlines suggestions for how compliance with the principles might be maintained.

Beutler, Moleiro, Malik, et al. (2003) conducted an independent, randomized clinical trial investigation of Prescriptive Therapy. A group of psychotherapists were selectively trained to use Prescriptive Therapy, cognitive therapy, or a form of narratively based therapy, to treat individuals who had concomitant depression and chemical abuse problems. Although some outcomes favored the prescriptive approach, as expected, the second level of analysis provided the most interesting and supportive findings. This aspect of the study sought to inspect the validity of those principles that defined the fit between classes of intervention and nondiagnostic aspects of the patient. Based on the principles previously defined, we extracted four treatment variables and corresponding patient qualities, the relationship of which were predicted to enhance outcomes beyond that associated with the main effects of treatments and patient qualities.

The results revealed that patient qualities (level of impairment, coping style, resistance levels, and distress) all predicted outcome at a low level. Likewise, the relative frequency of using directive interventions, those focused on symptom change, and those designed to facilitate emotional processing, contributed as a group to both short and long-term outcomes. These relationships were in the direction and of the magnitude predicted. Moreover, the quality of the therapeutic relationship also added some predictive power to the estimates, as would be expected, but of a lesser strength than originally anticipated.

The fit between the patient's personal characteristics and the nature of the interventions used added a substantial and surprising degree of additional and independent predictive power to the equation. Even procedures, like directiveness, that were generally effective, were much less so or not at all so, among certain types of patients (i.e., those who were highly resistant). Even more than what procedures were used, the fit between the procedures selected and the nature of the patient's level of receptivity to these procedures were implicated in long-term outcomes. Thus, the use of principles of change provided a way of balancing various contributors and assessing complex relationships among patient, therapy, relationship, and other factors that relate to change.

A Principle-Based Treatment for Treating Mass Trauma

A third example of the use of a principle-based treatment combines empirically derived principles of change with two empirically supported treatment models. Unlike Prescriptive Therapy, which is an example of the application of the STS model, this newer illustration is an example of an intervention that blends the "Common" and "Unique" principles identified by the Division 12/NASPR Task Force (Castonguay & Beutler, 2006) and empirically supported treatment approaches (Bryant, Harvey, Guthrie, & Moulds, 2000). The treatment, in this case, is being developed as a response to anticipated natural and terrorist-initiated disasters that affect large groups of people, and that may tax the system's ability to respond.

Housley and Beutler (in press) have outlined a three-stage intervention to be initiated in the hours immediately following a mass trauma. Each stage is governed by a designated list of Division 12/NASPR principles, on which are superimposed a set of procedures that have received independent validation. Thus, in the first stage, employed in the first 3–5 days following the crisis, and at a time when it is still not possible to clearly identify who among the victims will require long-term or intensive care, trained lay persons can implement empirically supported procedures of Psychological First Aid. These procedures include helping identified victims connect with social support systems, ensuring that they obtain information about their families and possessions, and helping them obtain suitable shelter and medical assistance.

This initial stage is also one at which information is obtained about those who are likely to be at significant risk for long-term problems. Thus, stage one interventions are guided by Task Force Principles that identify those who will need follow-up. These principles include:

1. Clients with a high level of impairment are less likely to benefit from therapy than those with a better level of functioning at pretreatment.
2. Clients who have been diagnosed with a personality disorder are less likely to benefit from treatment than those who have not.
3. Clients who face financial or occupational difficulties may benefit less from treatment than those who do not.
4. Clients who experienced significant interpersonal problems during their early development may have difficulty responding to psychotherapy.
5. Client's expectations are likely to influence treatment outcome.

Accordingly, lay counselors are trained to obtain information about symptom severity, pre-existing mental health problems, prior exposure to violence and trauma, quality of interpersonal relationships, and loss of hope as well as other negative expectations. Those who have indicators of being at long-term risk are followed in stage two of the intervention.

The second intervention stage is initiated after about 5 days following the signal event and lasts up to 3 months. By the end of this time, symptoms are generally stabilizing and those whose resiliency is low will become apparent.

During this second stage, the empirically derived interventions rely on the healing powers of a therapeutic alliance. The Task Force Principles that guide the interventions at this stage fall within three different domains.

Quality of the Therapeutic Relationship

1. Therapy is likely to be beneficial if a strong working alliance is established and maintained during the course of treatment.
2. Clients are likely to benefit from group therapy if a strong level of group cohesion is developed and maintained during therapy.
3. Therapists should attempt to facilitate a high degree of collaboration with clients during therapy.

Therapist Interpersonal Skills

1. Therapists should relate to their clients in an empathic way.
2. When adopted by therapists, an attitude of caring, warmth, and acceptance is likely to be helpful in facilitating therapeutic change.
3. Therapists are likely to facilitate change when adopting an attitude of congruence or authenticity.

Therapist Clinical Skills

1. Therapists should use relational interpretations quite sparingly.
2. When relational interpretations are used, they are likely to facilitate improvement if they are accurate.
3. Therapists can resolve ruptures to the alliance by addressing such ruptures in an empathic and flexible way.

The emphasis on building and maintaining a therapeutic relationship is supplemented by some specific procedures that are designed to help develop problem-solving skills. These latter interventions are extracted largely from the work of Bryant and his colleagues (e.g., Bryant & Harvey, et al., 2000), and consist of identifying problems and the steps to their resolution, monitoring progress and outcomes, and testing assumptions. At this point, the victims may also be taught relaxation skills to help them manage anxiety and to find social resources that are needed to cope. Insight and exposure methods are avoided at this time in favor of skills with more objective ways of monitoring progress.

Victims who fail to benefit from two or three brief sessions on coping and problem solving are followed into stage three of the intervention. At this stage, explorative psychotherapy begins and victims are offered two alternative sets of interventions—continuing support based on the relationship and alliance-building procedures initiated at stage two, or exposure-based interventions designed to uncover unhelpful thoughts and emotions. Some of the common principles that guide the therapist at this stage relate to the therapists style.

Therapeutic Stance and General Interpersonal Style

1. Positive change is likely if the therapist provides a structured treatment and remains focused in the application of his/her interventions.
2. Therapists should be able to skillfully use nondirective or self-directive as well as directive interventions.

Other principles relate to the way the intervention is framed and positioned within a continuum of intensity.

Framework of Intervention

1. Time-limited therapy can be beneficial.
2. Therapeutic change may be facilitated by, or even require, intense therapy if a personality disorder or severe problem is present.

Still other principles relate to the need to address both interpersonal and intrapersonal environments.

Interpersonal/Systemic versus Intrapersonal/Individual Procedures

1. The therapist may be more effective if he/she does not restrict him/herself to individual procedures: Being with others during treatment can be beneficial for some clients.
2. Effective therapy may require therapists to address intrapersonal aspects of the client's functioning.
3. Therapy outcome is likely to be enhanced if therapy addresses interpersonal issues related to clinical problems.

The degree and balance of taking a symptom focus versus an adaptive focus on skill development are also addressed in the Principles of Change.

Thematic/Insight-Oriented versus Symptom/Skill Building Procedures, as Well as the Use of Emotion-Focused Procedures

1. Therapy is likely to be beneficial if the therapist facilitates change in clients' cognitions.
2. The client is likely to benefit from therapy if therapist helps him/her modify maladaptive behavioral, emotional, or physiological responses.
3. Facilitating client self-exploration can be helpful.

4. Therapeutic change is likely if the therapist helps clients accept, tolerate, and, at times, fully experience their emotions.
5. Interventions aimed at controlling emotions can be helpful.

Finally, many of the governing principles help the therapist to select interventions that are tailored to a particular problem or patient:

1. Patients with high levels of initial impairment respond better when they are offered long-term, intensive treatment, than when they receive non-intensive and brief treatments, regardless of the particular model and type of treatment assigned. Patients with low impairment seem to do equally well in high and low intensive treatments.
2. Patients whose personalities are characterized by impulsivity, social gregariousness, and external blame for problems, benefit more from direct behavioral change and symptom reduction efforts, including building new skills, and managing impulses, than they do from procedures that are designed to facilitate insight and self-awareness.
3. Patients whose personalities are characterized by low levels of impulsivity, indecisiveness, self-inspection, and overcontrol, tend to benefit more from procedures that foster self-understanding, insight, interpersonal attachments, and self-esteem, than they do from procedures that aim at directly altering symptoms and building new social skills.

This third stage of treatment may go on as long as the patient continues to have difficulty adjusting, sleeping, and relating. These are the most impaired victims and those with the most serious disturbances.

CONCLUSION

The goal of the present integrative approach is to provide a general strategy by which an individual clinician, regardless of theoretical orientation, can tailor a treatment plan in order to maximize outcomes for a particular patient. Based upon the identification of Principles of Therapeutic Change That Work (Castonguay & Beutler, 2006) and the principles found in both Systematic Treatment Selection and Prescriptive Psychotherapy, this approach allows for the development of a unified and empirically based treatment. Perhaps more importantly, it fosters the expression of scientific practices and the artistic implementation of current and new procedures. We argue that principles offer clinicians a high degree of flexibility in their practice allowing them, for instance, to chose from a variety of techniques (within or across different orientations) to achieve a particular therapeutic goals. In addition, this integrative approach provides clinicians with established guidelines even when they are working with clinical problem for which a specific manual has not been developed.

Principles provide a structure upon which to base treatment prognosis, develop new and innovative techniques, undertake long-term treatment planning, develop and maintain the therapeutic alliance and employ a wide range of effective interventions. Rather than asking clinicians to rely primarily or exclusively on one set of therapeutic factors, they allow therapists to build an integrated treatment that incorporates techniques, relationship, and participant factors, while using empirically based methods of therapeutic change.

REFERENCES

Bernal, G., & Scharrón-Del-Río, M. R. (2001). Are empirically supported treatments valid for ethnic minorities? Toward an alternative approach for treatment research. *Cultural Diversity and Ethnic Minority Psychology, 7*(4), 328–342.

Beutler, L. E., Alomohamed, S., Moleiro, C., & Romanelli, R. (2002). Systemic treatment selection and prescriptive therapy. In F. W. Kaslow (Eds.), *Comprehensive handbook of psychotherapy: Integrative/eclectic*, vol. 4 (pp. 255–271). Hoboken, NJ: Wiley.

Beutler, L. E., & Clarkin, J. F. (1990). *Systematic treatment selection: Toward targeted therapeutic interventions*. Philadelphia, PA: Brunner/Mazel.

Beutler, L. E., & Harwood, T. M. (2000). *Prescriptive psychotherapy: A practical guide to systematic treatment selection*. New York: Oxford University Press.

Beutler, L. E., & Johannsen, B. E. (2006). Principles of change. In J. C. Norcross, L. E. Beutler, & R. F. Levant (Eds.), *Evidence-based practices in mental health* (pp. 226–234). Washington, DC: American Psychological Association.

Beutler, L. E., Clarkin, J. F., & Bongar, B. (2000). *Guidelines for the systematic treatment of the depressed patient*. New York: Oxford University Press.

Beutler, L. E., Machado, P. P. P., & Neufeld S. A. (1994). Therapist variables. In A. E. Bergin & S. L. Garfield (Eds.), *Handbook of psychotherapy and behavior change* (4th ed., pp. 299–269). Oxford: Wiley.

Beutler, L. E., Moleiro, C., Malik, M., Harwood, T. M., Romanelli, R., Gallagher-Thompson, D., & Thompson, L. (2003). A comparison of the Dodo, EST, and ATI indicators among co-morbid stimulant dependent, depressed patients. *Clinical Psychology & Psychotherapy, 10*, 69–85.

Blatt, S. J., & Zuroff, D. C. (2005). Empirical evaluation of the assumptions in indentifying evidence based treatments in mental health. *Clinical Psychology Review, 25*, 459–486.

Blatt, S. J., Sanislow, C. A., III, Zuroff, D. C., & Pilkonis, P. A. (1996). Characteristics of effective therapists: Further analyses of data from the National Institute of Mental Health Treatment of Depression Collaborative Research Program. *Journal of Consulting and Clinical Psychology, 64*(6), 1276–1284.

Bohart, A. A. (2006). The active client. In J. C. Norcross, L. E. Beutler, & R. F. Levant (Eds.), *Evidence-based practices in mental health* (pp. 218–226). Washington, DC: American Psychological Association.

Bryant, R. A., A. G. Harvey, Guthrie, R. M., & Moulds, M. L. (2000). "A prospective study of psychophysiological arousal, acute stress disorder and posttraumatic stress disorder." *Journal of Abnormal Psychology, 109*(2), 341–344.

Castonguay, L. G., & Beutler, L. E. (2006). *Principles of therapeutic change that work*. New York: Oxford University Press.

Castonguay, L. G., Schut, A. J., Constantino, M. J., & Halperin, G. S. (1999). Assessing the role of treatment manuals: Have they become necessary but non-sufficient ingredients of change? *Clinical Psychology: Science and Practice, 6,* 449–455.

Chambless, D. L., Baker, M. J., Baucom, D. H., Beutler, L. E., Calhoun, K. S., Crits-Christoph, P., et al. (1998). Update on empirically validated therapies, II. *The Clinical Psychologist, 51,* 3–16.

Chambless, D. L., Sanderson, W. C., Shoham, V., Johnson, S. B., Pope, K. S., Crits-Christoph, P., et al. (1996). An update on empirically validated therapies. *The Clinical Psychologist, 49*(2), 5–14.

Chambless, D. L., & Crits-Christoph, P. (2006). The treatment method. In J. C. Norcross, L. E. Beutler, & R. F. Levant (Eds.), *Evidence-based practices in mental health* (pp. 191–200). Washington, DC: American Psychological Association.

Chambless, D. L., & Hollon, S. D. (1998). Defining empirically supported therapies. *Journal of Counseling and Clinical Psychology, 66*(1), 7–18.

Chambless, D. L., & Ollendick, T. H. (2001). Empirically supported psychological interventions: Controversies and evidence. *Annual Review of Psychology, 52*(1), 685–716.

Clarkin, J. F., & Levy, K. N. (2004). The influence of client variables on psychotherapy. In M. J. Lambert (Ed.), *Handbook of psychotherapy and behavior change* (5th ed., pp. 194–226). New York: Wiley.

Crits-Christoph, P., & Mintz, J. (1991). Implications of therapist effects for the design and analysis of comparative studies of psychotherapies. *Journal of Consulting and Clinical Psychology, 59*(1), 20–26.

Eysenck, H. J. (1952). The effects of psychotherapy: An evaluation. *Journal of Counseling Psychology, 16,* 319–324.

Frank, J. D. (1973). *Persuasion and healing: A comparative study of psychotherapy* (rev. ed.). Baltimore: The Johns Hopkins University Press.

Goldfried, M. R. (1980). Toward the delineation of therapeutic change principles. *American Psychologist, 35,* 991–999.

Hofmann, S. G., & Tompson, M. C. (Eds.). (2002). *Treating chronic and severe mental disorders: A handbook of empirically supported interventions*. New York: Guilford Press.

Housley, J., & Beutler, L. E. (in press). *Treating victims of mass trauma and terrorism*. Gottengen: Hogrefe & Huber.

Lambert, M. J. (1992). Psychotherapy outcome research: Implications for integrative and eclectic therapists. In J. C. Norcross & M. R. Goldfried (Eds.), *Handbook of psychotherapy integration* (pp. 94–129). New York: Basic Books.

Lambert, M. J., & Ogles, B. M. (1988). Treatment manuals: Problems and promise. *Journal of Integrative and Eclectic Psychotherapy, 7,* 187–204.

Luborksy, L., Rosenthal, R., Diguer, L., Andrusyna, T. P., Berman, J. S., Levitt, J. T., et al. (2002). The dodo bird verdict is alive and well—mostly. *Clinical Psychology: Science and Practice, 9*(1), 2–12.

Luborsky, L., Singer, B., & Luborsky, L. (1975). Comparative studies of psychotherapies. *Archives of General Psychiatry, 32,* 995–1008.

Nathan, P. E., & Gorman, J. M. (2002). Treatments that work—and what convinces us they do. In Nathan, P. E. & Gorman, J. M. (Eds.), *A guide to treatments that work* (2nd ed., pp. 35–25). New York: Oxford University Press.

Norcross, J. C. (Ed.). (2002). *Psychotherapy relationships that work: Therapist contributions and responsiveness to patient needs.* New York: Oxford University Press.

Norcross, J. C., & Lambert, M. J. (2006). The therapy relationship. In J. C. Norcross, L. E. Beutler, & R. F. Levant (Eds.), *Evidence-based practices in mental health* (pp. 208–218). Washington, DC: American Psychological Association.

Ollendick, T. H., & King, N. J. (2006). Empirically supported treatments typically produce outcomes superior to non-empirically supported treatment therapies. In J. C. Norcross, L. E. Beutler, & R. F. Levant (Eds.), *Evidence-based practices in mental health* (pp. 308–317). Washington, DC: American Psychological Association.

Smith, M. L., Glass, G. V., & Miller, T. I. (1980). *The benefits of psychotherapy.* Baltimore, MD: Johns Hopkins University Press.

Sue, S., & Zane, N. (2006). How well do both evidence-based practices and treatment as usual satisfactorily address the various dimensions of diversity? In J. C. Norcross, L. E. Beutler, & R. F. Levant (Eds.), *Evidence-based practices in mental health* (pp. 329–374). Washington, DC: American Psychological Association.

Task Force on Promotion and Dissemination of Psychological Procedures. (1995). Training in and dissemination of empirically validated psychological treatments: Report and recommendations. *The Clinical Psychologist, 48*(1), 3–23.

Wallerstein, R. S., & DeWitt, K. N. (1997). Intervention modes in psychoanalysis and in psychoanalytic psychotherapies: A revised classification. *Journal of Psychotherapy Integration, 7,* 129–150.

Wampold, B. E. (2001). *The great psychotherapy debate: Models, methods, and findings.* Hillsdale, NJ: Erlbaum.

Wampold, B. E. (2006). Not a scintilla of evidence to support empirically supported treatments as more effective than other treatments. In J. C. Norcross, L. E. Beutler, & R. F. Levant (Eds.), *Evidence-based practices in mental health* (pp. 299–308). Washington, DC: American Psychological Association.

Woody, S. R., & Ollendick, T. H. (2006). Technique factors in treating anxiety disorders. In I. G. Castonguay & L. E. Beutler (Eds.), *Principles of therapeutic change that work* (pp. 167–186). New York: Oxford University Press.

8

Alliance Ruptures
Theory, Research, and Practice

KARYN D. RUIZ-CORDELL AND JEREMY D. SAFRAN

More than half a century of psychotherapy research has yielded compelling evidence implicating the quality of the therapeutic alliance as one of the most robust predictors of overall treatment success (Horvath & Symonds, 1991; Martin, Garke, & Davis, 2000). This is a finding replicated multiples times across treatment modalities. Other findings indicate that poor outcome cases demonstrate greater evidence of negative interpersonal process (e.g., hostile interactions between patient and therapist or deterioration in the quality of the alliance) than good outcome cases (e.g., Coady, 1991; Henry, Schacht, & Strupp, 1986; Samstag, 1999). There is also evidence that therapists who are more helpful are better able to facilitate the development of a therapeutic alliance (e.g., Luborsky, McLellan, Diguer, Woody, & Seligman, 1997). Taken together, these findings suggest that recognizing and attending to negative interpersonal process or ruptures in the therapeutic alliance may play a valuable role in successful treatments.

Impasses or ruptures in the therapeutic alliance may be understood as moments of tension or breakdown in communication between patient and therapist (Safran & Muran, 2000). These moments may fluctuate in strength from seemingly trivial tensions, of which the patient or therapist may only be partially conscious, to significant breakdowns in collaboration and communication that if not resolved may result in premature termination or treatment failure. Alliance ruptures manifest in various ways. Sometimes the existing tension between patient and therapist is obvious and is addressed and resolved quickly. In other cases, a pseudoalliance or alliance based on a false self develops between the patient and therapist. In such cases a complete treatment can occur without the patient being impacted in any real or beneficial manner (Balint, 1958; Winnicott, 1965).

A number of studies have demonstrated that resolving ruptures in the therapeutic alliance can play an important role in treatment process and outcome (e.g., Foreman & Marmer, 1985; Lansford, 1986; Rhodes, Hill, Thompson, & Elliot, 1994; Safran & Muran, 1996; Stiles et al., 2004; see Safran, Muran, Samstag, & Stevens, 2002, for a review). A review of the research identifies three common themes in successful resolution processes: (1) therapist recognition of ruptures at the time of enactment, (2) patient verbalization of their concerns or negative feelings regarding the treatment and the therapist, and (3) the therapist's ability to maintain a nondefensive and empathic stance (Safran et al., 2002). At the same time, the research indicates that it is often difficult for therapists to negotiate alliance ruptures in a successful fashion. The data indicate that even skilled therapists may have difficulty recognizing alliance ruptures when they occur (Hill, Nutt-Williams, Heaton, Thompson, & Rhodes, 1996; Hill, Thompson, Cogar, & Denman, 1993; Regan & Hill, 1992; Rennie, 1994; Rhodes et al., 1994). Moreover, when therapists do become aware of alliance ruptures, they are often unable to address them in an effective fashion. A number of studies have found that therapists commonly increase their adherence in a rigid manner to their treatment model, rather responding flexibly, when addressing problems in the alliance (Castonguay, Goldfried, Wiser, Raue, & Hayes, 1996; Piper, Azim, Joyce, & McCullum, 1991; Piper et al., 1999). The Vanderbilt II Study (Henry, Strupp, Butler, Schacht, & Binder, 1993) demonstrated that experienced therapists who participated in a training program designed to help them manage negative interpersonal process became technically adherent, but actually displayed an increase in negative interpersonal process (e.g., hostile or incongruent communications). Thus it seems critical to further refine our understanding of how to help therapists negotiate alliance ruptures in a constructive fashion.

RUPTURE RESOLUTION AND THE THERAPEUTIC ALLIANCE

The concept of the alliance has an extensive history, beginning with Freud's early statements about the importance of making a "collaborator" of the patient (Breuer & Freud, 1893–1895) and followed by his introduction of the "unobjectionable positive transference," or that aspect of the transference that should not be analyzed because it provides the patient with the motivation to continue in the treatment (Freud, 1921). This conceptualization was later followed by formulations of the alliance advanced by a number of theorists including Richard Sterba (1934), Elizabeth Zetzel (1956), Lawrence Friedman (1969), and Ralph Greenson (1967). Current conceptualizations of the alliance, while differing in various respects, all converge on the notion that the therapeutic alliance involves the capacity of the patient and therapist to work collaboratively in treatment.

As Wolfe and Goldfried (1988) maintain, the therapeutic alliance is the "quintessential integrative variable." Recognition by diverse therapeutic traditions of the importance of the therapeutic alliance can be attributed, at least in part, to its centrality in the psychotherapy research community (e.g., Hovarth & Greenberg, 1994; Horvath & Luborsky, 1993), where there has been a proliferation of measures and evidence demonstrating the predictive validity of the concept spanning nearly 20 years (Gaston, 1990; Hartley, 1985; Horvath & Symonds, 1991). Interest in this concept among researchers can be partially attributed to the search for understanding common mechanisms of change, given that no particular treatment has been shown to be consistently more effective than others (Smith, Glass, & Miller, 1980). It was also catalyzed by the early empirical work of Lester Luborsky (1976), demonstrating the predictive validity of the alliance. Another important influence was Edward Bordin (1979), who attracted considerable attention within the psychotherapy research community with his transtheoretical reformulation of the alliance concept. Bordin suggested that a good alliance is a prerequisite for change in all forms of psychotherapy. He conceptualized the alliance as consisting of three interdependent components: *tasks*, *goals*, and the *bond*. According to him, the strength of the alliance is dependent on the degree of agreement between the patient and therapist about the tasks and goals of therapy, and on the quality of the relational bond between them.

The *tasks of therapy* consist of the specific activities (either explicit or implicit) that the patient must engage in to benefit from the treatment. For example, classical psychoanalysis requires the patient to try to free-associate by attempting to say whatever comes to mind without censoring it. An important task in cognitive therapy may consist of completing a behavioral assignment between sessions. Gestalt therapists may ask their patients to engage in a dialogue between two different parts of the self.

The *goals of therapy* are the general objectives toward which the treatment is directed. For example, ego psychologists assume that the problems people bring into therapy result from a maladaptive way of negotiating conflict between instincts and defenses, and that the goals concern developing a more adaptive way of negotiating that conflict. A behavior therapist, in contrast, may see the goal of treatment as one of removing a specific behavior or symptom.

The *bond* component of the alliance consists of the affective quality of the relationship between patient and therapist (e.g., the extent to which the patient feels understood, respected, valued, and so on). Goal, task, and bond dimensions of the alliance influence one another in an ongoing fashion. For example, if therapist and patient agree about the therapeutic tasks and goals from the outset, it will have a positive influence on the bond dimension of the alliance. On the other hand, when there is an initial disagreement about the goals of therapy, the presence of an adequate bond will assist the therapist and patient in negotiating an agreement.

Different therapeutic tasks place different demands on patients and will tend to be experienced by them as more or less helpful depending on their own capacities and characteristic ways of relating to themselves and others. One patient may experience a structured cognitive-behavioral task as reassuring and containing. Another may experience it as domineering and controlling. One may experience the task of free associating as liberating. Another may experience it as a form of pressure.

While the quality of the alliance is critical in all therapeutic approaches, the specific variables mediating this quality will vary as a function of a complex, interdependent, and fluctuating matrix of therapist, patient, and approach-specific features. Bordin's formulation thus highlights the complex and multidimensional nature of the alliance. This conceptualization of the alliance has a number of important implications. First, this formulation highlights the interdependence of technical and relational factors in treatment (Safran, 1993b). Although it may be possible to distinguish between technical and relational factors conceptually, in reality they are indivisible. Second, rather than basing one's therapeutic approach on some inflexible and idealized criterion such as therapeutic neutrality, one can be guided by an understanding of what a particular therapeutic task means to a particular patient in a given moment. Third, as Stolorow and colleagues (Stolorow, Brandchaft, & Atwood, 1994) have highlighted, ruptures in the therapeutic alliance are the royal road to understanding the patient's core organizing principles.

Building upon Bordin's (1979) model of the alliance, we conceptualize the alliance as a process of *negotiation* between patient and therapist about the tasks and goals of therapy (Safran & Muran, 2000). In this conceptualization, the alliance is viewed as a bi-directional emergent aspect of the relationship, rather than as a static quality. More traditional conceptualizations of the alliance assume that there is only one therapeutic task (i.e., rational collaboration with the therapist on the task of self-observation), or at least privilege this task over others. Although Sterba, Zetzel, and Greenson emphasized the importance of the therapist acting in a supportive fashion in order to facilitate the development of the alliance, ultimately they assume that the patient will identify with the therapist and adapt to the therapist's conceptualization of the tasks and goals of therapy or accept the therapist's understanding of the value of the tasks and goals. In contrast, Safran and Muran's (2000) conceptualization of the alliance assumes that there will be an ongoing negotiation between therapist and patient at both conscious and unconscious levels about the tasks and goals of therapy and that this process of negotiation both establishes the necessary conditions for change to take place and is an intrinsic part of the change process.

This conceptualization is consistent with an increasingly influential way of conceptualizing therapeutic process in relational psychoanalytic thinking. Jessica Benjamin (1990), for example, argues that the process of negotiation between two different subjectivities is at the heart of the change process. Mitchell (1993) emphasizes that the negotiation between the patient's desires and those of the therapist is a critical therapeutic mechanism. Pizer (1992) also describes the essence of therapeutic action as constituted by the engagement of two persons in a process of negotiation. This line of thought deepens our understanding of the significance of negotiation between therapists and patients about therapeutic tasks and goals. It suggests that this process is not purely about negotiation toward consensus. At a deeper level, it taps into fundamental dilemmas of human existence, such as negotiation of one's desires with those of another, the struggle to experience oneself as a subject while at the same time recognizing the subjectivity of the other (Safran, 1993a), and the tension between the need for agency versus the need for relatedness (Safran & Muran, 2000).

Therapeutic alliance ruptures highlight the tensions that are inherent in negotiating relationships with others and bring into relief the inevitable barriers to authentic relatedness. They highlight for patients their separateness and lack of omnipotence (Safran, 1993a; 1999). Expressing one's disappointment to a therapist who accepts this criticism and survives is an important part of the process of developing a sense of agency. Learning to will or to express one's will, however, is only half the battle. The other half consists of coming to accept that the world and the people in it exist independent of one's will, that the events of the world run according to their own plan, and that other people have wills of their own (Safran, 1999). As Winnicott (1965) pointed out, an important part of the maturational process consists of seeing that the other is not destroyed by one's aggression, since this establishes the other as having a real, independent existence as a subject, rather than as an object. Although this type of disillusionment is a difficult and painful part of the maturational process, it ultimately helps to establish the other as capable of confirming oneself as real (Safran, 1993a, 1999). In this way, the groundwork is laid for relationships in which reciprocal confirmation can take place.

Coming to accept both self and other are thus mutually dependent processes that can be facilitated by working through ruptures in the therapeutic alliance. For the patient, establishing the therapeutic relationship requires negotiation at both the interpersonal and intrapsychic level, necessitating constant negotiation that balances the patient's requirements for agency with their needs for relatedness. The therapist, by empathizing with the patient's experience and reaction to the rupture, demonstrates that potentially divisive feelings (e.g., anger, disappointment) are acceptable and that experiencing nurturance and relatedness are not contingent on disowning part of oneself. He or she demonstrates that relatedness is possible in the very face of separateness and that nurturance is possible even though it can never completely fill that void that is part of the human condition. If the therapist is *good enough*, the patient will gradually come to accept the therapist with all of his or her imperfections. The exploration and working through of alliance ruptures thus paradoxically entails an exploration and affirmation of both the separateness and togetherness of self and other (Safran, 1993a).

→ RUPTURE RESOLUTION: PROCESS AND RESEARCH

Our research program on alliance ruptures began in the late 1980s (e.g., Safran, Crocker, McMain, & Murray, 1990). During that period, the concept of the therapeutic alliance was emerging as an important focus for psychotherapy researchers, and evidence regarding the predictive validity of the therapeutic alliance in various forms of treatment was emerging (Gaston, 1990; Hartley, 1985; Horvath

& Symonds, 1991). Our research program has focused on investigating how strained or ruptured alliances can be re-established or repaired.

We have identified two major forms of ruptures: *withdrawal* and *confrontation* ruptures (Safran & Muran, 2000). In a *withdrawal* rupture the patient responds to tension in the therapeutic relationship by disconnecting or withdrawing from the therapist, or from some aspect of his or her experience. Various processes are employed by the patient including: denial, minimal responsiveness, random alternating of presented topics, and intellectualization. For example, a patient may deny feeling anger that he or she expressed indirectly toward the therapist. Or a patient may comply or defer to the therapist.

In a *confrontation* rupture, anger is expressed in a blaming, aggressive, or entitled fashion. This anger is directed at the therapist, the therapeutic process, or a blend of both. For example, the patient may complain about the therapist as a person, criticizing his or her interested manner as meddlesome, or the patient may find the therapist's comments of no use and question the therapist's ability. Patients who present primarily with withdrawal ruptures tend to favor the needs for relatedness over the needs for agency. Patients who present primarily with confrontation ruptures often have difficulty expressing their needs for relatedness. The resolution of an alliance rupture thus not only facilitates the implementation of a particular therapeutic task, it also provides an opportunity for patients to learn to constructively negotiate their needs for both agency and relatedness.

Over the years we have used the task analysis research paradigm (Greenberg, 1986; Rice & Greenberg, 1984), to develop and refine a stage-process model explicating the rupture resolution process (Safran et al., 1990; Safran & Muran, 1996; Safran, Muran & Samstag, 1994). Task analysis involves a combination of intensive analysis of single cases, and hypothesis testing studies that use group comparison designs. The model that has emerged is comprised of four stages: (1) *Attending to the Rupture Marker*, (2) *Exploring the Rupture Experience*, (3) *Exploring the Avoidance*, and (4) the *Emergence of the Wish/Need*. Although resolution begins with the process of *Attending to the Rupture Marker*, and usually ends with the *Emergence of the Wish/Need*, repetition and cycling between the states in an ongoing fashion typically occurs throughout.

When *Attending to the Rupture Marker*, the first stage in the resolution process, the therapist becomes aware of and draws the patient's attention to an interactional cycle that is taking place between them. At this point, both therapist and patient are embedded in the relational configuration, and the therapist may possess only limited recognition of the nature of his or her own contribution to the impasse. Therapists begin by drawing the patient's attention to the rupture and initiating a collaborative exploration of both partner's contribution to the impasse. Through reflecting and explicitly owning his or her own contribution, the therapist is able to initiate the disembedding process and begin the movement toward the resolution. At this point, the use of *metacommunication* is often helpful. Metacommunication is an attempt to bring ongoing awareness to bear on the interactive process as it unfolds. It facilitates the process of stepping outside of the relational cycle being enacted by treating it as the focus of collaborative explo- ration and communicating about the transaction or implicit communication that is taking place. For example, a therapist who finds his or her attention wandering could metacommunicate by explicitly disclosing this experience to the patient and then inquiring about the patient's experience. For example, the therapist may remark: "I'm aware of losing my ability to focus on what you're saying as you speak. It's not clear to me as to why, yet I'm wondering if it's connected at all to a distance that I hear in your voice, a disconnectedness. Any sense of what's going on for you right now?" In reaction to this intervention, the patient is able to recognize this withdrawal as directly connected to feeling wounded by some- thing the therapist said previously. Metacommunication may also be useful in the context of a confrontation rupture. In this context, the therapist might remark: "I feel very uncomfortable saying anything to you, because I feel criticized when I attempt address your questions and concerns." A comment such as this provides the patient with feedback that might, for example, ultimately help him or her to explore dissociated feelings of anger toward the therapist.

The second stage, *Exploring the Rupture Experience*, develops as the patient begins the process of self-exploration and the expression of feelings associated with the alliance rupture. The therapist's task at this point is to assist the patient in unpacking his or her experience of the interaction through working to illumi- nate the subtle nuances of the patient's construal, and to help the patient begin to articulate that which is not yet fully explicit. For example, in a withdrawal rupture, patients typically begin to become aware of and express negative feelings in a qualified or indirect manner; whereas in a confrontation rupture, the patient's mode of expression will be primarily critical or accusatory in nature. Thus, in the case of a withdrawal rupture, the therapist may ask the patient to explore the direct articulation of any unacceptable feelings that the therapist believes may have been pushed away or rejected, a task then followed by asking the patient to be present for any feelings that may have emerged during the exercise. Importantly, when exploring confrontation ruptures, it is essential that patients experience any feelings of anger, pain, or rapprochement that present as real, allowable, and endurable, even prior to the process of exploring existing longings that are more vulnerable in nature. The acknowledgement of these existing underlying needs must surface in an organic manner from the therapeutic relationship through the negotiation and working through of the particular hostile interaction. This process is facilitated through empathic holding on the part of the therapist.

In the third stage, *Exploring the Avoidance*, the therapist and patient explore the defensive mechanisms blocking the acceptance and articulation of feelings about the therapist or underlying wishes that are being avoided. The avoidance is indicated by the patient engaging in defensive strategies such as switching topics, monotone speech, and presenting overly general topics rather than remaining in the here-and-now. These mechanisms function to avoid or manage the emotions associated with the rupture experience. There is often an alternation between *Exploring the Avoidance* and *Exploring the Rupture Experience*. *Exploring the*

Avoidance acts to free up and facilitate further *Exploration of the Experience* when it becomes blocked and *Exploring the Experience* creates an increased anxiety state and defensive process, thus requiring more extensive *Exploring of the Avoidance*. There are two common defensive processes in this context. The first consists of expectations, hopes, and fears the patient has regarding the therapist's potential reaction to his or her feelings or underlying needs. The second common defensive process in this context is the patient's internalized criticism of his or her own needs or wishes. These introjected criticisms impede the exploration of feelings the patient has about the therapeutic impasse. Overall, it is helpful for the therapist to assist the patient in distinguishing and exploring these various emotion states in context. Therapists can help to refocus the patient's awareness to the ways in which she or he moves to a self-critical stance when self-assertive feelings are triggered and thus facilitate an understanding of this experience as a conflict between two variant aspects of the self. The therapist can then ask the patient to begin a dialogue between these conflicting parts of the self, explicitly articulating and alternating between the self that desires to directly assert and the part that criticizes that wish (Safran & Muran, 2000). This process enables the patient to develop an experientially grounded appreciation of the way in which feelings associated with the rupture are blocked by intrapsychic conflict.

In the fourth state, the *Emergence of the Wish/Need*, the patient articulates wishes or needs that develop in the context of the therapeutic relationship and that are blocked by defensive processes. In withdrawal ruptures, this typically takes place in the form of self-assertion and often involves the overt expression of negative feelings (e.g., expressed resentment toward the therapist due to perceived failings). In confrontation ruptures, the expression of the underlying wish or need is typically linked to an experience of vulnerability (e.g., the desire for support or nurturance from the therapist).

Once the patient has begun to accept and then express an underlying wish, it is important for the therapist to respond in an empathic and nonjudgmental way. This kind of response plays an important role in challenging the expectations (both conscious and unconscious) that have made it difficult for the patient to self-assert or express a wish in the first place. A common pattern is for patients to initially assert themselves in a manner that is structured by their characteristic relational schema—for example, a patient whose father was tyrannical and critical, asks the therapist to be more confrontative. When the patient asserts in this manner, the therapist should try to empathize with the patient's desire, rather than to immediately interpret it as a reflection of an old relational schema. The latter response risks discouraging patients from asserting themselves more and can lead to them to further submerge their underlying wishes. In contrast, when therapists empathize with their patient's desires, it helps them to assert themselves in a fashion that is less likely to be structured by their old schema. Thus, the patient in the above example may ultimately be able to ask the therapist to be more supportive.

The therapist's capacity to genuinely empathize with the patient's pain and despair can represent an important new experience—one that helps the patient begin to emerge from his or her feelings of isolation and alienation, and to develop more self-compassion. By responding to the patient's despair in a compassionate and understanding fashion, the therapist provides the patient with the experience of being cared for and connected to another in his or her pain.

RUPTURE RESOLUTION AND PRACTICE: METACOMMUNICATION

An important part of the therapist's task when utilizing this kind of exploration with the patient is to discover and reflect on his or her own feelings and use them as a point of departure for collaborative exploration. Different forms of exploration and discovery are possible. The therapist may give the patient feedback regarding the ways in which he or she impacts others. For example: "I feel cautious with you … as if I'm walking on eggshells." Or, "I feel like it's difficult to really make contact with you. On the one hand, the things you're talking about really seem important. But on the other, there's a level at which it is difficult for me to really feel you." Or, "I feel judged by you." Comments such as these provide an opening for the exploration of the patient's dissociated actions and self-states. For example, the therapist can add, "Does this feedback make any sense to you? Do you have any awareness of judging me?" It is often useful for therapists to pinpoint specific instances of patients' eliciting actions. For example, "I feel dismissed or shut out by you, and I think it's connected to your tendency not to pause and reflect in a way that suggests that you are actually considering what I'm saying."

Below are described a number of general principles underlying the skillful use of therapeutic metacommunication:

1. Explore with skillful tentativeness and emphasize one's own subjectivity.
   Therapists should communicate observations in a tentative and exploratory manner. The message at both explicit and implicit levels should be one of inviting patients to participate in a collaborative effort to understand what is taking place, rather than one of conveying information with objective status. It is also essential to highlight the subjectivity of one's perceptions since this encourages patients to use the therapist's observations as a stimulus for self-exploration rather than to react to them either as authoritative statements in a positive or negative fashion.
2. Do not assume a parallel with other relationships.
   Therapists should be wary of prematurely attempting to establish a link between the interpersonal cycle that is being enacted in the therapeutic relationship and other relationships in the patient's life. Attempts to draw parallels of this type (while useful in some contexts) can be experienced by patients as blaming (especially in the context of an alliance rupture) and may serve a defensive function for therapists. Instead the focus should be one exploring patient's internal experience and actions in a nuanced fashion, as they present in the here-and-now.

3. Ground all formulations in awareness of one's own feelings and accept responsibility for one's own contributions.

All observations and formulation should be grounded in the therapist's feelings. Failure to do so increases the risk of distorted understanding that is influenced by unconscious factors. It is crucial to accept responsibility for one's own contributions to the interaction. We are always unwittingly contributing to the interaction and a central aspect to this undertaking consists of exploring the nature of this contribution in an ongoing fashion. In some situations, the process of explicitly accepting responsibility for one's contributions to patients can be a particularly potent intervention. First, this process can help patients become aware of unconscious or semiconscious feelings that they have difficulty articulating. For example, conceding that one has been critical enables patients to articulate their feelings of hurt and resentment. Second, by validating the patient's perceptions of the therapist's actions, the therapist can reduce his or her need for defensiveness.

4. Start where you are.

Collaborative exploration of the therapeutic relationship should integrate feelings, intuitions, and observations that are emerging for the therapist in the moment. What was true one session may not be true the next and what was true one moment may change the next. Two therapists will react differently to the same patient, and each therapist must begin by making use of his or her own unique experience. For example, although a third observer may be able to adopt an empathic response toward an aggressive patient, therapists cannot conceptually manipulate themselves into an empathic response they do not feel. They must begin by fully accepting and working with their own feelings and subjective reactions.

5. Focus on the concrete and specific and the here-and-now of the therapeutic relationship.

Whenever possible, questions, observations, and comments should focus on concrete instances in the here and now rather than generalizations. This promotes experiential awareness rather than abstract, intellectualized speculation.

6. Collaborative exploration of the therapeutic relationship and disembedding take place at the same time.

It is not necessary for therapists to have a clear formulation prior to metacommunicating. In fact, the process of thinking out loud about the interaction often helps the therapist to unhook from the cycle that is being enacted by putting into words the subtle perceptions that might otherwise remain implicit. Moreover, the process of telling patients about an aspect of one's experience that one is in conflict over, can free the therapist up to see the situation more clearly.

7. Remember that attempts to explore what is taking place in the therapeutic relationship can function as new versions of an ongoing unconscious interpersonal cycle.

For example, the therapist articulates a growing intuition that the patient is withdrawing and says: "It feels to me like I'm trying to pull teeth." In response, the patient withdraws further and an intensification of the interpersonal cycle ensues in which the therapist escalates his attempts to break through and the patient becomes more defended. It is critical to track the quality of patients' responsiveness to all interventions and to explore their experience of interventions that have not been facilitative. Does the intervention deepen the patient's self-exploration or lead to defensiveness or compliance? The process of exploring the ways in which patients experience interventions that are not facilitative helps to refine the understanding of the unconscious interpersonal cycle that is taking place.

RUPTURE RESOLUTION AND THERAPIST INTERNAL PROCESSES

In recent years we have become increasingly interested in investigating the type of internal processes that help therapists to negotiate alliance ruptures (Safran, 2003). Since therapeutic impasses often evoke difficult, painful, and conflictual feelings in therapists, it is important for them to develop the capacity to reflect on these feelings (e.g., rage, impotence, self-loathing, and despair) without defining themselves by these reactions and without dissociating them. This involves engaging in a process of "letting go" and yielding to one's experience, while simultaneously holding and reflecting on it in a nonjudgmental manner. In fact, one important function of metacommunication is to facilitate the development of this state of mind, through articulating feelings, which seem unacceptable or unsayable (Safran, 2003; Safran & Muran, 2000).

This state of mind can be cultivated through the use of mindfulness training. Mindfulness involves the ongoing observation of experience as it emerges in the here-and-now. It is comprised of three essential elements or skills: (1) the direction of attention, (2) remembering or reconstructing, and (3) nonjudgmental awareness (Safran & Muran, 2000). An important byproduct of mindfulness practice is the discovery of internal space (Safran & Muran, 2000). This consists of the loosening of attachments to one's cognitive-affective processes, with the objective of viewing them as constructions of the mind. This, in turn, reduces the experience of constriction resulting from an over-identification with these processes, and allows one to reflect on them and to use them therapeutically. Mindfulness involves radical self-acceptance of thoughts, feelings, and behaviors. It is vital in this practice that therapists work to develop true acceptance through awareness of the subtle and not so subtle aspects of what they deem unacceptable in their attitudes and actions. True compassion develops through struggling and finally accepting one's own pain, limitations, failures, and internal conflicts (Safran, 1999). Of course, personal therapy can contribute to the development of this type of self-acceptance, but mindfulness practice constitutes a valuable additional tool. During moments of conflict, it is only through radical acceptance of their own disavowed and undesirable feelings that therapists can begin to become more accepting of their patients. Just as patients cannot change by forcing themselves to be one way rather than another, therapists cannot will themselves into a more empathic stance. Self-acceptance plays a critical role in allowing therapists to free themselves up to recognize their own contributions to the impasse and to see new possibilities for resolving it.

BRIEF RELATIONAL PSYCHOTHERAPY (BRT)

Drawing upon the concepts and research described above, we have developed and manualized a treatment approach specifically designed to be used for the purposes of negotiating or resolving ruptures in the therapeutic alliance (Safran, 2002; Safran & Muran, 2000). The approach is referred to as Brief Relational Therapy (BRT). At the level of overall outcome, we have conducted research evaluating the efficacy this treatment approach that has been influenced by our process research as well as current developments in contemporary psychoanalysis (e.g., relational theory). BRT is a manualized treatment designed to be conducted in a time limited manner (although it can be administered as a long-term treatment as well). The approach is based both upon findings emerging from our own research program and principles from relational psychoanalysis. We have found that adherence to the principles of BRT can be reliably assessed and that therapists conducting BRT can be distinguished from therapists administering either short-term cognitive therapy or short-term dynamic therapy of a more traditional nature (Muran, Safran, Samstag, & Winston, 2005; Safran, Muran, Samstag, & Winston, 2005).

The central principles of BRT are as follows: (1) it assumes a two-person psychology (i.e., it assumes that both the patient and therapist contribute to the interpersonal cycle that is being enacted; (2) there is an intensive focus on the here-and-now of the therapeutic relationship; (3) there is an ongoing collaborative exploration of the patients' as well as the therapists' contributions to the interaction; (4) it emphasizes in-depth exploration of the nuances of patients' experience in the context of unfolding therapeutic enactments and is cautious about making transference interpretations that speculate about generalized relational patterns; (5) it makes intensive use of countertransference disclosure; (6) it emphasizes the subjectivity of the therapist's perceptions; and (7) It assumes that the relational meaning of interventions is critical (Safran, 2002).

Training in BRT and rupture resolution includes an important emphasis on experiential learning and self-exploration. Therapists are trained to attend to and explore their own feelings as important sources of information about what is going on in the therapeutic relationship. We often use role-playing exercises in order to provide therapists with the opportunity to simulate working with difficult patients and experimenting with metacommunication. The purpose of these exercises is not just to provide them with the opportunity to practice technical skills, but also to develop the skill of exploring their own feelings and internal conflicts as they emerge during alliance ruptures. These are referred to as "awareness-oriented role plays" (Safran & Muran, 2000). Supervision employs mindfulness training for the purposes of helping therapists refine their capacity to observe their own inner experience as well as the nature of their own contributions to alliance ruptures. Through this training, therapists learn to refine their capacity to investigate their own experience and observe their own actions in a nonjudgmental fashion. In fact, we conceptualize metacommunication as a type of "mindfulness in action" (Safran & Muran, 2000).

We have evaluated the efficacy of BRT relative to two more traditional models of short-term treatment: short-term dynamic psychotherapy (STDP) and short-term cognitive-behavior therapy (CBT) (Muran, Safran, Samstag, & Winston, 2005). Although the three treatments were found to be equally effective, there were fewer dropouts in the BRT condition than in the other treatment conditions. A related small sample pilot study was conducted to explicitly assess the effectiveness of BRT as a treatment strategy for treating patients with whom it is difficult to establish a therapeutic alliance. Patients receiving STDP and CBT were monitored over the first few sessions of treatment, and poor alliance patient/therapist dyads were identified using a set of empirically established criteria. These patients were offered the option of transferring to another therapist in another treatment condition. Those who accepted were randomly assigned to either to BRT or to a control condition depending on the type of treatment in which they began (CBT for those patients beginning in STDP and STDP for those patients beginning in CBT). The results indicated that patients who had been transferred to BRT showed more improvement than patients in the other two treatments (Safran, Muran, Samstag and Winston, 2005). Taken together, these findings suggest that BRT may have some advantage over the other two treatments in addressing strained alliances.

CONCLUSION

Although our research program began a number of years ago, in many ways it is still in its early stages. An overarching principle guiding us has been an attempt to achieve a meaningful integration between the art and science of psychotherapy. We attempt to respect and acknowledge the complexity of the therapeutic process while at the same time identifying generalizable principles of change and testing them where possible. This is daunting challenge, and sometimes gains in knowledge can be slow. Nevertheless we remain convinced of the importance of pursuing this type of integration.

REFERENCES

Balint, M. (1958). *The basic fault.* London: Tavistock.

Benjamin, J. (1990). An outline of intersubjectivity: The development of recognition. *Psychoanalytic Psychology, 7,* 33–46.

Bordin, E. (1979). The generalizability of the psychoanalytic concept of the working alliance. *Psychotherapy: Theory, Research, and Practice, 16,* 252–260.

Breuer, J., & Freud, S. (1893–1895/1955). Studies on hysteria. In J. Strachey (ed. and trans.), *The standard edition of the complete psychological works of Sigmund Freud* (Vol. 2, pp. 1–31). London: Hogarth Press.

Castonguay, L. G., Goldfried, M. R., Wiser, S., Raue, P. J., & Hayes, A. M. (1996). Predicting the effect of cognitive therapy for depression: A study of unique and common factors. *Journal of Consulting & Clinical Psychology, 64,* 497–504.

Coady, N. (1991). The association between client in therapist interpersonal processes and outcome on psychodynamic psychotherapy. *Research on Social Work Process, 1,* 122–138.

Foreman, F. A., & Marmer, C. R. (1985). Therapist actions that address initially poor therapeutic alliances in psychotherapy. *American Journal of Psychiatry, 142,* 922–926.

Freud, S. (1921). *The dynamics of transference.* Standard Edition, 12:97–108. London: Hogarth Press

Friedman, L. (1969). The therapeutic alliance. *International Journal of Psycho-Analysis, 50,* 139–153.

Gaston, L. (1990). The concept of the alliance and its role in psychotherapy: Theoretical and empirical considerations. *Psychotherapy: Theory, Research, and Practice, 27,* 143–153.

Greenberg, J. (1986). Theoretical models and the analyst's neutrality. *Contemporary Psychoanalysis, 22,* 87–106.

Greenson, R. (1967). *The technique and practice of psychoanalysis.* New York: International University Press.

Hartley, D. E. (1985). Research on the therapeutic alliance in psychotherapy. In R. Hales & A. Frances (Eds.), *Psychiatry update* (pp. 532–549). Washington, DC: American Psychiatric Association Press.

Henry, W. P., Schacht, T. E., & Strupp, H. H. (1986). Structural analysis of social behavior: Application to a study of interpersonal process in differential psychotherapeutic outcome. *Journal of Consulting & Clinical Psychology, 54,* 27–31.

Henry, W. P., Strupp, H. H., Butler, S. F., Schacht, T. E., & Binder, J. L. (1993). Effects of training in time-limited psychotherapy: Changes in therapist behavior. *Journal of Counseling & Clinical Psychology, 61,* 434–440.

Hill, C. E., Nutt-Williams, E., Heaton, K. J., Thompson, B. J., & Rhodes, R.H. (1996). Therapist retrospective recall of impasses in long-term psychotherapy: A qualitative analysis. *Journal of Counseling Psychology, 43,* 207–217.

Hill, C. E., Thompson, B. J., Cogar, M. C., & Denman, D. W. (1993). Beneath the surface of long-term therapy: Therapist and client report of their own on each other's covert processes. *Journal of Counseling Psychology, 40,* 278–287.

Horvath, A. O., & Symonds B. D. (1991). Relation between working alliance and outcome in psychotherapy: A meta-analysis. *Journal of Counseling Psychology, 38,* 139–149.

Hovarth, A. O., & Greenberg, L. S. (Eds.). (1994). *The working alliance: Theory, research, and practice.* New York: Wiley.

Hovarth, A. O., & Luborsky, L. (1993). The role of therapeutic alliance in psychotherapy. *Journal of Consulting and Clinical Psychology, 61,* 561–573.

Lansford, E. (1986). Weakenings and repairs of the working alliance in short-term psychotherapy. *Professional Psychology: Research & Practice, 17,* 364–366.

Luborsky, L. (1976). Helping alliances in psychotherapy. In J. L. Claghorn (Ed.), *Successful psychotherapy* (pp. 92–116). New York: Brunner/Mazel.

Luborsky, L., McLellan, A. T., Diguer, L., Woody, G., & Seligman, D. A. (1997). The psychotherapist matters: Comparison of outcomes across twenty-two therapists and seven patient samples. *Clinical Psychology Science & Practice, 4,* 53–65.

Martin, D. J., Garke, J. P., & Davis, M. K. (2000). Relation of the therapeutic alliance with outcome and other variables: A meta-analytic review. *Journal of Consulting and Clinical Psychology, 68,* 438–450.

Mitchell, S. A. (1993). *Hope and dread in psychoanalysis.* New York: Basic Books.

Muran, J. C., Safran, J. D., Samstag, L., & Winston, A. (2005). Evaluating an alliance-focused intervention for personality disorders. *Psychotherapy, 42,* 532–545.

Piper, W. E., Azim, H., Joyce, A. S., & McCullum, M. (1991). Transference interpretations, therapeutic alliance, and outcome in short term individual psychotherapy. *Archives of General Psychiatry, 48,* 946–953.

Piper, W. E., Ogrodniczuk, J. S., Joyce, A. S., McCullum, M., Rosie, J. S., O'Kelly, J. G., & Steinberg, P. I. (1999). Predicting of dropping out in time-limited, interpretive individual psychotherapy. *Psychotherapy, 36,* 114–122.

Pizer, S. A. (1992). The negotiation of paradox in the analytic process. *Psychoanalytic Dialogues, 2,* 215–240.

Regan, A. M., & Hill, C. E. (1992). Investigation of what clients and counselors do not say in brief therapy. *Journal of Counseling Psychology, 39,* 168–174.

Rennie, D. L. (1994). Clients' deference in psychotherapy. *Journal of Counseling Psychology, 41,* 427–437.

Rhodes, R. H., Hill, C. E., Thompson, B. J., & Elliot, R. (1994). Client retrospective recall of resolved and unresolved misunderstanding events. *Journal of Counseling Psychology, 41,* 473–483.

Rice, L. N., & Greenberg, L. S. (1984). *Patterns of change: Intensive analysis of psychotherapy process.* New York: Guilford.

Safran, J. D. (1993a). Breaches in the therapeutic alliance: An area for negotiating authentic relatedness. *Psychotherapy: Theory, Research, and Practice, 30,* 11–24.

Safran, J. D. (1993b). The therapeutic alliance as a transtheoretical phenomenon: Definitional and conceptual issues. *Journal of Psychotherapy Integration, 3,* 33–49.

Safran, J. D. (1999). Faith, will and despair in psychoanalysis. *Contemporary Psychoanalysis, 35,* 5–23.

Safran, J. D. (2002). Brief relational psychoanalytic treatment. *Psychoanalytic Dialogues, 12,* 171–195.

Safran, J. D. (2003). The relational turn, the therapeutic alliance, and psychotherapy research: Strange bedfellows or postmodern marriage? *Contemporary Psychoanalysis, 39,* 449–473.

Safran, J. D., Crocker, P., McMain, S., & Murray, P. (1990). Therapeutic alliance rupture as a therapy event for empirical investigation. *Psychotherapy, 27,* 154–165.

Safran, J. D., & Muran, J. C. (1996). The resolution of ruptures in the therapeutic alliance. *Journal of Consulting & Clinical Psychology, 64,* 447–458.

Safran, J. D., & Muran, J. C. (2000). *Negotiating the therapeutic alliance: A relational treatment guide*. New York: Guilford.

Safran, J. D., Muran, J. C., & Samstag, L. W. (1994). Resolving therapeutic alliance ruptures: A task analytic investigation. In A. O. Horvarth & L. S. Greenberg (Eds.), *The working alliance: Theory, research, and practice* (pp. 225–255). New York: Wiley.

Safran, J. D., Muran, J. C., Samstag, L. W., & Stevens, C. (2002). Repairing alliance ruptures. In J. C. Norcross (Ed.), *Psychotherapy relationships that work: Therapist contributions and responsiveness to patients* (pp. 235–254). New York: Oxford University Press.

Safran, J. D., Muran, J. C., Samstag, L., & Winston, A. (2005). Evaluating an alliance focused treatment for potential treatment failures. *Psychotherapy, 42*, 512–531.

Samstag, L. W. (1999). Difficult dyads and unsuccessful treatments: A comparison of dropout, poor, and good outcome groups in brief psychotherapy. *Dissertation Abstracts International, 59*, 5109.

Smith, M. L., Glass, G. V., & Miller, M. I. (1980). *The benefits of psychotherapy*. Baltimore: Johns Hopkins University Press.

Sterba, R. (1934). The fate of the ego in analytic therapy. *International Journal of Psycho-Analysis, 15*, 117–126.

Stiles, W. B., Glick, M. J., Osatuke, K., Hardy, G. E., Shapiro, D.A., Agnews-Davies, R., Rees, A., & Barkham, M. (2004). Patterns of alliance development and rupture-repair hypothesis: Are productive relationships U-shaped or V-Shaped? *Journal of Counseling Psychology, 51*, 81–92.

Stolorow, R., Brandchaft, B., & Atwood, G. (1994). *Psychoanalytic treatment: An inter-subjective approach*. Hillsdale, NJ: Analytic Press.

Winnicott, D. W. (1965). *The maturational process of the facilitating environment*. New York: International Universities Press.

Wolfe, B. E., & Goldfried, M. R. (1988). Research on psychotherapy integration: Recommendations and conclusions from NIMH workshop. *Journal of Consulting and Clinical Psychology, 56*, 448–451.

Zetzel, E. (1956). Current concepts of transference. *International Journal of Psycho-Analysis, 37*, 369–375.

9

Understanding and Working with Resistant Ambivalence in Psychotherapy
An Integrative Approach

HAL ARKOWITZ AND DAVID ENGLE

Resistance to change is an important and pervasive phenomenon in psychotherapy and health care. The term usually refers to the observation that many people who try to change on their own or with professional assistance often engage in behaviors that interfere with their making the desired changes. In the field of psychotherapy, resistance is seen as both an impediment to change and a phenomenon that can provide valuable information about the client. Helping people overcome their resistance can lead to significantly higher success rates for psychotherapy and health care.

The fragmentation of the field of psychotherapy into numerous "schools," with each having its own theory of resistance and how to work with it, has slowed progress toward a more unified and integrated view of resistance. Aspiring to find some common ground among the major theories, Wachtel (1982) invited representatives from each of the major therapy schools to describe their views on resistance and to comment on other contributions. What emerged was lively disagreement but little consensus.

In this chapter, we will take an integrative approach (Arkowitz, 1997) to understanding and working with resistance. Engle and Arkowitz (2006) reviewed the major theories of resistance, searching for common themes across the different therapies. We found that once we translated the theoretical jargon of each into

Table 9.1 Reasons for Not Changing from Different Therapy Theories

- *Diablos Conocidos:* Our "familiar devils" are at least familiar and predictable. Change leads to less predictable situations, and people seek familiarity and predictability, even if it has many negative aspects for them.

- *Fear of Changing:* Positive change is associated with new challenges and new situations, and we may be unsure how we will respond to them.

- *Fears of Failing:* People may be afraid to try once again to change, thinking that if they fail again they will feel even worse.

- *Faulty Beliefs:* These are beliefs that relate to oneself and change, which may be conscious or unconscious and that interfere with the occurrence of change.

- *Reactance:* Our internal dialogues about change often involve a struggle between a part of us that says that we *should* change, why we should change, why our life would be better, etc. This side is often bossy and gives orders and lectures. Just as we often resist others' attempts to directly change us, we resist when our internal monologues are mostly *shoulds* as opposed to *desires* about changing.

- *The functions of the undesirable behavior:* Although the present pattern of behavior is undesirable, it persists because it still serves some functions for the person. For example, drugs and alcohol temporarily help people escape from stress. People often feel that change means giving up a pattern that works a little for one that may not work at all.

common language, a number of similarities emerged. Finding these common themes about why people resisted change, however, was only part of the story. We were also struck by the fact that in most cases, resistance occurred in the context of seeking to change. This observation led us to formulate resistance as ambivalence.[1] To tie these two concepts together, we will refer to "resistant ambivalence" in the remainder of this chapter. We believe that recasting resistance as ambivalence can go a long way toward a better understanding of it and toward helping people overcome obstacles to change.

A WORKING MODEL OF RESISTANT AMBIVALENCE

Resistant ambivalence refers to patterns of behavior in which people express some desire to change, believe that the change will improve their lives, believe that effective strategies are available, have adequate information about executing those strategies, but nonetheless do not employ them sufficiently for change; these patterns are usually accompanied by negative affect (Engle & Arkowitz, 2006).

In our search across different therapies for common themes relating to resistant ambivalence, several interesting ones emerged. The ones that characterize most or all of the theories are summarized in everyday language in Table 9.1. When these reasons are juxtaposed with the observation that people also seek and desire change, the relevance of the construct of ambivalence becomes clear.

A central assumption of our model is that (1) *the data of resistant ambivalence provides important information about people and their problems, which can best be understood from the clients' perspective.* This stands in sharp contrast to a view of resistance as a problematic obstacle to be overcome.

Case Illustration

The case of Roger illustrates both the information value of resistant ambivalence and the value of understanding it from the client's perspective. Roger, a 50-year-old married man with two children, was referred for therapy by his physician because he was not complying with the recommended dietary and life-style changes, nor was he taking the prescribed medication to control his life-threatening hypertension. Sessions with him were oriented toward understanding his perspective on why he was acting this way. He stated that "My life is ok, my marriage is ok, my kids are ok, my job is ok … but when I sit down to a plate of ribs, I'm in heaven!" The only passion he seemed to experience in life was when he was eating foods that he enjoyed, but which also contributed to his problems with hypertension. He also described how his parents lived. They were in their eighties and according to Roger, examined every morsel of food before eating it to determine whether it was healthy or not. Further, he mentioned how they lined up all of their medications in the morning and went to great pains to ensure that they took them properly. In describing them, he said "I don't want to live like that," indicating that he'd rather die younger and enjoy his life than to live longer as they did. Roger's behavior makes sense when understood from his perspective, but didn't make sense to his doctor or wife. They didn't appreciate the importance of the reasons that mattered most to him, and as a result found his behaviors puzzling and frustrating. The only ambivalence Roger had was due to the discomfort caused by his wife's and doctor's unhappiness with his not changing.

A second assumption is that (2) *resistant ambivalence is intrapersonal and reflects relationships (discrepancies and congruencies) among self-schemas relevant to change.* We have found it useful to start our inquiries about resistant ambivalence by stating that most people have a side that wants to change and another that struggles against change, and that we want to understand both sides. This serves to normalize ambivalence, reducing some of the stigma that may be associated with not wanting to change. This format also serves as a catalyst for identifying and understanding the schemas that constitute the person's ambivalence.

Researchers in social cognition (e.g., Higgins, 1987, 1996; Markus & Nurius, 1986) have studied self-schemas extensively. Their work suggests that it is the dynamic relationships among self-schemas that are most relevant for understanding emotion and behavior, rather than any one schema. For example, Higgins developed an open-ended measure called the Selves Questionnaire in which subjects were asked to describe the characteristics of different aspects of their self, including their Actual, Desired, and Ideal selves. Each entry on one pair of lists was compared with all entries on the other. Using a thesaurus, the entries were rated as a match if they were synonyms, a mismatch if they were antonyms, and a mismatch of degree if they were to some extent dissimilar. Studies by Higgins and his associates found that discrepancies between the Actual and Should Selves were associated with anxiety and that discrepancies between the Actual and Desired selves were associated with depression (Higgins, 1987; Higgins, Bond, Klein, & Strauman, 1986, Higgins, Klein, & Strauman, 1985; Strauman, 1992). Of most relevance to the present discussion, Van Hook and Higgins (1988) found that subjects who had discrepancies between their Should and Desired Selves (or what Higgins and his associates call the "Ought" and "Ideal" selves, respectively) were more likely to experience confusion-related emotions (e.g., unsure of self or goals, muddled, and confused about identity). This confusion is related to what Van Hook and Higgins (1988) refer to as a double approach–avoidance conflict (see Heilizer, 1977) in which each end state has both a positive and negative valence. The more one meets one goal, the more one fails to meet the other, resulting in positive feelings from the former and negative feelings from the latter. This discrepancy and the associated emotion of confusion seem to relate nicely to ambivalence.

In the integrative model, we take a discovery-oriented approach in which the therapist seeks to identify the discrepancies that are associated with resistant ambivalence for each client. We have observed several common relationships between schemas that are associated with resistant ambivalence. These emerged from our clinical observations and most have not yet been studied in research.

One pattern, described earlier in the work of Van Hook and Higgins (1988), consists of discrepancies between our desires and "shoulds." When there are discrepancies between what we desire and what we believe we should do, ambivalent resistance will result. For example, one client expressed a desire to be more relaxed and carefree, but also believed that he should be more ambitious, hard driving, and successful. The more time he took to relax, the more uncomfortable he felt for not working, and the more he worked, the more uncomfortable he felt about not relaxing enough. This resulted in a pattern of approach and avoidance to work as well as to relaxation. (e.g., unsure of self or goals, muddled, and confused about identity).

Another pattern consists of discrepancies between our shoulds and our tendencies to respond to them in a reactant way. In this discrepancy, the movement toward achieving the characteristics of the Should self is countered by a Reactant self that responds negatively and oppositionally to those directives. While Brehm and Brehm (1981) and others who have written about reactance have emphasized its interpersonal determinants, we believe that reactance is a phenomenon that can also occur intrapersonally, i.e., when we are the one who both gives and receives the directive. Just as directives from others may be perceived as limiting our freedoms, our directives to ourselves (our "shoulds") are also experienced as limiting our freedoms and may elicit reactance and oppositional behavior. A few years ago, the first author decided to begin a vegetarian diet. Even though he typically ate meat only once every few weeks, he chose to eliminate meat from his diet by telling himself, in effect, "You shouldn't eat meat any more." In the next few weeks, his craving for meat drastically increased and he ate more meat on this diet than off it. He finally decided that he would eat less meat by allowing himself to eat meat than by restricting his freedom to do so. In the clinical situation, internalized self-critical directives are often met with active or passive resistance, even if the directive is in the person's best interest. Wegner (1989) has referred to such phenomena as "ironic processes."

A third relationship we have observed consists of congruencies between desires and fears. In some instances, resistant ambivalence may result from our being afraid of achieving what we also desire to achieve. In this instance, the person both desires and fears change, leading to a pattern of ambivalence and resistance. The first author worked with a young man who sought therapy in order to lose weight so that he could more easily meet women and have an intimate relationship (his "Desired" self). As we began to focus on weight loss, he became quite ambivalent. He neglected the agreed upon between-sessions exercises of self-monitoring his food intake, and weighing himself weekly. In discussing this with him, what emerged were his fears relating to successfully losing weight and then having to deal with sexuality, sexual performance, and intimacy. Essentially, the thought of attaining his desired self (thinner, having a relationship with a woman) activated his feared self (sexually inadequate, unable to deal with an intimate relationship), resulting in ambivalent resistance.

These three patterns are presented for illustrative purposes and by no means exhaust the possibilities. We believe that a discovery-oriented therapy approach will reveal many more patterns that relate to resistant ambivalence in different clients. The three are discussed here because they illustrate our point and also because we have observed them frequently.

A third assumption of the model is that (3) *resistant ambivalence is also interpersonal and needs to be understood in the interpersonal context in which it occurs.* A consistent finding in the psychotherapy literature is that a positive therapeutic relationship is one of the most important predictors of therapeutic change (e.g., Lambert & Barley, 2002). As a result, problems in the therapeutic relationship, or what Safran, Muran, Samstag, and Stevens (2002) have called "alliance ruptures," can cause resistance and interfere with the change process. In this regard, therapist directiveness may be a particularly noteworthy source of resistance and will be discussed more fully below.

A fourth assumption of the model is that (4) *people may not be fully aware of their self-schemas or the relationships among them that cause resistant ambivalence.* Further, we believe that (5) *resistant ambivalence can best be understood as a state rather than as a trait.* It seems obvious that people can be ambivalent about some areas of their lives but not about others. For this reason, we believe that ambivalence is best viewed as a situation-specific state rather than as a cross-situational trait. For some people who show resistant ambivalence across a wide range of situations, we may consider it a trait, but we prefer to let data show that this is the case rather than making an a priori assumption that it is a trait.

In reviewing theories of resistance in psychotherapy, Engle and Arkowitz (2006) noted that most theories suggest that (6) *desires to change are often countered by fears that change will lead to unpredictability and uncontrollability compared with the safety and predictability of the status quo.* Barlow (2002) has emphasized the significance of perceptions of unpredictability and uncontrollability in anxiety. Although we approach change because we believe that it will have obvious benefits to us, it makes our world less stable and secure resulting in resistant ambivalence as an approach-avoidance conflict.

The final assumption of our integrative model relates to working with resistant ambivalence in psychotherapy: (7) *approaches based on empathy and support are more likely to facilitate change than more directive approaches.* Numerous studies support the conclusion that more directive attempts to get someone to change are less likely to work than those that are based on empathy and support (Burns & Nolen-Hoeksma, 1991, 1992; Miller, Benefield, & Tonigan, 1993; Patterson & Chamberlain, 1994). In many cases, it seems that the more we try to directly change people through advice, persuasion, or exhortation, the less they change. By contrast, change is more likely to occur when we are accepting and supportive of their attempts to change, but do not become advocates for change. Miller and Rollnick (1991, 2002) have based their Motivational Interviewing approach on these ideas and focus on ways to increase the other person's intrinsic motivation to change rather than on direct attempts to effect change.

STRATEGIES FOR WORKING WITH RESISTANT AMBIVALENCE

Our search for ways of working with resistant ambivalence was guided by this last assumption. We particularly sought less directive approaches that were based on empathy and support. We found two well-developed treatment approaches that seemed particularly appropriate, both of which have a supporting body of research associated with them: Motivational Interviewing (MI) (Miller & Rollnick, 2002) and Two-Chair work used in Emotion-Focused Therapy (EFT) (Greenberg, Rice, & Elliott, 1993; Greenberg & Watson, 2006)[2]. Engle and Arkowitz (2006) discussed other potentially useful strategies as well. However, because these are not as well-developed and lack a solid research base, they will not be discussed here.

One particularly interesting feature of both the MI and Two-Chair approach is the variety of ways that they can be employed: as a pre-treatment to other established approaches such as CBT to prepare clients for change by reducing resistant ambivalence, as a stand-alone treatment, and combined or integrated with other therapies.

In addition, both approaches are compatible with the integrative model that we have proposed. They both emphasize the importance of a therapeutic relationship characterized by acceptance, support, and empathy. They share a common emphasis on the importance of ambivalence and of client agency in change. Perhaps most importantly, they both use the therapist's role to tap into the client's inner resources to effect change, rather than taking the role of external change agent. In this sense, both are client-centered, seeking to make the client the advocate and agent of change, and avoiding therapist directiveness that may elicit resistant ambivalence.

Motivational Interviewing (MI)

Motivational Interviewing, developed by Miller and Rollnick (1991, 2002), began as a way of working with alcohol and substance abuse problems. However, it is now being expanded to a number of other areas (Arkowitz, Westra, Miller, & Rollnick, in press) including depression and anxiety disorders (Arkowitz & Westra, 2004), eating disorders (Treasure & Schmidt, in press), compulsive gambling (Hodgins, in press), and suicide (Zerler, in press).

Principles and Strategies of MI

Miller and Rollnick (2002) describe MI as a client-centered *and* directive approach. It is client-centered in its basic humanistic underpinnings, in how people and change are viewed. It also draws heavily from client-centered therapy including its emphases on reflection and empathy. It is directive only in a subtle sense. MI does not try to directly influence people to change. In fact, any therapist who adopts the stance of "change advocate" is not doing MI. Instead, the MI therapist seeks to increase intrinsic motivation and reduce ambivalence about changing. With these changes, it is assumed that behavior change will occur naturally, with the client perceiving the locus of change as internal rather than residing in the therapist. Miller and Rollnick (2002) describe four basic principles of MI: (1) express empathy, (2) develop discrepancy, (3) roll with resistance, and (4) support self-efficacy.

In MI, empathy is primarily communicated through reflective listening (or accurate empathy) as described by Carl Rogers (1951). Underlying this principle of empathy is a client-centered attitude of "acceptance," wherein client ambivalence or reluctance to change is viewed as a normal part of the human experience rather than as pathology or defensiveness. Reflective statements are more than a simple "parroting" of what the clients says. Instead, they are *guesses* at the client's meanings and experience. For example, a client might say: "My parents have been bugging me a lot this week." The therapist might respond with the statement: "So, you've been pretty angry at your parents this week." The therapist's statement is just a small step beyond the client's statement and makes a reasonable guess that the client feels angry when bugged by parents. But it's an attempt to deepen the client's experience and check the therapist's understanding of it.

Developing discrepancy, the second principle of motivational interviewing, is where MI begins to depart from classic client-centered therapy. A key goal in motivational interviewing is to increase the importance of change from the client's perspective. This is accomplished using specific types of questions, along with selective reflections that direct the client toward the discrepancy between his/her problem behavior and important personal values. For example, a drug-addicted woman may see, through the therapist's reflections, that such behavior conflicts with her strong value on being a good mother to her child.

The third basic principle of motivational interviewing is to roll with the resistance rather than opposing it. This involves accepting the client's concerns about changing as valid without trying to directly challenge them. A useful strategy in this regard is the use of a decisional balance framework in which the pros and cons of change from the client's perspective are both fully explored. During work on decisional balance, and throughout MI, the therapist tries to highlight behavior-value discrepancies and elicit, reflect, and reinforce talk relating to commitment to change (Amhrein, Miller, Yahne, Palmer, & Fulcher, 2003) in order to help tip the balance toward change.

The fourth guiding principle of motivational interviewing, therefore, is to enhance the client's confidence in his or her ability to cope with obstacles and to succeed in changing. This confidence, which Bandura (1997) has described as self-efficacy, is an essential element in motivation and a good predictor of treatment outcome. This too is done by the therapist evoking (e.g., asking about success in past change attempts), reflecting, and reinforcing statements relating to confidence in changing.

When the therapist thinks the client may be ready for change, the therapist elicits the client's thoughts about how to go about making that change. Throughout MI, the therapist is a consultant to the client's change program, but the client is always in the lead. As a consultant, however, the therapist can and should offer advice and suggestions about change strategies that may be helpful. The therapist asks to be "invited in" by statements and questions like: "I have some thoughts about what's been helpful for other people with similar problems that might be helpful for you. Would you be interested in hearing them?" The client is then free to accept, reject, or modify the therapist's suggestions.

While MI has been used as a stand-alone treatment to prepare clients for change and to work with them during the action stage, it has also been used extensively as a prelude to other more directive treatments like cognitive-behavior therapy and 12-step approaches (see reviews by Burke, Arkowitz, & Menchola, 2003; Hettema, Steele, & Miller, 2005). Several studies have found that MI pretreatments enhance the outcomes of these therapies, even compared to other types of pretreatments. MI seems to increase motivation to change sufficiently that clients are "ready to go" and respond favorably even to more directive treatments once they are ready.

Case Illustration

This case illustrates the use of MI as a stand-alone therapy for depression (see also Arkowitz and Burke, in press). Brad sought therapy with the first author for depression and anxiety. He was a college junior who lived at home and who felt "lost" because he had no idea what he wanted to do with his life after he graduated. In the first few sessions, the therapist primarily utilized open-ended questions and reflections to hear Brad's story and to understand his frame of reference. In the process, we began to examine the decisional balance relating to his depression. Brad listed the many obvious disadvantages of being depressed including feeling sad, not being able to do things, having no interest in anything, etc. The advantages of being depressed were explored from Brad's point of view in a nonjudgmental manner, and without the therapist advocating for the advantages of change. Brad reported that if his depression and anxiety improved, he would have to deal with the difficult question of what to do with his life. He stated that this was one of the issues that may have precipitated the depression. In addition, if his symptoms improved, he expected that his parents would "be more on my case to get a job or do something, and I don't know what I want to do." Using reflections, value-behavior discrepancies, and elicitation and reinforcement of change talk, Brad began to engage in behaviors (e.g., socialize more) that he believed would help him reduce his depression.

Research on the Efficacy of MI

A meta-analysis by Burke, Arkowitz, and Menchola, (2003) reviewed 30 outcome studies of MI with problems that included alcohol and drug abuse, smoking, diet and exercise, and HIV-risk behaviors. They found that across problem areas, MI was more effective than no treatment or placebo, and as effective as other treatments to which it was compared. Interestingly, the effect size for MI as a prelude was greater than for MI as a stand-alone treatment. When MI efficacy for specific problem areas was examined, results supported the efficacy of MI for problems involving alcohol, drugs, and diet and exercise. Results did not support the efficacy of MI for smoking and HIV-risk behaviors, although it should be noted that the number of studies in each of these categories was quite small. A later meta-analysis of 72 studies (Hettema, Steele, & Miller, 2005) also found considerable support for the efficacy of MI.

More recently, Westra and Dozois (in press) compared CBT for anxiety disorders with and without an MI prelude. The MI-CBT group showed significantly greater reductions in anxiety, scored significantly higher on a self-rating measure of CBT homework compliance, and significantly increased scores on a measure of optimism after MI. A greater percentage of the MI-CBT group completed treatment than the CBT only group, but this difference only approached significance.

Overall, there is considerable support for the efficacy of MI in a variety of areas. However, the mechanism that accounts for this remains unclear. Although MI does work with ambivalence, we cannot conclude that it was the resolution of ambivalence that accounted for the observed changes since we do not yet have adequate measures of resistant ambivalence. Further research will be needed to ascertain this and to clarify why MI works.

The Two-Chair Approach

The Two-Chair method has its roots in the Gestalt therapy of Perls, Hefferline, and Goodman (1951). This therapy makes use of "experiments" that are semi-structured novel experiences related to the problem under discussion and constructed jointly by the therapist and client. They are discovery-oriented and designed to increase the client's awareness of feelings and change dysfunctional ways of thinking about themselves and others. They may take place during or between therapy sessions. For example, Perls and colleagues (1951) described the use of two-chair experiments in which the client engages in a dialogue between conflicting aspects of the self. The client may take one role (e.g., the critical self) in one chair and another (e.g., the rebellious self) in the other chair, with the therapist facilitating a dialogue between the two. In recent years, Greenberg and his associates have expanded on this work and developed Emotion-Focused Therapy (EFT) (e.g., Greenberg & Safran, 1987; Greenberg, Rice, & Elliott, 1993; Greenberg & Watson, 2006) that builds upon Rogers' (1951) client-centered therapy as well as Gestalt therapy. The part of their work that is most relevant to ambivalence is what Greenberg, Rice, and Elliot (1993) call "conflict splits." Here, there is a sense of struggle between the two selves that pull a person in different directions, e.g., "Part of me wants this, but another part of me wants that." We built on this work to develop a two-chair procedure specifically aimed at resistant ambivalence and its resolution.

In our version of the conflict split, one self advocates for change and another self struggles against change. The markers we employ for inviting a client to participate in this experiment are statements and behaviors that suggest ambivalence about change. The dialogue is structured so that the client takes turns speaking from each of two chairs that face one another. In one chair, the client is asked to speak from the perspective of the part of self that moves toward change (the "Change Self") and, in the other, the part of self that struggles against change (the "No Change Self"). Clients are usually fairly aware of the former, but much less aware of the latter. The experiment is more "discovery-oriented" than hypothesis-testing, and is aimed at both bringing the contents of both sides to full awareness, and resolving conflicts between them. The role of the therapist is to facilitate this dialogue and work from the client's perspective rather than imposing an external perspective. As a facilitator, the therapist does not side with either of the selves. More detailed discussions of the two-chair experiment can be found in Engle and Arkowitz (2006) and Greenberg, Rice, and Elliot (1993).

The dialogue is usually continuously evolving as the experiment proceeds. For example, we have seen experiments start with the Change side expressing desires to change and the No Change expressing fears of change. This then developed into a Should and Reactant dialogue with the Should side often evolving into a critical parent. It is important for the therapist to follow the client's lead in these experiments, but also to be attuned to underlying meanings and feelings and to help bring these into awareness.

The initial stage of the Two-Chair experiments emphasizes *separation* of the selves in each chair. Clients will often shift into the self in the other chair, while remaining in their current chair. When this happens, the therapist tries to establish separation by asking the client to move to the other chair so that the different selves remain coherent and relatively distinct.

Often, the first few minutes of the dialogue involve the two selves talking *at* rather than *with* one another. They are each staking out their territory without being particularly responsive to the other. At this point, the task of the therapist is to encourage *contact* between the selves. To accomplish this, the therapist might make suggestions like "Tell her (the self in the other chair) how she makes you feel when she says that."

As contact is made, the therapist tries to encourage expression of wants and needs, particularly in the self that is experiencing more emotion (e.g., the reactant self being criticized by the should self). For example, the self that was initially reactant may respond to the should self by saying "Your criticisms make me even more afraid and unwilling to change. I need you to back off from these criticisms. If you do I might be more willing to try changing."

Toward the end of a successful experiment, the client will often become aware that both sides are trying to help, but in different ways. The two sides begin to negotiate with each other in a genuine attempt to resolve the conflict between them and work together in the person's interests. Resolution of the conflict leads to an *integration* of the two sides.

Throughout the process, the therapist is particularly attuned to tacit emotions, and gently encourages the client to express them. Emotional expression facilitates greater contact between the two sides, and often leads to the awareness and expression of material that is deeply felt, but censored from expression in the nonemotional state.

Case Illustration

Sarah was an attractive single 20-year-old with a young son. She had been in a two-year relationship with a 36-year-old divorced man whom she described as emotionally abusive. He had other relationships with women, disappeared for days at a time with no explanation, stole money, and lied to her. He yelled at her and demeaned her for things that were not her fault. She made several failed attempts to end the relationship, always resuming it after a couple of weeks. Her parents and friends urged her to end the relationship. Although she knew they were right, she was unable to do so. Her statements during the interview clearly reflected her ambivalence about staying with him or leaving.

The Two-Chair experiment took place over several sessions. In speaking from the Change side, she described the boyfriend as abusive, unfaithful, and untrustworthy, leading to her unhappiness in the relationship and a desire to end it. The No Change side stated that "You know he loves you" and "… maybe things will change, maybe things will work out." As the experiment continued, the Change side became angry at the other side for keeping her trapped in the relationship, while the No Change side was sad, clinging to belief that he could change and the relationship could work. At this point in the dialogue, there were the beginnings of contact, but both sides were still firmly entrenched in their respective positions. She renamed the two sides the "emotional self" that wanted to stay and the "logical self" that wanted to leave.

At the end of the second dialogue there was an emerging understanding between the selves, and the anger was mostly gone. In response to a prompt for the logical self to tell the emotional self what she needed from that side, she said: "You're a part of my life that I need. I need your ability to trust. I need your ability to love. I need who you are. I would like for us to be able to work together and not be at such odds. I'm sure there is somebody out there that will fit both of our needs … and not just yours, and not just mine." This was the first overture toward resolving the conflict between the selves and working cooperatively. The dialogue continued to reflect an increasing sense of cooperation between the two selves. In the following session, there were remnants of fear about "being a loser" if she left the relationship and if her boyfriend very quickly found someone else and she did not. However, she also expressed how tired both sides were of the endless struggle. A strong desire to meet in the middle emerged, with a *bridge* being a central image. Subsequently, the logical self moved more toward accepting the idea of her leaving and the emotional self asked for support and help from the logical self in leaving. The dialogue continued with mutual support as the theme and without conflict. The different selves were now working out how to give and receive the support needed to leave. Sarah subsequently did leave the relationship, and a year later had not gotten back together with him, despite frequent requests on his part to do so.

Research on the Two-Chair Approach

There have been several studies that bear on efficacy of the Two-Chair procedure. Early studies (Greenberg & Clarke, 1979; Greenberg & Dompierre (1981); Greenberg & Higgins, 1980) compared empathic reflection (derived from Carl Rogers' Client-Centered Therapy) with Two-Chair work for clients who were experiencing ambivalence about a decision. Both groups made considerable progress toward behavioral goals, but were not significantly different from one another.

Another study used volunteers who were having trouble making a difficult decision. Greenberg and Webster (1982) gave these subjects a six-week treatment consisting mainly of Two-Chair work. After the treatment, subjects were divided into "Resolvers" and "Non-Resolvers" based on whether they had manifested three components of a proposed model of conflict resolution during treatment: expression of criticism by one side; expression of feelings and wants by the other; and a "softening" in the attitude of the critic. After treatment, Resolvers were significantly less indecisive and anxious than Non-Resolvers.

Clarke and Greenberg (1986) employed subjects who sought counseling to help them resolve a conflictual decision. They were randomly assigned to two sessions of either a Two-Chair intervention, a problem-solving cognitive-behavioral intervention (CBT), or a no-treatment control group. The Two-Chair group improved more than the CBT group and the control group on one measure of indecisiveness. The two groups did not differ significantly on the other measure; both improved significantly more than the no treatment control group.

Arkowitz and Engle (1995) conducted a small single-group pilot study on the Two-Chair procedure for resolving ambivalence. People who were having trouble making an important change in their lives were recruited from advertisements in the campus newspaper. Seven respondents were deemed appropriate for the study. Their focal problems included: two women who wanted to leave what they considered to be bad relationships but were unable to do so; one smoker who wished to stop; one who was trying to lose weight; one who was messy to the point of embarrassment about having people visit her; one who was indecisive in her career choice, and a depressed man who was unable to move ahead on many of the goals he set for himself. Each subject received four half-hour sessions devoted almost entirely to the Two-Chair procedure applied to the focal problem. Of the seven, there were clear resolutions and behavioral changes in four, improvement but short of full resolution change in two cases, and no change at all in one.

Greenberg and Watson (1998) conducted a study of patients who met the criteria for Major Depression. They compared 15–20 sessions of either Client-Centered Therapy (CCT) or Emotion-Focused Therapy (EFT), which includes the two-chair method. The EFT therapy included a base of CCT in the context of which the therapist used several different Gestalt techniques including, but not limited to, Two-Chair dialogues for conflict splits. Overall, both groups showed considerable improvement with treatment. The effects seemed clinically significant when compared to effect sizes in other treatment studies of depression that employed a No-Treatment Control Group. At post-treatment, the EFT group showed greater improvements in self-esteem, interpersonal functioning, and symptom distress than did the CCT group. Further, EFT seemed to work faster, showing greater changes than CCT at mid-treatment. Treatment gains were maintained at six-month follow-up, but differences between the two treatments disappeared. A replication and extension of this study (Goldman, Greenberg, & Angus, in press) demonstrated that EFT was significantly more effective in the treatment of Major Depression that CCT, and this difference was maintained at follow-up. Another study by Watson, Gordon, Stermac, Kaleogerakos, and Steckley (2003) compared EFT and CBT in the treatment of Major Depression. Overall, both therapies were equally effective, but several measures showed an advantage for EFT.

Although results for the Two-Chair procedure are promising, the jury is still out on whether it is efficacious. As with MI, it is also not clear that this procedure effects change through the resolution of ambivalence.

CONCLUDING COMMENTS

A major goal of this chapter has been to draw attention to resistant ambivalence as an important set of processes that can be worked with to facilitate change. We have taken an integrative approach to accomplish this. The movement toward psychotherapy integration has made great strides in recent years (see Norcross and Goldfried, 2005) and our work is in the integrative tradition in several respects. First, we started by identifying common processes that cut across different schools of therapy. We believe that many therapies have a great deal to offer in understanding and facilitating change, but that the commonalities among them are often lost in the different jargons. Competition among types of therapies has also contributed to an unwillingness to look to other therapies to see what can be learned. Second, we looked to a variety of sources to inform our thinking, including therapy theories as well as other areas of psychology such as on social cognition. We also looked across therapies to find ways of working with resistant ambivalence that are potentially useful. Third, our suggestions for understanding and working with resistant ambivalence can be combined or integrated with virtually any type of therapy (see Engle and Arkowitz, 2006, for a fuller discussion of this point). Finally, our work reflects an integration between research and practice. Both authors have been active researchers as well as psychotherapy practitioners. We value the interplay between the two, and believe that knowledge generated from only one of these sources may have serious limitations.

Our work also reflects an alternative approach to the current movement toward empirically supported therapies (ESTs), which are lists of specific therapies for specific problems that have met certain criteria for having research support. The EST movement has provoked sharp and divisive controversy in the field that will hopefully evolve into a more unifying force. We believe that this can occur as we move away from an emphasis on therapy techniques and toward principles and processes of change (Arkowitz & Lilienfeld, 2006; Rosen and Davison, 2003). Serious questions have been raised about how important these specific therapy techniques are compared to the contributions of the therapeutic relationship and other processes (e.g., see Wampold, 2001). We believe that the field can make more progress and do so in a more unified way by emphasizing common processes of change and by moving toward the concept of evidence-based practice (American Psychological Association, 2005) in which psychotherapy practice is informed not only by research on therapy techniques, but by research in the entire field of psychology. We agree with Sechrest and Smith's (1994) comment that "Psychotherapy is the practice of psychology."

There are many questions about resistant ambivalence that need to be answered. We believe that one of the first of these, and one that needs to be on a research agenda, is the measurement of ambivalence. There have been some attempts in this direction by Engle and Arkowitz (2006). However, these are still very preliminary. Without good measures relating to resistant ambivalence, we cannot draw any clear conclusions about its role in resistance or noncompliance and about whether resolving ambivalence does indeed lead to change as we have discussed. Hopefully, this chapter will stimulate research on resistant ambivalence and contribute to practicing psychotherapists thinking more integratively about the construct.

REFERENCES

APA Presidential Task Force on Evidence Based Practice (2006). Evidence-based practice in psychology, *American Psychologist*, *61*, 271–285.

Amrhein, P. C., Miller, W. R., Yahne, C. E., Palmer, M., & Fulcher, L. (2003). Client commitment language during motivational interviewing predicts drug use outcome. *Journal of Consulting and Clinical Psychology*, *71*, 862–878.

Arkowitz, H. (1997). Integrative theories of therapy. In P. W. Wachtel & S. M. Messer (Eds.), *Theories of psychotherapy: Origins and evolution* (pp. 227–288). Washington, DC: American Psychological Association Press.

Arkowitz, H., & Burke, B. (in press). Motivational interviewing and depression. In H. Arkowitz, H. A. Westra, W. R. Miller, & Rollnick, S. (Eds.), (in press). *Motivational interviewing and psychotherapy*. To be published by Guilford Press.

Arkowitz, H., & Engle, D. (1995, April). *Working with resistance to change in psychotherapy*. Paper presented at the Meetings of the Society for the Exploration of Psychotherapy Integration. New York, New York.

Arkowitz, H., & Lilienfeld, S. O. (2006). Psychotherapy on trial? *Scientific American Mind*, *17*, 41–48.

Arkowitz, H., & Westra, H. A. (2004). Integrating motivational interviewing and cognitive behavioral therapy in the treatment of depression and anxiety. *Journal of Cognitive Psychotherapy*, *18*, 337–350.

Arkowitz, H., Westra, H. A., Miller, W. R., & Rollnick, S. (Eds.). (in press). *Motivational interviewing and psychotherapy*. To be published by Guilford Press.

Bandura, A. (1997). *Self-efficacy: The exercise of control*. New York: Worth Publishers.

Barlow, D. (2002). *Anxiety and its disorders*. New York: Guilford Press.

Brehm, S. S., & Brehm, J. W. (1981). *Psychological reactance: A theory of freedom and control*. New York: Academic Press.

Burke, B., Arkowitz, H., & Menchola, M. (2003). The efficacy of motivational interviewing: A meta-analysis of controlled clinical trials. *Journal of Consulting and Clinical Psychology*, *71*, 843–861.

Burns, D., & Nolen-Hoeksma, S. (1991). Coping styles, homework compliance, and the effectiveness of cognitive-behavior therapy. *Journal of Consulting and Clinical Psychology*, *59*, 305–311.

Burns, D., & Nolen-Hoeksma, S. (1992). Therapeutic empathy and recovery from depression: A structural equation model. *Journal of Consulting and Clinical Psychology*, *92*, 441–449.

Clarke, K. M., & Greenberg, L. S. (1986). Differential effects of a Gestalt two-chair intervention and problem-solving in resolving decisional conflict. *Journal of Counseling Psychology*, *33*, 11–15.

Engle, D., & Arkowitz, H. (2006). *Ambivalence in psychotherapy: Facilitating readiness to change*. New York: Guilford Press.

Goldman, R., Greenberg, L., & Angus, L. (in press). The effects of adding specific emotion-focused interventions to the therapeutic relationship in the treatment of depression. *Psychotherapy Research*.

Greenberg, L. S., & Clarke, K. M. (1979). Differential effects of the two-chair experiment and empathic reflection at a conflict marker. *Journal of Counseling Psychology*, *26*, 1–8.

Greenberg, L. S., & Dompierre, L. (1981). The specific effects of Gestalt two-chair dialogue on intrapsychic conflict in counseling. *Journal of Counseling Psychology*, 28, 288–296.

Greenberg, L. S., & Higgins, H. (1980). Effects of a two-chair dialogue on focusing and conflict resolution. *Journal of Counseling Psychology*, 27, 221–224.

Greenberg, L. S., Rice, L. N., & Elliott, R. (1993). *Facilitating emotional change: The moment-by-moment process*. New York: Guilford.

Greenberg, L. S., & Safran, J. D. (1987). *Emotion in psychotherapy*. New York: Guilford Press.

Greenberg, L. S., & Watson, J. C. (1998). Experiential therapy of depression: Differential effects of client-centered relationship conditions and process experiential interventions. *Psychotherapy Research, 8*, 210–224.

Greenberg, L. S., & Watson, J. C. (2006). *Emotion-Focused Therapy for Depression*. Washington, D.C.: American Psychological Association.

Greenberg, L. S., & Webster, M. (1982). Resolving decisional conflict by Gestalt two-chair dialogues: Relating process to outcome. *Journal of Counseling Psychology*, 29, 468–477.

Heilizer, F. (1977). A review of theory and research on Miller's response competition (conflict) models. *The Journal of General Psychology, 97*, 227–280.

Hettema, J., Steele, J., & Miller, W. R. (2005). Motivational interviewing. *Annual Review of Clinical Psychology, 1*, 91–111.

Higgins, E. T. (1987). Self-discrepancy: A theory relating self and affect. *Psychological Review, 94*, 319–340.

Higgins, E. T. (1996). The "Self Digest": Self-knowledge serving self-regulatory functions. *Journal of Personality and Social Psychology, 71*, 1062–1073.

Higgins, E. T., Bond, R. T., Klein, R., & Strauman, T. (1986). Self-discrepancies and emotional vulnerability: How magnitude, accessibility, and type of discrepancy influence affect. *Journal of Personality and Social Psychology, 51*, 5–15.

Higgins, E. T., Klein, R., & Strauman, T. (1985). Self-concept discrepancy theory: A psychological model for distinguishing among different aspects of depression and anxiety. *Social Cognition, 3*, 51–76.

Hodgins, D. (in press). Motivational interviewing and problem and pathological gambling. In H. Arkowitz, H. A. Westra, W. R. Miller, & Rollnick, S. (Eds.), (in press). *Motivational interviewing and psychotherapy*. To be published by Guilford Press.

Lambert, M., & Barley, D.E. (2002). Research summary on the therapeutic relationship and psychotherapy. In J. Norcross (Ed.), *Psychotherapy relationships that work* (pp. 17–36). New York: Oxford University Press.

Markus, H., & Nurius, P. (1986). Possible selves. *American Psychologist, 42*, 954–969.

Miller, W. R., Benefield, R. G., & Tonigan, J. S. (1993). Enhancing motivation for change in problem drinking: A controlled comparison of two therapist styles. *Journal of Consulting and Clinical Psychology, 61*, 455–461.

Miller, W. R., & Rollnick, S. (1991). *Motivational interviewing: Preparing people to change addictive behavior*. New York: Guilford Press.

Miller, W. R., & Rollnick, S. (2002). *Motivational interviewing: Preparing people for change* (2nd ed.). New York: Guilford.

Norcross, J. C., & Goldfried, M. R. (2005). *Handbook of psychotherapy integration* (2nd ed.). New York: Oxford University Press.

Patterson, G., & Chamberlain, P. (1994). A functional analysis of resistance during parent training. *Clinical Psychology: Research and Practice, 1*, 53–70.

Perls, F., Hefferline, R., & Goodman, P. (1951). *Gestalt therapy.* New York: Julian Press.

Rogers, C. R. (1951). *Client-centered therapy.* Boston: Houghton-Mifflin.

Rosen, G. M., & Davison, G. C. (2003). Psychology should list empirically supported principles of change (ESPs) and not credential trademarked therapies or other treatment packages. *Behavior Modification, 27*, 300–312.

Safran, J. D., Muran, J. C., Samstag, L. W., and Stevens, C. (2002). Repairing alliance ruptures. In J. C. Norcross (Ed.), *Psychotherapy relationships that work: Therapist contribution and responsiveness to patients* (pp. 235–254). New York: Oxford Press.

Sechrest, L., & Smith, B. (1994). Psychotherapy is the practice of psychology. *Journal of Psychotherapy Integration, 4*, 1–30.

Strauman, T. (1992). Self-guides, autobiographical memory, and anxiety and dysphoria: Toward a cognitive model of vulnerability to emotional distress. *Journal of Abnormal Psychology, 101*, 87–95.

Treasure, J., & Schmidt, U. (in press). Motivational interviewing and eating disorders. In H. Arkowitz, H. A. Westra, W. R. Miller, & Rollnick, S. (Eds.), (in press). *Motivational interviewing and psychotherapy.* To be published by Guilford Press.

Van Hook, E., & Higgins, E. T. (1988). Self-related problems beyond the self-concept: Motivational consequences of discrepant self-guides. *Journal of Personality and Social Psychology, 55*, 625–633.

Wachtel, P. W. (Ed.). (1982). *Resistance: Psychodynamic and behavioral approaches.* New York: Plenum Press.

Wampold, B. E. (2001). *The great psychotherapy debate: Models, methods, and findings.* Mahwah, NJ: Erlbaum

Watson, J. C., Gordon, L. B., Stermac, L., Kalogerakos, F., & Steckely, P. (2003). Comparing the effectiveness of process–experiential with cognitive–behavioral psychotherapy in the treatment of depression. *Journal of Consulting and Clinical Psychology, 71*, 773–781.

Wegner, D. (1989). White bears and other unwanted thoughts: Suppression, obsession, and the psychology of mental control. New York: Guilford.

Westra, H. A., & Dozois, D. J. A. (in press). Preparing clients for cognitive behavioural therapy: A randomized pilot study of motivational interviewing for anxiety. *Cognitive Therapy and Research.*

Westra, H., & Dozois, D. (in press). Integrating motivational interviewing into the treatment of anxiety. In H. Arkowitz, H. A. Westra, W. R. Miller, & Rollnick, S. (Eds.), (in press). *Motivational interviewing and psychotherapy.* To be published by Guilford Press.

Zerler, H. (in press). Motivational interviewing and suicide. In H. Arkowitz, H. A. Westra, W. R. Miller, & Rollnick, S. (Eds.), (in press). *Motivational interviewing and psychotherapy.* To be published by Guilford Press.

ENDNOTES

1. We should note that there are some instances of what might be labeled as resistance that do not reflect ambivalence, e.g., people may appear resistant to change when they simply do not *want* to change or do not *know how* to change.

2. Emotion-Focused Therapy is the general name for a treatment that includes the two-chair method, Process-Experimental Therapy is the name of the manualized version that has been used in research. For the sake of consistency, we will refer only to Emotion-Focused Therapy.

Section *III*
TREATMENTS OF
AXIS I DISORDERS

10

General Principles for the Treatment of Emotional Disorders Across the Lifespan

JILL T. EHRENREICH, BRIAN A. BUZZELLA,
AND DAVID H. BARLOW

SHARED FACTORS IN THE DEVELOPMENT OF EMOTIONAL DISORDERS

The search for a parsimonious set of psychological treatment procedures that may be efficacious across the emotional disorders must necessarily begin with an understanding of how much these disorders overlap in terms of their occurrence and etiology. We know that disorders characterized by high levels of emotional dysregulation and inappropriate emotional responding, particularly anxiety and unipolar depressive disorders, are common. These disorders are also chronic and extremely costly, begin in late childhood and continue through adulthood, and tend to co-occur at high rates (Angold, Costello, & Erklani, 1999; Barlow, 2002; Kovacs & Devlin, 1998). As noted by Orvaschel, Lewinsohn, and Seeley (1995), experience of a childhood or adolescent anxiety disorder may not only predict the presentation of later anxiety symptomatology, it may also be associated with the development of a mood disorder. These authors found that roughly two-thirds (64.5%) of adolescents with a primary anxiety disorder diagnosis later developed a diagnosis of a depressive disorder. Similarly, rates of current and lifetime comorbidity between emotional disorders in adulthood are very high. Brown, Campbell, Lehman, Grisham, and Mancill (2001) indicate that of 1,127 patients carefully assessed for anxiety and depressive disorders using the Anxiety Disorders Interview Schedule for the *DSM-IV*, Lifetime Version (ADIS-IV-L, 1994), 55% presented with a principal mood or anxiety disorder and at least one additional mood or anxiety disorder at the time of assessment, even with conservative *DSM-IV* hierarchical diagnostic rules applied. When lifetime prevalence rates were calculated, this figure increased to 76% of patients experiencing an additional anxiety or mood disorder sometime in their lifespan (Brown et al., 2001).

The high rate of co-occurrence between anxiety and depressive disorders is less surprising when considering the multitude of similar factors in their development, along with their potentially shared latent structure (Allen, Ehrenreich, & Barlow, 2005). For instance, findings from investigations employing a behavioral genetic design indicate that the genetic influences on anxiety and depression are almost entirely shared (Eley, 1997; Eley & Stevenson, 1999; Eley, 2001; Thapar & McGuffin, 1997). Multiple studies have also supported the notion that anxiety and depression share a common, although often differently named, temperamental risk factor (Barlow, Chorpita, & Turovsky, 1996; Brady & Kendall, 1992; King, Ollendick, & Gullone, 1991; Watson & Clark, 1984). Brown, Chorpita, and Barlow (1998), Zinbarg and Barlow (1996) and others have sought to describe the latent structure of anxiety and depression, with some general consensus given to what is called the "tripartite model" of emotional disorders, first described by Clark and Watson (1991). In this model, negative affect (NA), the first factor in the model, is a common factor to both anxiety and depression. NA is described by Clark and Watson (1991) as "the extent to which a person is feeling upset or unpleasantly engaged rather than peaceful, and encompasses various affective states, including upset, angry, guilty, afraid, sad, scornful, disgusted, and worried" (p. 321). Positive affect (PA), the second factor, on the other hand, distinguishes depression from anxiety; depression seems to involve a reduction in PA, along with increases in NA, while anxiety may be characterized by NA alone. PA "reflects the extent to which a person feels a zest for life and is most clearly defined by such expressions of energy and pleasurable engagement as active, delighted, interested, enthusiastic, and proud" (Clark & Watson, 1991, p. 321). The third factor, physiological arousal (PH), is independent of the other two, and most likely, in our view, represents the phenomena of panic (Barlow, 2002). One of the intriguing findings from this line of research is that mood disorders show greater overlap with certain anxiety disorders, such as GAD, than do other anxiety disorders, supporting and reinforcing the commonalities of depression and anxiety at a phenomenological level (Brown et al., 1998; Clark, Steer, & Beck, 1994; Mineka, Watson, & Clark, 1998). The tripartite model has also been well supported in the child and adolescent literature, indicating that the same pattern of variations in NA and PA seen in adults characterize anxiety and depression symptoms in youth (Chorpita, Albano, & Barlow, 1998; Joiner, Catanzaro, & Laurent, 1996; Phillips, Lonigan, Driscoll, & Hooe, 2002; Turner & Barrett, 2003).

Alternative explanations can also be forwarded to explain the degree of comorbidity between anxiety and depressive disorders. These include issues with overlapping diagnostic criteria, artifactual reasons, such as differing base rates of occurrence in certain settings, and evidence of sequential disorder development, such as anxiety disorders possibly acting as risk factors for future depression (Brown & Barlow, 2002) or vice versa (Costello, Mustillo, Erkanli, Keeler, & Angold, 2003). But, supported by the "common factors" argument, these data largely suggest the existence of a "general neurotic syndrome" (Andrews, 1990; Andrews, 1996; Tyrer, 1989) in those with anxiety and depressive disorders. Under this conceptualization, heterogeneity in the expression of emotional disorder symptoms (e.g., individual differences in social anxiety, intrusive thoughts, worry, the presence of panic attacks, anhedonia, etc.) is considered to be largely trivial variation in the manifestation of a broader syndrome. Taken together, these early vulnerabilities, considered in concert with the phenomenological evidence reviewed above, strongly suggest the presence of common factors in the genesis and presentation of emotional disorders.

CURRENT TREATMENTS FOR EMOTIONAL DISORDERS IN YOUTH AND ADULTHOOD

When examining the empirical status of current, efficacious treatments for anxiety and depressive disorders, several overarching themes emerge. For instance, most of these treatments possess a cognitive-behavioral (CBT) framework and result from large-scale clinical trials, frequently conducted across several treatment sites, a process which often endows them with a relatively large N and sufficient control for allegiance effects (Barlow, Allen, & Choate, 2004). When aggregating findings across these studies, it appears that between 50% and 80% of patients receiving treatment for one or more emotional disorders will achieve "responder" status at post-treatment and early follow-up points, although the definition of who exactly a treatment "responder" is may vary from study to study. In most cases, a "responder" has achieved this status by making some clinically significant improvements, although they may not be "cured" or considered symptom-free. Moreover, these outcomes are typically better than some credible psychological treatment or "placebo" for just about every anxiety disorder, although this issue may be slightly less clear for depressive disorders (Barlow, 2001; Nathan & Gorman, 2002).

Despite this positive state of affairs in the CBT literature for emotional disorders, a number of significant caveats can be identified that might point us toward areas of potential innovation regarding treatment of the emotional disorders. Clearly, not all patients respond to cognitive-behavioral treatment, leaving room for improvement to such approaches. Since most researchers manualize their cognitive-behavioral approaches to the treatment of very specific problems or disorders, the resultant state is one in which multiple manuals, workbooks, and protocols co-exist, including many for the same disorder (Barlow, Allen, & Choate, 2004). While this state of affairs is marginally better in the child and adolescent anxiety literature, where protocols such as those by Kendall (1990) target a slightly larger breadth cluster of anxiety disorders, including GAD, Social Phobia and Separation Anxiety Disorder, additional manuals and workbooks still exist to treat both this same cluster of anxiety disorders and the plethora of other emotional disorders in youth. Finally, because these manuals are often complex, their dissemination to community treatment providers is a large obstacle (Barlow, Levitt, & Bufka, 1999). Recently, NIMH set forth a task force to specifically address this issue in the area of depression, specifying a priority for the development of more "user friendly" protocols to treat depressive disorders (Hollon et al., 2002). One way to conceptualize an increase in such "user friendliness" might be through the development of a more integrated treatment protocol that is inherently responsive to the commonly co-occurring variations in emotional and behavioral symptoms often seen in more naturalistic treatment settings (Weisz, 2004).

Promising evidence for the utility of single treatment protocols for a larger array of emotional disorders can be found in research (cited above) suggesting the presence of a "general neurotic syndrome" among those with emotional disorders. For example, psychological treatments for a given anxiety disorder produce significant improvement in additional comorbid anxiety or mood disorders, even those not specifically addressed in treatment (Borkovec, Abel, & Newman, 1995; Brown, Antony, & Barlow, 1995). In the field of child and adolescent anxiety intervention, Rapee (2000) indicates that his family-based, CBT group treatment program for child and adolescent anxiety disorders, may "be of value to the full range of anxiety disorders seen in general clinical practice" (p. 128). Findings from Kendall, Brady, and Verduin (2001) yield support for this contention, demonstrating a positive impact of CBT targeted at a small range of child anxiety disorders (i.e., GAD, separation anxiety disorder, or social phobia) on other comorbid anxiety disorders, in children between the ages of eight and 13. Some investigations of anxious youth have also observed a significant decrease in self-reported depression levels following CBT for anxiety (Barrett, Rapee, Dadds, & Ryan, 1996; Kendall et al., 1997; Mendlowitz et al., 1999) and the maintenance of such decreases at long-term follow-up (Kendall, Safford, Flannery-Schroeder, & Webb, 2004). Furthermore, comorbid anxiety symptoms may also improve during the course of treatment targeting child and adolescent depression (Mufson, Weissman, Moreau, & Garfinkel, 1999; Reynolds & Coats, 1986; Stark, Reynolds, & Kaslow, 1987).

Within the adult literature, new examples of the beneficial effect of treatment for a principal anxiety disorder on co-occurring emotional disorders have recently appeared. For example, the presence of additional diagnoses in a sample of 126 patients treated for Panic Disorder with Agoraphobia (PDA) at the Center for Anxiety and Related Disorders was recently examined (Barlow, Allen, & Choate, 2004). At pretreatment, 26% had an additional diagnosis of GAD, but the rate of comorbid GAD declined significantly at post-treatment to 9%, and remained at this level at a two-year follow-up. Whether these findings represent the generalization of elements of treatment to independent facets of both disorders, or a way of effectively addressing "core" features of emotional disorders, is not significant to our purpose here. In both cases, the efficiency of a unified treatment protocol is suggested. Moreover, the fact that a wide range of emotional disorders (e.g., Major Depressive Disorder [MDD], Dysthymia, Obsessive-Compulsive Disorder [OCD], and PDA) respond similarly to antidepressant medications has also been interpreted as indicative of a shared pathophysiology among these symptoms (e.g., Hudson & Pope, 1990).

THE DEVELOPMENT OF A NEW APPROACH TO THE TREATMENT OF EMOTIONAL DISORDERS

After considering the shared etiologic pathways, structural commonalities, and treatment response to similar psychological and pharmacologic interventions across anxiety and depressive disorders, Barlow (1988) proposed that, in line with emotion theorists such as Izard (1971), a more singular, coherent approach to the treatment of emotional disorders was most likely to result from emotion theory. Consistent with this notion and the concurrent work of Lang (1968), Rachman (1981), and Wilson (1982), Barlow (1988) outlined components of any affective therapy, with a primary tenant that there was likely no better or faster way to change a dysregulated emotional state than the modification of *emotionally driven behaviors* (EDB) associated with a specific, disordered emotion. This model of therapeutic change also held that other essential targets for intervention included a sense of controllability or predictability over events in one's environment; decreasing the avoidance that occurs during self-focused attention on nontask-related consequences of excess emotionality; as well as attention to other treatment targets, such as emotional cognitions, coping skills, social support networks and heightened arousal levels (see Barlow [1988] for a full review of these latter components).

In 2004, Barlow and colleagues revisited this initial model of essential treatment components and set out to further review emerging science in the areas of learning, emotional development and regulation, and cognitive science, postulating that research in these domains added to and coalesced particularly well with our existent knowledge regarding the treatment techniques that reliably produce symptom relief across emotional disorders. Based on this theory and associated research (reviewed in extensive detail in Campbell-Sills and Barlow [in press]), a common set of three therapeutic change elements with potential applicability across the emotional disorders was proposed. From these elements, they also formulated a pragmatic approach to the amelioration of these emotional disorders entitled the "Unified Protocol for the Treatment of Emotional Disorders" (Barlow, Allen, & Choate, 2006; Campbell-Sills & Barlow, in press). For the remainder of this chapter, we will concentrate on a description of the central change principles associated with the Unified Protocol (UP) and initial evidence supporting this protocol's potential efficacy across the emotional disorders. First, we will turn our attention to a thorough description of the common change principles targeted in the UP. Next, we will illustrate some practical applications of this treatment approach. Finally, we will discuss initial evidence of the UP's potential to produce positive therapeutic change across emotional disorders in both adolescence and adulthood.

THE UNIFIED PROTOCOL FOR THE
TREATMENT OF EMOTIONAL DISORDERS

As noted, three primary therapeutic components have been developed and operationalized during the past several years, serving as the backbone of our unified treatment approach. After providing some general psychoeducation on the nature of emotions and their relationship to behavior (a component common to most cognitive behavioral treatments), the following three components are introduced to the patient: (1) altering antecedent cognitive reappraisals; (2) preventing emotional avoidance—a global effort that extends beyond more traditional attempts to prevent behavioral avoidance by targeting cognitive, somatic, and behavioral avoidance (examples of each type of avoidance and their manifestations across several types of emotional disorders are presented in Table 10.1); and (3) modifying emotionally driven behaviors to incorporate new, adaptive responses to emotions. Our treatment reinforces these three components via a series of discussions and exercises designed to provoke emotional expression (emotion exposure), using cognitive, somatic, and situational triggers. In this regard, the treatment differs between patients only in the specific exercises and stimuli used to elicit emotions. While standard mood induction techniques may be utilized to provoke emotions in most patients, other provocation techniques may vary from patient to patient, and can be customized to some degree to address the patient's presenting concerns. Importantly, we are not conceptualizing "exposure" as the mechanism of action in this treatment approach; rather, successful emotion provocation serves as a setting condition for the implementation of treatment strategies, such as those described above.

Antecedent Cognitive Reappraisal

Theory and techniques associated with cognitive therapy (Beck, 1972; Beck, Rush, Shaw, & Emery, 1979) are a fundamental part of most psychological treatments for the emotional disorders, in which clinicians typically focus on the appraisals and interpretations that individuals with emotional disorders make about internal and external events. It is fair to say that emotional disorders are, in part, characterized by their cognitive biases, such as the tendency to overestimate the likelihood that negative events may occur and underestimate one's ability to cope with such events. Cognitive therapy was first developed to treat depression, at which time this modality's primary developer, Aaron T. Beck, hypothesized a "cognitive triad" through which individuals created and maintained negative beliefs about themselves, the world, and their future. This concept was later extended to anxiety disorders (Beck, Emery, & Greenberg, 1985), and negative appraisals about internal events (e.g., somatic sensations) were also discussed.

The aim of cognitive therapy is to objectively evaluate the probability of these negative appraisals and eventually utilize more realistic, evidence-based appraisals of potential situational outcomes. On the surface, this technique can appear to be

Table 10.1 Examples of Emotional Avoidance

Emotional Avoidance Strategy	Disorder Most Usually Associated
1. Subtle Behavioral Avoidance	
• Avoid eye contact	Social Phobia
• Avoid drinking coffee	PDA
• Attempt to control breathing	PDA
• Avoid exercise/physiological arousal (interoceptive avoidance)	PDA
• Avoid touching sink/toilet	OCD
• Procrastination (avoiding emotionally salient tasks)	GAD
2. Cognitive Avoidance	
• Distraction (reading a book, watching television)	PDA
• "Tuning out" during a conversation	Social Phobia
• Reassuring self that everything is okay	GAD
• Worrying	GAD
• Rumination	Depression
• Trying to prevent thoughts from coming into mind	OCD
• Distractions from reminders of trauma	PTSD
• Thought suppression	All disorders
3. Safety Signals	
• Carry cell phone	PDA/GAD
• Carry empty medication bottles	PDA
• Hold onto "good luck" charms	OCD
• Carry items that are associated with positive experiences (e.g., teddy bears, pictures)	GAD
• Having mace at all times	PTSD
• Carry water bottle	PDA
• Having reading material/prayer books on hand	GAD
• Carry sunglasses or items to hide face/eyes	Social Phobia

Note: PDA = panic disorder with agoraphobia; OCD = obsessive-compulsive disorder; GAD = generalized anxiety disorder; PTSD = posttraumatic stress disorder.

a way of suppressing or controlling negative thoughts by "rationalizing" them, and occasionally, this is how cognitive therapy is incorrectly applied, as noted by Hayes, Strosahl, and Wilson (1999). Importantly, this technique can also be conceptualized from an emotion-regulation perspective, if reappraisals of threat and negativity are made *prior to* the emotionally arousing situation. Data from the emotion regulation literature has evidenced that altering appraisals before experiencing increased levels of emotional arousal can have a salutary effect on the later expression of negative emotions (Gross, 1998; Richards & Gross, 2000; Thayer, 2000). Antecedent cognitive reappraisal has also been shown to reduce the subjective experience of negative emotion (Gross, 1998).

A well-known investigation utilizing a manipulation of perceived control over a potential threat provides a good illustration of the impact of antecedent appraisals within the context of emotional disorders (Sanderson, Rapee, & Barlow, 1989). In this study, a standard CO_2 inhalation paradigm was utilized and patients with PDA were told that they would be able to control the flow of carbon dioxide (CO_2) by turning a dial when a light appeared. For approximately half the patients, the light was never illuminated, which lead them to think they possessed no control over the flow of CO_2. However, for the other half, the light did appear, suggesting that they could control the flow of CO_2 by using the dial. In actuality, this dial had no effect on the flow of CO_2, with all patients receiving the same flow of CO_2 for the entire experiment. Thus, the dial served only to give participants the illusion of control (perceived control), and, in fact, no one actually tried to use the dial. Nonetheless, those in the perceived control condition reported experiencing a lesser number of panic attacks during the experiment, as compared to the control group. Although many different types of antecedent misappraisals have been identified across emotional experiencing, the majority of clinical research from our Center has focused on two fundamental antecedent misappraisals: the probability of a negative event happening (probability overestimation) and the potential consequences of the negative event, if it did happen (catastrophizing) (Barlow & Craske, 2000; Craske & Barlow, 2006). These antecedent misappraisals are directly targeted in the UP.

Emotional Avoidance

An increasing body of evidence supports the notion that as humans attempt to down-regulate or avoid their unexpected, excessive emotions they inevitably experience increasingly intense emotional states. This process is hypothesized to be central to emotional states, such as depression, anger, and excitement (mania) in addition to fear (Barlow, 1988). Even within nonclinical populations, the frequency of untriggered emotions seems to suggest a high usage of maladaptive strategies for controlling emotional states (Craske, Brown, Meadows, & Barlow, 1995). In a laboratory-based study using another sample of nonclinical subjects, Feldner, Zvolensky, Eifert, and Spira (2003) divided patients into categories of high and low emotional avoiders and subjected them to four breaths of 20% CO_2-enriched air. Half of each group was instructed to suppress uncomfortable emotions, while the other half was instructed to simply observe their emotions. High emotional avoiders reported greater distress and anxiety, regardless of suppression or observation instructions, as compared to low emotional avoiders.

In considering the impact of emotional avoidance on those with emotional disorders, Roemer, Litz, Orsillo, and Wagner (2001) found that veterans with Posttraumatic Stress Disorder (PTSD) were more likely to withhold negative *and* positive emotions, as compared to veterans without PTSD. At our clinic, Levitt, Brown, Orsillo, and Barlow (2004) randomized 60 patients with PDA into one of three groups. Each of these groups listened to a 10-minute audiotape with a description of one or two emotion regulation techniques (acceptance or suppression) or a neutral narrative. After undergoing a 15-minute, 5.5% CO_2

challenge, all patients were asked to undergo a second challenge. Consistent with the findings reported above on the effects of emotional avoidance, the acceptance group in this study reported significantly less anxiety and less avoidance than either the suppression or control groups during the first challenge, and showed a greater willingness to participate in the second challenge.

Importantly, evidence on the potentially negative impact of avoidance strategies may also extend to breathing and relaxation techniques, which were a significant part of earlier treatment protocols (Barlow & Cerny, 1988). When relaxation strategies are used specifically for the purpose of reducing uncomfortable emotions in the moment, these techniques can actually become counterproductive. Schmidt et al. (2000) found that the addition of breathing retraining did not add any significant benefit to a treatment package consisting of psychoeducation, cognitive restructuring, and situational exposures for individuals with panic disorder. In fact, breathing retraining appeared to be associated with lower outcome functioning on both self-report and clinician-rated measures. Similar results have been obtained when examining the impact of distraction techniques in treatment (Craske, Street, & Barlow, 1989; Craske, Street, Jayaraman, & Barlow, 1991; Kamphuis & Telch, 2000) and safety signals (Salkovskis, Clark, Hackmann, Wells, & Gelder, 1999; Sloan & Telch, 2002; Wells et al., 1995).

With regard to the use of maladaptive emotion regulation strategies across both anxiety and mood disorders, data from our own lab are useful. Sixty patients with an anxiety or mood disorder and 30 individuals with no history of emotional disorders subjected themselves to possible negative feelings while watching an emotional film. In the first study (Campbell-Sills, Barlow, Brown, & Hofmann, in press), spontaneous emotion appraisals and emotion regulation strategies were seen in both samples. The participants with an anxiety or mood disorder reported significantly different emotional appraisals and emotion regulation strategies, as compared to the nonclinical sample. Clinical patients reported both a greater sense of anxiety about their emotions, as well as less emotional clarity. These participants also reported using maladaptive emotion regulation strategies (e.g., suppression, avoidance, cognitive rehearsal), and rated their emotions as less acceptable. Higher levels of emotional suppression were associated with increased physiological response, as well as poorer recovery from distress. In the second study (Campbell-Sills, Barlow, Brown, & Hofmann, in press), participants were instructed to either use emotional suppression strategies or acceptance strategies during the same emotion induction exercise. Individuals who used suppression were unable to recover from the distressing experience and manifested a different heart rate pattern. Specifically, heart rate increased from the beginning to the end of the film for the suppression group, whereas heart rate decreased in this time frame for the acceptance group. Overall, these data provide strong evidence that patients with emotional disorders endorse more negative emotional appraisals and use maladaptive strategies for regulating emotions, as compared to individuals without emotional disorders.

Modifying Emotionally Driven Behaviors (Action Tendencies)

Izard (1971), utilizing ideas from emotion theory, suggested that the most efficient and effective way to change emotions is through an alteration of the responses to those emotions. Simply stated, "the individual learns to act his way into a new way of feeling" (p. 410). This means that the Emotionally Driven Behaviors (EDB) currently associated with a particular emotional experience must be resisted during exposure activities. Awareness of, and attention to, both the existing EDBs and the EDBs being developed are critical components of treatments for anxious and depressive disorders (Barlow, 1988). In fact, this clinical utility is reflected in the prominent role the creation of new EDBs plays in several successful treatments for depression. The treatment for depression by Beck, Rush, Shaw, and Emery (1979), for instance, incorporates a change in EDBs such that patients no longer behave in a "passive, retarded, and apathetic manner" in response to their depressive feelings (p. 312). In a similar vein, behavioral activation strategies are becoming increasingly common in newer treatments for depression (Jacobson, Martell, & Dimidjian, 2001).

Although the alteration of EDBs has recently received additional research attention, these strategies have existed for many years and have been applied in a range of areas. In 1960, for example, Frankl induced laughter, humor, and related facial expressions that were not related to the EDBs during paradoxical intention experiments. Ascher (1980) utilized these same strategies to effectively counteract fear. Linehan (1993) has successfully adapted the strategy of modifying EDBs (referred to as "opposite action tendencies") to treat individuals with borderline personality disorder (a disorder which may, at its core, represent a severe emotional disorder). More recently, Hayes and colleagues conceptualized EDBs in their Acceptance and Commitment Therapy (ACT; Hayes, Strosahl, & Wilson, 1999), emphasizing the importance of using alternative coping strategies, with the goal of providing a sense of control over one's responses to emotions, instead of attempting to reduce the occurrence of unwanted internal events. Originally, it was thought that modifying EDBs results in the induction of cognitive changes. At this time, it also seems plausible to suggest that these strategies operate by preventing behavioral responses and altering the EDBs (i.e., facial expressions) an individual associates with a given emotion.

APPLICATION OF THE UNIFIED APPROACH TO EMOTIONAL DISORDERS

As noted previously, the goal of the Unified Protocol is to apply a set of fundamental therapeutic strategies to each of the emotional disorders. We believe it is possible to apply these strategies in a manner that effectively treats the events associated with an array of emotional disorders. Antecedent cognitive reappraisal, for instance, is characterized by two distinct biases seen in every emotional disorder: overestimating the likelihood of negative events (probability overestimation) and underestimating one's ability to cope with the negative event (catastrophizing). A substantial amount of evidence also supports the existence of cognitive and behavioral avoidance strategies—including mental rituals, distraction, and emotion suppression—that cut across emotional disorders. For instance, individuals with PDA often choose their activities in order to avoid experiencing interoceptive and somatic cues that might produce a panic attack or panic sensations. Cognitive and behavioral rituals are a central part of OCD, although these events are also evidenced in the rumination and "worry behaviors" of those with GAD (e.g., checking behaviors, seeking reassurance, perfectionism, etc.) (Craske & Barlow, 2006). These rituals are likely an attempt to assert control and reduce the distress and negative affect associated with a lack of control over future outcomes (Frost, Heimberg, Holt, Mattia, & Neubauer, 1993; Scott & Cervone, 2002). Similarly, behavioral tendencies toward withdrawal seem to function as a way of avoiding contexts and interactions that may induce negative affect, examples of which can be seen in Table 10.1.

To modify the EDB associated with a particular emotion, one must first provoke the emotion, usually through emotion-inducing exposure-based procedures. Next, one must change the EDB usually associated with the emotion in question. Using the example of an individual with a specific phobia, approaching the feared stimuli instead of engaging in avoidance behaviors is one way of modifying EDBs. An additional step might be to provoke an entirely different emotion (such as a smiling or laughing) in the presence of the feared stimuli. Treatment of GAD, on the other hand, might involve assigning "nonperfect" behavior in the home, school, or workplace counteracting the emotionally driven perfectionistic tendencies associated with GAD. To address anger concerns, passivity and detachment may be appropriate behaviors to recommend, while positive, active coping skills would be useful for depression. Additional examples are provided in Table 10.2. The use of avoidance behaviors (e.g., distraction and the use of "safety behaviors"), while engaging in emotion-provocation exercises, often prevent the full experience of emotion and reduce the effectiveness of a given exposure. In fact, the prevention of emotional avoidance while modifying EDBs associated with the emotion is crucial to successful emotional exposures.

Case Example

We now present a more detailed explication of the treatment of one patient seen by one of the authors (DHB), using an initial draft of the UP. This patient "Mike" was a 24-year-old single male currently enrolled in a Master's degree program in creative writing. He was referred by a community mental health agency and presented with problems "arranging things, counting, and repetitive ritual things." A thorough assessment revealed a principal diagnosis of obsessive compulsive disorder (OCD) and no additional comorbid disorders that rose to a clinically significant level. Mike noted that he was seeking treatment at this time because his medication was not working well. Mike had

Table 10.2 Modifying Emotionally Driven Behaviors

List of EDBs	Disorder Most Usually Associated	List of Incompatible Behaviors
Calling home to check on safety	GAD	Restricting contact/calling relatives
Perfectionist behavior at work or home	GAD	Leaving things untidy or unfinished
Checking locks, stove, or other appliances	OCD	Repeatedly locking/unlocking and turning on/off until memory is unclear
Leaving (escaping from) a theater, religious service, other crowded area	PDA	Move to the center of the crowd. Smile or produce nonfearful facial expressions
Leaving (escaping) a social situation	Social Phobia	Staying in situation and approaching people
Verbally/physically attacking someone when in a argument	PTSD	Remove self from situation and/or practice relaxation techniques
Hypervigilance	All disorders	Focus attention on specific task at hand; meditation; relaxation

Note: PDA = panic disorder with agoraphobia; OCD = obsessive-compulsive disorder; GAD = generalized anxiety disorder; PTSD = posttraumatic stress disorder.

sought treatment several times during the previous years and each time had been prescribed Zoloft. Upon presentation, he was taking 200 mg per day.

Principal obsessions included doubting (e.g., doubting that he had locked a door or turned off an appliance) as well as some thoughts of aggressive themes. He was also "obsessed" with the idea that he had caused his girlfriend, with whom he had recently broken up, or perhaps some other girl to become pregnant, thereby ruining their lives and his as well. He was fully aware rationally that this was highly unlikely. Mike also engaged in compulsions, including counting (letters, numbers, and other objects in the environment), checking (locks, appliances, faucets, and the placement of things), adhering to certain rules or sequences (e.g., assuring symmetry and engaging in ritualistic acts, such as tapping his hand a certain number of times), and practicing extreme orderliness and neatness. He noted that he "sometimes thinks he is going crazy" and reported being "incredibly anxious and frustrated about negative things throughout the day." Further assessment revealed mild to moderate social anxiety which did not reach a clinical level.

As per the protocol, initial sessions were spent explaining the rationale, as well as carefully monitoring emotional activity, identifying triggers and cognitive, physiological, and behavioral facets of emotions. Mike was asked about the different emotions he experienced on a daily basis (frustration, anxiety, anger, sadness) and how these emotions affected his life. Any physical sensations associated with different emotional experiences were considered and explored. Subtle strategies for avoiding the experience of intense emotion were evaluated, such as distraction, as well as what sorts of actions (emotion-driven behaviors) "he felt like doing" when he was anxious (such as escaping, making things right, or just lying down). A rationale was presented accounting for the progression of normal intense emotions into emotional disorders. Careful monitoring and observing of naturally occurring emotions became the context for explicating these concepts. Antecedent cognitive reappraisal began in session four based on our usual and customary process of identifying probability overestimations and tendencies to catastrophize outcomes. Following the tenets of the emotional regulation literature, an emphasis was placed on practicing these techniques at nonanxious times prior to entering any high-risk situations (antecedent). Emotion-provoking exercises, specifically interoceptive stimulation, began in session five. Much to his surprise, several of the exercises, particularly spinning (and accompanying slight feelings of nausea), provoked the very same anxious feelings and immediate attempts to escape that occurred in response to an obsession and prior to ritualistic activity. This training continued, as well as the beginnings of provoking emotions in situational context.

This strategy was coupled with avoidance prevention strategies and modification of EDBs. In the case of Mike, uncertainty and lack of order were obsessional triggers for anxiety. Thus, instead of ritualistically cleaning his apartment, Mike was instructed to mess up his apartment and leave many things out of place. Continued monitoring and emotional awareness training revealed that he scuffed his shoes while he walked, a compulsion of which he had not been aware. This action was functionally related to intense, obsessionally provoked anxiety. The behavior of walking smoothly to music was substituted. Situational emotional exposure continued with exercises focused on turning appliances on and off to the point where he had difficulty remembering if they were off (which provoked strong emotion) in place of the action tendency of checking appliances. By session eight, he discontinued Zoloft, a long-term goal that was reached more quickly than he had planned since his insurance coverage for the medication had run out. After several days of discontinuation symptoms, including marked somatic symptoms associated with his intense emotions that he had been provoking with interoceptive exercises, he was handling these symptoms very well and determined that he no longer needed medication. Remaining sessions continued to focus on provoking emotions in context while modifying (ritualistic) responses and utilizing appropriate antecedent cognitive reappraisal prior to the exercises. In addition, EDBs of escape (vs. avoidance) were modified by planned approach to emotion-provoking triggers combined with continued awareness training. Mike did very well in treatment and reported significant improvement in levels of distress, ritualizing, occurrence of obsessions, and more generalized anxiety. At a six-month follow-up conducted by an independent evaluator, his Clinical Severity Rating (CSR) on the ADIS-IV-L was 2 (at intake Mike's

OCD was rated at a 5; these ratings are on a 0–8 scale). He reported that he was essentially better, although he would still, on occasion, have an intrusive thought or two. However, he reported that these thoughts were no longer distressing, and he did not act on them.

CURRENT STATUS OF TREATMENT

Although intended for use with individual clients, the UP was first tested in three diagnostically heterogeneous adult patient therapy groups. This group format was chosen to allow an examination of the best format for presenting the UP's therapeutic principles to a wide range of patients. Based on these experiences, the treatment developers were able to review and consolidate their own conceptualizations of the treatment principles and alter the protocol's specified style of presentation.

More recently, the Unified Protocol has been examined in the individual treatment of six adult and three adolescent patients (Allen, Ehrenreich, & Barlow, 2005; Goldstein & Ehrenreich, 2005). These nine patients presented with a range of anxious and unipolar depressive principal diagnoses, including dysthymia, MDD, GAD, OCD, co-principal MDD and social phobia, co-principal MDD and GAD, and anxiety disorder not otherwise specified (Allen, Ehrenreich, & Barlow, 2005; Goldstein & Ehrenreich, 2005).

Upon completion of the treatment, five of the six adult patients reported a reduction in principal diagnostic symptomatology such that their symptoms no longer reached clinical levels. In addition, several of those patients who reported this reduction in symptomatology also noted an improvement of comorbid conditions, which included OCD related to hoarding, bulimia, PTSD, and cannabis use (Allen, Ehrenreich, & Barlow, 2005). One adult patient, who had been diagnosed with co-principal MDD and social phobia, still reported clinical levels of distress and impairment at the completion of treatment, but had demonstrated improvements in functioning in several life domains. Overall, this improvement reflects an 83% reduction of principal diagnostic symptomatology to subclinical levels.

In the adolescent sample, all three of the adolescent patients and their parent(s) reported a reduction in the severity and interference of principal diagnostic symptoms upon completing treatment. In addition, all three evidenced an even further reduction of symptoms at a six-month follow-up interview such that all symptoms warranting a clinical diagnosis at the pretreatment assessment were significantly reduced to subclinical levels or completely absent (Goldstein & Ehrenreich, 2005). This reduction in symptoms, observed among both adult and adolescent samples appears to be at least comparable, and perhaps even better, than those found in cognitive-behavioral treatments for more diagnostically homogeneous populations, although the sample is very small. These findings suggest that the treatment techniques utilized in the Unified Protocol may be effective in the reduction of a broad range of emotional disorder symptoms presenting during childhood development or in adulthood.

REFERENCES

Allen, L. B., Ehrenreich, J. T., & Barlow, D. H. (2005). A unified treatment for emotional disorders: Applications with adults and adolescents. *Japanese Journal of Behavior Therapy, 31*, 3–31.

Andrews, G. (1996). Comorbidity and the general neurotic syndrome. *The British Journal of Psychiatry, 168*, 76–84.

Andrews, G. (1990). Neurosis, personality, and cognitive behaviour therapy. In M. McNaughton & G. Andrews (Eds.), *Anxiety* (pp. 3–14). New Zealand: University of Otago Press.

Angold, A., Costello, E. J., & Erkanli, A. (1999). Comorbidity. *Journal of Child Psychology and Psychiatry, 40*, 57–87.

Ascher, L. M. (1980). Paradoxical intention. In A. Goldstein & E. B. Foa (Eds.), *Handbook of behavioral interventions: A clinical guide*. New York: Wiley.

Barlow, D. H. (1988). *Anxiety and its disorders: The nature and treatment of anxiety and panic*. New York: Guilford.

Barlow, D. H. (2002). *Anxiety and its disorders: The nature and treatment of anxiety and panic* (2nd ed.). New York: Guilford.

Barlow, D. H. (Ed.). (2001). *Clinical handbook of psychological disorders: A step-by-step treatment manual* (3rd ed.). New York: Guilford.

Barlow, D. H., Allen, L., & Choate, M. L. (2006). The Unified Protocol for Treatment of the Emotional Disorders. Unpublished manuscript, Boston University.

Barlow, D. H., Allen, L. B., & Choate, M. L. (2004). Toward a unified treatment for emotional disorders. *Behavior Therapy, 35*, 205–230.

Barlow, D. H., & Cerny, J. A. (1988). *Psychological treatment of panic*. New York: Guilford.

Barlow, D. H., Chorpita, B. F., & Turovsky, J. (1996). Fear, panic, anxiety, and disorders of emotion. In D. A. Hope (Ed.), *Perspectives on anxiety, panic, and fear* (pp. 251–328). Lincoln: University of Nebraska Press.

Barlow, D. H., & Craske, M. G. (2000). *Mastery of your anxiety and panic: Client workbook for anxiety and panic* (3rd ed.). London: Oxford University Press.

Barlow, D. H., Levitt, J. T., & Bufka, L. F. (1999). The dissemination of empirically supported treatments: A view to the future. *Behaviour Research and Therapy, 37*, S147–S162.

Barrett, P. M., Rapee, R. M., Dadds, M. R., & Ryan, S. M. (1996). Family enhancement of cognitive style in anxious and aggressive children. *Journal of Abnormal Child Psychology, 24*, 187–203.

Beck, A. T. (1972). *Depression: Clinical, experimental, and theoretical aspects*. New York, Harper & Row, 1967. Republished as *Depression: Causes and treatment*. Philadelphia: University of Pennsylvania Press.

Beck, A. T., Emery, G., & Greenberg, R. L. (1985). *Anxiety disorders and phobias: A cognitive perspective*. New York: Basic Books.

Beck, A. T., Rush, A. J., Shaw, B. F., & Emery, G. (1979). *Cognitive therapy of depression*. New York: Guilford.

Borkovec, T. D., Abel, J. L., & Newman, H. (1995). Effects of psychotherapy on comorbid conditions in generalized anxiety disorder. *Journal of Consulting and Clinical Psychology, 63*, 479–83.

Brady, E. U., & Kendall, P. C. (1992). Comorbidity of anxiety and depression in children and adolescents. *Psychological Bulletin, 111*, 244–255.

Brown, T. A., Antony, M. M., & Barlow, D. H. (1995). Diagnostic comorbidity in panic disorder: Effect on treatment outcome and course of comorbid diagnoses following treatment. *Journal of Consulting and Clinical Psychology, 63,* 408–418.

Brown, T. A., & Barlow, D. H. (2002). Classification of anxiety and mood disorders. In: D. H. Barlow (Ed.), *Anxiety and its disorders: The nature and treatment of anxiety and panic* (2nd ed.) New York: Guilford.

Brown, T. A., Campbell, L. A., Lehman, C. L., Grisham, J. R., & Mancill, R. B. (2001). Current and lifetime comorbidity of the DSM-IV anxiety and mood disorders in a large clinical sample. *Journal of Abnormal Psychology, 110,* 585–599.

Brown, T. A., Chorpita, B. F., & Barlow, D. H. (1998). Structural relationships among dimensions of the DSM-IV anxiety and mood disorders and dimensions of negative affect, positive affect, and autonomic arousal. *Journal of Abnormal Psychology, 107,* 179–192.

Campbell-Sills, L. & Barlow, D.H. (in press). Incorporating emotion regulation into conceptualization and treatment of anxiety and mood disorders. In J. J. Gross (Ed.), *Handbook of emotion regulation.* New York: Guilford Press.

Campbell-Sills, L., Barlow, D. H., Brown, T. A., & Hofmann, S. G. (in press). Effects of emotional suppression and acceptance in individuals with anxiety and mood disorders. *Behavior Research and Therapy.*

Campbell-Sills, L., Barlow, D. H., Brown, T. A., & Hofmann, S. G. (in press). Acceptability and suppression of negative emotion in anxiety and mood disorders. *Emotion.*

Clark, D. A., Steer, R. A., & Beck, A. T. (1994). Common and specific dimensions of self-reported anxiety and depression: Implications for the cognitive and tripartite models. *Journal of Abnormal Psychology, 103,* 645–654.

Clark, L. A., & Watson, D. (1991). Tripartite model of anxiety and depression: Psychometric evidence and taxonomic implications. *Journal of Abnormal Psychology, 100,* 316–336.

Chorpita, B. F., Albano, A. M., & Barlow, D. H. (1998). The structure of negative emotions in a clinical sample of children and adolescents. *Journal of Abnormal Psychology, 107,* 74–85.

Costello, E. J., Mustillo, S., Erkanli, A., Keeler, G., & Angold, A. (2003). Prevalence and development of psychiatric disorders in childhood and adolescence. *Archives of General Psychiatry, 60,* 837–844.

Craske, M. G., & Barlow, D. H. (2006). *Mastery of your anxiety and worry.* London: Oxford University Press.

Craske, M. G., Brown, T. A., Meadows, E. A., & Barlow, D. H. (1995). Uncued and cued emotions and associated distress in a college sample. *Journal of Anxiety Disorders, 9,* 125–137.

Craske, M. G., Street, L., & Barlow, D. H. (1989). Instructions to focus upon or distract from internal cues during exposure treatment for agoraphobic avoidance. *Behaviour Research and Therapy, 27,* 663–672.

Craske, M. G., Street, L. L., Jayaraman, J., & Barlow, D. H. (1991). Attention versus distraction during in vivo exposure: Snake and spider phobias. *Journal of Anxiety Disorders, 5,* 199–211.

Eley, T. C. (2001). Contributions of behavioral genetics research: Quantifying genetic, shared environmental and nonshared environmental influences. In M. W. Vasey & M. R. Dadds (Eds.), *Developmental psychopathology of anxiety* (pp. 45–59). London: Oxford University Press.

Eley, T. C. (1997). Depressive symptoms in children and adolescents: Etiological links between normality and abnormality: A research note. *Journal of Child Psychology and Psychiatry, 38*, 861–865.

Eley, T. C., & Stevenson, J. (1999) Using genetic analyses to clarify the distinction between depressive and anxious symptoms in children and adolescents. *Journal of Abnormal Child Psychology, 27*, 105–114.

Feldner, M. T., Zvolensky, M. J., Eifert, G. H., & Spira, A. P. (2003). Emotional avoidance: An experimental test of individual differences and response suppression using biological challenge. *Behaviour Research and Therapy, 41*, 403–411.

Frankl, V. E. (1960). Paradoxical intention: A logotherapeutic technique. *American Journal of Psychotherapy, 14*, 520–535.

Frost, R. O., Heimberg, R. G., Holt, C. S., Mattia, J. I., & Neubauer, A. L. (1993). A comparison of two measures of perfectionism. *Personality and Individual Differences, 14*, 119–126.

Goldstein, C. R., & Ehrenreich, J. T. (2005). Unified Protocol for the Treatment of Emotional Disorders in Adolescents: A Pilot Study. Unpublished manuscript, Boston University.

Gross, J. J. (1998). Antecedent- and response-focused emotion regulation: Divergent consequences for experience, expression, and physiology. *Journal of Personality and Social Psychology, 74*, 224–237.

Hayes, S. C., Strosahl, K. D., & Wilson, K. G. (1999). *Acceptance and commitment therapy: An experiential approach to behavior change.* New York: Guilford Press.

Hollon, S. D., Munoz, R. F., Barlow, D. H., Beardslee, W. R., Bell, C. C., Guillermo, B., et al. (2002). Psychosocial intervention development for the prevention and treatment of depression: Promoting innovation and increasing access. *Biological Psychiatry, 52*, 610–630.

Hudson, J. I., & Pope, H. G. (1990). Affective spectrum disorder: Does antidepressants response identify a family of disorders with a common pathophysiology? *American Journal of Psychiatry, 147*, 552–564.

Izard, C. E. (Ed.). (1971). *The face of emotion.* New York: Appleton-Century-Crofts.

Jacobson, N. S., Martell, C. R., & Dimidjian, S. (2001). Behavioral activation treatment for depression: Returning to contextual roots. *Clinical Psychology: Science and Practice, 8*, 255–270.

Joiner, T. E., Catanzaro, S. J., & Laurent, J. (1996). Tripartite structure of positive and negative affect, depression, and anxiety in child and adolescent psychiatric inpatients. *Journal of Abnormal Psychology, 105*, 401–409.

Kamphuis, J. H., & Telch, M. J. (2000). Effects of distraction and guided threat reappraisal on fear reduction during exposure based treatments for specific fears. *Behaviour Research and Therapy, 38*, 1163–1181.

Kendall, P. C. (1990). *Coping Cat Workbook.* Philadelphia: Temple University.

Kendall, P. C., Brady, E. U., & Verduin, T. L. (2001). Comorbidity in childhood anxiety disorders and treatment outcome. *Journal of the American Academy of Child and Adolescent Psychiatry, 40*, 787–794.

Kendall, P. C., Flannery-Schroeder, E., Panichelli-Mindel, S. M., Southam-Gerow, M., Henin, A., & Warman, M. (1997). Therapy for youths with anxiety disorders: A second randomized clinical trial. *Journal of Consulting and Clinical Psychology, 65*, 366–380.

Kendall, P. C., Safford, S., Flannery-Schroeder, E., & Webb, A. (2004). Child anxiety treatment: Outcomes in adolescence and impact on substance use and depression at 7.4-year follow-up. *Journal of Consulting and Clinical Psychology, 72,* 276–287.

King, N. J., Ollendick, T. H., & Gullone, E. (1991). Negative affectivity in children and adolescents: Relations between anxiety and depression. *Clinical Psychology Review, 11,* 441–459.

Kovacs, M. & Devlin, B. (1998). Internalizing disorders in childhood. *Journal of Child Psychology and Psychiatry, 39,* 47–63.

Lang, P. J. (1968). Fear reduction and fear behavior: Problems in treating a construct. In J. M. Shlien (Ed.), *Research in psychotherapy* (Vol. 3). Washington, DC: American Psychological Association.

Levitt, J. T., Brown, T. A., Orsillo, S. M., & Barlow, D. H. (2004). The effects of acceptance versus suppression of emotion on subjective and psychophysiological responses to carbon dioxide challenge in patients with panic disorder. *Behavior Therapy, 35,* 747–766.

Linehan, M. M. (1993). *Skills training manual for cognitive behavioral treatment of borderline personality disorder.* New York: Guilford.

Mendlowitz, S. L, Manassis, K., Bradley, S., Scapillato, D., Miezitis, S., & Shaw, B. R. (1999). Cognitive-behavioral group treatments in childhood anxiety disorders: The role of parental involvement. *Journal of the American Academy of Child and Adolescent Psychiatry, 38,* 1223–1229.

Mineka, S., Watson, D., & Clark, L. A. (1998). Comorbidity of anxiety and unipolar mood disorders. *Annual Review of Psychology, 49,* 377–412.

Mufson, L., Weissman, M. M., Moreau, D., & Garfinkel, R. (1999). Efficacy of interpersonal psychotherapy for depressed adolescents. *Archives of General Psychiatry, 56,* 573–579.

Nathan, P. E., & Gorman, J. M. (Eds.). (2002). *A guide to treatments that work.* London: Oxford University Press.

Orvaschel, H., Lewinsohn, P. M., & Seeley, J. R. (1995). Continuity of psychopathology in a community sample of adolescents. *Journal of the American Academy of Child and Adolescent Psychiatry, 34,* 1525–1535.

Phillips, B. M., Lonigan, C. J., Driscoll, K., & Hooe, E. S. (2002). Positive and negative affectivity in children: A multitrait-multimethod investigation. *Journal of Clinical Child and Adolescent Psychology, 31,* 465–479.

Rachman, S. (1981). The primacy of affect: Some theoretical implications. *Behaviour Research and Therapy, 19,* 279–290.

Rapee, R. M. (2000). Group treatment of children with anxiety disorders: Outcome and predictors of treatment responses. *Australian Journal of Psychology, 52,* 125–130.

Reynolds, W. M., & Coats, K. I. (1986). A comparison of cognitive-behavioral therapy and relaxation training for the treatment of depression in adolescents. *Journal of Consulting and Clinical Psychology, 54,* 653–660.

Richards, J. M., & Gross, J. J. (2000). Emotion regulation and memory: The cognitive costs of keeping one's cool. *Journal of Personality and Social Psychology, 79,* 410–424.

Roemer, L., Litz, B. T., Orsillo, S. M., & Wagner, A. W. (2001). A preliminary investigation of the role of strategic withholding of emotions in PTSD. *Journal of Traumatic Stress, 14,* 143–150.

Salkovskis, P. M., Clark, D. M., Hackmann, A., Wells, A., & Gelder, M. G. (1999). An experimental investigation of the role of safety-seeking behaviors in the maintenance of panic disorder with agoraphobia. *Behaviour Research and Therapy, 37,* 559–574.

Sanderson, W. C., Rapee, R. M., & Barlow, D. H. (1989). The influence of an illusion of control on panic attacks induced via inhalation of 5.5% carbon dioxide-enriched air. *Archives of General Psychiatry, 46,* 157–164.

Schmidt, N. B., Woolaway-Bickel, K., Trakowski, J., Santiago, H., Storey, J., Koselka, M., et al. (2000). Dismantling cognitive-behavioral treatment for panic disorder: Questioning the utility of breathing retraining. *Journal of Consulting and Clinical Psychology, 68,* 417–424.

Scott, W. D., & Cervone, D. (2002). The impact of negative affect on performance standards: Evidence for an affect-as-information mechanism. *Cognitive Therapy and Research, 26,* 19–37.

Sloan, T., & Telch, M. J. (2002). The effects of safety-seeking behavior and guided threat reappraisal on fear reduction during exposure: An experimental investigation. *Behaviour Research and Therapy, 40,* 235–251.

Stark, K. D., Reynolds, W. M., & Kaslow, N. J. (1987). A comparison of the relative efficacy of self-control therapy and a behavioral problem-solving therapy for depression in children. *Journal of Abnormal Child Psychology, 15,* 91–113.

Thapar, A., & McGuffin, P. (1997). Anxiety and depressive symptoms in childhood: A genetic study of comorbidity. *Journal of Child Psychology and Psychiatry, 38,* 651–656.

Thayer, R. E. (2000). Mood regulation and general arousal systems. *Psychological Inquiry, 11,* 202–204.

Turner, C. M., & Barrett, P. M. (2003). Does age play a role in structure of anxiety and depression in children and youths? An investigation of the tripartite model in three age cohorts. *Journal of Consulting and Clinical Psychology, 71,* 826–833.

Tyrer, P. (1989). *Classification of neurosis.* Oxford, England: Wiley.

Watson, D., & Clark, L. A. (1984). Negative affectivity: The disposition to experience aversive emotional states. *Psychological Bulletin, 96,* 465–490.

Weisz, J. R. (2004). *Psychotherapy for children and adolescents: Evidence-based treatments and case examples.* Cambridge: Cambridge University Press.

Wells, A., Clark, D. M., Salkovskis, P. M., Ludgate, J., Hackmann, A., & Gelder, M. (1995). Social phobia: The role of in-situation safety behaviors in maintaining anxiety and negative beliefs. *Behavior Therapy, 26,* 153–161.

Wilson, G. T. (1982). Psychotherapy process and procedure: The behavioral mandate. *Behavior Therapy, 13,* 291–312.

Zajonc, R. B. (2001). Mere exposure: A gateway to the subliminal. *Current Directions in Psychological Science, 10,* 224–228.

Zinbarg, R. E., & Barlow, D. H. (1996). Structure of anxiety and the anxiety disorders: A hierarchical model. *Journal of Abnormal Psychology, 105,* 181–93.

11

The Art of Evidence-Based Treatment of Trauma Survivors

BRETT T. LITZ AND KRISTALYN SALTERS-PEDNEAULT

Evidence-based practices are critically important for reasons we will discuss in this chapter, but science only takes us so far. In our view, this is especially true when considering psychological treatment of trauma-linked disorders and difficulties, such as posttraumatic stress disorder (PTSD). First, the emotional, psychological, and spiritual legacy of trauma, especially interpersonal trauma and betrayal (particularly in childhood), is often ineffable and can shape behavior and experience in immeasurable and uncertain ways. Second, the trajectory of posttraumatic adjustment is variably expressed and intricately moderated by numerous person and contextual variables, which can frustrate nomothetic prescriptions for care. Third, in order to be effective, the treatment of trauma requires a patient to self-disclose and be vulnerable, which can only happen in an intimate human context. Fourth, it is often the case that therapists need to go beyond the information given to uncover formerly concealed, avoided, or even freshly acknowledged elements of trauma histories and their impact, which requires artful openness, probing, and exploration. Thus, in trauma treatment, the scientifically measurable outcomes and the strategies used to target them are limited. Treatment often needs to be delivered and tailored in highly individualized and artful ways and therapists' ability to appeal to, and manifest, their own humanity and to manage what are, in effect, matters of the heart are important to efficacy. In this chapter, we first review the state of evidenced-based treatment for PTSD, detail the limitations of scientifically informed treatment schemes and the need to consider artful elements to care, provide some practical considerations for addressing art in helping traumatized individuals, address training and practice implications, and end with explicating some pitfalls and caveats.

EVIDENCE-BASED PRACTICES

There is considerable evidence from randomized controlled trials (RCT) to support the use of relatively brief, manualized, cognitive-behavioral therapy (CBT) to target PTSD (e.g., Bradley, Greene, Russ, Dutra, & Westen, 2005). CBT may offer particular advantages over medications (Otto, Pollack, & Penava, 1999) and CBT for PTSD benefits patients who are unresponsive to medications (Otto et al., 2003). At present, there is no single set of CBT procedures but rather a family of options, with no single approach conferring significant advantage over the others. In practice, nearly all evidence-based CBT involves a combination of exposure to trauma-related memories (imaginal) and contexts (in vivo), cognitive restructuring, and negative affect and arousal management techniques (e.g., Foa et al., 1999). Exposure-focused interventions have been the most studied, maintain very large effect sizes over time, and may lead to more rapid change (e.g., Foa, Hembree, & Cahill, 2005; Taylor, Thordarson, & Maxfield, 2003).

Yet, there is room for improvement. At posttreatment intervals, approximately 40–50% of patients retain a PTSD diagnosis (e.g., Bradley et al., 2005; Foa et al., 1999) and dropout rates are approximately 25%. In addition, despite the relative success in civilian contexts, the efficacy of CBT in targeting PTSD in veterans is marginal (e.g., Schnurr et al., 2003). Arguably, cases that have more chronic PTSD and associated impairment such as social adjustment and relationship difficulties, work disruption, aggression, substance abuse, and revictimization experiences require more intensive and extensive intervention. These types of patients are also likely to have various sources of current adversity, logistical, financial, and emotional obstacles to engaging in treatment, as well as difficulties meeting the boundary conditions of CBT (e.g., therapeutic alliance, homework compliance).

Notwithstanding the limitations of CBT, there is sufficient scientific evidence to justify the widespread routine use of systematic CBT to target posttraumatic difficulties whenever possible. This is also the conclusion of a series of practice guidelines published by the International Society for Traumatic Stress (Foa, Keane, & Friedman, 2000), the American Psychiatric Association (Ursano et al., 2004), and the Departments of Veterans Affairs and Defense (2003). In an ideal world, all professionals who treat trauma patients would have sufficient training in evidence-based CBT and therapists would start from the premise that one of the questions that their assessment and case conceptualization needs to address is which CBT strategies should be used to target various trauma-related problems.

However, this is not the current state of affairs. CBT for PTSD is extraordinarily underutilized, despite often being rated as the most credible and desirable treatment (Zoellner, Feeny, Cochran, & Pruitt, 2003). Despite some promising results from one dissemination trial (Foa et al., 2005), evidence-based CBT, especially exposure therapy, is not widely used outside of specialty clinics and research settings (e.g., Rosen, Chow, & Finney, 2004). Only 17% of psychologists who treat PTSD patients report using exposure therapy for PTSD (Becker, Zayfert, & Anderson, 2004). A number of professional barriers likely exist, including lack of familiarity or comfort with exposure procedures and beliefs that exposure interventions are overly intrusive and invasive (Astin & Rothbaum, 2000). One-third of behaviorally-oriented trauma therapists, most of whom are well trained in, and comfortable with exposure therapy, reported that they never used exposure to treat PTSD (Becker et al., 2004). Much of this is likely due to a generic problem in the field with training and dissemination in evidence-based practices (Barlow, Levitt, & Bufka, 1999). However, even experts state that they use exposure therapy for PTSD in approximately 50% of instances (Litz, Blake, Gerardi, & Keane, 1990).

Given the enormous public health and societal costs associated with chronic PTSD (e.g., Kessler, Sonnega, Bromet, Hughes, & Nelson, 1995), we would argue that the dissemination of evidence-based practices is one of the biggest current challenges for the field. Most people do not get the care they need or are provided inert palliative interventions or systematic interventions that have no evidence to support their use. The dangers are that people will suffer in isolation or when they approach a professional they will not be provided with state of the art care, may waste their time and resources, and in the worse case, get involved in something that may be harmful or may destroy their motivation to seek care in the future. Given that the psychosocial burden of trauma can be manifest across the lifespan for many, the latter is particularly troublesome.

One of the factors that keep therapists from considering CBT is that many believe that exposure therapy is likely to increase risk for dropout (Becker et al., 2004). This is not unexpected, given that exposure procedures increase anguish in the short-term. However, exposure therapy is not associated with higher rates of dropout than CBTs without exposure elements (Hembree, Foa, & Dorfan, 2003), and exposure is associated with a higher likelihood of treatment completion in clinical settings (Zayfert et al., 2005). An examination of the broader literature demonstrates that dropout rates from *all* forms of CBT are higher than from non-CBT interventions, leading to speculation that it is not the level of distress, per se, associated with *exposure* that may lead to dropout.

It could be that CBT training, and the increased structure demanded of CBT treatment, limits therapists' attention to the necessary nonspecific artful factors of psychotherapy (Hembree et al., 2003). Although no one who writes CBT manuals for PTSD would argue that effective participant-observation, empathic communication, and other stylistic elements are irrelevant to CBT interventions, they would argue that it is their job to focus primarily on theory-based systematization of intervention strategies, measurement, and replicability. Of course, it is no less important to attend to the therapeutic context for successful CBT for PTSD and efficacy is inevitably mediated by these factors, as it is generally (see Norcross, 2001). While RCTs of CBT have traditionally attempted to control for therapist effects, a meta-analysis suggests that the therapist has a robust effect (5–9%) on psychotherapy outcome (Crits-Christoph, Baranackie, & Kurcias, 1991). This equals the effect of many treatments, which are estimated to contribute 5–15% of variance in outcome (e.g., Wampold, 2001).

Because the artful elements to care are relatively overlooked (and perhaps assumed) in CBT training and CBT manuals, therapists may infer that they are not very important, they may be caught off guard when things do not go as planned, or CBT for trauma will be eschewed by those that may be predisposed to reject systematic approaches to behavior change. Given that the treatment of traumatized individuals is an intensely emotional and impactful experience, it is unhelpful, if not unacceptable, that insufficient attention is paid to therapy process and delivery issues. Also, given the need to disseminate evidence-based practices, providing excuses for rejection of science is problematic for the field. It is important for research-oriented training programs to grapple with the challenge of providing experiences for their students to nurture and develop the human and artful elements of care. And, CBT manuals need to speak to therapist, therapy context, and relationship issues and to embrace latitude and flexibility in clinical decision making. Attending to algorithms for greater flexibility within evidence-based practices and artful means of accomplishing various therapy goals will create better therapists, future supervisors and trainers, and better treatments. Creativity within therapy will lead to innovation in technology, which can then be examined scientifically. Science and art are reciprocal processes in psychotherapy; neither is sufficient to help people with trauma-related difficulties. When the CBT models of care are able to facilitate the convergence of art and science, the most powerful psychotherapies for trauma will emerge.

COMPLEXITY MATTERS

There are arguably many valid reasons why well-trained and well-intentioned clinicians fail to rely upon science in their decision making about intervention. Some patients present with problems and individual differences that negatively affect their capacity to build a therapeutic alliance and their ability to comply with the active components of CBT, which are fundamental and necessary features of successful CBT, especially exposure therapy. Patients who present with trauma histories are also commonly very complex and do not fit well into the *DSM* model of PTSD and, as a result, do not have the circumscribed problems of patients used in CBT trials. Many of these cases receive the signification of "complex PTSD," which is a fuzzy set of enduring symptoms and problems observed in patients who have extensive trauma histories, especially early betrayal by caregivers and various forms of neglect and abuse akin to the affect dysregulation and self- and other-disorganization that typifies borderline personality disorder (e.g., Herman, 1995).

We would argue that the more complex a case is, the more artfulness is required. It is generally true that cases that entail single incident, adult-onset trauma with few complications and intact social and self-esteem resources should be approached straightforwardly and succinctly, applying manualized CBT. A good deal of what we offer below entails recommendations to leverage the artful elements so that science-based interventions are possible for the complex cases. In many ways, this boils down to finding ways of building and maintaining therapeutic relationships, using assessment data wisely, conceptualizing cases in a sophisticated manner, using in-session process to promote new learning, and planning a course of treatment with provisions for various high probability pitfalls and snags.

Consider the conceptual underpinnings and the implied therapeutic mechanisms behind exposure therapy for PTSD. Exposure therapy entails repeated emotionally intense disclosure of traumatic experiences and, when applicable, in vivo confrontations with contexts that trigger traumatic memories, strategies that were developed directly from basic animal models of fear learning and maintenance (Bouton, 2002). A schematic of the process by which negative affect and arousal is acquired in response to a motor vehicle accident entails: a set of unconditioned stimuli (UCS; in this case the accident) elicits unconditioned responses (e.g., intense fear), which are paired with previously neutral stimuli (conditioned stimuli (CS), e.g., various aspects of the road situation), leading to conditioned responses (CR; e.g., fear) in the presence of CSs (driving in cars). Avoidance maneuvers prevent natural extinction of CRs and nonsustained exposure to CSs promote higher order learning to various contexts and cues and broad stimulus generalization, furthering maladaptive behavior in otherwise safe contexts. This is a model of discreet fear acquisition that is a relatively straightforward and elegant translation from basic infrahuman and human research. In this context, exposure therapy would entail imagining the accident in a sustained and focused fashion (and driving in various in vivo contexts) while preventing avoidance maneuvers, which leads to extinction and the acquisition of new nondanger associations.

However, consider the complex conditioning and learning that occurs as a result of repeated physical and sexual abuse by caregivers in development. Consider also the array of acquired and overlearned emotional, appraisal, and social behavior traits that likely arise from such experiences. In these instances, the person is likely to have diffuse and generalized trauma memories that affect well-being and functioning, impairments in the building blocks to self-esteem and relational success, and various coincident adversities and life problems. These cases are also going to be compromised in their ability to build trust and form a therapeutic alliance, to acquire insight into internal processes, and to be aware of and able to manage emotional experiences.

Well-controlled studies of treatment for PTSD and other trauma-linked disorders began to emerge just over 20 years ago. While there has been great progress in this area, there is still much we do not know about treating survivors of trauma. In particular, there has been scant attention paid to: the factors that might assist clinicians with difficult and complex trauma cases, matching interventions to patients, the moderating influence of therapist variables (a noteworthy exception can be found in Cloitre, Koenen, Cohen, & Han, 2002; Cloitre, Chase Stovall-McClough,

Miranda, & Chemtob, 2004), the role of therapist and patient expectancies, and effectiveness of practice in real-world clinical settings (e.g., Zayfert et al., 2005). As a result, there is a limited scientific basis to inform recommendations for the artful elements of trauma treatment. We argue for research into the artful elements in the care of traumatized individuals in a variety of practice settings and much greater attention to these issues in training contexts.

ART IN THE TREATMENT OF PTSD
Maintaining Flexibility

The promise of science in the treatment of traumatized individuals is that all patients would be provided state-of-the-art interventions that have been shown to be helpful to achieve measurable and well-monitored goals. Mental health professionals who have had to refer a person dear to them for psychotherapy for a trauma-related problem will have struggled with questions about what a given professional knows and how rigorous they are; accountability and replicability matter. On the other hand, professionals familiar with the state of the science are not going to be concerned with how many sessions are required to achieve specific goals or whether manuals and protocols are followed religiously. And, those who practice CBT know that with any set of problems, it is nearly impossible to stay on protocol all the time, and that it can be viewed as invalidating by patients when we do. Both patients engaged in CBT in the course of living a life full-time outside of therapy and the therapist must be responsive to concerns that arise, without allowing those concerns to derail therapeutic progress.

Empirically validated trauma therapies should be construed as collections of techniques founded on evidence-based principals of change (e.g., Rosen & Davison, 2003), and clinical judgment should inform the inclusion, alteration, or omission of particular strategies or a particular sequence of interventions. Psychotherapy for trauma in most cases mandates flexible application of protocols. Although there is no empirical rationale for this suggestion (and there is preliminary evidence that flexible approaches may not be any more effective than standardized application of protocols; Schulte, Künzel, Pepping, Schulte-Bahrenberg, 1992), it may be that the lack of flexibility in CBT accounts for the high rate of treatment failures or dropout because of the complexity of issues around trauma.

In practice, it can also be very useful to glean different interventions from different treatment manuals or frameworks (and the mindsets they confer). For example, we have conducted trauma-focused therapy with patients incorporating elements of *Dialectical Behavior Therapy* (Linehan, 1993), *Prolonged Exposure* (Foa & Rothbaum, 1997), and *Cognitive Processing Therapy* (Resick & Schnicke, 1993), while attending carefully to process observations in the therapeutic relationship to help shape behavior toward therapeutic goals informed by the case conceptualization (described well by Kohlenberg & Tsai, 1991). Each package named above has been shown to be efficacious with trauma-related emotional difficulties (and comorbid problems, such as depression), and there is a strong theoretical rationale for the active ingredients (and considerable overlap; each is part of the CBT family of therapies for PTSD). Each model offers very useful specific clinical heuristics and nuanced strategies that can be employed to address a variety of unanticipated twists and turns. Rather than winging it, artful trauma therapists should tune-up their case conceptualization and incorporate tried-and-true recommendations from different evidence-based schemes or protocols.

Therapist Characteristics and the Therapeutic Relationship

We believe that the quality of the relationship between the patient and therapist has particular importance in treating trauma-linked difficulties. Although very little empirical evidence supports this assertion, Cloitre and colleagues (2004) found a much stronger effect of alliance on treatment outcome for childhood abuse-related PTSD than has been found in the general treatment literature (e.g., Martin, Garske, & Davis, 2000). As we discuss below, although the consequences of many forms of trauma may make alliance-building more challenging, they may also afford a unique opportunity to affect change.

For many, the traumatic event represents a catastrophic violation of established beliefs and personal norms, such as the belief that the world is a safe place and that those who occupy it are basically benevolent or at least neutral. In the multiply traumatized, a given subsequent traumatic event may reinforce maladaptive beliefs, while in the case of interpersonal trauma, the impact on thinking and appraisal is even more robust if it is perpetrated by loved ones or trusted others. And, because others may attribute responsibility for the event to the survivor (e.g., Pollard, 1992), the newly acquired or confirmed belief that others cannot be relied upon may be reinforced in a vicious cycle. As a result, many survivors experience disruptions in their ability to trust, to form attachments, and to take advantage of disconfirming interpersonal successes when they arise.

A variety of posttraumatic symptoms and problems, such as irritability and low frustration tolerance, apparent emotional numbing, and a variety of defensive and avoidance maneuvers can also hinder alliance-building. Avoidance symptoms may also lead to inconsistent attendance and disengagement. Patients with significant emotional numbing symptoms may have difficulty feeling connected to the therapist, just as the therapist may have difficulty forging a strong bond with the patient because of a lack of give and take and poignant expression of emotion. In their study of CBT for trauma-related anger symptoms in Vietnam veterans, Chemtob, Novaco, Hamada, and Gross (1997) found that despite efforts by the research team to match patients to therapists with characteristics meant to lend credibility and trustworthiness (e.g., other Vietnam War veterans), anger often led to breaks in the alliance and treatment termination.

It is often necessary to focus on obstacles to an effective therapeutic relationship in the treatment of trauma. There are inevitable trauma-links to the reasons that a person has difficulty engaging and sustaining intimacy in the therapeutic relationship. As a result, if a positive therapeutic relationship can be success-fully forged and maintained, this can serve as an agent of change. The process of allying with a therapist may serve as a corrective emotional experience, disconfirm maladaptive beliefs about relationships and the consequences of self-disclosure and vulnerability (and the costs of concealment), serve as an extinction training context, and boost treatment credibility and adherence.

Attention to the therapeutic relationship is not static but is an unfolding dynamic process (see also chapters 6–9 of this volume). For example, the alliance may be important in the early stages of treatment to promote engagement with procedures that may be unfamiliar, terrifying, or effortful (e.g., Meyer et al., 2002), whereas a progressively stronger therapeutic alliance is needed (Joyce & Piper, 1998) as the therapist encourages the patient to disclose very personal information, approach instinctively avoided stimuli, and engage in counterintuitive behaviors (such as is the case in exposure). A strong alliance with a confident therapist facilitates this process, whereas a weak alliance opens the door to resistance, drop out, and poor outcome (e.g., Yoemans, Gutfreund, & Selzer, 1994).

The corrective new learning that can occur in the therapeutic relationship can generalize either spontaneously or strategically to other relationships, and thus have considerable added value. Generally, attention should be paid to the characteristics of the relationship that will maximize therapeutic change based on patients' previous learning history. Contextual factors related to the trauma may be highly germane (e.g., if the trauma occurred in the context of an emotionally invalidating social environment). The therapeutic alliance may also disconfirm patients' maladaptive beliefs, or lead to extinction of generalized fear associa-tions (e.g., example, in the case of sexual assault, the belief that all men are threatening).

Outside of therapy, many trauma survivors are given unhelpful, shaming, and often very destructive messages by intimates or the culture. Examples include that they are: (1) responsible for the event (e.g., they are careless or provocative); (2) weak for experiencing enduring psychological distress related to the event (e.g., "Why aren't you over this already!"); or (3) they are unduly needy and not pulling their weight. If the trauma is isolated and recent, the impact of these interpersonal experiences can be relatively easily challenged and overcome. If the trauma is repeated and the outcome chronic, the person will have a well-organized schema that they will employ to assimilate difficulties in therapy. For example, they may maintain a helplessly and hopelessly flawed construction of themselves or experi-ence shame as a result of the slightest provocation, both of which reduce motiva-tion and expectations of personal agency. As the therapy progresses, the therapist needs to become increasingly challenging, balancing the dialectic of acceptance and change (Linehan, 1993), but this process must be founded in a context of support and nonjudgment. Further, given that trauma may be related to beliefs that the world/other people are unpredictable and uncontrollable, the therapist must appreciate the importance of respect, structure, and boundaries. Different therapists likely have different approaches or comfort levels in these areas, but the structure and boundaries of the particular therapeutic relationship must be openly discussed, agreed upon, and strictly enforced.

The art in this context is finding ways to balance a caring, patient, understanding, and empathic manner and pushing the envelope via challenge, confrontation, and focusing on dreaded and charged interpersonal experiences in real-time. The effective therapist needs to fully appreciate how scary and new the intimacy demands of psychotherapy are for many traumatized individuals and how much courage it takes to reveal details of traumatic histories and the emotional aftermath of trauma.

A trauma therapist needs to use assessment data to anticipate obstacles to a therapeutic alliance, conceptualize the trauma-linked nature of these difficulties (when applicable), and generate a plan to redress problems. The therapist also needs to evaluate the prognosis for targeting obstacles and develop a treatment plan that compensates for apparent unmodifiable interpersonal repertoires or repertoires that go beyond the therapist's expertise to address. This kind of decision making requires taking into account the chances of success with the consequences of failure and the resources of the patient.

Choosing the Right Intervention

In 1990, our group published clinical decision-making guidelines for selecting treatment options for PTSD (Litz et al., 1990) in which we suggested that patient factors such as the inability to tolerate intense negative affect and arousal, emotional and physiological reactivity to specific trauma cues, imagery ability, motivation for treatment, and presence of certain comorbid difficulties (e.g., substance abuse disorders), are contraindications for exposure therapy. Although empirical support for some of these factors has emerged, others have been found to be unrelated to compliance or outcome (see van Minnen, Arntz, & Keijsers, 2002). For example, comorbid alcohol abuse predicts treatment drop out (van Minnen et al., 2002), but factors such as previous trauma (e.g., Tarrier, Sommerfield, Pilgrim, & Faragher, 2000), and chronicity of trauma (e.g., Jaycox, Foa, & Morral, 1998) have not been consistently supported. In its current state, the literature suggests that although it is important to match the patient to the treatment, many previously held reasons for excluding patients from exposure therapy are unfounded. Historically, many clinicians believed that multiple traumas and chronic symptoms would not respond well to trauma-focused treatment; however there is an emerging consensus that this is not the case (Astin & Rothbaum, 2000).

Although matching the patient to a particular modality of care is important, therapist factors that may influence treatment choice must also be considered. Foremost, therapists should not attempt therapeutic techniques they have not been taught to deliver. CBT manuals, while helpful for seasoned clinicians and supervised trainees, are not substitutions for training. Exposure therapies also require the therapist to tolerate not only the anguish and distress that naturally emerges when patients focus on memories of their trauma but also the distress that arises in the person when they hear about such awful experiences. Because sustained emotional engagement is central to change from exposure therapy (Foa & Kozak, 1986), a therapist who is prone to shift to less distressing content may not be well-suited for this type of therapy.

Related to alliance issues, treatment choice and goal-setting should be approached as collaborative activities in trauma therapy. Given the intrusive nature of traumatic events, the introduction of trauma-focused work must not be thrust upon the patient, even if, in the clinician's view, this is the most viable option. The goals of trauma-focused work should be arrived at collaboratively, with the clinician carefully attending to and challenging avoidance, but also respecting the patient's free will and personal control. In our view, the patient's expertness is sometimes not fully honored in the decision-making process. The clinician has access to a wide range of information about available treatments, research literatures supporting those approaches, and patient factors predicting outcomes. The patient is an expert about their personal preferences, values, beliefs, and learning styles. Within the constellation of evidence-based modalities for trauma treatments, a discussion about the advantages and disadvantages of each can be approached in therapy, and a mutually satisfactory approach arrived upon.

Imparting Confidence and Positive Expectations

Exposure techniques can be destabilizing and unsettling for therapists and threaten their confidence because patients can appear worse before they improve; exposure therapy can reveal aspects of a patient's experience that were unanticipated, typically event details or responses to events that trigger intense shame (e.g., the work may unveil acts of perpetration). Patients will also be alarmed by shifts in the intensity and frequency of their suffering, so they will look to the therapist for reassurance. Relatively low therapist confidence will exacerbate a patient's nascent fears, lower confidence, reduce motivation, reinforce beliefs that the material needs to stay buried, and invite treatment drop out or poor outcome. The antidote to breaches in confidence comes from extensive training in exposure-based therapy, education in the theoretical and empirical bases for these strategies, supervision or consultation, as well as therapist personal experiences with treatment success.

When patients are asked to disclose details of horrific events and their peritraumatic responses and focus their attention while doing so (i.e., not avoid), they are asked to take a leap of faith. Most of their experiences with the content of the traumatic memory have been either in the context of the trauma itself or in the context of re-experiencing. Re-experiencing is very disturbing, uncontrollable, and likely interpreted by the brain as equally dangerous as the actual event (see LeDoux, 1996). Imparting faith to the patient is a cognitive-emotional process, although therapists may be tempted to rely too heavily on the cognitive aspects, trying to convince the patient with strong logic that this will help them. Psychoeducation about the rationale for exposure may impart some degree of rational belief in the procedures, but at the level of emotional/experiential knowledge, the patient has no basis for belief that approaching these memories, thoughts, feelings, and sensations will be helpful. A large degree of their re-experiencing is arguably precognitive (e.g., Davidson, 2001) and, therefore, likely less subject to verbal argument. They will probably not truly "believe" in a rational sense until they experience the changes. For a good while, the therapist must then genuinely, deeply, and confidently believe that this course of action is best, normalize the anticipatory dread and fear, acknowledge the need for a leap of faith, and connect with their own emotional knowledge that their patient can be helped in this manner.

Bearing Witness to Trauma

While therapists must instill faith, hope, and courage, they also abide the important task of bearing witness to the trauma. In trauma-focused work, a patient will be charged with speaking about and reliving events that may be regarded by society as literally unspeakable. This may be another unmeasured mechanism of change in therapy; there are positive consequences to simply disclosing strategically concealed emotional events (see Lumley, 2004). The therapist's reaction during the retelling will shape and impact the process considerably. The reaction must be strategic, to promote therapeutic processing and to maximize new learning, influenced by the patient's frame of reference for the event, and genuinely based on the therapist's own human emotional reaction. If, as is frequently the case, a patient blames him or herself for the event, a reaction of strong negative emotion such as disgust or fear from the therapist may be misinterpreted as blame toward or disgust with the patient. Even when sitting with the stories of a perpetrator, a therapist must find the elements around which true empathic connection can be summoned. Maintaining an empathic and caring expression and stance is recommended during the retelling or reliving of events, even if the content of the event is horrifying. Judgment, shock, intense emotional reaction, and hesitation are to be avoided at all costs. In this context, it is important for trauma therapists to have considerable pathos, as well as an appreciation of the dark and evil things that humans can do to one another, and an idea of the primitiveness, rawness, and nonrational nature of victimization experiences and what might happen when desperation ensues.

Therapist Self-Care

Trauma treatment can significantly impact the practitioner. At a minimum, therapists who bear witness to varied and numerous traumas and the damage done to their patients will experience strong emotions that may not dissipate easily. Some therapists have an uncanny temperament and very thick skins that allow them to fairly readily recover a sense of well-being and positive expectancies. Others will have emotional and psychological experiences that linger and pose a burden of some kind.

The most damaging forms of psychological impact have been described as "secondary traumatization" or "vicarious traumatization" (e.g., Figley, 1995).

Unfortunately, these terms are used far too broadly and may overly pathologize a phenomenon that is not necessarily abnormal or unhealthy. Because it is so essential that trauma therapists be open, humane, and caring in their work, it leaves them understandably vulnerable. The risk is to overaccommodate information about trauma and to, consequently, see the world as unfair, unjust, horrible, and threatening, and to exaggerate personal vulnerability. In this context, it helps if therapists have strong generally positive (but not Pollyannaish) self- and other-schemas that allow them to assimilate what they learn from their patients. On the other hand, it is entirely normal to respond to stories of abuse, assault, and other victimization with strong emotions. In fact, a therapist who does not experience some raw emotional response in this context should consider another line of work. The therapists' job is to know themselves well, to self-monitor effectively, and to anticipate shifts in thoughts or behaviors related to the stories they hear. For example, a therapist working with female sexual assault victims may suddenly feel uncomfortable in a room full of men. These experiences of nascent fear can trigger anger or avoidance, which needs to be actively countered. However, these experiences need to be used to improve understanding of a patient's experiences. The clinician can also use mirrored experiences as an impetus for enacting the behaviors that are critical for their patients: enhance awareness, promote non-avoidance, and apply self-care skills.

Trauma therapy can be enormously rewarding but it can also be emotionally draining. Trauma therapists are reminded constantly that terrible things happen and that we all have a shared vulnerability. Clinicians should employ primary and secondary prevention in the service of minimizing the negative impact of their very human responses on themselves and on their capacity to help their patients. If a therapist spends a significant percentage of his work week hearing about tragedy and intense human suffering, or if she has many difficult and taxing cases, and if he has noteworthy current adversity and life-stress, a therapist needs to pay very close attention to the personal impact of the work and should double-up on self-care. There are excellent resources available that promote self-care for trauma therapists (e.g., Saakvitne & Pearlman, 1995), and their importance cannot be overstated. Maintaining scheduled breaks between patients, and time for relaxation, exercise, sleep, and meals is important. Seeking supervision, support, validation, and compassion from a fellow professional can also relieve some of the burden.

Self-Disclosure and Emotional Presence

Self-disclosure is a somewhat controversial aspect of the art of psychotherapy, and yet it can be helpful in trauma therapy when delivered in a strategic and careful manner (see Knox & Hill, 2003 for a full review of the merits of therapist self-disclosure). Although maintaining boundaries is important in trauma therapy, it is also important to underscore shared humanity. Trauma patients will likely feel alone in their suffering. They may feel deeply tainted and tarnished and expect others to be unable to fathom what happened to them. Although we would not endorse the therapist disclosing if they themselves have a trauma history, the disclosure of less personal but nonetheless forthcoming experiences of vulnerability may be warranted. For example, it may be helpful for therapists to disclose one of their own experiences with anxiety (e.g., "When I have to speak in front of a group of people I notice all kinds of anxious thoughts, such as 'I wonder if I'll make an idiot of myself?'"). The therapist should not compare this suffering to that experienced by their patient, but rather use disclosure to impart that everyone suffers in their own way and that the therapist is not immune (even though the therapist may be viewed by the patient as having a privileged struggle-free life). This provides a coping model rather than a mastery model, which arguably has a higher likelihood of motivating patients.

We have used an adaptation of the "mountain metaphor" from Hayes and colleagues' Acceptance and Commitment Therapy (ACT; Hayes, Strosahl, & Wilson, 1999) to address the problem when patients communicate that they feel the therapist cannot understand their pain and therefore lack credibility in proposing a solution. In using this metaphor, patients imagine that life is like climbing a mountain, that everyone has his or her own mountain, and that each is unique. We must acknowledge that some of the mountains are less steep, or have fewer obstacles. The therapist, too, has a mountain to climb, but is in the position of being able to look over to the patient's mountain and say things like "Hey, there's a big boulder in the way, move right." Therapists, then, have experience with climbing mountains in general, probably have had a few boulders (sources of pain) of their own, and because they spend a lot of time observing others' mountains, and are on their own separate mountain, can be objective about what may be helpful for the patient.

Maximizing Emotional Engagement

A small but growing empirical literature has supported the supposition that emotional engagement is an important mediator to adjustment to trauma and response to treatment. For example, strategic emotional withholding (Roemer, Litz, Orsillo, & Wagner, 2001), emotionally avoidant coping styles (e.g., Marx & Sloan, 2002), and constricted emotionality (Lisak, Hopper, & Song, 1996) are associated with poorer posttraumatic outcomes. In treatment, facial expressions of fear during imaginal recall has been shown to index emotional engagement, which predicts symptom improvement (Foa, Riggs, Massei, & Yarczower, 1995), and individuals with high initial emotional engagement are more likely to benefit from exposure treatment (Jaycox et al., 1998).

An aspect of trauma-focused therapy that heavily relies on art is the process of guiding the patient's emotional engagement within a session and over the course of therapy. There is unanimous agreement that the degree of a patient's emotional engagement is critical to outcome in trauma-focused work. In Foa and Kozak's (1986) model of emotional processing, new learning, in the form of exposure to corrective experience, occurs when the "fear network" is accessed fully, which includes stimulus, response, and meaning cues or elements. In our experience, the latter provides a very useful heuristic to guide therapists in their trauma-focused work. Motivated by strategic and nonconscious avoidance, patients may characteristically prefer a certain mode of disclosing and processing their traumatic memories. Typically, patients will shy away from focusing on their emotional reliving. Therapists should keep a watchful eye out for systematic biases so they can direct the patient's attention to other cue categories. Equal weight should be given to the stimulus (e.g., sights, sounds, smells), response (e.g., not being able to breathe), and meaning (e.g., "I feel abandoned") elements.

The following are basic questions that can be asked while conducting exposure therapy to direct a patient's attention to different elements of a trauma memory in the present tense, first person, which is the prescribed mode to maximize engagement: (1) What are you seeing (alternatively, what are you sensing or hearing, and so on?; (2) What are you feeling (now) as you are seeing (hearing, smelling, etc.) _____?; and (3) What comes to mind as you feel _____?.

It can be extremely difficult to facilitate an emotionally numb or strategically avoidant individual's focus on deeply distressing content. Patients are highly motivated to evade this material and have developed and employed avoidance strategies that have, over time, become deeply entrenched and automatized, particularly in the case of chronic PTSD. In addition to the experience of emotions as frightening and overwhelming, childhood trauma survivors may have received messages during development that any level of emotional response is dangerous ("If you cry you will be harmed," or "Emotions in others mean something really bad is going to happen."). Patients may come to therapy with the belief that if they let go and focus freely on their emotions they will be destroyed by them; some fear "going crazy." Moving a numb or avoidant patient toward emotional engagement requires flexibility, patience, and trial and error.

Some patients may require practice with emotional engagement or initial emotion regulation training (such as that provided by Cloitre and colleagues' treatment model; Cloitre et al., 2002) before they move into trauma-focused work, in order to feel they are prepared when emotions arise. Although it may seem counterintuitive, training in effective and flexible emotion modulation can impart a sense of safety and predictability around emotions that facilitates the abandonment of overused or rigid control strategies. The use of mindfulness to increase awareness and acceptance of emotions (as described in Linehan, 1993) may also be valuable. Mindfulness training may provide patients with the learning experience that emotional responses are not objectively dangerous and can be experienced without alteration or suppression.

Although it is not necessary to unearth every single possible detail of a traumatic experience to accomplish therapeutic goals, it is often the case that patients have difficulty staying with the emotional disclosure in a sufficiently vivid and sustained manner. As a result, it is often necessary to help them by emphasizing certain aspects of a traumatic experience. And, some patients need to go "beyond the information given" and explore previously avoided aspects of traumatic experiences and their implications. In each of these scenarios, the art is found in getting under someone's skin, and, based on the case conceptualization, emotion knowledge, personal experience, and expectations of possible trauma scenarios, hypothesize where the stuck-points might be and what is being left out from a trauma narrative.

Facilitating emotional engagement during imaginal exposure requires the clinician to be keenly attuned to the patient's emotional response, and to the specific aspects of the trauma memory that are particularly painful; the clinician's job is to push the patient, encouraging him or her to stay with and notice pain. As described above, it also requires the therapist to remain open to and aware of the elements of the memory that may be avoided, or to parts of the narrative that seem incongruent or not sufficiently fleshed out. When done artfully, this process is flowing and dynamic, taking into account the personality of the patient and the quality of the therapeutic relationship. The therapist must be intuitive but not overly presumptuous, testing the patient's emotional response to different aspects of the memory, and learning what must be approached more fully, all the while being empathically present. In some ways, this process may be counter to the natural desire to ease the patient's suffering, so the clinician must be vigilant for urges to back away and the subtle ways this may manifest itself (e.g., feeling compelled to hand the patient a tissue, which may interrupt poignant and focused moments).

Another potential difficulty is the possibility of dissociation during exposure, a problem that might be conceptualized as excessive immersion in the recall experience. In our experience, clinicians, too, often err on the side of caution with the emotional responses of trauma survivors, but we acknowledge the possibility that dissociation or even full immersion flashbacks (however poorly these phenomena are operationalized and described in the literature) may occur during exposure. Hypothetically, dissociation should be avoided because, if present-moment safety cues are not consciously accessible, the contextual inhibitory learning that occurs during extinction (see Bouton, 2002) is disrupted, rendering exposure inert, and introducing the possibility of sensitization. If someone is known to be prone to dissociation, initial emotion regulation training may be indicated. If dissociation happens unexpectedly during exposure, so-called "grounding techniques," such as having the patient observe aspects of the current situation (e.g., the feel of his or her feet on the floor) may help the patient re-engage with the present moment. Dissociation may not be a contraindication for exposure, but may require clinical ingenuity. The clinician may employ more gradually graded exposure by choosing less threatening memories in the trauma fear hierarchy, or may continue to approach the same memory in a graded fashion.

Overcoming Resistance

It is not uncommon for patients to be considerably resistant to approaching traumatic material and reminder contexts (see also chapter 9 of this volume). A patient's efforts in-session and outside of therapy and their persistence in the face of emotional challenges are key determinants of outcome. Effort and persistence can only come if the patient has positive efficacy and outcome expectancies.

The psychotherapy outcome research literature demonstrates that resistive patients are more vulnerable to treatment drop out and poor outcome in directive therapies compared to less directive approaches (Beutler, Moleiro, & Talebi, 2002). CBT therapists are sometimes trained to "go for the avoidance" wherever it lives, which may account for the high drop out in CBT for trauma. Certainly, we would not suggest that CBT be abandoned if the patient demonstrates resistance (especially given that there is weak empirical evidence for the efficacy of non-directive interventions such as psychodynamic therapy for PTSD; see Kudler, Blank, & Krupnick, 2000), but we do suggest that the therapist is likely to be more effective in encouraging change by being less authoritative.

Sometimes resistance takes the form of anger or threats of termination and other times patients are passively obstructive. Therapists must be mindful of the gestalt of the case, use their case conceptualization, and take into account where patients are in the course of their therapy. Some patients may report that external forces preclude their engagement in aspects of the therapy (e.g., "I do not have a room in my home to play my exposure tapes,"), or may come to each imaginal exposure session with an immediate concern to be addressed. Although a wise therapist will be vigilant about the possibility of secondary gain, the most parsimonious hypothesis is that the patient is not confident in his or her abilities or the outcome that will result from the pain of the process. The course of action that should result from this way of thinking about resistance is inquiring about self- and outcome expectations, finding ways of promoting, in small ways, agency and hope, having the patient self-monitor obstacles to compliance, and finding solutions to various obstacles.

Therapists must remain confident in their conviction that approach of this material is what is most helpful for patients; however, they must also balance directiveness with gentleness. A significant push for change may be viewed by the patient as invalidating or misunderstanding the horror of the trauma (e.g., by suggesting I confront this you must not fully appreciate how awful it is).

Anecdotally, we have found it helpful to use elements of motivational interviewing (Miller & Rollnick, 2002) in working with resistance. Many of our patients have struggled for years with the residue of trauma, but find comfort in the familiarity of their suffering. Their ambivalence is often addressed by having them imagine the positive and negative consequences of engaging in exposure; patients often come to realize that the thoughts, feelings, and memories they try so desperately to avoid are part of their daily lives anyway, and that exposure can't make these any worse than they already are.

Caveats and Cautions

In the trauma field, there are many examples of techniques and interventions offered by charismatic clinicians who claim scientific validity to legitimize techniques that, in reality, have no empirical basis. Trauma is uniquely stigmatizing and there are considerable logistic, financial, time, and psychological barriers to trauma survivors getting the proper care they need. The danger for the field of trauma is that practices may be promoted and disseminated that waste patients valuable time and emotional and financial resources.

The majority of our suggested artful practices are based on clinical experience and a construction of the common pitfalls in trauma therapy. Generating ideas about how art can assist the translation of science into practice is needed to advance the field and to disseminate best practices broadly.

In closing, there are several reasons why art and artfulness should not be unduly overemphasized in the treatment of traumatized individuals. First, therapists must strike a balance between evidence-based practices and artful approaches to carry them out. Second, professionals are at risk for being seduced by artful strategies because it can be highly reinforcing to successfully introduce some dramatic, but likely short-lived, shift in patients awareness and behavior. The means to accomplish therapeutic goals should not become ends unto themselves. We should also be mindful of the tendency for patients to be "people pleasing," which would motivate them to provide positive feedback to therapists in order to make them feel better or to maintain their commitment. Third, trainees may have lowered self-efficacy because they are exposed to particularly charismatic supervisors or lecturers who have a uniquely successful and stylized artfulness. We recommend modeling and fostering humility in the face of significant trauma-related difficulties in therapy and the need to be driven by theory and an iterative case conceptualization. Therapists should evaluate their patients systematically and monitor various specific targets in order to maintain quality control (and evaluate efficacy). We also suggest supervising trainees in a manner that fosters their sense of agency and confidence and nurtures their potential. They should be allowed to work toward articulating their own unique style and voice as therapists.

REFERENCES

Astin, M. C., & Rothbaum, B. O. (2000). Exposure therapy for the treatment of posttraumatic stress disorder. *National Center for PTSD Clinical Quarterly, 9,* 49–54.

Barlow, D. H., Levitt, J. T., & Bufka, L. F. (1999). The dissemination of empirically supported treatments: A view to the future. *Behaviour Research and Therapy, 37,* S147–S162.

Becker, C. B., Zayfert, C., & Anderson, E. (2004). A survey of psychologists' attitudes towards and utilization of exposure therapy for PTSD. *Behaviour Research and Therapy, 42,* 277–292.

Beutler, L. E., Moleiro, C., & Talebi, H. (2002). Resistance in psychotherapy: What conclusions are supported by research? *Journal of Clinical Psychology, 58,* 207–217.

Bouton, M. E. (2002). Context, ambiguity, and unlearning: Sources of relapse after behavioral extinction. *Biological Psychiatry, 52,* 976–986.

Bradley, R., Greene, J., Russ, E., Dutra, L., & Westen, D. (2005). A multidimensional meta-analysis of psychotherapy for PTSD. *American Journal of Psychiatry, 162,* 214–227.

Chemtob, C. M., Novaco, R. W., Hamada, R. S., & Gross, D. M. (1997). Cognitive-behavioral treatment for severe anger in posttraumatic stress disorder. *Journal of Consulting and Clinical Psychology, 65,* 184–189.

Cloitre, M., Chase Stovall-McClough, K., Miranda, R., & Chemtob, C. M. (2004). Therapeutic alliance, negative mood regulation, and treatment outcome in child abuse-related posttraumatic stress disorder. *Journal of Consulting and Clinical Psychology, 72,* 411–416.

Cloitre, M., Koenen, K. C., Cohen, L. C., & Han, H. (2002). Skills training in affective and interpersonal regulation followed by exposure: A phase-based treatment for PTSD related to childhood abuse. *Journal of Consulting and Clinical Psychology, 70,* 1067–1074.

Crits-Christoph, P., Baranackie, K., & Kurcias, J. S. (1991). Meta-analysis of therapist effects in psychotherapy outcome studies. *Psychotherapy Research, 1,* 81–91.

Davidson, R. J. (2001). The neural circuitry of emotion and affective style: Prefrontal cortex and amygdala contributions. *Social Science Information, 40,* 11–37.

Department of Veterans Affairs and Health Affairs, Department of Defense Management of Posttraumatic Stress. (2003). *VA/DoD clinical practice guidelines.* (Office of Quality and Performance publication 10Q-CPG/PTSD-04). Washington, DC: Author.

Figley, C. R. (1995). *Compassion fatigue: Coping with secondary traumatic stress disorder in those who treat the traumatized.* Philadelphia: Brunner/Mazel.

Foa, E. B., Hembree, E. A., & Cahill, S. P. (2005). Randomized trial of prolonged exposure for posttraumatic stress disorder with and without cognitive restructuring: Outcome at academic and community clinics. *Journal of Consulting and Clinical Psychology, 73,* 953–964.

Foa, E. B., & Kozak, M. J. (1986). Emotional processing of fear: Exposure to corrective information. *Psychological Bulletin, 99,* 120–135.

Foa, E. B., Dancu, C. V., Hembree, E. A., Jaycox, L. H., Meadows, E. A., & Street, G. P. (1999). A comparison of exposure therapy, stress inoculation training, and their combination for reducing posttraumatic stress disorder in female assault victims. *Journal of Consulting and Clinical Psychology, 67,* 194–200.

Foa, E. B., Keane, T. M., & Friedman, M. J. (2000). *Effective treatments for PTSD: Practice guidelines from the International Society for Traumatic Stress Studies.* New York: Guilford.

Foa, E., Riggs, E., Massie, E., & Yarczower, M. (1995). The impact of fear activation and anger on the efficacy of exposure treatment of posttraumatic stress disorder. *Behavior Therapy, 26,* 487–499.

Foa, E. B., & Rothbaum, B. O. (1997). *Treating the trauma of rape: Cognitive behavioral therapy for PTSD.* New York: Guilford.

Hayes, S. C., Strosahl, K. D., & Wilson, K. G. (1999). *Acceptance and commitment therapy: An experiential approach to behavior change.* New York: Guilford.

Hembree, E. A., Foa, E. B., & Dorfan, N. M. (2003). Do patients drop out prematurely from exposure therapy for PTSD? *Journal of Traumatic Stress, 16,* 555–562.

Herman, J. L. (1995). Complex PTSD: A syndrome in survivors of prolonged and repeated trauma. In G. S. Everly Jr. & J. M. Lating (Eds.), *Psychotraumatology: Key papers and core concepts in posttraumatic stress* (pp. 87–100). New York: Plenum.

Jaycox, L. H., Foa, E. B., & Morral, A. R. (1998). Influence of emotional engagement and habituation on exposure therapy for PTSD. *Journal of Consulting and Clinical Psychology, 66,* 185–192.

Joyce, A. S., & Piper, W. E. (1998). Expectancy, the therapeutic alliance, and treatment outcome in short-term individual psychotherapy. *Journal of Psychotherapy Practice & Research, 7,* 236–248.

Kessler, R. C., Sonnega, A., Bromet, E., Hughes, M., & Nelson, C. B. (1995). Posttraumatic stress disorder in the National Comorbidity Survey. *Archives of General Psychiatry, 52,* 1048–1060.

Knox, S., & Hill, C. E. (2003). Therapist self-disclosure: Research-based suggestions for practitioners. *Journal of Clinical Psychology, 59,* 529–539.

Kohlenberg, R. J., & Tsai, M. (1991). *Functional analytic psychotherapy: Creating intense and curative therapeutic relationships.* New York: Plenum.

Kudler, H. S., Blank, A. S. Jr., & Krupnick, J. L. (2000). Psychodynamic therapy. In E. B. Foa, T. M. Keane, & M. J. Friedman (Eds.), *Effective treatments for PTSD: Practice guidelines from the International Society for Traumatic Stress Studies* (pp. 176–198). New York: Guilford.

LeDoux, J. E. (1996). *The emotional brain: The mysterious underpinnings of emotional life.* New York: Simon & Schuster.

Linehan, M. M. (1993). *Cognitive-behavioral treatment of borderline personality disorder.* New York: Guilford.

Lisak, D., Hopper, J., & Song, P. (1996). Factors in the cycle of violence: Gender rigidity and emotional constriction. *Journal of Traumatic Stress, 9,* 721–743.

Litz, B. T., Blake, D. D., Gerardi, R. G., & Keane, T. M. (1990). Decision making guidelines for the use of direct therapeutic exposure in the treatment of posttraumatic stress disorder. *The Behavior Therapist, 18,* 91–93.

Lumley, M. A. (2004). Alexithymia, emotional disclosure, and health: A program of research. *Journal of Personality, 72,* 1271–1300.

Martin, D. J., Garske, J. P., & Davis, M. K. (2000). Relation of the therapeutic alliance with outcome and other variables: A meta-analytic review. *Journal of Consulting and Clinical Psychology, 68,* 438–450.

Marx, B. P., & Sloan, D. M. (2002). The role of emotion in the psychological functioning of adult survivors of childhood sexual abuse. *Behavior Therapy, 33,* 563–577.

Meyer, B., Pilkonis, P. A., Krupnick, J. L., Egan, M. K., Simmens, S. J., & Sotsky, S. M. (2002). Treatment expectancies, patient alliance, and outcome: Further analysis from the National Institute of Mental Health Treatment of Depression Collaborative Research Program. *Journal of Consulting and Clinical Psychology, 70,* 1051–1055.

Miller, W. R., & Rollnick, S. (2002). Motivational interviewing: Preparing people for change (2nd ed). New York: Guilford.

Norcross, J. C. (2001). Purposes, processes and products of the task force on empirically supported therapy relationships. *Psychotherapy: Theory, Research, Practice, Training, 38,* 345–356.

Otto, M. W., Pollack, M. H., & Penava, S. J. (1999). Group cognitive-behavior therapy for patients failing to respond to pharmacology for panic disorder: A clinical case series. *Behaviour Research and Therapy, 37,* 763–770.

Otto, M. W., Hinton, D., Korbly, N. B, Chea, A., Phalnarith, B., Gershuny, B. S., et al. (2003). Treatment of pharmacotherapy-refractory posttraumatic stress disorder among Cambodian refugees: A pilot study of combination treatment with cognitive-behavior therapy vs. sertraline alone. *Behaviour Research and Therapy*, *41*, 1271–1276.

Pollard, P. (1992). Judgments about victims and attackers in depicted rapes: A review. *British Journal of Social Psychology*, *31*, 307–326.

Resick, P. A., & Schnicke, M. K. (1993). Cognitive processing therapy for rape victims: A treatment manual. Thousand Oaks, CA: Sage.

Roemer, L., Litz, B. T., Orsillo, S. M. & Wagner, A. (2001). A preliminary investigation of the role of strategic withholding of emotions in PTSD. *Journal of Traumatic Stress*, *14*, 149–156.

Rosen, C. S., Chow, H. C., & Finney, J. F. (2004). VA practice patterns and practice guidelines for treating posttraumatic stress disorder. *Journal of Traumatic Stress*, *17*, 213–222.

Rosen, G. M., & Davison, G. C. (2003). Psychology should list empirically supported principles of change (ESPs) and not credential trademarked therapies or other treatment packages. *Behavior Modification*, *27*, 300–312.

Saakvitne, K. W., & Pearlman, L. A. (1995). *Transforming the pain: A workbook on vicarious traumatization*. New York: Norton.

Schnurr, P. P., Friedman, M. J., Foy, D. W., Shea, T. M., Hsieh, F. Y., Lavori, P. W., et al. (2003). Randomized trial of trauma-focused group therapy for posttraumatic stress disorder: Results from a Department of Veterans Affairs cooperative study. *Archives of General Psychology*, *60*, 481–489.

Schulte, D., Künzel, R., Pepping, G., & Schulte-Bahrenberg, T. (1992). Tailor-made versus standardized therapy of phobic patients. *Advances in Behaviour Research & Therapy*, *14*, 67–92.

Tarrier, N., Sommerfield, C., Pilgrim, H., & Faragher, B. (2000). Factors associated with outcome of cognitive-behavioural treatment of chronic posttraumatic stress disorder. *Behaviour Research and Therapy*, *38*, 191–202.

Taylor, S., Thordarson, D. S., & Maxfield, L. (2003). Comparative efficacy, speed, and adverse effects of three PTSD treatments: Exposure therapy, EMDR, and relaxation training. *Journal of Consulting and Clinical Psychology*, *71*, 330–338.

Ursano, R. J., Bell, C., Eth, S., Friedman, M., Norwood, A., Pfefferbaum, B., et al. (2004). Practice guideline for treatment of patients with acute stress disorder and post-traumatic stress disorder. *American Journal of Psychiatry*, *161*, 3–31.

van Minnen, A., Arntz, A., & Keijsers, G. P. J. (2002). Prolonged exposure in patients with chronic PTSD: Predictors of treatment outcome and dropout. *Behaviour Research and Therapy*, *40*, 439–457.

Wampold, B. E. (2001). *The great psychotherapy debate: Models, methods, and findings*. Mahwah, NJ: Erlbaum.

Yeomans, F. E., Gutfreund, J., & Selzer, M. A. (1994). Factors related to drop-outs by borderline patients: Treatment contract and therapeutic alliance. *Journal of Psychotherapy Practice & Research*, *3*, 16–24.

Zayfert, C., DeViva, J. C., Becker, C. B., Pike, J. L., Gillock, K. L., & Hayes, S. A. (2005). Exposure utilization and completion of cognitive behavioral therapy for PTSD in a "real world" clinical practice. *Journal of Traumatic Stress*, *18*, 637–645.

Zoellner, L. A., Feeny, N. C., Cochran, B., & Pruitt, L. (2003). Treatment choice for PTSD. *Behaviour Research and Therapy*, *41*, 879–886.

Section *IV*
TREATMENTS OF AXIS II DISORDERS

12

Personality Diagnosis with the Shedler-Westen Assessment Procedure (SWAP)
Bridging the Gulf Between Science and Practice

JONATHAN SHEDLER

During a routine medical exam, a friend had an abnormal finding on a lab test. His physician ordered more tests, then referred him to an oncologist. The oncologist ordered more tests, then referred him to a team of oncology specialists, researchers at the cutting edge of their discipline. My friend underwent a liver biopsy. The oncologists diagnosed advanced liver cancer and told him he had only months to live.

In the ensuing panic there were few voices of reason. One happened to be that of a psychiatrist, my friend's senior colleague. She asked a simple question: Had he been *feeling* sick? He had not. The psychiatrist raised an eyebrow. Her wordless gesture spoke volumes: Something did not add up. The pieces did not fit. If my friend had advanced liver cancer, he would likely be deathly ill.

Indeed, he did not have cancer. After additional biopsies (and ineffable emotional turmoil), the oncologists eventually concluded that his liver had an area of dense blood vessel growth (hemangioma) that had probably been present from birth and was of no medical consequence. One might reasonably ask how these research-oriented oncologists had gotten it so wrong and why an elderly psychiatrist who had not practiced medicine in decades had shown greater diagnostic acumen. No doubt many factors were at work, but I believe one factor is that the oncologists focused on laboratory findings to the exclusion of other meaningful data, including the data afforded by their own eyes and ears. Additionally, they failed to consider how the data *fit together*. Had the laboratory findings been contextualized by what else the doctors knew or could have know about their patient, they may have regarded them differently—as pieces of a diagnostic puzzle, not the diagnostic picture in its entirety. To the extent that they relied on laboratory technology to the exclusion of clinical observation, judgment, and inference, the oncologists functioned more as *technicians* than as *clinicians*.

In recent decades, the mental health professions have also emphasized data from the research laboratory over data from the clinical consulting room. Personality diagnosis once depended on expert clinical judgment and inference about subtle, textured, and nuanced personality processes. Clinicians considered a range of data, relying not just on what patients said but also on how they said it, drawing complexly determined inferences from patients' accounts of their lives and important relationships, from their manner of interacting with the clinician, and from their own emotional reactions to the patient. For example, expert clinicians tend not to assess lack of empathy, a diagnostic criterion for narcissistic personality disorder, by administering self-report questionnaires or asking direct questions. Often, an initial sign of lack of empathy on the part of the patient is a subtle sense on the part of the clinician of being interchangeable or replaceable, of being treated as a sounding board rather than as a fellow human being. The clinician might go on to consider whether she consistently feels this way with this particular patient and whether such feelings are characteristic for her in her role as therapist. She might then become aware that the patient's descriptions of important others come across as somewhat two-dimensional, or that he tends to describe others more in terms of the functions they serve or the needs they meet than in terms of who they are as people. The clinician might further consider whether and how these issues dovetail with the facts the patient has provided about his life, with the problems that brought him to treatment, with information gleaned from family members or other collateral contacts, and so on. When clinicians function as clinicians and not as technicians, it is this kind of thinking, reasoning, and inference that they engage in.

It is just such clinical judgment and inference that psychiatry and psychology have turned away from. As successive editions of the *Diagnostic and Statistical Manual* (*DSM*) have minimized the role of clinical judgment and inference, personality diagnosis has evolved into a largely technical task of tabulating behavioral signs and symptoms with relatively little consideration for how they fit together, the psychological functions they serve, their meanings, the developmental trajectory that gave rise to them, or the present-day factors that maintain them. Indeed, the diagnostic "gold standard" in personality disorder research is the structured research interview. Such assessment methods are designed to achieve inter-rater reliability by minimizing the role of clinical judgment. Instead of relying on clinical knowledge, complexly determined inferences, and consistent impressions made on the harnessed subjectivities of seasoned therapists (McWilliams, 1999), such assessment procedures substitute standardized questions and decision rules. Indeed, they are typically not administered by expert clinicians at all, but by research assistants or trainees. Like the oncologists in the story, practitioners who rely on such diagnostic methods are functioning more as technicians than as clinicians.

We must also keep in mind that the *DSM*, and the structured assessment instruments it spawned, developed in the directions they have for good reason. Prior to *DSM-III*, psychiatric diagnosis was unsystematic, overly subjective, and of questionable scientific merit. It often revealed more about the clinician's background and theoretical commitments than it did about the patient. The *DSM* and structured personality assessment methods evolved in the service of science and in reaction against the unsystematic and overly subjective diagnostic methods of the past. In the evolution of diagnosis from a largely subjective, clinical enterprise to a largely technical, research-driven enterprise, much has been gained, just as much has been lost. The solution cannot be to turn back the clock and abandon the technical developments of the past decades, any more than it would make sense for oncologists to disregard the most advanced laboratory tests available. The solution, rather, may be a marriage of the best aspects of clinical wisdom and empirical rigor. We need not choose between empiricism devoid of clinical realism versus a return to a pre-empirical past. To borrow the paradoxical title of a popular movie, progress may lie in going back to the future

This chapter describes the Shedler-Westen Assessment Procedure (SWAP), an approach to personality assessment designed to *harness* clinical judgment and inference rather than eliminate it, and to combine the best features of the clinical and empirical traditions in personality assessment. It renders clinical constructs accessible to empirical investigation and provides a means of assessing personality that is both clinically relevant and empirically grounded.

This chapter will (1) review problems inherent in the current *DSM* diagnostic system, (2) discuss difficulties associated with the use of clinical observation and inference in research, (3) describe the development of the SWAP and its use in systematizing clinical observation, (4) present a clinical case illustrating how the SWAP provides a bridge between descriptive psychiatry and clinical case formulation, and (5) discuss recommendations for revising and refining *DSM* Axis II based on empirical findings from a national sample of patients.

WHY REVISE AXIS II?

The approach to PD (personality disorder) diagnosis codified by *DSM* finds little favor with either clinicians or researchers. There is a consensus that the *DSM* classifications system for PDs requires major reconfiguration. Some of the problems with *DSM*-Axis II include the following (see Westen & Shedler, 1999a, 2000):

1. The diagnostic categories do not rest on a solid empirical foundation and often disagree with empirical findings from cluster and factor analyses (Blais & Norman, 1997; Clark, 1992; Harkness, 1992; Livesley & Jackson, 1992; Morey, 1988).
2. *DSM*-Axis II artificially dichotomizes continuous variables (diagnostic criteria) into present/absent, which is neither theoretically nor statistically sensible (e.g., how little empathy constitutes "lack of empathy?").
3. *DSM*-Axis II commits arbitrarily to a categorical diagnostic system. It may be more useful to conceptualize borderline pathology, for example, on a continuum ranging from none through moderate to severe, rather than classifying borderline PD as present/absent (Widiger, 1993).
4. *DSM*-Axis II lacks the capacity to weight criteria that differ in their diagnostic importance (Davis, Blashfield, & McElroy, 1993).
5. Comorbidity between PD diagnoses is unacceptably high. Patients who receive any PD diagnosis often receive 4 to 6 out of a possible 10 (Blais & Norman, 1997; Grilo, Sanislow & McGlashan, 2002; Oldham et al., 1992; Pilkonis et al., 1995; Watson & Sinha, 1998), indicating lack of discriminant validity of the diagnostic constructs, the assessment methods, or both.
6. In trying to reduce comorbidity, *DSM* work groups have been forced to gerrymander diagnostic categories and criteria, sometimes in ways faithful neither to clinical observation nor empirical data. For example, they excluded lack of empathy and grandiosity from the diagnostic criteria for antisocial PD to minimize comorbidity with narcissistic PD, despite evidence that these traits are associated with both disorders (Widiger & Corbitt, 1995).
7. Efforts to define PDs more precisely have led to narrower criterion sets over time, progressively eroding the distinction between personality *disorders* (multifaceted *syndromes* encompassing cognition, affectivity, motivation, interpersonal functioning, and so on) and simple personality *traits*. The diagnostic criteria for paranoid PD, for example, are essentially redundant indicators of one trait, chronic suspiciousness. The diagnostic criteria no longer describe the multifaceted personality syndrome recognized by most clinical theorists and practitioners (Millon, 1990; Millon & Davis, 1997).
8. *DSM*-Axis II fails to consider personality strengths that might rule out personality disorder diagnoses for some patients. For example, differentiating between a patient with narcissistic personality disorder and a

much healthier person with prominent narcissistic dynamics may not be a matter of counting symptoms, but rather of noting whether the patient has such positive qualities as the capacity to love and to sustain meaningful relationships characterized by mutual caring.

9. *DSM*-Axis II does not encompass the spectrum of personality pathology that clinicians see in practice. Among patients receiving treatment for personality pathology (defined as enduring, maladaptive patterns of emotion, thought, motivation, or behavior that lead to distress or dysfunction), fewer than 40% can be diagnosed on axis II (Westen & Arkowitz-Westen, 1998).

10. The categories and criteria are not as clinically useful or relevant as they might be. For example, knowing whether a person meets *DSM-IV* diagnostic criteria for avoidant PD or dependent PD tells us little about the meaning of the person's symptoms, which personality processes to target for treatment, or how to treat them.

11. The algorithm used for diagnostic decisions (counting symptoms) diverges from the methods clinicians use, or could plausibly be expected to use, in real-world practice. Research in cognitive science indicates that clinicians are unlikely to make diagnoses by additively tabulating symptoms. Rather, they gauge the overall "match" between a patient and a cognitive template or prototype of the disorder (i.e., they consider the features of a disorder as a configuration or gestalt), or they use causal theories that make sense of the functional relations between the different symptoms (Blashfield, 1985; Cantor & Genero, 1986; Kim & Ahn, 2002; Westen, Heim, Morrison, Patterson, & Campbell, 2002).

12. The instruments used to assess personality disorders do not meet the standards for validity normally expected in psychological research (Perry, 1992; Skodol, Oldham, Rosnick, Kellman, & Hyler, 1991; Westen, 1997) and show poor test-retest reliability at intervals greater than 6 weeks (First et al., 1995; Zimmerman, 1994). The lack of test-retest reliability is especially problematic given that personality disorders are, by definition, enduring and stable over time.[1]

Most of the proposed solutions to these problems share the assumption that progress lies in further minimizing the role of the clinician, either by developing increasingly behavioral and less inferential diagnostic criteria, or by bypassing clinical judgment entirely through self-report questionnaires. Such attempted solutions may, however, be part of the problem. By eliminating clinical observation and inference, we may unintentionally be eliminating from study the psychological phenomena that are of greatest relevance and importance. The empathically attuned clinician may still be the only "measurement instrument" sensitive enough to register crucial psychological phenomena (Shedler, Mayman, & Manis, 1993). An alternative to eliminating clinical observation and inference is to *harness* it for scientific use.

THE PROBLEM WITH CLINICAL DATA

The problem with clinical observation and inference is *not* that it is inherently unreliable, as some researchers assume. The problem is that it tends to come in a form that does not lend itself readily to systematic study (Shedler, 2002). Rulers measure in inches and scales measure in pounds, but what metric do psychotherapists share? Imagine three clinicians reviewing the same case material. One might speak of schemas and belief systems, another of conditioning history, and the third of transference and resistance. Even among clinicians who share similar theoretical commitments, there may still be little overlap in constructs and terminology. For example, one psychodynamic clinician might speak of conflict and compromise formation, a second of object relations, and the third of self defects.

It is not readily apparent whether the hypothetical clinicians can or cannot make similar observations and inferences. There are three possibilities: (1) They may be observing and describing the same thing but using different language and metaphor systems to express it. (2) They may be attending to different aspects of the clinical material, as in the parable of the elephant and the blind men. (3) They may not be able to make the same clinical observations at all. *If we want to know whether clinicians can make the same observations and inferences, we must ensure that they speak the same language and attend to the same range of clinical phenomena.*

A STANDARD VOCABULARY FOR CASE DESCRIPTION

The *Shedler-Westen Assessment Procedure* (SWAP) is an assessment instrument designed to provide clinicians of all theoretical orientations with a standard vocabulary with which to express their observations and inferences about personality functioning (Shedler & Westen, 1998, 2004a, 2004b; Westen & Shedler, 1999a, 1999b). The vocabulary consists of 200 statements, each printed on a separate index card. Each statement may describe a given patient very well, somewhat, or not at all. A clinician who knows a patient well can describe the patient by ranking or ordering the statements into eight categories, from those that are most descriptive of the patient (assigned a value of 7) to those that are not descriptive (assigned a value of 0). Thus, the SWAP yields a score from 0 to 7 for each of 200 personality-descriptive variables. (Web-based software will soon allow clinicians to input SWAP scores and receive computer-generated diagnostic reports. The program can be previewed at http://www.SWAPassessment.org).

The standard vocabulary of the SWAP allows clinicians to provide in-depth psychological descriptions of patients in a systematic and quantifiable form. It also ensures that all clinicians attend to the same spectrum of clinical phenomena. SWAP statements are written in a manner close to the data (e.g., "Tends to be passive and unassertive," or "Emotions tend to spiral out of control, leading to extremes of anxiety, sadness, rage, etc."), and statements that require inference about internal processes are written in clear and unambiguous language (e.g., "Tends to blame own failures or shortcomings on other people or circumstances; attributes his/her difficulties to external factors rather than accepting responsibility for own conduct or choices."). Writing items in this jargon-free manner minimizes idiosyncratic and unreliable interpretive leaps. It also makes the item set useful for all clinicians regardless of their theoretical commitments.

The SWAP is based on the Q-Sort method, which requires clinicians to place a predetermined number of statements in each category (i.e., it uses a "fixed distribution"). The SWAP distribution resembles the right half of a normal distribution or "bell-shaped curve." One-hundred items are placed in the "0" or not descriptive category and progressively fewer items are placed in the higher categories. Only eight items are placed in the "7" or most descriptive category. The use of a fixed distribution has important psychometric advantages and eliminates much of the measurement error or "noise" inherent in standard rating procedures[2] (see Block, 1978, for the psychometric rationale underlying the Q-sort method).

The SWAP item set was drawn from a wide range of sources including the clinical literature on PDs written over the past 50 years (e.g., Kernberg, 1975, 1984; Kohut, 1971; Linehan, 1993); Axis II diagnostic criteria included in *DSM-III* through *DSM-IV*; selected *DSM* Axis I items that could reflect aspects of personality (e.g., depression and anxiety); research on coping and defense mechanisms (Perry & Cooper, 1987; Shedler, Mayman, & Manis, 1993; Vaillant, 1992; Westen, Muderrisoglu, Fowler, Shedler, & Koren, 1997); research on interpersonal pathology in patients with PDs (Westen, 1991, Westen, Lohr, Silk, Gold, & Kerber, 1990); research on personality traits in nonclinical populations (e.g., Block, 1971; John, 1990; McCrae & Costa, 1990); research on PDs conducted since the development of Axis II (see Livesley, 1995); extensive pilot interviews in which observers watched videotaped interviews of patients with PDs and described them using earlier versions of the item set; and the clinical experience of the authors.

Most importantly, the SWAP-200 (the first major edition of the SWAP) is the product of a seven-year iterative revision process that incorporated the feedback of hundreds of clinician-consultants who used earlier versions of the instrument (Shedler & Westen, 1998) to describe their patients. We asked each clinician-consultant one crucial question: "Were you able to describe the things you consider psychologically important about your patient?" We added, rewrote, and revised items based on this feedback, then asked new clinician-consultants to describe new patients. We repeated this process over many iterations until most clinicians could answer "yes" most of the time. A newer, revised version of the SWAP item set, the SWAP-II incorporates the additional feedback of over 2,000 clinicians of all theoretical orientations. The iterative item revision process was designed to ensure both the comprehensiveness and the clinical relevance of the SWAP item sets.

Because the SWAP is jargon-free and clinically comprehensive, it has the potential to serve as a universal language for describing personality pathology. Our studies demonstrate that experienced clinicians of diverse theoretical orientations understand the items and can apply them reliably to their patients. In one study, a nationwide sample of 797 experienced psychologists and psychiatrists of diverse theoretical orientations, who had an average of 18 years practice experience post training, used the SWAP-200 to describe patients with personality pathology (Westen and Shedler, 1999a). These experienced therapists provided similar SWAP-200 descriptions of PDs regardless of their theoretical commitments, and fully 72.7% agreed with the statement, "I was able to express most of the things I consider important about this patient" (the highest rating category). In a subsequent sample of 1,201 psychologists and psychiatrists who used the SWAP-II, over 80% "agreed" or "strongly agreed" with the statement, "The SWAP-II allowed me to express the things I consider important about my patient's personality" (less than 5% disagreed). The ratings were unrelated to clinicians' theoretical orientation. Virtually identical agreement rates were obtained in a national sample of clinicians who used the adolescent version of the instrument, the SWAP-II-A.

AN ILLUSTRATION:
BORDERLINE PERSONALITY PATHOLOGY

Some clinicians may doubt that a finite set of 200 statements can capture the richness and complexity of clinical case description. However, SWAP statements can be combined in virtually infinite patterns to express subtle clinical concepts. The mathematically inclined reader might note that there are 200 factorial possible orderings of the SWAP statements, which is an inexpressibly large number. The musically inclined reader might note that all of Western music can be notated using combinations of only twelve tones.

Many clinical theorists consider *splitting*, *projective identification*, and *identity disturbance* to be hallmarks of borderline personality pathology (e.g., Clarkin, Yeomans, & Kernberg, 2006; Kernberg, 1975, 1984; Linehan, 1993; McWilliams, 1994). Consider, for example, the items reproduced below from the original SWAP-200 item set. The three items, *taken in combination*, convey something of the defensive splitting seen in patients with borderline personality pathology:

SWAP Item #	SWAP Item Text
162	Expresses contradictory feelings or beliefs without being disturbed by the inconsistency; has little need to reconcile or resolve contradictory ideas.
45	Tends to idealize certain others in unrealistic ways; sees them as "all good," to the exclusion of commonplace human defects.
79	Tends to see certain others as "all bad," and loses the capacity to perceive any positive qualities the person may have.

The following items, from the SWAP-II, capture some additional meanings of the concept *splitting*.

9	When upset, has trouble perceiving both positive and negative qualities in the same person at the same time (e.g., may see others in black or white terms, shift suddenly from seeing someone as caring to seeing him/her as malevolent and intentionally hurtful, etc.).
18	Tends to stir up conflict or animosity between other people (e.g., may portray a situation differently to different people, leading them to form contradictory views or work at cross purposes).

The next group of items, *taken in combination*, captures at least one meaning of the term *projective identification*:

116	Tends to see own unacceptable feelings or impulses in other people instead of in him/herself.
76	Manages to elicit in others feelings similar to those s/he is experiencing (e.g., when angry, acts in such a way as to provoke anger in others; when anxious, acts in such a way as to induce anxiety in others).
154	Tends to draw others into scenarios, or "pull" them into roles, that feel alien or unfamiliar (e.g., being uncharacteristically insensitive or cruel, feeling like the only person in the world who can help, etc.).

The concept *identity disturbance* (or *identity diffusion*) subsumes a wide range of phenomena (Wilkinson-Ryan & Westen, 2000). When the same term has been used in the literature in different ways, or used differently by different theorists, we wrote multiple SWAP items to cover the multiple meanings. The following SWAP-II items illustrate some of the manifestations and facets of identity disturbance:

15	Lacks a stable sense of who s/he is (e.g., attitudes, values, goals, and feelings about self seem unstable or ever-changing).
151	Appears to experience the past as a series of disjointed or disconnected events; has difficulty giving a coherent account of his/her life story.
90	Is prone to painful feelings of emptiness (e.g., may feel lost, bereft, abjectly alone even in the presence of others, etc.).
172	Seems unable to settle into, or sustain commitment to, identity-defining life roles (e.g., career, occupation, lifestyle, etc.).

SWAP Item #	SWAP Item Text
150	Tends to identify with admired others to an exaggerated degree, taking on their attitudes, mannerisms, etc. (e.g., may be drawn into the "orbit" of a strong or charismatic personality).
87	Sense of identity revolves around a "cause," movement, or label (e.g., adult child of alcoholic, adult survivor, environmentalist, born-again Christian, etc.); may be drawn to extreme or all-encompassing belief systems.
38	Tends to feel s/he is not his/her true self with others; may feel false or fraudulent.
102	Has a deep sense of inner badness; sees self as damaged, evil, or rotten to the core (whether consciously or unconsciously).

The next group of items helps flesh out a picture of a certain kind of borderline patient, addressing issues of affect regulation, interpersonal relations, cognition, and so on:

191	Emotions tend to change rapidly and unpredictably.
12	Emotions tend to spiral out of control, leading to extremes of anxiety, sadness, rage, etc.
185	Is prone to intense anger, out of proportion to the situation at hand (e.g., has rage episodes).
157	Tends to become irrational when strong emotions are stirred up; may show a significant decline from customary level of functioning.
117	Is unable to soothe or comfort him/herself without the help of another person (i.e., has difficulty regulating own emotions).
98	Tends to fear s/he will be rejected or abandoned.
11	Tends to become attached quickly or intensely; develops feelings, expectations, etc. that are not warranted by the history or context of the relationship.
167	Is simultaneously needy of, and rejecting toward, others (e.g., craves intimacy and caring, but tends to reject it when offered).
153	Relationships tend to be unstable, chaotic, and rapidly changing.
52	Has little empathy; seems unable or unwilling to understand or respond to others' needs or feelings.
176	Tends to confuse own thoughts, feelings, or personality traits with those of others (e.g., may use the same words to describe him/herself and another person, believe the two share identical thoughts and feelings, etc.).
41	Appears unable to describe important others in a way that conveys a sense of who they are as people; descriptions of others come across as two-dimensional and lacking in richness.
29	Has difficulty making sense of other people's behavior; tends to misunderstand, misinterpret, or be confused by others' actions and reactions.

The last group of items, below, includes descriptors that might apply to a more disturbed type of borderline patient, perhaps one likely to be seen in an inpatient setting (Gunderson, 2001):

SWAP Item #	SWAP Item Text
134	Tends to act impulsively (e.g., acts without forethought or concern for consequences).
142	Tends to make repeated suicidal threats or gestures, either as a "cry for help" or as an effort to manipulate others.
109	Tends to engage in self-mutilating behavior (e.g., self-cutting, self-burning, etc.).
188	Work-life and/or living arrangements tend to be chaotic or unstable (e.g., job or housing situation seems always temporary, transitional, or ill-defined).
44	When distressed, perception of reality can become grossly impaired (e.g., thinking may seem delusional).

The items reproduced here are illustrative only and are not intended to describe "the" borderline patient or any particular borderline patient. They are intended only to illustrate that it is possible to describe clinically sophisticated constructs without succumbing to either reductionism or jargon. Further, such descriptions are empirically testable.

TREATMENT IMPLICATIONS

DSM diagnostic criteria are largely descriptive, emphasizing behavioral signs and symptoms. They provide little guidance for the clinician trying to understand the meaning and function of the symptoms, or how to intervene. For example, *DSM* tells us that borderline patients are characterized by "a pattern of unstable and intense interpersonal relationships." The statement is descriptively accurate, but *why* does the patient have unstable relationships and how can the clinician help? Because the SWAP addresses underlying personality processes that give rise to these characteristics, it suggests some answers.

Consider the following personality process (item 9 in the SWAP-II item set): "When upset, has trouble perceiving both positive and negative qualities in the same person at the same time (e.g., may see others in black or white terms, shift suddenly from seeing someone as caring to seeing him/her as malevolent and intentionally hurtful, etc.)." The item describes the phenomenon known to psychodynamic clinicians as *splitting* and to cognitive-behavioral clinicians as *dichotomous thinking*. If the patient's perceptions of others gyrate between extremes, it follows that his relationships will be unstable. This implies a specific treatment strategy: The therapist will intervene effectively if she can help the patient recognize the extremes of thinking and see others in a more balanced light. For example, the therapist might observe, "When you are angry with your partner, you seem unable to remember that there is anything you like about him. By the same token, when you are feeling close to him, it is hard to remember that he has human flaws and limitations." Interventions of this kind are designed to develop the patient's capacity to integrate contradictory perceptions of others and see them in more complex, modulated, and balanced ways.

Likewise, *DSM* tells us that borderline patients may have "transient, stress-related paranoid ideation" but leaves us in the dark about why this occurs or how to intervene. Suppose the patient has high scores on the following SWAP items: "Is prone to intense anger, out of proportion to the situation at hand" (item 185) and "Tends to see own unacceptable feelings or impulses in other people instead of in him/herself" (item 116). The items, considered in combination, suggest a hypothesis about the meaning and function of paranoid ideation: The patient may become paranoid (i.e., see the world as dangerous and hostile) because, in times of intense agitation, he sees his own hostility wherever he looks. The interventions that follow from this formulation are straightforward, if difficult to implement. The therapist must help the patient develop the capacity to recognize and tolerate anger and find more adaptive ways to regulate it.

A CASE ILLUSTRATION

At present, descriptive psychiatric diagnosis and clinical case formulation are largely independent activities. The former is aimed at classification (a nomothetic approach) whereas the latter is aimed at understanding an individual patient (an idiographic approach). The SWAP bridges these activities. It generates dimensional diagnosis scores for each PD included in *DSM-IV* (as well as for the additional PDs proposed in the *DSM-IV* appendix) and it generates richly detailed clinical case narratives relevant to clinical case formulation and treatment planning.

Dimensional PD scores measure the "fit" or "match" between a patient and a prototype SWAP description representing each PD in its "ideal" or pure form (e.g., a prototype description of paranoid personality disorder). Thus, each PD is diagnosed on a continuum, where a low PD score indicates that the patient does not fit or match the PD syndrome and a high score indicates that the patient matches it well (with intermediate scores indicating varying degrees of "fit"). The PD scores can be graphed to create a PD profile resembling an MMPI profile, as illustrated in Figure 12.1. Dimensional PD diagnosis is consistent with clinical thinking and advocated by virtually all contemporary personality researchers (Widiger & Simonsen, 2005).

A clinical case example may best illustrate these diagnostic applications of the SWAP.[3]

Case Background

Melania is a 30-year-old Caucasian woman. Her presenting complaints included substance abuse and inability to extricate herself from an emotionally and physically abusive relationship. The initial assessment included a psychiatric intake interview and administration of both the Structured Clinical Interview for DSM-IV (SCID) and Structured Clinical Interview for DSM-IV Personality Disorders (SCID-II) structured interviews. She met SCID criteria for an Axis I diagnosis of substance abuse and SCID-II criteria for an Axis II diagnosis of borderline PD with histrionic traits. The intake interviewer assigned a score of 45 on the Global Assessment of Functioning (GAF) scale, indicating severe symptoms and impairment in functioning.

Melania's early family environment was marked by neglect and parental strife. A recurring family scenario is illustrative: Melania's mother would scream at her husband, telling him he was a failure and that she was going to leave him; she would then slam the door and lock herself in her room, leaving Melania frightened and in tears. Both parents would then ignore Melania, often forgetting to feed her. Melania's parents divorced when she was eight. After the divorce, Melania lived with her mother, who showed little concern for her needs or welfare.

By adolescence, Melania had developed behavioral problems. She often skipped school and spent her days sleeping or wandering the streets. At age 18, she left home and began what she described as "life on the streets." She engaged in a series of impulsive, chaotic, and rapidly changing sexual relationships which led to three abortions by age 24. She abused street drugs, eventually developing a pattern of cocaine and heroine abuse (snorting). She also engaged in petty criminal activity, including shoplifting and stealing from employers.

Melania held a series of low paying jobs that were not commensurate with her intelligence or education. She failed to hold any job for more than a few months and was fired from each when she was caught stealing. In her mid-twenties, Melania moved in with her boyfriend, a small-time drug dealer who exploited her financially and abused her physically. He spent his days sleeping or watching television while Melania worked to pay the rent. She often had sex with other men to obtain money or drugs for her boyfriend. He sometimes beat her when he was dissatisfied with what she brought home.

Melania began psychodynamic therapy at a frequency of three sessions per week. The first ten psychotherapy sessions were tape recorded and transcribed. Two clinicians (blind to all other data) reviewed the transcripts and provided SWAP-200 descriptions of Melania, based on the information contained in the session transcripts. The SWAP-200 scores were then averaged across the two clinical judges to obtain a single SWAP-200 description.[4] After two years of psychotherapy, 10 consecutive psychotherapy sessions were again recorded and transcribed and the SWAP assessment procedure was repeated.

PD Diagnosis

The solid line in Figure 12.1 shows Melania's PD scores at the beginning of treatment for the 10 PDs included in *DSM-IV*. A "healthy functioning" index is graphed as well, which reflects clinicians' consensual understanding of healthy personality

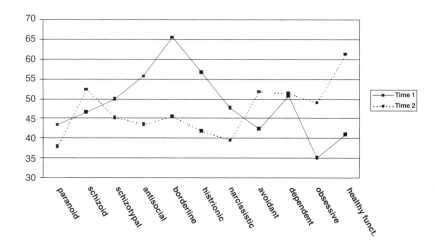

Figure 12.1 PD Score Profile

functioning (Westen & Shedler, 1999a). For ease of interpretation, the PD scores have been converted to T-scores (Mean = 50, SD = 10) based on norms established in a psychiatric sample of patients with axis II diagnoses (Westen & Shedler, 1999a). Although the SWAP assesses PDs dimensionally and treats each PD diagnosis as a continuum, we have established cutoff scores for "backward compatibility" with *DSM-IV*. To maintain continuity with the *DSM-IV* categorical diagnostic system, we have suggested T = 60 as a threshold for making a categorical PD diagnosis, and T = 55 as a threshold for diagnosing "features."[5]

Melania's PD profile shows a marked elevation for borderline PD (T = 65.4, approximately one and a half standard deviations above the sample mean), with secondary elevations for histrionic PD (T = 56.6) and antisocial PD (T = 55.7). Applying the recommended cutoff scores, her *DSM-IV* axis II diagnosis is borderline PD with histrionic and antisocial features. Also noteworthy is the T-Score of 41 for the "healthy functioning" index, nearly a standard deviation below the mean in a reference sample of patients with Axis II diagnoses. The low score indicates significant impairment in functioning and parallels the low GAF score assigned by the intake interviewer.

Narrative Case Description

We can generate a narrative case description by listing the SWAP items assigned the highest scores in the patient's SWAP description (e.g., items with scores of 5, 6, and 7). Below is a narrative case description for Melania based on the top 30 most descriptive SWAP-200 items. We have grouped together conceptually related items. To aid the flow of the text, we have made some minor grammatical changes and added connecting text. However, the SWAP-200 items are reproduced essentially verbatim. The narrative description is based on the same data used to generate the PD score profile in Figure 12.1.

Melania experiences severe depression and dysphoria. She tends to feel unhappy, depressed, or despondent, appears to find little or no pleasure or satisfaction in life's activities, feels life is without meaning, and tends to feel like an outcast or outsider. She tends to feel guilty, and to feel inadequate, inferior, or a failure. Her behavior is often self-defeating and self-destructive. She appears inhibited about pursuing goals or successes, is insufficiently concerned with meeting her own needs, and seems not to feel entitled to get or ask for things she deserves. She appears to want to "punish" herself by creating situations that lead to unhappiness, or actively avoiding opportunities for pleasure and gratification. Specific self-destructive tendencies include getting drawn into and remaining in relationships in which she is emotionally or physically abused, abusing illicit drugs, and acting impulsively and without regard for consequences. She shows little concern for consequences in general.

Melania shows many personality traits associated specifically with borderline PD. Her relationships are unstable, chaotic, and rapidly changing. She has little empathy and seems unable to understand or respond to others' needs and feelings unless they coincide with her own. Moreover, she tends to confuse her own thoughts, feelings, and personality traits with those of others, and she often acts in such a way as to elicit her own feelings in other people (for example, provoking anger when she herself is angry, or inducing anxiety in others when she herself is anxious).

Melania expresses contradictory feelings without being disturbed by the inconsistency, and she seems to have little need to reconcile or resolve contradictory ideas. She is prone to see certain others as "all bad," losing the capacity to perceive any positive qualities they may have. She lacks a stable image of who she is or would like to become (e.g., her attitudes, values, goals, and feelings about self are unstable and changing) and she tends to feel empty. Affect regulation is poor: She tends to become irrational when strong emotions are stirred up and shows a noticeable decline from her customary level of functioning. She also seems unable to soothe or comfort herself when distressed and requires the involvement of another person to help her regulate affect. Both her living arrangements and her work life tend to be chaotic and unstable.

Finally, Melania's attitudes toward men and sexuality are problematic and conflictual. She tends to be hostile toward members of the opposite sex (whether consciously or unconsciously) and she associates sexual activity with danger (e.g., injury or punishment). She appears afraid of commitment to a long-term love relationship, instead choosing partners who seem inappropriate in terms of age, status (e.g., social, economic, intellectual), or other factors.

The narrative description provides a detailed portrait of a severely troubled patient with borderline personality pathology. The description helps illustrate the difference between descriptive psychiatry (aimed at establishing a diagnosis) and clinical case formulation (aimed at understanding an individual). In this instance, however, all findings are derived from the same assessment procedure and grounded in quantitative data.

Assessing Change in Therapy

The case of Melania has a happy ending. After two years of psychotherapy, the SWAP assessment revealed significant personality changes. The changes parallel concrete behavior changes as well as changes in Melania's life circumstances (e.g., ending her drug abuse, getting and keeping a good job, ending her involvement with her abusive boyfriend, and no longer engaging in theft, promiscuous sex, or prostitution).

The dotted line in Figure 12.1 shows Melania's PD scores after two years of treatment. Her scores on the borderline, histrionic, and antisocial dimensions have dropped below T = 50 and she no longer warrants a PD diagnosis. Her score on the healthy functioning index has increased by two standard deviations, from 41.0 to 61.2.

To assess change in an ideographic, more fine-grained manner, we created a change score for each individual SWAP item by subtracting the item score at Time 1 from the score at Time 2. The narrative description of change, below, is comprised of the SWAP items with change scores > 4. Again, we have made some minor grammatical changes and added connecting text to aid the flow of the text, but the SWAP-200 items are reproduced essentially verbatim.

Melania has developed strengths and inner resources that were not evident at the Time 1 assessment. She has come to terms with painful experiences from the past, finding meaning in, and growing from, these experiences; she has become more articulate and better able to express herself in words; she has a newfound ability to appreciate and respond to humor; she is more capable of recognizing alternative viewpoints, even in matters that stir up strong feelings; she is more empathic and sensitive to other's needs and feelings; and she is more likeable.

There is marked improvement in many areas associated specifically with borderline psychopathology. With respect to affect regulation, Melania is less prone to become irrational when strong emotions are stirred up, is more likely to express affect appropriate in quality and intensity to the situation at hand, and is better able to soothe or comfort herself when distressed. She is less prone to confuse her own thoughts and feelings with those of others, less manipulative, and less likely to devalue others and see them as "all bad." She has come to terms with negative feelings toward her parents.

Melania is also less impulsive, more conscientious and responsible, and more aware of the consequences of her actions. Her living arrangements are more stable, as is her work life. Melania's use of illicit drugs has decreased significantly, and she is no longer drawn to abusive relationships.

As the more severe aspects of borderline personality pathology have receded, other conflicts and symptoms have moved to the fore. For example,

Melania appears to have developed somewhat obsessional defenses against painful affect. She adheres more rigidly to daily routines and becomes anxious or uncomfortable when they are altered. She is more prone to think in an abstract and intellectualized manner, and tries to see herself as more logical and rational, less influenced by emotion.

Despite her wish to act more logically and rationally, Melania seems engaged in an active struggle to control her affect and impulses. She tends to oscillate between undercontrol and overcontrol of needs and wishes, either expressing them impulsively or disavowing them entirely. She has more difficulty allowing herself to experience strong pleasurable emotions (e.g., excitement, joy). She is more prone to repress, "forget," or otherwise distort distressing events.

Finally, there are changes in Melania's relationships and orientation toward sexuality. Whereas before she presented in a histrionic manner (i.e., with exaggerated feminine traits), she is now more disparaging of traditionally feminine traits, instead emphasizing independence and achievement. Whereas previously she engaged in multiple chaotic sexual relationships, she now seems conflicted about her intimacy needs. She craves intimacy but tends to reject it when offered. She has more difficulty directing both sexual and tender feelings toward the same person, seeing men as either respectable and virtuous, or sexy and exciting, but not both. She is more likely to hold grudges.

We leave it to readers to judge the clinical relevance of the SWAP as an assessment tool and the value of the diagnostic profiles and narrative case descriptions it provides. Note, however, that the standard vocabulary of the SWAP ensures that different clinicians will describe the same patient in much the same way, once they learn to use the SWAP reliably. Had other clinicians described Melania using the SWAP, the narrative descriptions would have been much the same, since the descriptive statements comprising the narrative were taken directly from the SWAP-200 item set.

RELIABILITY AND VALIDITY

Researchers in psychology and psychiatry have often assumed that clinical observation and judgment are unreliable; a well-established literature documents the limitations of "clinical judgment." Unfortunately, studies of clinical judgment have often asked clinicians to make judgments about things that fall well outside their legitimate area of expertise (just as unfortunate, some clinicians have been all too willing to offer such prognostications). Equally problematic, the studies have typically conflated clinicians' ability to make accurate observations and inferences (which they do well) with their ability to combine and weight variables to derive optimal predictions (a task *necessarily* performed better by statistical methods such as regression equations). In fact, a substantial literature documents the reliability and validity of clinical observation and inference *when it is quantified and used appropriately* (see Westen & Weinberger, 2004, for a detailed discussion and literature review).

The SWAP differs from past approaches in that it harnesses clinical judgment using psychometric methods developed specifically for this purpose, then applies statistical and actuarial methods to the resulting variables. In short, it relies on clinicians to do what they do best: making specific behavioral observations and inferences about the individual patients they know well. It relies on statistical algorithms to do what they do best: combining data optimally to derive reliable and valid diagnostic scales and indices.

Inter-rater reliability of SWAP-200 PD scale scores (Figure 12.1) and other diagnostic scales derived from the SWAP is above .80 for all scales in all studies conducted to date (e.g., Westen & Muderrisoglu, 2003, in press) and is often above .90 (e.g., Marin-Avellan, McGauley, Campbell, & Fonagy, 2005). These reliability coefficients are at least as high as those typically reported for self-report instruments and highly structured research interviews that avoid clinical inference and "just stick to the facts" (i.e., *DSM-IV* diagnostic criteria). Additionally, the SWAP diagnostic scales correlate highly with a wide range of external criterion measures in both adult and adolescent samples, including, e.g., genetic history variables such as psychosis in first- and second-degree relatives, substance abuse in first- and second-degree relatives, developmental history variables such as childhood sexual and physical abuse, life events such as psychiatric hospitalizations and suicide attempts, ratings of adaptive functioning, and so on (see Shedler & Westen, 2004b; Westen & Muderrisoglu, 2003; Westen & Shedler, 1999a; Westen, Shedler, Durrett, Glass, & Martens, 2003; Westen & Weinberger, 2004).

We will describe some illustrative studies in detail.[6] Westen and Muderrisoglu (2003) interviewed a small sample of outpatients using the Clinical Diagnostic Interview (CDI; Westen, 2002), a systematic interview (2 to 3 hours in length) designed to systematize the personality assessment methods employed by knowledgeable clinicians in real-world practice (Westen, 1997). The CDI does not ask patients to describe their own personality traits but instead elicits narrative descriptions of patients' lives and important relationships. The narrative descriptions allow clinical interviewers to draw inferences about patients' characteristic ways of thinking, feeling, regulating emotions and impulses, relating interpersonally, and so on (much as a skilled clinician might do in the first two to four meeting with a new patient).

The primary aims of the study were to (1) assess inter-rater reliability of SWAP diagnostic scales as assessed by independent clinicians who either conducted or observed (on videotape) the CDI interview, and (2) to assess convergent validity between these independent raters and the treating clinicians, whose SWAP scores were based on extensive contact with their patients over time. All of the clinical assessors were blind to the data provided by the others. The study examined the reliability and validity of ten SWAP PD scores plus seven other SWAP diagnostic indices (see Westen & Shedler, 1999b).

Inter-rater reliability between independent interviewers averaged greater than .80 for all SWAP scores. Convergent validity coefficients between interviewers and treating clinicians were also above .80 for all scores. Discriminant validity coefficients (i.e., correlations between unrelated diagnostic scales) were excellent, hovering near zero. To provide some reference points with which to compare these values, convergent validity between PD diagnoses derived from structured research interviews and diagnoses based on the longitudinal evaluation using all available data (LEAD) standard (Spitzer, 1983) have ranged from .00 to .40 in prior studies, and discriminant validity has been notably poor (see Pilkonis et al., 1991, 1995). Similarly, a meta-analysis of PD dimensions assessed via self- and informant-report yielded a median correlation of only .36 (Klonsky, Oltmanns, & Turkheimer, 2002).

A second study (Bradley & Westen, 2003) examined convergence between SWAP scores and patient self-report data for borderline and antisocial PD (the two PDs for which self-report and informant-report data tend to converge). Advanced clinical psychology graduate students used the SWAP-200 to describe 54 outpatients after the fifth clinical contact hour. The patients completed the Personality Assessment Inventory (PAI; Morey, 1991). Convergence validity was high, with SWAP antisocial and borderline PD scores differentially predicting antisocial and borderline scores on the PAI. Discriminant validity coefficients were desirably low, indicating excellent diagnostic specificity. The data provide further evidence for the validity of the SWAP-200 as an assessment tool.

A study from a research group other than our own reported comparable findings (Marin-Avellan, McGauley, Campbell, & Fonagy, 2005). The investigators applied the SWAP-200 to audiotaped Adult Attachment Interviews (AAI; Main, Kaplan, & Cassidy, 1985) plus chart records for a sample of inpatients at a maximum security forensic hospital. Inter-rater reliability between independent assessors was high for all SWAP-200 PD scales, with a median inter-rater correlation of r = .91. The SWAP PD scores differentiated patients who had committed violent versus nonviolent offenses, whereas SCID-II diagnosis did not. The SWAP-200 also proved superior to the SCID-II in predicting ward behavior, assessed independently by ward nurses (blind to all other data) using a 49-item interpersonal rating scale. SWAP antisocial PD scores correlated significantly with dominance behavior and coercive behavior observed on the ward, and correlated negatively with submissive behavior and compliant behavior observed on the ward. In contrast, the SCID-II predicted only dominance behavior. The findings demonstrate incremental validity of the SWAP-200 relative to a widely used PD instrument that relies substantially on patient self-report.

In sum, experienced clinicians can make highly reliable observations and inferences about personality dynamics, given a suitable technology for harnessing their judgments. The belief that clinicians cannot reliably assess psychodynamic and other complex clinical constructs is mistaken.

TOWARD *DSM-V*: AN EMPIRICAL APPROACH TO REVISING AND REFINING DIAGNOSTIC CRITERIA

As noted above, the approach to personality diagnosis codified by *DSM-IV* has elicited little enthusiasm from either clinicians or researchers. Ultimately, revisions to the diagnostic categories and criteria over successive editions of the *DSM* reflect committee decision processes, which can be influenced by group dynamics, the opinions of individual committee members, the sociopolitical *zeitgeist*, and other such factors. Here we describe an alternative, empirical approach to identifying PD diagnostic criteria.[7]

Identifying Core Features of PDs

Because the SWAP quantifies clinical case description, it allows investigators to statistically combine case descriptions to obtain a composite description of a particular grouping of patients. This is accomplished by averaging (aggregating) the values assigned to each SWAP item across a relevant patient sample. For example, if we obtain SWAP descriptions for a representative sample of patients diagnosed with paranoid PD, we can average the values for each SWAP items to obtain a composite description of the prototypical paranoid patient.

A fortunate statistical consequence of averaging is that only SWAP items ranked highly for virtually all patients will have a high ranking in the composite description. If a descriptor does not apply to all or most patients in the sample, the item will not achieve a high score. Thus, examination of the highest-ranking items in the composite description for paranoid PD reveals the *core psychological features* shared by paranoid patients treated in the community. This represents a purely empirical procedure for identifying the core features of a personality syndrome.

Method

A national sample of 530 experienced psychiatrists and clinical psychologists recruited from the rosters of the American Psychiatric Association and the American Psychological Association used the SWAP-200 to describe a current patient with a specified PD diagnosis (for a more complete description of the study methods, see Shedler & Westen, 2004a). We aggregated the SWAP descriptions across all patients with a given PD diagnosis to create a *composite description* for each PD diagnosis included in *DSM-IV*. The composite descriptions were highly reliable (coefficient alpha > .90 for all descriptions), indicating that the sample sizes were adequate to obtain stable and reproducible personality descriptions.[8]

Results

We will describe the findings for only a few PDs. For a complete account of the study findings for all ten PDs, see Shedler & Westen (2004a).

Cluster A: The "Odd" Cluster

Tables 12.1a–12.1c list the SWAP-200 items that received the highest scores or rankings in each composite description, along with the item's mean score or ranking in the composite (indicating its centrality or importance in defining the PD). Two findings are noteworthy. First, the descriptions differ systematically from those of the *DSM-IV* and include psychological features absent from the *DSM* criterion sets, especially items addressing inner life or intrapsychic experience. Second, there is considerable overlap in item content between the disorders. Thus, there are psychological features that are central to two or all three of the Cluster A disorders (e.g., difficulty making sense of other people's behavior, problematic reality testing, a propensity to feel misunderstood or mistreated, a tendency toward social isolation). If we consider each composite description as a *whole* (that is, if we consider the "gist" or gestalt of the 15 to 20 most descriptive statements), the descriptions are readily distinguishable. However, if we limit the descriptions to just the first 8 to 9 items—the number included in *DSM-IV* criterion sets—it is more difficult to distinguish them. This suggests that criterion sets of 8 to 9 items are too small to provide PD descriptions that are both clinically accurate and adequately distinct (Shedler & Westen, 2004b; Westen & Shedler, 2000).

Paranoid PD

Empirically observable features of Paranoid PD include aggression ("tends to be angry or hostile") and the defenses of externalization ("tends to blame own one's failures or shortcomings on others") and projection ("tends to see own unacceptable feelings or impulses in other people instead of in him/herself"). The findings are consistent with the view that projection of aggression is a central dynamic in paranoid personality (i.e., paranoid patients perceive the world as dangerous because they see their own hostility wherever they look). Similar findings emerged when we stratified the data by clinician theoretical orientation and omitted data provided by clinicians who described their theoretical orientation as psychoanalytic or psychodynamic. (It is therefore highly unlikely that the reporting clinicians were simply describing their personality theories, rather than the observed characteristics of their patients.) Other empirically observable characteristics of paranoid PD absent from DSM-IV include feelings of victimization, difficulties understanding others' actions, hypersensitivity to slights, lack of close friendships and relationships, and the tendency for reasoning to become severely impaired under stress.

Cluster B: The "Dramatic" Cluster

Tables 12.2a–12.2d list the SWAP-200 items that received the highest ranking in the composite descriptions for the Cluster B disorders. Again, the PD descriptions differ systematically from the DSM-IV descriptions and place greater emphasis on inner life. Once again there is significant item overlap, but the disorders are readily distinguishable when the descriptions are considered in total.

Table 12.1a Composite Description of Patients Diagnosed with Paranoid PD

Item	Mean
Tends to feel misunderstood, mistreated, or victimized.	6.19
Is quick to assume that others want to harm or take advantage of him/her; tends to perceive malevolent intentions in others' words and actions.	5.97
Tends to be angry or hostile (whether consciously or unconsciously).	5.74
Tends to hold grudges; may dwell on insults or slights for long periods.	5.55
Tends to blame others for own failures or shortcomings; tends to believe his/her problems are caused by external factors.	5.26
Tends to avoid confiding in others for fear of betrayal; expects things she/he says or does will be used against him/her.	5.03
Tends to be critical of others.	5.03
Tends to react to criticism with feelings of rage or humiliation.	4.94
Lacks close friendships and relationships.	4.52
Tends to get into power struggles.	4.48
Has difficulty making sense of other people's behavior; often misunderstands, misinterprets, or is confused by others' actions and reactions.	4.48
Perception of reality can become grossly impaired under stress (e.g., may become delusional).	4.32
Tends to feel like an outcast or outsider; feels as if she/he does not truly belong.	4.26
Tends to express intense and inappropriate anger, out of proportion to the situation at hand.	4.23
Tends to feel helpless, powerless, or at the mercy of forces outside his/her control.	4.16
Tends to see own unacceptable feelings or impulses in other people instead of in him/herself.	4.03

Table 12.1b Composite Description of Patients Diagnosed with Schizoid PD

Item	Mean
Lacks close friendships and relationships.	5.85
Lacks social skills; tends to be socially awkward or inappropriate.	5.59
Appears to have a limited or constricted range of emotions.	5.44
Tends to feel like an outcast or outsider; feels as if she/he does not truly belong.	5.13
Tends to be inhibited or constricted; has difficulty allowing self to acknowledge or express wishes and impulses.	5.08
Tends to be shy or reserved in social situations.	4.95
Appearance or manner seems odd or peculiar (e.g., grooming, hygiene, posture, eye contact, speech rhythms, etc. seem somehow strange or "off").	4.56
Tends to avoid social situations because of fear of embarrassment or humiliation.	4.46
Has difficulty making sense of other people's behavior; often misunderstands, misinterprets, or is confused by others' actions and reactions.	4.31
Has difficulty acknowledging or expressing anger.	4.28
Tends to feel unhappy, depressed, or despondent.	4.23

continued

Table 12.1b (continued) Composite Description of Patients Diagnosed with Schizoid PD

Item	Mean
Has difficulty allowing self to experience strong pleasurable emotions (e.g., excitement, joy, pride).	4.18
Tends to be passive and unassertive.	4.13
Appears to find little or no pleasure, satisfaction, or enjoyment in life's activities.	4.00
Tends to feel she/he is inadequate, inferior, or a failure.	3.97
Appears to have little need for human company or contact; is genuinely indifferent to the presence of others.	3.92
Appears inhibited about pursuing goals or successes; aspirations or achievements tend to be below his/her potential.	3.90
Tends to be anxious.	3.59

Table 12.1c Composite Description of Patients Diagnosed with Schizotypal PD

Item	Mean
Lacks close friendships and relationships.	6.17
Appearance or manner seems odd or peculiar (e.g., grooming, hygiene, posture, eye contact, speech rhythms, etc. seem somehow strange or "off").	6.08
Reasoning processes or perceptual experiences seem odd and idiosyncratic (e.g., may make seemingly arbitrary inferences; may see hidden messages or special meanings in ordinary events).	5.17
Tends to feel like an outcast or outsider; feels as if she/he does not truly belong.	4.79
Lacks social skills; tends to be socially awkward or inappropriate.	4.79
Has difficulty making sense of other people's behavior; often misunderstands, misinterprets, or is confused by others' actions and reactions.	4.71
Perception of reality can become grossly impaired under stress (e.g., may become delusional).	4.63
Appears to have a limited or constricted range of emotions.	4.50
Tends to become irrational when strong emotions are stirred up; may show a noticeable decline from customary level of functioning.	4.08
Tens to be shy or reserved in social situations.	4.04
Tends to be anxious.	3.88
Tends to feel unhappy, depressed, or despondent.	3.83
Tends to feel helpless, powerless, or at the mercy of forces outside his/her control.	3.71
Tends to feel misunderstood, mistreated, or victimized.	3.58
Tends to avoid social situations because of fear of embarrassment or humiliation.	3.54
Has little psychological insight into own motives, behavior, etc.; is unable to consider alternate interpretations of his/her experiences.	3.54
Lacks a stable image of who she/he is or would like to become (e.g., attitudes, values, goals, and feelings about self may be unstable and changing).	3.50

Table 12.2a Composite Description of Patients Diagnosed with Antisocial PD

Item	Mean
Takes advantage of others; is out for number one; has minimal investment in moral values.	5.64
Tends to be deceitful; tends to lie or mislead.	5.50
Tends to engage in unlawful or criminal behavior.	5.36
Tends to be angry or hostile (whether consciously or unconsciously).	5.29
Has little empathy; seems unable to understand or respond to others' needs and feelings unless they coincide with his/her own.	5.04
Appears to experience no remorse for harm or injury caused to others.	4.93
Tends to blame others for own failures or shortcomings; tends to believe his/her problems are caused by external factors.	4.89
Tends to act impulsively, without regard for consequences.	4.89
Tends to show reckless disregard for the rights, property, or safety of others.	4.86
Tries to manipulate others' emotions to get what she/he wants.	4.75
Tends to be unconcerned with the consequences of his/her actions; appears to feel immune or invulnerable.	4.39
Tends to be unreliable and irresponsible (e.g., may fail to meet work obligations or honor financial commitments).	4.32
Has little psychological insight into own motives, behavior, etc.; is unable to consider alternate interpretations of his/her experiences.	4.21
Tends to get into power struggles.	4.07
Appears to gain pleasure or satisfaction by being sadistic or aggressive toward others.	4.04
Tends to abuse alcohol.	4.04
Tends to be critical of others.	4.00
Tends to be conflicted about authority (e.g., may feel she/he must submit, rebel against, win over, defeat, etc.).	4.00
Tends to seek power or influence over others (whether in beneficial or destructive ways).	3.93
Has an exaggerated sense of self-importance.	3.75

Table 12.2b Composite Description of Patients Diagnosed with Borderline PD

Item	Mean
Emotions tend to spiral out of control, leading to extremes of anxiety, sadness, rage, excitement, etc.	5.05
Tends to feel unhappy, depressed, or despondent.	4.88
Tends to feel she/he is inadequate, inferior, or a failure.	4.42
Tends to fear she/he will be rejected or abandoned by those who are emotionally significant.	4.40
Is unable to soothe or comfort self when distressed; requires involvement of another person to help regulate affect.	4.28

continued

Table 12.2b (continued) Composite Description of Patients Diagnosed with Borderline PD

Item	Mean
Tends to feel helpless, powerless, or at the mercy of forces outside his/her control.	4.19
Tends to be angry or hostile (whether consciously or unconsciously).	4.05
Tends to be anxious.	4.05
Tends to react to criticism with feelings of rage or humiliation.	3.95
Tends to be overly needy or dependent; requires excessive reassurance or approval.	3.93
Tends to feel misunderstood, mistreated, or victimized.	3.79
Tends to become irrational when strong emotions are stirred up; may show a noticeable decline from customary level of functioning.	3.74
Tends to get into power struggles.	3.56
Tends to "catastrophize"; is prone to see problems as disastrous, unsolvable, etc.	3.51
Emotions tend to change rapidly and unpredictably.	3.51
Lacks a stable image of who she/he is or would like to become (e.g., attitudes, values, goals, and feelings about self may be unstable and changing).	3.49
Tends to feel like an outcast or outsider; feels as if she/he does not truly belong.	3.47
Tends to express intense and inappropriate anger, out of proportion to the situation at hand.	3.40

Table 12.2c Composite Description of Patients Diagnosed with Histrionic PD

Item	Mean
Expresses emotion in exaggerated and theatrical ways.	5.00
Tends to fear she/he will be rejected or abandoned by those who are emotionally significant.	4.66
Tends to be anxious.	4.43
Emotions tend to spiral out of control, leading to extremes of anxiety, sadness, rage, excitement, etc.	4.40
Tends to be overly needy or dependent; requires excessive reassurance or approval.	4.34
Tends to develop somatic symptoms in response to stress or conflict (e.g., headache, backache, abdominal pain, asthma, etc.).	3.77
Tends to get into power struggles.	3.63
Tends to become attached quickly or intensely; develops feelings, expectations, etc. that are not warranted by the history or context of the relationship.	3.60
Tends to be overly sexually seductive or provocative, whether consciously or unconsciously (may be inappropriately flirtatious, preoccupied with sexual conquest, prone to "lead people on," etc.).	3.60
Seeks to be the center of attention.	3.57
Tends to feel misunderstood, mistreated, or victimized.	3.54
Is articulate; can express self well in words.	3.46

continued

Table 12.2c (continued) Composite Description of Patients Diagnosed with Histrionic PD

Item	Mean
Tends to become irrational when strong emotions are stirred up; may show a noticeable decline from customary level of functioning.	3.46
Tends to feel helpless, powerless, or at the mercy of forces outside his/her control.	3.37
Is unable to soothe or comfort self when distressed; requires involvement of another person to help regulate affect.	3.34
Emotions tend to change rapidly and unpredictably.	3.34
Tends to "catastrophize;" is prone to see problems as disastrous, unsolvable, etc.	3.29
Tends to feel unhappy, depressed, or despondent.	3.29
Tends to use his/her physical attractiveness to an excessive degree to gain attention or notice.	3.26
Tends to be angry or hostile (whether consciously or unconsciously).	3.17

Table 12.2d Composite Description of Patients Diagnosed with Narcissistic PD

Item	Mean
Appears to feel privileged and entitled; expects preferential treatment.	4.95
Has an exaggerated sense of self-importance.	4.68
Tends to be controlling.	4.53
Tends to be critical of others.	4.40
Tends to get into power struggles.	4.28
Tends to feel misunderstood, mistreated, or victimized.	4.28
Tends to be competitive with others (whether consciously or unconsciously).	4.25
Is articulate; can express self well in words.	4.25
Tends to react to criticism with feelings of rage or humiliation.	4.22
Tends to be angry or hostile (whether consciously or unconsciously).	4.15
Has little empathy; seems unable to understand or respond to others' needs and feelings unless they coincide with his/her own.	4.10
Tends to blame others for own failures or shortcomings; tends to believe his/her problems are caused by external factors.	4.00
Seeks to be the center of attention.	3.63
Tends to be arrogant, haughty, or dismissive.	3.63
Seems to treat others primarily as an audience to witness own importance, brilliance, beauty, etc.	3.50
Has fantasies of unlimited success, power, beauty, talent, brilliance, etc.	3.43
Tends to hold grudges; may dwell on insults or slights for long periods.	3.40
Expects self to be "perfect" (e.g., in appearance, achievements, performance, etc.).	3.38

Antisocial PD

The composite description of antisocial patients includes multiple traits associated with the construct of psychopathy that preceded the current antisocial PD diagnosis (Cleckley, 1941; Patrick & Zempolich, 1998). Included in the composite description, but absent from the *DSM-IV* criterion set, are items addressing lack of empathy, sadism, emotional manipulativeness, imperviousness to consequences, and externalization of blame. In contrast, *DSM-IV* emphasizes behaviors associated with criminality (and would therefore miss the more "successful" psychopathic personalities who express their pathology in the world of business or politics).

Cluster C: The "Anxious" Cluster

Avoidant and Dependent PD

The empirical portraits of avoidant and dependent PD in Tables 12.3a and 12.3b help explain the high comorbidity between the disorders observed in virtually every study to date, including our own (Millon & Martinez, 1995; Westen & Shedler, 1999a). Patients diagnosed with these disorders share *a depressive* or *dysphoric core* that appears to pervade all areas of functioning. This depression or dysphoria is not captured by the current *DSM* criteria. Patients diagnosed by their clinicians with avoidant PD attempt to deal with dysphoria by keeping their distance from others whereas those diagnosed with dependent PD attempt to cope by clinging to others. However, both groups experience depression and despondency, feelings of inferiority, guilt, shame, anxiety, self-criticism, self-blame, passivity, and inhibitions. Clinicians appear to be using these diagnostic categories to describe patients who might be better conceptualized in terms of depressive PD.

Discussion of Empirical Findings

Advantages of Expanded Criterion Sets

A consistent theme running through the findings is that *DSM-IV* criterion sets are too narrow. They do not capture the richness and complexity of the personality syndromes observed, empirically in patients treated in the community, nor do they capture the complexity of PDs as they are defined by *DSM-IV* itself. The preamble to axis II defines PDs in terms of multiple domains of functioning including cognition, affectivity, interpersonal relations, and impulse regulation. However, the PD criterion sets do not actually encompass these domains of functioning (Millon, 1990; Millon & Davis, 1997).

DSM-IV limits the number of diagnostic criteria to 8 or 9 criteria (items) per disorder, but it is clinically and psychometrically impossible for such small item sets simultaneously to describe personality syndromes in their complexity, and to describe distinct (nonoverlapping) syndromes. Certain traits play central roles in more than one PD (e.g., lack of empathy is characteristic of both narcissistic and antisocial PD; hostility is characteristic of paranoid, antisocial, borderline, and narcissistic PDs). Excluding these traits from the PD criterion sets leads to clinically inaccurate descriptions, but including the same items in multiple

Table 12.3a Composite Description of Patients Diagnosed with Avoidant PD

Item	Mean
Tends to feel she/he is inadequate, inferior, or a failure.	6.34
Tends to be shy or reserved in social situations.	6.26
Tends to avoid social situations because of fear of embarrassment or humiliation.	5.94
Tends to feel ashamed or embarrassed.	5.71
Tends to be anxious.	5.60
Tends to feel like an outcast or outsider; feels as if she/he does not truly belong.	5.51
Tends to be inhibited or constricted; has difficulty allowing self to acknowledge or express wishes and impulses.	5.31
Tends to be passive and unassertive.	5.29
Tends to feel unhappy, depressed, or despondent.	5.20
Tends to be self-critical; sets unrealistically high standards for self and is intolerant of own human defects.	4.91
Lacks close friendships and relationships.	4.89
Tends to blame self or feel responsible for bad things that happen.	4.86
Tends to fear she/he will be rejected or abandoned by those who are emotionally significant.	4.83
Tends to feel guilty.	4.77
Lacks social skills; tends to be socially awkward or inappropriate.	4.74
Appears inhibited about pursuing goals or successes; aspirations or achievements tend to be below his/her potential.	4.49

Table 12.3b Composite Description of Patients Diagnosed with Dependent PD

Item	Mean
Tends to be overly needy or dependent; requires excessive reassurance or approval.	6.13
Tends to fear she/he will be rejected or abandoned by those who are emotionally significant.	5.55
Tends to feel she/he is inadequate, inferior, or a failure.	5.47
Tends to feel unhappy, depressed, or despondent.	5.26
Tends to be ingratiating or submissive (e.g., may consent to things she/he does not agree with or does not want to do, in the hope of getting support or approval).	5.24
Tends to feel helpless, powerless, or at the mercy of forces outside his/her control.	5.16
Tends to feel guilty.	4.89
Tends to be passive and unassertive.	4.76
Tends to be anxious.	4.55
Tends to blame self or feel responsible for bad things that happen.	4.53
Has difficulty acknowledging or expressing anger.	4.53
Tends to feel ashamed or embarrassed.	4.39

continued

Table 12.3b (continued) Composite Description of Patients Diagnosed with Dependent PD

Item	Mean
Is unable to soothe or comfort self when distressed; requires involvement of another person to help regulate affect.	4.37
Has trouble making decisions; tends to be indecisive or to vacillate when faced with choices.	4.26
Appears inhibited about pursuing goals or successes; aspirations or achievements tend to be below his/her potential.	4.21
Tends to express aggression in passive and indirect ways (e.g., may make mistakes, procrastinate, forget, become sulky, etc.).	4.03
Tends to get drawn into or remain in relationships in which she/he is emotionally or physically abused.	3.79

Table 12.3c Composite Description of Patients Diagnosed with Obsessive-Compulsive PD

Item	Mean
Tends to be conscientious and responsible.	5.83
Tends to be self-critical; sets unrealistically high standards for self and is intolerant of own human defects.	5.20
Has moral and ethical standards and strives to live up to them.	5.17
Tends to be overly concerned with rules, procedures, order, organization, schedules, etc.	4.89
Tends to be anxious.	4.86
Tends to be controlling.	4.80
Tends to become absorbed in details, often to the point that she/he misses what is significant in the situation.	4.74
Expects self to be "perfect" (e.g., in appearance, achievements, performance, etc.).	4.69
Tends to blame self or feel responsible for bad things that happen.	4.49
Tends to feel guilty.	4.43
Tends to adhere rigidly to daily routines and become anxious or uncomfortable when they are altered.	4.29
Is troubled by recurrent obsessional thoughts that she/he experiences as senseless and intrusive.	4.26
Is articulate; can express self well in words.	4.26
Tends to be inhibited or constricted; has difficulty allowing self to acknowledge or express wishes and impulses.	4.14
Is excessively devoted to work and productivity, to the detriment of leisure and relationships.	4.11
Tends to feel unhappy, depressed, or despondent.	4.09
Has difficulty allowing self to experience strong pleasurable emotions (e.g., excitement, joy, pride).	3.97

criterion sets leads to high comorbidity (i.e., low specificity). As now constituted, Axis II cannot transcend this catch 22.

The catch 22 could be resolved by (1) expanding the size of the criterion sets, and (2) diagnosing PDs as configurations or gestalts rather than by tabulating individual symptoms (for discussion of such an approach to diagnosis, which we call "prototype matching," see Shedler & Westen, 2004a; Westen & Shedler, 2000). For example, the composite descriptions of narcissistic and antisocial PD contain numerous overlapping traits, yet they are conceptually distinct and would be difficult to confuse. Expanding the size of the criterion sets would (1) help bridge the gap between science and practice by making *DSM* PD descriptions more faithful to clinical reality, (2) make the PD descriptions more faithful to the conceptual definition of *personality* disorder (i.e., multifaceted syndromes encompassing multiple domains of functioning), and (3) reduce comorbidities among PDs by making the diagnostic categories more distinct from one another.

Addressing Intrapsychic Processes and Inner Experience

DSM-IV tends to underemphasize inner experience or intrapsychic processes that are centrally defining of PDs, which limits both its clinical relevance and its empirical fidelity. For example, the data strongly indicate that aggression and the defenses of externalization and projection are defining features of paranoid PD, yet they are not included in the *DSM-IV* criterion set. The data indicate that hostility, sadism, lack of empathy, lack of insight, self-importance, and power-seeking are defining of antisocial PD. However, these aspects of mental life are absent from the DSM description, which instead emphasizes behavioral markers such as criminality and lack of stable employment. Feelings of inadequacy and inferiority, shame, embarrassment, passivity, depression, anxiety, self-blame, and guilt appear centrally defining of both avoidant and dependent PD (which should probably be subsumed by a depressive PD diagnosis); instead, *DSM-IV* emphasizes behavioral indicators of social avoidance in the former and dependency in the latter.

Identifying Optimal Diagnostic Groupings

This analysis focused on the diagnostic categories currently included in *DSM-IV* but the findings raise broader questions about these categories. For example, the composite descriptions of avoidant and dependent PD overlap substantially and contain numerous features that would be better characterized in terms of a depressive personality syndrome (e.g., the tendency to feel unhappy, depressed, despondent, inadequate, inferior, or a failure; to blame themselves for bad things that happen; to be inhibited about pursuing goals or successes; to feel ashamed or embarrassed; to fear rejection and abandonment; etc.). A depressive PD category deserves consideration for *DSM-V*. (See Shedler & Westen [2004a] for additional recommendations regarding reconfiguration of the axis II categories).

CONCLUSION: INTEGRATING SCIENCE AND PRACTICE

A clinically useful diagnostic system should encompass the spectrum of personality pathology seen in clinical practice and have meaningful implications for treatment. An empirically sound diagnostic system should facilitate reliable and valid diagnoses: Independent clinicians should be able to arrive at the same diagnosis, the diagnoses should be relatively distinct from one another, and each diagnosis should be associated with unique and theoretically meaningful correlates, antecedents, and sequelae (Livesley & Jackson, 1992; Millon, 1991; Robins & Guze, 1970).

One obstacle to achieving this ideal has been an unfortunate schism in the mental health professions between science and practice. Too often, research has been conducted in isolation from the crucial data of clinical observation. The results often strike clinicians as naïve and of dubious clinical relevance. Ultimately, the most empirically elegant diagnostic system will have little impact if clinicians do not find it helpful for understanding their patients (Shedler & Westen, 2005). On the other hand, clinical theory has too often developed with little regard for questions of falsifiability or empirical credibility. The results have often struck researchers as scientifically naïve.

The SWAP represents an effort to bridge the schism between science and practice by quantifying clinical wisdom and expertise and making clinical constructs accessible to empirical study. It relies on clinicians to do what they do best, namely, making observations and inferences about individual patients they know and treat. It relies on quantitative methods to do what they do best, namely, aggregating observations to discern relationships and commonalities, and combining data to yield optimal predictions (cf. Sawyer, 1966). The findings raise possibilities for developing a classification of personality disorders that is both empirically sound and clinically (and psychodynamically) meaningful; for integrating descriptive psychiatric diagnosis with clinical case formulation; for assessing personality change (not just symptom remission) in psychotherapy; and for assessing individual patients in ways that integrate the best features of clinical judgment and psychometric rigor. The SWAP attempts to provide a "language" for case description that is at once clinically rich enough to describe the complexities of the patients we treat, and empirically rigorous enough to meet the requirements of science. There remains a sizeable schism between clinical practitioners and empirical researchers. Perhaps this new language will be a step toward one that all parties can speak.

Note: This chapter is adapted from a chapter of the same title previously published in the *Psychodynamic Diagnostic Manual* (Shedler & Westen, 2006).

REFERENCES

Blais, M., & Norman, D. (1997). A psychometric evaluation of the DSM-IV Personality Disorder Criteria. *Journal of Personality Disorders, 11,* 168–176.

Blashfield, R. (1985). Exemplar prototypes of personality disorder diagnoses. *Comprehensive Psychiatry, 26,* 11–21.

Block, J. (1971). *Lives through time.* Berkeley, CA: Bancroft.

Block, J. (1978). *The Q-sort method in personality assessment and psychiatric research.* Palo Alto, CA: Consulting Psychologists Press.

Bradley, R., & Westen, D. (2003). *Validity of SWAP-200 personality diagnosis in an outpatient sample.* Unpublished manuscript, Emory University.

Cantor, N., & Genero, N. (1986). Psychiatric diagnosis and natural categorization: A close analogy. In Contemporary directions in psychopathology. In G. L. Klerman (Ed.), *Toward the DSM-IV* (pp. 233–256). New York: Guilford.

Clark, L. (1992). Resolving taxonomic issues in personality disorders: The value of larger scale analyses of symptom data. *Journal of Personality Disorders, 6,* 360–376.

Clarkin, J. F., Yeomans, F. E., & Kernberg, O. F. (2006). *Psychotherapy for borderline personality: Focusing on object relations.* Washington, DC: American Psychiatric Press.

Cleckley, H. (1941). *The mask of sanity.* St. Louis, MO: Mosby Co.

Davis, R., Blashfield, R., & McElroy, R. (1993). Weighting criteria in the diagnosis of a personality disorder: A demonstration. *Journal of Abnormal Psychology, 102,* 319–322.

First, M., Spitzer, R., Gibbon, M., Williams, J., Davies, J. B., Howes, M., et al. (1995). The structured clinical interview for DSM-III-R Personality Disorders (SCID-II). Part II: Multi-site test-retest reliability study. *Journal of Personality Disorders, 9,* 92–104.

Grilo, C. M., Sanislow, C. A., & McGlashan, T. H. (2002). Co-occurrence of DSM-IV personality disorders with borderline personality disorder. *Journal of Nervous and Mental Disease, 190*(8), 552–553.

Gunderson, J. G. (2001). *Borderline personality disorder: A clinical guide.* Washington, DC: American Psychiatric Publishing, Inc.

Hare, R. D., Harpur, T. J., Hakstian, A. R., Forth, A. E., Hart, S. D., & Newman, J. P. (1990). The revised Psychopathy Checklist: Reliability and factor structure. *Psychological Assessment: A Journal of Consulting and Clinical Psychology, 2,* 338–341.

Harkness, A. (1992). Fundamental topics in the personality disorders: Candidate trait dimensions from lower regions of the hierarchy. *Psychological Assessment: A Journal of Consulting and Clinical Psychology, 4,* 251–259.

John, O. (1990). The 'big five' factor taxonomy: Dimensions of personality in the natural language and in questionnaires. In L. Pervin (Ed.), *Handbook of personality: Theory and research* (pp. 66–100). New York: Guilford.

Kernberg, O. (1975). *Borderline conditions and pathological narcissism.* New York: Jason Aronson.

Kernberg, O. (1984). *Severe personality disorders.* New Haven, CT: Yale University Press.

Kim, N. S., & Ahn, W. (2002). Clinical psychologists' theory-based representations of mental disorders predict their diagnostic reasoning and memory. *Journal of Experimental Psychology, 131*(4), 451–476.

Klonsky, E. D., Oltmanns, T. F., & Turkheimer, E. (2002). Informant-reports of personality disorder: Relation to self-reports and future research directions. *Clinical Psychology: Science & Practice, 9,* 300–311.

Kohut, H. (1971). *The analysis of the self.* New York: International Universities Press.

Lingiardi, V., Shedler, J., & Gazillo, F. (2006). Assessing personality change in psychotherapy with the SWAP-200: A case study. *Journal of Personality Assessment, 86,* 23–32.

Linehan, M. M. (1993). *Cognitive-behavioral treatment of borderline personality disorder.* New York: Guilford.

Livesley, W. J. (Ed.). (1995). *The DSM-IV personality disorders.* New York: Guilford.

Livesley, W. J., & Jackson, D. N. (1992) Guidelines for developing, evaluating, and revising the classification of personality disorders. *Journal of Nervous and Mental Disease, 180*(10), 609–618.

MacKinnon, R., & Michels, R. (1971). *The psychiatric interview in clinical practice.* Philadelphia: WB Saunders.

Main, M., Kaplan, N., & Cassidy, J. (1985). Security in infancy, childhood, and adulthood: A move to the level of representation. *Monographs of the Society for Research in Child Development, 50*(1–2, Serial No. 209).

Marin-Avellan, L., McGauley, G., Campbell, C., & Fonagy, P. (2005). Using the SWAP-200 in a personality-disordered forensic population: Is it valid, reliable and useful? *Journal of Criminal Behaviour and Mental Health, 15*, 28–45.

McCrae, R., & Costa, P. (1990). *Personality in adulthood.* New York: Guilford.

McWilliams, N. (1994). *Psychoanalytic diagnosis: Understanding personality structure in the clinical process.* New York: Guilford.

McWilliams, N. (1999). *Psychoanalytic Case Formulation.* New York: Guilford.

Millon, T. (1990). *Toward a New Psychology.* New York: Wiley.

Millon, T. (1991). Classification in psychopathology: Rationale, alternatives and standards. *Journal of Abnormal Psychology, 100*, 245–261.

Millon, T., & Davis, R. D. (1997). The place of assessment in clinical science. In T. Millon (Ed.), *The Millon Inventories: Clinical and Personality Assessment* (pp. 3–20). New York: Guilford.

Millon, T., & Martinez, A. (1995). Avoidant personality disorder. In W. J. Livesley (Ed.), *The DSM-IV personality disorders* (pp. 218–233). New York: Guilford.

Morey, L. C. (1988). Personality disorders in DSM-III and DSM-III-R: Convergence, coverage, and internal consistency. *American Journal of Psychiatry, 145*, 573–577.

Morey, L. C. (1991). *The Personality Assessment Inventory: Professional manual.* Odessa, FL: Psychological Assessment Resources.

Oldham, J., Skodol, A., Kellman, H. D., Hyler, S., Rosnick, L., & Davies, M. (1992). Diagnosis of DSM-III-R personality disorders by two semistructured interviews: Patterns of comorbidity. *American Journal of Psychiatry, 149*, 213–220.

Patrick, C. J., & Zempolich, K. A. (1998). Emotion and aggression in the psychopathic personality. *Aggression and Violent Behavior, 3*(4), 303–338.

Perry, J. C. (1992). Problems and considerations in the valid assessment of personality disorders. *American Journal of Psychiatry, 149*, 1645–1653.

Perry, J. C., & Cooper, S. H. (1987). Empirical studies of psychological defense mechanisms. In J. Cavenar & R. Michels (Eds.), *Psychiatry.* Philadelphia: JB Lippincott.

Pilkonis, P. A., Heape, C. L., Proietti, J. M., Clark, S. W., McDavid, J. D., & Pitts, T. E. (1995). The reliability and validity of two structured diagnostic interviews for personality disorders. *Archives of General Psychiatry, 52*, 1025–1033.

Pilkonis, P. A., Heape, C. L., Ruddy, J., & Serrao, P. (1991). Validity in the diagnosis of personality disorders: The use of the LEAD standard. *Psychological Assessment, 31*, 46–54.

Robins, E., & Guze, S. (1970). The establishment of diagnostic validity in psychiatric illness: Its application to schizophrenia. *American Journal of Psychiatry, 126*, 983–987.

Sawyer, J. (1966). Measurement and prediction, clinical and statistical. *Psychological Bulletin, 66,* 178–200.

Shedler, J. (2002). A new language for psychoanalytic diagnosis. *Journal of the American Psychoanalytic Association, 50*(2), 429–456.

Shedler J., Mayman, M., & Manis, M. (1993). The illusion of mental health. *American Psychologist, 48,* 1117–1131.

Shedler, J., & Westen, D. (1998). Refining the measurement of Axis II: A Q-sort procedure for assessing personality pathology. *Assessment, 5*(4), 333–353.

Shedler, J., & Westen, D. (2004a). Refining DSM-IV Personality Disorder Diagnosis: Integrating science and practice. *American Journal of Psychiatry, 161,* 1350–1365.

Shedler, J., & Westen, D. (2004b). Dimensions of personality pathology: An alternative to the five factor model. *American Journal of Psychiatry, 161,* 1743–1754.

Shedler, J., & Westen, D. (2005). A simplistic view of the Five Factor Model: Drs. Shedler and Westen reply. *American Journal of Psychiatry, 162,* 1551.

Shedler, J. & Westen, D. (2006). Personality diagnosis with the Shedler-Westen Assessment Procedure (SWAP): Bridging the gulf between science and practice. In Alliance Task Force (Ed.), *Psychodynamic Diagnostic Manual (PDM)*. Silver Spring, MD: Alliance of Psychoanalytic Organizations.

Skodol, A., Oldham, J., Rosnick, L., Kellman, D., & Hyler, S. (1991). Diagnosis of DSM-III-R personality disorders: A comparison of two structured interviews. *International Journal of Methods in Psychiatric Research, 1,* 13–26.

Spitzer, R. L. (1983). Psychiatric diagnosis: Are clinicians still necessary? *Comprehensive Psychiatry, 24,* 399–411.

Vaillant, G. (Ed.) (1992). *Ego mechanisms of defense: A guide for clinicians and researchers.* Washington, DC: American Psychiatric Press.

Watson, D., & Sinha, B. K. (1998). Comorbidity of DSM-IV personality disorders in a nonclinical sample. *Journal of Clinical Psychology, 54*(6), 773–780.

Westen, D. (1991). Social cognition and object relations. *Psychology Bulletin, 109,* 429–455.

Westen, D. (1997). Divergences between clinical and research methods for assessing personality disorders: Implications for research and the evolution of Axis II. *American Journal of Psychiatry, 154,* 895–903.

Westen, D. (2002). *Clinical Diagnostic Interview.* Unpublished manual, Emory University. Available from http://www.psychsystems.net/lab.

Westen, D., & Arkowitz-Westen, L. (1998). Limitations of Axis II in diagnosing personality pathology in clinical practice. *American Journal of Psychiatry, 155,* 1767–1771.

Westen, D., Heim, A. K., Morrison, K., Patterson, M., & Campbell, L. (2002). Classifying and diagnosing psychopathology: A prototype matching approach. In M. Malik (Ed.), *Rethinking the DSM: Psychological perspectives* (pp. 221–250). Washington, DC: APA Press.

Westen, D., Lohr, N., Silk, K., Gold, L., & Kerber, K. (1990). Object relations and social cognition in borderlines, major depressives, and normals: A TAT analysis. *Psychological Assessment: A Journal of Consulting and Clinical Psychology, 2,* 355–364.

Westen, D., & Muderrisoglu, S. (2003). Reliability and validity of personality disorder assessment using a systematic clinical interview: Evaluating an alternative to structured interviews. *Journal of Personality Disorders, 17,* 350–368.

Westen, D. & Muderrisoglu, S. (in press). Clinical assessment of pathological personality traits. *American Journal of Psychiatry.*

Westen, D., Muderrisoglu, S., Fowler, C., Shedler, J., & Koren, D. (1997). Affect regulation and affective experience: Individual differences, group differences, and measurement using a Q-sort procedure. *Journal of Consulting and Clinical Psychology, 65,* 429–439.

Westen, D., & Shedler, J. (1999a). Revising and assessing Axis II: I. Developing a clinically and empirically valid assessment method. *American Journal of Psychiatry, 156*(2), 258–272.

Westen, D., & Shedler, J. (1999b). Revising and assessing Axis II: II. Toward an empirically based and clinically useful classification of personality disorders. *American Journal of Psychiatry, 156*(2), 258–272.

Westen D., & Shedler, J. (2000) A prototype matching approach to diagnosing personality disorders toward DSM-V. *Journal of Personality Disorders, 14*(2), 109–126.

Westen D., Shedler, J., Durrett, C., Glass, S., & Martens, A. (2003). Personality diagnosis in adolescence: DSM-IV axis II diagnoses and an empirically derived alternative. *American Journal of Psychiatry, 160,* 952–966.

Westen, D., & Weinberger, J. (2004). When clinical description becomes statistical prediction. *American Psychologist, 59,* 595–613.

Widiger, T. A. (1993). The DSM-III-R categorical personality disorder diagnoses: A critique and an alternative. *Psychological Inquiry, 4*(2), 75–90.

Widiger, T. A., & Corbitt, E. M. (1995). Antisocial personality disorder. In J. W. Livesley (Ed.), *The DSM-IV personality disorders. Diagnosis and treatment of mental disorders* (pp. 103–126). New York: Guilford.

Widiger, T. A., & Simonsen, E. S. (2005). Alternative dimensional models of personality disorders: Finding common ground. *Journal of Personality Disorders, 19,* 110–130.

Widiger, T. A., Hare, R., Rutherford, M., Corbitt, E. M., Hart, S. D., Woody, G., et al. (1996). DSM-IV antisocial personality disorder field trial. *Journal of Abnormal Psychology, 105,* 3–16.

Wilkinson-Ryan, T., & Westen, D. (2000). Identity disturbance in borderline personality disorder: An empirical investigation. *American Journal of Psychiatry, 157,* 528–541.

Zimmerman, M. (1994). Diagnosing personality disorders: A review of issues and research methods. *Archives of General Psychiatry, 51,* 225–245.

ENDNOTES

1. Poor test-retest reliability has led some researchers to suggest that PDs are less stable than previously believed. An alternative hypothesis is that the assessment instruments overemphasize transitory behavioral symptoms (e.g., self-cutting in borderline patients) and underemphasize underlying personality processes that are much more stable over time (e.g., emotional dysregulation and self-hatred in borderline patients).

2. One way it reduces measurement error is by ensuring that raters are "calibrated" with one another. Consider the situation with rating scales, where raters can use any value as often as they wish. Inevitably, certain raters will tend toward extreme values (e.g., values of 0 and 7 on a 0–7 scale) whereas others will tend toward middle values (e.g., values of 4 and 5). Thus, the ratings reflect not only the characteristics of the patients but also the calibration of the raters. The Q-Sort method, with its fixed distribution, eliminates this kind of measurement error, because all clinicians must assign each value the same number of times. If use of a standard item set gives clinicians a common vocabulary, use of a fixed distribution can be said to give them a common "grammar" (Block, 1978).

3. The material presented in this section is adapted from Lingiardi, Shedler, & Gazzillo (2006). See the original publication for a more complete description of the case, treatment methods, and findings.

4. Averaging across raters enhances the reliability of the resulting scores.

5. The relatively low thresholds reflect the fact that the reference sample consisted of patients with PD diagnoses. Thus, a T-score of 50 indicates "average" functioning among patients with PD diagnoses, and a T-score of 60 represents an elevation of one standard deviation relative to other patients with PD diagnoses.

6. The material presented here is adapted from Westen & Weinberger (2004).

7. The material in this section is adapted from Shedler & Westen, 2004a.

8. The reliability of a composite or aggregate personality description is measured by coefficient alpha, which reflects the intercorrelations between the patients (columns of data) included in the aggregate description. The logic is identical to computing the reliability of a psychometric scale, except that patients are treated as scale "items" (columns in the data file) and SWAP-200 items are treated as cases (rows in the data file). See note 4 for additional details.

13

The "Art" of Interpreting the "Science" and the "Science" of Interpreting the "Art" of the Treatment of Borderline Personality Disorder

KENNETH N. LEVY AND LORI N. SCOTT

Borderline personality disorder (BPD) is characterized by affective instability, angry outbursts, frequent suicidality and parasuicidality, as well as marked deficits in the capacity to work and to maintain meaningful relationships. BPD has prevalence rates of nearly 1–4% in the general population, 10% in psychiatric outpatient samples, and up to 20% in psychiatric inpatient samples (e.g., Paris, 1999; Torgersen, Kringlen, & Cramer, 2001; Weissman, 1993; Widiger & Frances, 1989; Widiger & Weissman, 1991). In addition, BPD is frequently comorbid with depression, anxiety disorders, eating disorders, posttraumatic stress disorder, and substance abuse, often with detrimental effects on the treatment of these disorders (for a review, see Skodol, Gunderson, Pfohl, Widiger, Livesley, & Siever, 2002). Furthermore, patients with BPD typically experience profound impairment in general functioning and have an estimated suicide completion rate of 8–10% (Oldham et al., 2001). Thus, BPD is a debilitating and life-threatening disorder that represents a serious clinical and public health concern.

Although patients with BPD are often deemed difficult to treat, there is some evidence that BPD may be a treatable disorder (Perry, Banon, & Ianni, 1999) and that psychotherapy is the recommended primary technique for its treatment (Oldham et al., 2001). Evidence for the efficacy of specific treatments for BPD now exists (Bateman & Fonagy, 1999; Giesen-Bloo et al., 2006; Koons et al., 2001; Linehan, Armstrong, Suarez, Allmon, & Heard, 1991; Linehan et al., 1999; Linehan et al., 2002; Turner, 2000; Verheul et al., 2003), with Dialectical Behavior Therapy (DBT; Linehan, 1993), to date, being perhaps the most extensively studied treatment in randomized controlled trials (RCTs). However, a number of other treatments for BPD have been developed that have demonstrated effectiveness (Blum, Pfohl, St. John, Monahan, & Black, 2002; Brown, Newman, Charlesworth, Crits-Christoph, & Beck, 2004; Clarkin et al., 2001; Levy, Clarkin, Schiavi, Foelsch, & Kernberg, 2006; Ryle & Golynkina, 2000; Stevenson & Meares, 1992). Meanwhile, additional studies testing the effectiveness and efficacy[1] of new treatments have recently been completed, presented at conferences but remain unpublished (Arnt, 2005; Clarkin, Levy, Lenzenweger, & Kernberg, 2006), or are currently being conducted (Markowitz, Skodal, Bleiberg, & Strasser-Vorus, 2004).

Despite the emergence of new treatments for BPD that have garnered empirical support in both effectiveness and efficacy studies, a growing number of researchers have espoused limiting psychotherapy practice and training to treatments that have demonstrated efficacy in RCTs (Calhoun, Moras, Pilkonis, & Rehm, 1998; Chambless & Hollon, 1998). In addition, managed health care companies often reimburse only for those treatments for BPD that have demonstrated efficacy data and refuse to reimburse for those that have not yet been tested in an RCT. With the proliferation of evidence for the efficacy of DBT and the increasing focus on the dissemination of empirically supported treatments (ESTs), the added value of naturalistic studies that bear on the ecological validity of ESTs is often overlooked. However, there are a number of important limitations to RCTs. RCTs are frequently limited in their generalizability to clinical practice (Borkovec & Castonguay, 1998; Goldfried & Wolfe, 1996; Goldfried & Wolfe, 1998; Morrison, Bradley, & Westen, 2003; Seligman, 1995; Westen & Morrison, 2001), and naturalistic studies may be necessary to help bridge the gap between practice and research (Morrison et al., 2003). Likewise, the utility of RCTs for evaluating a treatment's putative mechanisms of action and underlying theoretical constructs is frequently indirect and limited. In other words, studies that compare purportedly distinct treatments can only tell us which treatment yields the most favorable outcome. The active ingredients or dimensions of the more effective therapy remain unknown and can only be indirectly inferred. Limiting research, practice, and training exclusively to treatments that have been validated in RCTs could impede reasonable avenues of study in the treatment of BPD and obstruct access to treatments that might be better-suited to specific patient subgroups.

In this chapter we will summarize the pros and cons of RCTs, present a hierarchical model of evidence in psychotherapy studies that balances concerns about adequate controls and generalizability, and examine more broadly the psychotherapy research which bears on BPD. We will then report results from a series of studies performed at the Personality Disorders Institute at Cornell Medical Center on the treatment of BPD. Finally, we will summarize conclusions that can be drawn from this broader examination of the literature.

PROS AND CONS OF RCTs

Efficacy studies are widely considered the gold standard in psychotherapy research for their emphasis on internal validity through their use of relevant control groups, treatment manuals, random assignment to treatment conditions, and well-defined, homogeneous groups of patients (Nathan, Stuart, & Dolan, 2000). The controls provided by these aspects of RCT designs are important for eliminating rival hypotheses and making specific causal inferences about what treatments are most effective for particular patients under specified conditions. However, RCTs are not immune to threats to internal validity. Particularly in the study of personality disorders, which frequently involve longer-term treatments, patient attrition over longer treatment studies can negate the control provided by randomization (Howard, Orlinsky, & Lueger, 1995). Moreover, randomization and control groups cannot account for every potentially intervening variable, including patient or therapist characteristics that can influence the effects of treatment (Clarkin & Levy, 2003; Howard et al., 1995). The time that elapses between interventions and outcome measurement can also introduce rival hypotheses because any number of unmeasured factors outside the therapy may influence outcome or interfere with treatment effects, especially with personality-based disorders which revolve around the ways that people interact in their daily lives rather than alleviation of symptoms. In addition, recent research has found that purportedly separate and distinct therapeutic approaches tend to overlap considerably in RCTs (Ablon & Jones, 2002), rendering conclusions regarding the efficacy of any one specific treatment package over another problematic. A related issue in many RCTs that detracts from internal validity is the lack of adherence and competency data to ensure that therapists are delivering therapy as prescribed by treatment manuals and not engaging in proscribed techniques. Also, measurement of treatment credibility is important to ruling out expectancy effects, which many RCTs neglect to incorporate into their designs (Borkovec & Nau, 1972). In addition, many of the existing RCTs lack sufficient follow-up to determine the long-term effects of these treatments. Because BPD is a long-term chronic disorder and patients may continue to improve or may deteriorate after the conclusion of the study, it is imperative that there be long-term follow-up (at least 2 to 5 years) of well-defined patient groups in well-characterized treatments. The types of changes that occur during the year or two of a treatment study, such as reduction of self-harm episodes and number and length of hospitalizations, might lead to further changes after the termination of treatment in other domains of patients' lives, such as increased capacity to work and improved stability in personal relationships, all of which go unnoticed without adequate follow-up data.

Moreover, the emphasis on internal validity in RCTs can reduce the relevance and ecological validity of findings (Borkovec & Castonguay, 1998; Goldfried & Wolfe, 1996; Goldfried & Wolfe, 1998; Morrison et al., 2003; Seligman, 1995). Controls in such studies are rigorous, usually involving strict inclusion and exclusion criteria that may produce treatment samples that are nonrepresentative of the comorbidity and heterogeneity usually seen in private practice (Guthrie, 2000), especially among patients with BPD who typically show a pattern of "complex comorbidity" (Zanarini et al., 1998). A number of studies have shown that patient groups typically excluded from RCTs tend to have poorer outcomes or require substantially longer treatments (Humphreys & Weisner, 2000; Mitchell, Hoberman, Peterson, Mussell, & Pyle, 1996; Thompson-Brenner, Glass, & Westen, 2003), suggesting that findings from rigidly controlled RCTs might not generalize to such patient groups. In addition, treatments are often manualized in efficacy studies with careful supervision to control for adherence and competency, a tactic which is rare in naturalistic settings. The randomization process itself can also impact external validity because both therapists and patients lose their freedom of choice; patients in private practice have a choice of service providers, and therapists in private practice decide which patients they can work with, and typically refer those with whom they cannot to other therapists (Blatt & Zuroff, 2005). Further, due to over-reliance on the drug-metaphor for designing treatment studies (Guthrie, 2000) and other pragmatic factors such as inadequate funding for long-term treatment studies and patient attrition, RCTs usually offer shorter doses of treatment for BPD than would be common in the community. Given these threats to external validity in many RCTs, it is often unclear whether or not treatments found to be efficacious in such studies are transportable and will work as well or in the same way when they are implemented in clinical settings.

The numerous limitations of efficacy studies have led many investigators to recommend searching for empirically supported principles (ESPs) of treatment, or evidence-based explanations of treatment, rather than credentialed, trademarked, brand-name, or evidence-based treatment packages (Ablon & Jones, 2002; National Institute of Mental Health Workshop Summary, 2002; Rosen & Davison, 2003). Likewise, Borkovec and Castonguay (1998) and Weisz (2003) recommend conducting well-controlled therapy trials in more naturalistic settings. Such hybrids of efficacy and effectiveness research may help to bridge the gap between science and practice (Carroll & Rounsaville, 2003). At the same time, however, there seems to be considerable data already in existence at multiple levels of scientific evidence that could be combined to form increasingly well-rounded inferences about the treatment of BPD. Thus, a broader definition of evidence may be necessary when evaluating the effects of psychotherapy for this complex disorder.

THE HIERARCHY OF TREATMENT EVIDENCE

Gabbard and colleagues (Gabbard, 2002; Gabbard, Gunderson, & Fonagy, 2002) and others (e.g., Clarke & Oxman, 1999) have discussed a stage model, or hierarchy, of treatment evidence as a function of internal and external validity. They have suggested that evidence from multiple sources within this model is necessary in order to build an empirically grounded framework for specific forms of psychotherapy. In ascending levels of internal validity and descending levels of external validity, the hierarchy of treatment evidence starts with the provision of an argument or the articulation of clinical innovation, and proceeds through clinical case studies, clinical case series, pre-post designs, quasi-experimental designs, and RCTs. We argue that this hierarchy, in combination with the examination of evidence for specific techniques and mechanisms of action (Levy, Clarkin, Yeomans et al. 2006), provides better breadth of evidence and better validity than focusing on RCTs alone. In the next section, relevant studies on psychotherapy for BPD will be discussed in terms of this hierarchy, beginning with pre-post designs. The goal will be to integrate these findings into coherent inferences having both internal and external validity.

Pre-Post Designs

Pre-post designs are those that employ neither randomization nor control groups, and instead use patients as their own controls by measuring the amount of change in outcome variables over time. In pre-post studies, the lack of a comparison group limits the interpretation of positive change as attributable to the treatment. That is, the changes observed in the patients may have occurred over time without treatment. However, such studies are useful for showing the feasibility of a treatment approach, generating initial effect sizes, and for identifying potential predictors of outcome. Therefore, pre-post designs are an ideal first step in establishing a new treatment's success with a specific patient population.

There are a number of pre-post design studies that have been carried out with borderline patients (e.g., Blum et al., 2002; Brown et al., 2004; Clarkin et al., 1992; Clarkin et al., 2001; Low, Jones, Duggan, Power, & MacLeod, 2001; Cookson, Espie, & Yates, 2001; Miller, Wyman, Huppert, Glassman, & Rathus, 2000; Ryle & Golynkina, 2000; Smith, Koenigsberg, Yeomans, Clarkin, & Selzer, 1995; Stevenson & Meares, 1992; Telch, Agras, & Linehan, 2000; Trupin, Stewart, Beach, & Boesky; 2002; Wildgoose, Clark, & Waller, 2001; Yeomans et al., 1994; Mental Health Center of Greater Manchester, 1998). Stevenson and Meares (1992) conducted a pre-post study that evaluated the effects of a nonmanualized psychodynamic treatment (based on the ideas of Kohut, Winnocott, and Hobson's conversational model) for patients with BPD. They found that compared to pretherapy, patients at the end of treatment showed an increase in time employed and decreases in number of medical visits, number of self-harm episodes, and number and length of hospitalizations. Although the inferences that can be drawn from these results are limited by the lack of a control group, these findings supported further development and study of psychodynamic treatments for BPD.

Other early pre-post studies of treatments for BPD (e.g., Clarkin et al., 1992; Smith et al., 1995; Yeomans et al., 1994) have identified risk factors for BPD patient dropouts from psychotherapy, having important implications for both researchers and clinicians working with this patient population. These studies have shown that younger patients and those high in hostility are most likely to drop out of treatment (Smith et al., 1995). In this early work, however, the establishment of a strong treatment contract was not emphasized, and dropout rates were generally high (36% at 6 months into treatment). The often ego-syntonic nature of personality disturbance may also account for premature drop-out in younger patients, who may not recognize the seriousness of their difficulties until later in life. Furthermore, hostility in BPD is likely to disturb the patient's capacity for relatedness to the therapist. Other pre-post studies have demonstrated the importance of establishing the treatment frame (i.e., the contract) with BPD patients for improving compliance and avoiding premature termination of therapy and violation of therapeutic boundaries (Yeomans et al., 1994).

More recent pre-post studies have tested manualized treatments or modifications of manualized treatments for BPD. For example, Bohus and colleagues (2000) showed that DBT, a manualized cognitive behavioral therapy that was developed for treating chronically suicidal or parasuicidal women in outpatient settings, could be adapted for inpatient use. DBT (Linehan, 1993) includes weekly individual psychotherapy that emphasizes validation and acceptance, balanced with behavioral strategies designed to promote change. DBT also incorporates weekly groups that focus on the acquisition of interpersonal, self-regulation, and distress-tolerance skills. Although originally intended as an outpatient treatment, Bohus and his colleagues developed an intensive three-month inpatient program based on DBT, including weekly individual therapy and skills training groups, as well as weekly mindfulness, psychoeducation, and peer groups. Compared to assessments at admission, patients showed significant improvements one month after discharge in reported anxiety, depression, dissociation, and global stress, and a highly significant decrease in parasuicidal acts. This research generated initial effect sizes for DBT with inpatients, paving the way for more controlled studies with inpatient populations. Other pre-post studies have extended DBT for use with incarcerated female juvenile offenders (Trupin et al., 2002), suicidal adolescents (Miller et al., 2000), and women with binge-eating disorder (Telch et al., 2000).

Non-DBT cognitive approaches have also been evaluated with the pre-post research methodology. Brown and colleagues (Brown et al., 2004) demonstrated preliminary support for cognitive therapy (CT) for BPD, which focuses on changing automatic dysfunctional thought patterns. Patients treated with one year of CT showed significant decreases in hopelessness, depression, suicidality, and BPD criteria at 18-month assessments, but effect sizes ranged from only .22 to .55, which were in the moderate range (Cohen, 1988).

Ryle and Golynkina (2000) conducted a pre-post study evaluating the effectiveness of a time-limited Cognitive Analytic Therapy (CAT) for treating BPD. The CAT model of BPD emphasizes collaboration between patient and therapist in the identification of the partial dissociation of personality into dysfunctional patterns of affect, self regulation, and interpersonal behavior. Diagrams of these patterns are collaboratively developed and modified with the patient during treatment. This study demonstrated that about half of the patients who completed 24 sessions of CAT no longer met full criteria for the BPD diagnosis at the end of treatment. In addition, at six-month follow-up, the patients who no longer met BPD diagnostic criteria were more likely to be employed and involved in long-term relationships. These authors found that more severe BPD features, history of parasuicide, alcohol abuse, and unemployment, were predictors of poorer outcomes, highlighting the influence of pretreatment severity on outcomes in BPD patients. Mean follow-up assessment scores showed continued improvement at 18-month post-treatment, but high attrition rates prohibited statistical analyses of follow-up assessments beyond the 18-month point.

Yet another pre-post study (Blum et al., 2002) evaluated the effects of Systems Training for Emotional Predictability and Problem Solving (STEPPS), a short-term treatment program designed for BPD patients in rural areas. STEPPS is a skills-based approach that utilizes cognitive-behavioral and psychoeducational techniques in a group format and is conceptualized as adjunct to a patient's existing treatment. Blum and colleagues found moderate to high levels of satisfaction in patients and therapists who participated in STEPPS, and decreases in patients' self-reported negative behaviors, negative mood, and depression. Although these results are promising, they must be interpreted cautiously for several reasons in addition to the lack of a control group to rule out maturational and history effects. First, structured interviews were not used to assess patients for BPD, so there may have been patients included in the study who were subthreshold for the disorder. This suggests that these results might not generalize to more severely disturbed patients with BPD. Second, this study suffers from inconsistent data collection and limited domains of outcome. That is, patients were asked to provide self-report data at STEPPS group sessions, and the incompleteness of the data suggests patient noncompliance. In other words, these results may have resulted from a selected sample of patients who attended regularly and were more satisfied with treatment than those who did not attend or refused to complete the required group assignments used to determine outcome. Therefore, issues such as reliable clinical diagnoses and multiple outcome domains may be just as important to the validity of psychotherapy research as control groups and randomization.

The Borderline Psychotherapy Research Project at New York Presbyterian Hospital-Weill Cornell Medical Center, headed by Drs. Otto Kernberg and John Clarkin, conducted a pre-post study (Clarkin et al., 2001) to evaluate the effects of Transference-Focused Psychotherapy (TFP; Clarkin, Yeomans, & Kernberg, 1999) a manualized and highly structured psychodynamic treatment based on Kernberg's (1984) object relations model of BPD. Kernberg's model focuses on the development of mental representations that are derived through the internalization of attachment relationships with caregivers. According to Kernberg's model, BPD is characterized by unintegrated and undifferentiated representations of self and other (i.e., identity diffusion) and immature defense mechanisms such as projection and splitting. The major goals of TFP are better behavioral control, increased affect regulation, more intimate and gratifying relationships, and the ability to pursue life goals. These goals are hypothesized to be accomplished through the modification of primitive defensive operations and the resolution of identity diffusion that perpetuates the fragmentation of the patient's internal representational world. Thus, in contrast to therapies that focus on the short-term treatment of symptoms, TFP has the ambitious goal of not just changing symptoms, but changing the personality organization, which is the context of the symptoms. In contrast to most manuals for CBT or short-term treatments, the TFP manual could be described as principle-based rather than sequentially based, which requires the clinician to be flexible and use clinical judgment. Using videotaped sessions and supervisor ratings, Kernberg and his colleagues have been able to train both senior clinicians and junior trainees at multiple sites to adherence and competence in applying the principles of TFP.

For the pre-post study (Clarkin et al., 2001), participants were recruited from varied treatment settings (i.e., inpatient, day hospital, and outpatient clinics) within the New York metropolitan area. Participants were 21[2] women between the ages of 18 and 50 who met criteria for BPD through structured interviews. All therapists (senior therapists to postdoctoral trainees) selected for this phase of the study were judged by independent supervisory ratings to be both competent and adherent to the TFP manual. Three senior supervisors rated the therapists for TFP adherence and competence. Throughout the study, all therapists were supervised on a weekly basis by Kernberg and at least one other senior clinician (A. Appelbaum, F. Yeomans, & M. Stone).

The one-year dropout rate was 19.1% and no patient committed suicide. Two out of the total of 21 patients dropped out after four months, and two dropped out after eight months of treatment. These results compare well with other treatments for BPD: Linehan et al. (1991) had a 16.7% dropout rate, and one suicide (4%); Stevenson and Meares' study (1992) had a 16% dropout rate and no suicides; and Bateman and Fonagy's study (1999) had a 21% dropout rate and no suicides. None of the treatment completers deteriorated or were adversely affected by the treatment. Therefore, it appears that TFP is well-tolerated.

Further, 52.9% of participants no longer met criteria for BPD after one year of twice-weekly outpatient treatment. This rate compares quite well with that found by others. Stevenson and Meares (1992) found that 30% of patients in their treatment study no longer met criteria for *DSM-III* (American Psychiatric Association, 1980) BPD at a one-year follow-up. Perry et al. (1999) note that naturalistic follow-up studies of patients with BPD yield an estimated recovery rate of only 3.7% per year and four active treatment studies for mixed personality disorders (with 53% having borderline personality disorder) produced a recovery rate of 25.8% per year.

Overall, the major finding in the Clarkin et al. (2001) pre-post study was that patients with BPD who were treated with TFP showed marked reductions in the severity of parasuicidal behaviors, fewer emergency room visits, hospitalizations, and days hospitalized. The effect sizes were large and no less than those demonstrated for other BPD treatments (Bateman & Fonagy, 1999; Bohus et al., 2000; Linehan et al., 1991). In addition, reliable increases in global functioning and a generally low dropout rate were observed in these patients. These results suggest the potential utility of TFP for treating BPD patients and that more research on TFP is warranted.

In summary, pre-post designs are limited in that the improvements seen may have been attributable to the effects of time, rather than the treatment itself. Without a comparison group, it is impossible to eliminate this possibility. In order to address this limitation, researchers will need to examine patients treated in their modalities as compared to patients treated in other modalities. Despite these weaknesses, pre-post studies are useful for establishing the feasibility and tolerability of a treatment, and for generating initial effect sizes. The results of these studies have revealed promising findings and provided initial evidence for psychodynamic (both based on Kernberg and Kohut's theorizing), non-DBT cognitive therapy (Brown et al., 2004), and an integrative cognitive-analytic outpatient program (Ryle & Golynkina, 2000). Further, pre-post studies have extended DBT for inpatient, forensic, and adolescent populations, and provided some cautious support for a supplemental skills-based approach (i.e., STEPPS; Blum et al., 2002). Pre-post studies have also importantly led to the identification of risk factors for dropout from treatment and of technical changes that may be necessary when treating patients with BPD (such as a treatment contract and a strong, consistent frame).

Quasi-experimental Designs

Next in the hierarchy of treatment evidence are quasi-experimental designs, which compare an experimental treatment with another treatment condition but do not employ random assignment like RCTs. Without randomization, however, the possibility of ruling out rival hypotheses is decreased because patient outcomes could be affected by any number of nonrandom factors, such as reliable differences between treatment groups in patient severity. Even if there are no differences between the treatment group and the comparison group in terms of demographic, diagnostic, or severity variables, groups may still differ on some unmeasured variable (e.g., reactance or psychological mindedness) that may relate to outcome.

Despite these limitations, many quasi-experimental studies of treatments for BPD have extended previous pre-post studies, increasing the confidence of the findings from these studies and suggesting the value of conducting RCTs to further validate specific treatments. For example, Meares, Stevenson, and Comerford (1999) conducted a quasi-experimental study that confirmed the results of an earlier pre-post study (Stevenson & Meares, 1992) evaluating psychodynamic psychotherapy for BPD. Meares et al. (1999) compared BPD patients treated twice weekly for one year with a manualized interpersonal-psychodynamic (IP) psychotherapy to BPD patients who were on a wait list and receiving treatment-as-usual (TAU) or no formal psychotherapy for the same period. Thirty percent of IP-treated patients no longer met criteria for a *DSM-III* (American Psychiatric Association, 1980) BPD diagnosis at the end of the treatment year, whereas all of the TAU patients still met criteria for the diagnosis. These results demonstrated that psychotherapy based on psychodynamic principles is generally beneficial to patients with BPD in a naturalistic setting, having strong ecological validity. However, the TAU group were essentially on a wait list for treatment (because not enough therapists were available at the time), and therefore, many received no treatment at all, making it difficult to infer more from these results than simply that IP is more effective than no treatment for BPD.

Another quasi-experimental study (Rathus & Miller, 2002) compared a group of suicidal adolescents treated with 12 weeks of DBT (modified to include family therapy) to a TAU group, and found that those treated with DBT had significantly fewer hospitalizations and were more likely to complete treatment than those in the TAU group. These results were especially noteworthy considering that the DBT group had reliably more depressive, anxiety, and substance abuse disorders, more Axis I diagnoses, more hospitalizations, and more BPD diagnoses at pre-treatment assessment than did the TAU group. In addition, this study was conducted in a hospital setting, suggesting that these results might have greater ecological validity than most previous studies of DBT, which were conducted in university research settings. Another interesting aspect of this study is that it was conducted in an urban area (New York City) with an ethnically diverse sample of adolescents (almost 70% of the total patient sample were Hispanic), extending the generalizability of DBT's effectiveness for a variety of populations. However, as acknowledged by the researchers, the lack of randomization to treatment groups is problematic because the groups differed in a number of variables. One potential confound noted by the authors is the possibility that adolescents who are more depressed or generally symptomatic, as were those in the DBT group, may be more responsive to psychotherapy. In addition, the investigators only reported completer analyses and did not report analyses including patients who began but did not complete the study (intent-to-treat analysis).

A quasi-experimental study conducted at the Borderline Psychotherapy Research Project at New York Presbyterian Hospital-Weill Cornell Medical Center (Levy, Clarkin, Schiavi, 2006) provided further support for the effectiveness of TFP in treating BPD. In this study, 30 women diagnosed with BPD and treated with TFP were compared to 17 patients in a TAU group. There were no significant pre-treatment differences between the treatment group and the comparison group in terms of demographic or diagnostic variables, severity of BPD symptomatology, baseline emergency room visits, hospitalizations, days hospitalized, or global functioning scores. Of the 17 patients in the comparison group, six patients entered once-weekly individual psychotherapy (three with private therapists affiliated with Cornell and three with therapists working in the NYPH Outpatient Department), seven patients entered treatment in a NYPH day program (five in Dialectical Behavioral Therapy, one in psychodynamic therapy, and one who spent six months in psychodynamic therapy and six months in DBT), and four patients were in and out of various treatments both at NYPH and outside the Cornell system. None of the TAU patients were discharged from the Outpatient Department. Individual psychotherapy was provided at the NYPH for all but two TAU participants. Both patients in psychotherapy outside NYPH's Outpatient Department were seen by therapists trained and with clinical appointments at Cornell Medical College. Overall, the TAU therapists represented a multidisciplinary group of therapists whose experience level generally falls somewhere between the first and second cohorts of therapists in the experimental condition. The one-year attrition rate for TFP was 13.3%.[3] Overall, of the 30 patients who completed the treatment contract and started TFP, four did not complete the year of treatment and no patients committed suicide.

Compared to those treated with TAU, patients treated with TFP showed significant decreases in suicide attempts, hospitalizations, and number of days hospitalized, as well as reliable increases in global functioning. All of the within-subjects and between-subject effect sizes for the TFP-treated participants indicated favorable change. The within-subject effect sizes ranged from 0.73 to 3.06 for the TFP-treated participants, with an average effect size of 1.19, which is well above what is considered "large" (Cohen, 1988). These findings confirmed the previous success of TFP with BPD patients (Clarkin et al., 2001) and justified further validating TFP in comparison to established treatments in an RCT (Clarkin, Levy, Lenzenweger, & Kernberg, 2004). Furthermore, because this study's participants were clinically referred polysymptomatic patients (representative of those seen in clinical practice), who were treated in clinicians' private offices, these results are likely to be high in external validity.

In summary, despite the potential confounds of between-group differences in demographics, severity of psychopathology or symptomatology, or unmeasured variables, the findings from quasi-experimental treatment studies with borderline patients suggest (1) greater confidence in the findings from earlier pre-post studies examining psychodynamic and interpersonally oriented treatments, and (2) the usefulness of DBT for urban, ethnically diverse suicidal adolescents. The fact that many quasi-experimental studies are conducted in naturalistic settings and patients often have more choice of treatment than in RCTs increases their ecological validity.

Randomized Controlled Trials

Gabbard and colleagues (Gabbard et al., 2002) as well as the Cochrane report (Clarke & Oxman, 1999), suggest that even within RCT designs there is a hierarchy of treatment evidence based on varying levels of control provided by different comparison groups. The most rigorous variety of RCT is the comparison of an experimental treatment with a well-established, well-delivered, alternative treatment. Less rigorous forms of RCTs, ordered according to levels of internal validity, are those that compare the experimental treatment with placebo, TAU, and wait-list control groups, all of which may suffer from decreased treatment credibility in control groups that could lead to confounding expectancy effects.

To date, there have been 11 RCTs with BPD patients across these various levels of control: comparison with well-established, well-delivered, alternative treatment (Clarkin et al., 2004), placebo (Geisen-Bloo et al., 2006; Linehan et al., 2002; Linehan et al., 2006; Munroe-Blum & Marziali, 1995; Turner, 2000), and TAU (Verheul et al., 2003; Koons et al., 2001; Linehan et al., 1999; Bateman & Fonagy, 1999; Linehan et al., 1991). Other controlled studies reported in the literature are difficult to interpret because the studies focused on either suicidal behavior or mixed types of personality disorders without specifying borderline cohorts (Evans et al., 1999; Guthrie et al., 2001; Liberman & Eckman, 1981; Piper, Joyce, McCallum, & Azim, 1998; Salkovskis, Atha, & Storer, 1990; Tyrer et al., 2003).

Wait-List Control

At the very lowest level of control in the proposed hierarchy is the wait-list control group design, which is least preferred in research with BPD patients due to ethical reasons (i.e., withholding treatment from individuals in acute distress) as well as the lack of control for therapist contact. Because of the seriousness of BPD and the risk for suicide, wait-list control groups are rarely used in prospective psychotherapy studies for this disorder; however, there was one wait-list control group used in a naturalistic quasi-experimental study (Meares et al., 1999) due to a shortage of therapists. This study, however, did not randomly assign patients to groups and was therefore reviewed previously in this chapter as a quasi-experimental study. Briefly, this study found that 30 percent of patients treated with manualized interpersonal-psychodynamic psychotherapy no longer met BPD criteria after one year of treatment, while all patients in the comparison group remained unchanged in diagnosis.

Treatment-As-Usual

Treatment-as-usual (TAU) comparisons have been employed with great success in RCTs for BPD (Bateman & Fonagy, 1999; Linehan et al., 1991). The rationale for a TAU group is that a no-treatment placebo control is not sufficient, ethical, or practical for patients with BPD who often present with severe symptoms, including suicidality. In addition, proponents of a TAU approach suggest that the first necessary step is to demonstrate that the experimental treatment produces effects superior to existing treatments. TAU controls for the effects of spontaneous remission, for the effects of reassessments on outcome measures, and for the beneficial effects of treatments other than the experimental group. However, TAU comparison groups tend to reduce the specificity of conclusions that can be drawn from findings due to the fact that little can be known about what is actually provided in "treatment-as-usual," and some TAU groups actually involve little to no treatment at all. For example, in Linehan's initial study (Linehan et al., 1991)

27% of the participants in the TAU immediately dropped out of treatment and at any given time only about 50% of the participants in the TAU were in any type of treatment at all. Likewise, in the Bateman and Fonagy study (1999), patients in the TAU group received no formal psychotherapy and, unless hospitalized, only received twice-monthly psychiatric services. Thus, with BPD patients, TAU may be better conceptualized as nontreatment-as-usual or chaotic-treatment-as-usual. Unfortunately, most RCTs evaluating treatments for BPD have used TAU designs (for exceptions, see Clarkin et al., 2006; Giesen-Bloo et al., 2006; Munroe-Blum & Marziali, 1994; Linehan et al., 2002; Linehan et al., 2006; Turner, 2000).

The first RCT to examine a specific treatment for BPD was conducted by Linehan and colleagues (Linehan et al., 1991) to evaluate the efficacy of DBT in comparison to TAU for chronically parasuicidal women with BPD. At the end of one year of treatment, participants randomized to DBT showed a reduction in the number and severity of suicide attempts and a decrease in the length of inpatient admissions compared to those in the TAU group. In addition, DBT participants were significantly more likely than TAU participants to begin therapy, maintain treatment with the same therapist throughout the year, and to continue therapy. This was a seminal study in psychotherapy research for BPD, generating the first results suggesting the efficacy of a manualized treatment for reducing suicidality and parasuicidality in BPD patients. However, the study was not without its flaws and limitations. Linehan and Heard (1993) later reported that whereas DBT subjects received free treatment, TAU subjects were given referrals to low-fee treatment settings and had to pay for therapy. This introduces a potential confounding difference between the two groups in the availability of treatment. In addition, as mentioned earlier and as noted in Scheel's (2000) critique, about 27% of the TAU patients actually received no therapy at all, the amount of therapy received by the remaining 73% of the TAU group was unreported, and only about half received stable therapy for the year. Given that DBT is an intensive therapy that involves at least three hours of therapist contact per week, there was likely to be a large difference between groups in therapist contact.[4] Moreover, a reduction in suicide attempts and hospitalizations in the DBT group is not surprising considering that DBT is a treatment that focuses explicitly on keeping patients out of the hospital (Linehan, 1993).

Follow-up data on the patients from the Linehan et al. (1991) RCT were mixed. At six-month follow-up (Linehan, Heard, & Armstrong, 1993), there were no differences between groups in the number of days hospitalized, reasons for living, and levels of hopelessness and depression. Further, at one-year follow-up, there were no differences between groups in the number of days hospitalized and in frequency of self-destructive acts, with some patients treated with DBT showing variable maintenance of treatment effects. In addition, the follow-up sample sizes were too small to reliably detect differences between those patients who had continued to receive treatment after the study's termination and those who had not, indicating that any maintenance of treatment effects in the DBT group could have resulted from more therapy. Unfortunately, follow-up data are not available for these patients beyond one year. These results highlight the importance of long-term follow-ups in the evaluation of treatment efficacy. Moreover, as noted by the authors, these findings are consistent with the general clinical consensus that one year of treatment is not sufficient for long-term change in patients with BPD. However, contrary to clinical folklore, this study showed that there could be significant and important concrete changes during the first year of treatment for borderline patients.

Subsequent RCTs comparing DBT to TAU have provided further evidence for the success of DBT in treating borderline patients, and have extended DBT to other patient populations. Linehan and colleagues (1999) compared DBT with TAU for drug-dependent women with BPD and found that DBT patients showed significantly greater reductions in drug abuse (as measured by drug-positive urines) and gains in social adjustment. However, DBT patients again had more treatment than the TAU patients (43.14 ± 10.67 vs. 21.88 ± 32.32 days), introducing the rival hypothesis that DBT patients may have improved more than TAU as a result of therapist contact or other common factors, rather than as a result of specific techniques of DBT. In addition, the sample size was small and there was a difference in dropout definitions (TAU patients were considered a dropout if they never went to therapy, or if they dropped out anytime following the first session, whereas, DBT patients were considered dropouts if they missed four consecutive weeks of group or individual sessions). Most importantly, there was a serious confound regarding the measurement of drug-positive urines. Drug screens were considered positive if the sample was late or absent. The TAU was conducted outside the medical center where the drug screens were performed. As a result, TAU patients had no reason to visit the medical center at least twice weekly, as required for drug screens. The TAU patients' samples may therefore have been more likely to be missing or late for reasons other than actually being positive for drugs. Thus, TAU patients may have been over-represented in positive drug screens.

In another RCT (Koons et al., 2001), outcome for women veterans diagnosed with BPD was evaluated after six months of DBT compared to TAU. Both groups showed decreases in suicidal ideation, hopelessness, depression, and anger expression, but the DBT group showed greater decreases than TAU. DBT also showed decreases in anger experienced and not expressed, parasuicide, and dissociation, whereas these symptoms did not decrease significantly in TAU. Neither group showed decreases in anxiety. These findings suggest that DBT can lead to rapid improvement for female BPD patients in terms of symptoms. Another important finding of this study is that DBT could be effective when provided by a collaborative research group that is somewhat independent of the treatment's developer, suggesting the portability of DBT. Further, the authors assessed adherence and competence using the DBT Expert Rating Scale (Linehan, Wagner, & Tutek, 1990). However, the sample size was small (only 10 patients in each group), indicating that analyses may have been underpowered; this also limits generalizability. In addition, there were pretreatment differences in anxiety and differences in treatment credibility and structure, which may have influenced outcome. Finally, the lack of intent-to-treat analyses limits conclusions about effectiveness.

Verheul et al. (2003) again evaluated the efficacy of DBT compared to TAU for 64 clinically referred women with BPD, and found that those treated with DBT showed significant decreases in self-mutilating behavior and less treatment dropout, although they found higher dropout rates than previous studies of DBT. One of the strengths of this study was the sampling which resulted in a broader group of BPD patients. Interestingly, the authors examined outcome as a function of severity of illness (as measured by frequency and severity of parasuicides), and the results suggested that DBT may be more successful for patients who are parasuicidal than for those who are not.

In an RCT, Bateman and Fonagy (1999) compared the effectiveness of 18 months of a psychoanalytically oriented day hospitalization program with routine general psychiatric care for patients with BPD. Patients randomly assigned to the psychoanalytic day hospital program, now called mentalization-based therapy (MBT; Bateman & Fonagy, 2004) showed statistically significant improvement in depressive symptoms and better social and interpersonal functioning, as well as significant decreases in suicidal and parasuicidal behavior and number of inpatient days. Patients were reassessed every three months for up to 18 months post-discharge (Bateman & Fonagy, 2001). Follow-up results indicate that patients who completed the MBT not only maintained their substantial gains but also showed continued steady and statistically significant improvement on most measures, suggesting that BPD patients can continue to demonstrate gains in functioning long after treatment has ended. At 18-month post-discharge follow-up, 59.1% of patients treated with MBT were below the BPD diagnostic threshold, compared to only 12.5% of those treated in routine general psychiatric care.

In summary, a number of RCTs with comparison to TAU groups exist (Bateman & Fonagy, 1999; Linehan et al., 1991; Linehan et al., 1999; Koons et al., 2001; Verheul et al., 2003). DBT clearly has marshaled the most evidence of this kind, although it is important to note that there is evidence for psychodynamic treatments as well (Bateman & Fonagy, 1999, 2001). It is also important to note that TAU comparisons are often ill-defined, unsupervised, and unmanualized treatments (or no treatment), limiting the conclusions that can be drawn from this type of data. In addition, studies comparing treatments to TAU groups do not provide efficacy data beyond TAU groups (i.e., efficacy over supervised or manualized treatments).

Placebo

Placebo conditions are intended to control for common factors such as therapist warmth, empathy, and attention, yet they are controversial due to the ethical dilemma of providing an "inert" treatment instead of one that is known to be effective. In addition, researchers must balance the inertness of a placebo treatment with strength of the placebo treatment. Often researchers choose or design placebo conditions that are intended to fail and thus do not provide the intended placebo control. Other times placebo treatments contain active ingredients of the experimental treatment or other active mechanisms that are beyond the control of common factors and attention. Finally, placebo treatments are often perceived by patients and therapists as less credible (Borkovec & Nau, 1972), creating the potential confounds of expectancy and therapist effects. However, RCTs that evaluate specific treatments for BPD in comparison to a placebo control condition allow for more specific and internally valid conclusions than the typical TAU study because often TAU is either poorly defined or actually consists of no treatment at all, whereas placebo conditions allow for more control by delivering a well-defined and well-organized comparison treatment.

One such placebo control study by Munroe-Blum and Marziali (1995) randomly assigned 79 women to an Interpersonal Group Psychotherapy (IGP) or Individual Expressive Psychodynamic Psychotherapy (IEPP), which was conceptualized as a placebo. IGP was based on Dawson's relationship approach, whereas IEPP control condition was modeled after Kernberg's expressive psychotherapy at that time (pretransference focused psychotherapy). This is a study where the placebo may have been too strong. The total cohort showed significant improvements on all major outcomes at completion of treatment, but there were no between-group differences. The authors note that IGP was briefer, less expensive, and can be offered by a range of service providers. However, therapists in the IEPP condition did not receive the same level of supervision and structure as the IGP condition, nor was there a manual for the IEPP condition. Thus, with supervision, structure, and a manual, the IEPP condition may have achieved even better results.

Another placebo control study (Turner, 2000) compared a psychodynamically modified DBT (PM-DBT) treatment to client-centered psychotherapy (CCT; intended to control for common factors). Modifications in the PM-DBT condition included the use of psychodynamically oriented therapists, psychodynamic techniques—including interpretations, and modified skills groups. In addition, to help control for therapist contact, both conditions received the modified skills group. To control for between-group therapist effects, the same therapists, all of whom were psychodynamic and family-systems oriented, treated patients in both conditions. However, there may have been therapist loyalty effects, such that therapists could have believed that one treatment was more credible than the other, which may have influenced results. Outcomes showed that the PM-DBT group improved more than the CCT group on most measures. These results revealed more about the potential mechanisms of action in DBT than previous efficacy studies. Although many clinical theorists have argued that DBT is primarily effective because of its use of skills groups, the fact that skills groups were utilized in both groups and the PM-DBT group still demonstrated better outcomes indicates that something beyond the skills group must be an important mechanism of action in the treatment of BPD. In these results, the quality of the therapeutic alliance accounted for as much of the outcome as did condition. In addition, three of the four therapists were more effective using DBT than CCT (one of four was more effective using

CCT than DBT), suggesting the importance of continuous supervision for maintaining therapist competence and maintaining the treatment frame. Importantly, this study showed that contrary to assertions made by Linehan (1993), psychodynamic techniques can be integrated with DBT, and psychodynamically trained therapists can competently learn and deliver DBT effectively without having a background in cognitive-behavioral therapy or principles of behavior therapy.

In another placebo control study, Linehan et al. (2002) evaluated DBT compared with comprehensive validation therapy with a 12-step program (CVT+12s) for opioid-dependent women with BPD. Both DBT and CVT+12s were manualized, delivered by experienced therapists, and conducted in an academic treatment setting. Thus, CVT+12s served as a "placebo" condition to control for the validation-based strategies employed in DBT (e.g., therapist warmth, responsiveness, and empathy). All patients were given opiate agonist therapy and access to telephone consultations and crisis intervention. The 12-step component of CVT+12s consisted of 12-step group meetings for two hours weekly and recommended additional group and sponsor meetings. Only the DBT group received individual skills coaching and skills group training. Results demonstrated that both DBT and CVT+12s were effective in reducing opioid use and maintaining the reduction of opioid use during a four-month follow-up, as well as in improving global functioning, with no between-group differences in these domains. However, CVT+12s was significantly superior to DBT in treatment retention (dropout in DBT was 36% compared to 0% in CVT+12s). These findings suggest that, for opioid-dependent women with BPD, 12-step groups (and not necessarily skills training) are important for maintaining treatment compliance and reducing substance use.

In summary, there are a few studies examining comparisons with placebo but they are difficult to interpret. Nevertheless, there are some important implications from these studies. First, it appears that psychodynamic techniques, such as interpretation of transference, can be integrated into DBT with good success. Second, it appears that both psychodynamic and family therapists can be taught relatively easily to be effective DBT therapists. Third, it appears that skills training may not be the active mechanism of change in DBT, and that 12-step groups might be more effective than skills groups for keeping substance-abusing borderline patients in treatment.

Comparison with Well-established, Well-delivered, Alterative Treatments

The only RCT to date that has compared an experimental treatment for BPD to an established alternative treatment has been the RCT conducted by The Personality Disorders Institute, funded in part by the Borderline Personality Disorders Research Foundation, to assess the efficacy of TFP compared with DBT and supportive psychotherapy (SPT) for patients with BPD (Clarkin et al., 2004, 2006). DBT, which has received preliminary empirical support for its effectiveness, was selected as the active comparison treatment. The putative mechanisms of change in these two treatments are conceived in very different ways. DBT is hypothesized to operate through the learning of emotion-regulation skills in the validating environment of the treatment (Lynch, Chapman, Rosenthal, Kuo, & Linehan, 2006). TFP is hypothesized to operate through the integration of conflicted, affect-laden conceptions of self and others via the understanding of these working models as they are actualized in the here-and-now relationship with the therapist (Levy, Clarkin, Yeomans et al., 2006). SPT (Appelbaum, 1981, 2005), was used in contrast to these two active treatments as a control for attention and support.

In this study, the BPD patients were recruited from New York City and adjacent Westchester County. Ninety-eight percent of the participants were clinically referred by private practitioners, clinics, or family members. Ninety male and female patients between the ages of 18 and 50 were evaluated using structured clinical interviews, and randomized to one of the three treatment cells. To date, all treatments have been completed, but follow-up evaluations are still in progress.

There are a number of methodological strengths of this study such as the use of multiple domains of change to measure outcome, including behavioral, observer-rated, phenomenological, and structural change (i.e., attachment representations, object relations, and mentalization skills). In addition, this study included a broad range of BPD patients and not exclusively those with parasuicidality, representing the full spectrum of BPD manifestations. Further, all therapists were experienced in their respective treatment model, had practice cases prior to beginning the study, and were rated for adherence and competence in their delivery of therapy during the study. Adding to the external validity of this research, treatments were delivered in community mental health settings, including outpatient hospitals and private offices of therapists. Results show that all three groups had significant improvement in both global and social functioning, and significant decreases in depression and anxiety. Both TFP and DBT-treated groups, but not the SPT group, showed significant improvement in suicidality, depression, anger, and global functioning. Only the TFP-treated group demonstrated significant improvements in verbal assault, direct assault, irritability (Clarkin et al., 2006), and personality structure as assessed by narrative coherence, reflectiveness, and attachment security (Levy, Clarkin, & Kernberg, in press).

Accumulating evidence indicates that TFP may be an effective treatment for BPD. As more data from the RCT is assessed, we will have a better understanding of how the treatment performs under more stringent experimental conditions. Because the RCT better controls for unmeasured variables through randomization, offers controls for attention and support, and compares TFP to an already established, well-delivered, alterative treatment, its outcome will be a strong indicator of the treatment's efficacy and effectiveness. In addition to assessment of outcome, the RCT has also generated process-outcome studies designed to assess the hypothesized mechanisms of action in TFP that result in the changes seen in these patients (Clarkin & Levy, 2006; Levy, Clarkin, Yeomans et al., 2006). Additionally, in the future, evaluating the long-term effectiveness through two-, three-, and five-year follow-up data is crucial to establish the long-term significance of a treatment for a chronic disorder (Westen, 2000)

SUMMARY OF RCTs

Overall, results from RCTs have found that a number of cognitive-behavioral (DBT, Schema Focused Therapy) and psychodynamic treatments (Mentalization Based Therapy and TFP) have efficacy, although outcomes are inconsistent with the exception for parasuicidality (especially for DBT in comparison to TAU and with highly parasuicidal patients). In addition, power is generally low and, although attrition has been reduced in the experimental conditions, it still remains a problem. As pointed out by Rossi (1990), low power is low power, and finding effects in low-powered studies is problematic. He outlines a number of reasons for this conclusion, noting that besides the obvious reason that low power results in an inability to detect a true difference, low power can also result in false positives. Rossi (1990) points out that in low power studies, the chance of Type II errors is only slightly more than the chance of a Type I error. This is because studies with low power are susceptible to the undue influence that may be exerted by outliers. Although this issue is less so with nonparametric tests, it remains a problem and is compounded by the fact that there are no good tests of power for nonparametric tests. Finally, low power often results in an inability to test alternative hypotheses for findings. For instance, if one wanted to test for therapist effects, or patient effects, a small sample size would make it unlikely that these effects could be identified in the data and conversely more likely that an outlier could cause an effect to be found. Generally speaking, domains of change are limited (e.g., focus on symptoms) and few studies have examined patient predictors of outcome (sans parasuicidality, inpatient status). Most importantly, thus far, few studies have investigated specific mechanisms of action or change (Clarkin & Levy, 2006; see Levy et al., in press, for an exception). Finally, given the chronicity of personality disorders, none of the studies have sufficient follow-up as yet that would determine the maintenance of treatment effects and clarify the long-term course of BPD after treatment termination.

Implications for Mechanisms of Change

Although there is accumulating evidence from outcome studies suggesting the effectiveness and efficacy of a number of different treatments for BPD, the probative importance of these studies for understanding a treatment's actual mechanisms of action are both indirect and limited (Garfield, 1990). Therefore, despite the support for the effectiveness and efficacy of existing treatments for borderline personality disorder, researchers are still confronted with a high degree of uncertainty about the underlying processes of change. Additionally, validation for the treatment occurs to the extent that the theoretically specified mechanisms of change are actually related to the treatments' effectiveness. It is very possible that these treatments may work due to unintended mechanisms such as typical common factors (e.g., expectancies; see Weinberger, 1995) or a specific technique factor that is essential to good outcome but not necessarily unique to any one treatment.

Along these lines, Bateman and Fonagy (1999) suggest that essential mechanisms in the treatment of BPD are a theoretically coherent multicomponent treatment approach, a focus on relationships, considerable efforts aimed at reducing dropout rates, and consistent application over a significant period of time. These components are consistent across studies examining MBT, DBT, TFP, schema focused therapy, and CBT and may explain the better-than-expected results as compared to treatment-as-usual groups and studies of naturalistic follow-ups, particularly with regard to the issue of attrition from treatment. All of these treatments provide principle-based manuals and institutional supports such as ongoing supervision, not only to stress specific techniques, but also to metabolize countertransference and to minimize iatrogenic effects of therapist enactments. Additionally, each of these treatments invests considerable efforts to increase communication between different treaters (e.g., individual therapist and psychopharmacologist).

Specific questions have been raised to various aspects of these different treatments. For example, given the considerable efforts geared toward supporting therapists, one could ask, "Does DBT training or supervision reduce therapist burnout?" The data, to date, suggest not (Little, 2000; Linehan, Cochran, Mar, Levensky, & Comtois, 2000). Little (2000) found that DBT training reduced burnout scores on the Personal Accomplishment component of the Maslach Burnout Scale (Maslach & Jackson, 1986), but did not reduce burnout on the Depersonalization and Emotional Exhaustion components. Linehan et al. (2000) found that the best predictor of DBT-trained therapists' burnout was patient's pre-treatment burnout.

Another question that arises is: "Are treatment contracts useful?" One of the important tactics in TFP is the use of treatment contracts, which occurs before the treatment begins. The function of the contract is to define the responsibilities of patient and therapist, protect the therapist's ability to think clearly and reflect, provide a safe place for the patient's dynamics to unfold, set the stage for interpreting the meaning of deviations from the contract as they occur later in therapy, and provide an organizing therapeutic frame that permits therapy to become an anchor in the patient's life. The contract specifies the patient's responsibilities, such as attendance and participation, paying the fee, and reporting thoughts and feelings without censoring. The contract also specifies the therapist's responsibilities, including attending to the schedule, making every effort to understand and, when useful, comment, clarifying the limits of his/her involvement, and predicting threats to the treatment. Essentially, the treatment contract makes the expectations of the therapy explicit (Clarkin, 1996). There is some controversy regarding the value of treatment contracting. The APA guidelines recommend that therapist contract around issues of safety. Others (Sanderson, Swenson,

& Bohus, 2002) have suggested that the evidence contraindicates their use and shows them to be ineffective (Kroll, 2000). However, the Kroll (2000) study was designed to determine the extent that no-suicide contracts were employed (which was found to be 57%) and, although 42% of psychiatrics who used no-suicide contracts had patients that either suicided or made a serious attempt, the design of the study does not allow for assessment of the efficacy of no-suicide contracts. Other data suggest the utility to contracting around self-destructive behavior and treatment threats (Yeomans et al., 1994; Smith et al., 1995; Clarkin et al., 2001; Clarkin et al., 2006; Levy, Clarkin, Schiavi et al., 2006). For example, Yeomans and colleagues (Yeomans et al., 1994) in a pre-post study of 36 patients with borderline personality disorder found that the quality of the therapist's presentation and handling of the patient's response to the treatment contract correlated with treatment alliance and the length of treatment. In addition, in our earlier work on TFP (Smith et al., 1995), when we did not stress treatment contracting, our dropout rates were high (31% and 36% at the three month and six month marks of treatment, respectively). However, based on the findings of Yeomans et al. (1994), Kernberg and colleagues further systematized and stressed the importance of the treatment contract and in later studies (Clarkin et al., 2001; Clarkin et al., 2006; Levy, Clarkin, Schiavi et al., 2006) our group found lower rates of dropout (19%, 13%, and 25%) over a year-long period of treatment. These findings taken together suggest that sensitively but explicitly negotiated treatment contracts may have at least one of the desired effects: resulting in less dropout and longer treatments. Future research will need to address the issue of treatment contracts more directly, particularly testing the effects on parasuicidality and suicidality.

Another question that arises with regard to DBT concerns the evidence for the skills group as a mechanism of change in DBT. Linehan suggests that the skills group is a key mechanism of change (Koerner & Linehan, 2000; Linehan, 1993; Lynch et al., 2006). Patients and therapists also view skills groups as critical for improvement (Araminta, 2000; Cunningham, Wolbert, & Lillie, 2004; Miller et al., 2000; Perseius, Ojehagen, Ekdahl, Asberg, & Samuelsson, 2003). However, the data available to date would suggest otherwise. Linehan et al. (2002) compared standard DBT to Comprehensive Validation Therapy with a 12-step program and found similar outcomes in the two treatments, suggesting that validation and not skills training may be the active ingredient in DBT for substance abusing BPD patients. Contrary to the recommendations of Linehan (1993), Turner (2000) modified DBT skills by removing them from the traditional group format and incorporating them into the briefer individual sessions (as well as incorporating psychodynamic techniques). Turner also provided patients in both the experimental and control conditions with six sessions of a modified DBT skills group. Turner found that the psychodynamically and skills modified DBT was more effective than the client-centered therapy with modified skills groups. This finding suggests that skills groups can be integrated into individual sessions and with psychodynamic techniques. The only study we could finding looking at the acquisition of skills in DBT was a dissertation by Puerling (2000). She found increases in skill usage over time but failed to show any relationship between changes in skills and outcome.

Is there evidence that increased reflective function (RF; Bateman & Fonagy, 2004) is the mechanism of change in MBT? Although it is tempting to hypothesize that RF is the mechanism of change in MBT and that the increases in good outcome continue after treatment termination due to change, in RF, there is no direct evidence to suggest that RF changes in MBT. Indirectly, findings from Bateman and Fonagy's (2001) follow-up, in which they find continued improvement in their MBT treated patients, suggest some internal change akin to RF may have taken place. There is evidence, however, that RF changes in Kernberg's TFP treatment (Levy et al., in press).

What patient variables predict outcome for BPD? There is surprisingly little data about patient characteristics as predictors of outcome in the treatment of BPD. Fonagy et al. (1996) found that pretreatment RF did not predict outcome for 85 outpatients with BPD; however, attachment status did. Those patients with dismissive attachment, as compared with those with enmeshed preoccupied attachment, showed significantly greater increases in GAF scores. Levy-Mack, Jeglic, Wenzel, Brown, and Beck (2005) examined the relation between patient attitudes toward treatment and outcome in a sample of patients seeking CBT for BPD. Those who had positive attitudes toward treatment, as opposed to those with negative attitudes toward treatment, were more likely to experience greater decreases in the number of BPD and depressive symptoms despite attending fewer therapy sessions than those with negative attitudes. These results suggest that techniques designed to enhance patients' attitudes toward treatment could increase the likelihood of benefiting from treatment. Linehan et al. (2000) found that patient pretreatment burnout predicted therapist burnout at four months into treatment. Yeomans et al. (1994) found that impulsivity was negatively related to the length of treatment. Smith et al. (1995) found that patient hostility and younger age predicted dropout from treatment. What therapist's factors predict outcome in the treatment of BPD? Linehan et al. (2000) found that high expectancy for therapeutic success leaves therapists vulnerable to increased emotional exhaustion at a later point.

In sum, little is known of the mechanisms by which treatments for BPD actually work or what actually happens to the patient that results in change. Preliminary evidence suggests that theoretically coherent, relationship-focused treatments that place considerable efforts on reducing dropout, increasing communication with auxiliary treaters, and providing ongoing supervision of therapists are important. There is some evidence that skills groups may not be the mechanism of action in DBT and that increasing the patient's capacity to think about mental states may be the mechanism of action in psychodynamic treatments. Regarding patient and therapist factors, less is known, but hostility, impulsivity, and young age appear to be risk factors for a higher client dropout rate.

An Integration of the Evidence

Linehan's (Linehan et al., 1991) seminal randomized clinical trial of DBT was a breakthrough for the research on BPD; the treatment has quickly gained popular acceptance. A number of managed care companies now define special benefits for DBT. Several state departments of mental health (Illinois, Connecticut, Massachusetts, New Hampshire, North Carolina, and Maine) have now enthusiastically endorsed and subsidized DBT as the treatment of choice for BPD or have mandated DBT training for state employees working with seriously disturbed patients. In Massachusetts, former DBT patients can now be reimbursed for coaching current DBT patients. Hundreds of marketing, seminars, and training programs in DBT are provided for inpatient and outpatient clinics, correctional institutes, and community treatment centers. Certainly, Linehan's efforts to develop, examine, and given the seriousness of BPD, to disseminate DBT are laudable. Her 1991 study was influential and changed the face of psychotherapy research; however, concerns have been raised that the dissemination of DBT has exceeded the evidence base, particularly with regard to state legislation and insurance reimbursements (Corrigan, 2001; Scheel, 2000; Smith & Peck, 2004; Westen, 2000). There is no doubt that the empirical base for DBT, in terms of the sheer number of studies, is stronger than for any other treatment. However, the actual findings themselves may not be as strong as developing folklore. The Cochrane Review (Binks et al., 2006) meta-analytic findings suggest that although some of the problems, particularly parasuicidality, may be amenable to DBT, it remains "experimental and the studies are too few and small to inspire full confidence in their results." In addition, there are a number of other treatments, including cognitive-behavioral and psychodynamic-based treatments, which warrant serious consideration.

Viewing the BPD treatment literature from a broad perspective, there is support from various levels of scientific rigor for the effectiveness (and in some cases, efficacy) of psychodynamic, interpersonal, cognitive, and cognitive-behavioral psychotherapies for treating BPD. In addition, evidence suggests the combination of individual psychotherapy with skills-based, psychoeducational, and family therapy groups. Although DBT (Linehan, 1993) has been the most extensively studied treatment for BPD in RCTs, there is emerging evidence for the effectiveness and efficacy of psychodynamically oriented treatments such as MBT (Bateman & Fonagy, 1999, 2001, 2004) and TFP (Clarkin et al., 2006; Levy, Clarkin, Schiavi et al., 2006), cognitive (Brown et al., 2004) and cognitive-analytic treatments (Ryle & Golynkina, 2000), and interpersonal psychotherapy (Meares et al., 1999). In addition, there is preliminary evidence to suggest that DBT might be more efficacious for highly parasuicidal BPD patients than it is for those who are less parasuicidal (Verheul et al., 2003), and that TFP might be more efficacious than DBT in generating changes in personality structure (Levy et al., in press). Further research examining the factors that moderate outcome in the treatment of

BPD can help to verify or refute these hypotheses. In addition, there is evidence to suggest that psychodynamic therapists can learn and apply DBT well, that psychodynamic techniques can be integrated into DBT, and that DBT skills groups can be modified and even incorporated into individual sessions (Turner, 2000). These issues warrant further study.

With the heterogeneity of BPD presentations, the question should not be simply "which treatment is most efficacious for treating BPD?", but rather, as Gordon Paul (1967) suggested "What treatment, by whom, is most effective for this individual with that specific problem, and under which set of circumstances?" (p. 111). We would also add "and by what mechanisms?" The maximization of treatment effects depends upon the examination of mechanisms of change, both at the level of changes within the patient as well as at the level of the specific techniques that affect such changes (Levy, Clarkin, Yeomans et al., 2006).

It is hoped that this chapter has demonstrated that, although RCTs are important in the evaluation of psychotherapy for BPD, they can be restricted in their explanatory power, external validity, and ability to identify mechanisms of change. Limitations of existing RCTs include the lack of adherence and competence ratings (Linehan et al., 1991; Bateman & Fonagy, 1999). Without knowing which techniques are prescribed and proscribed by the experimental treatment and whether or not therapists adequately followed the principles and techniques of a given therapy, inferences regarding the components of therapy that actually lead to change cannot be made. Future studies of psychotherapy for BPD could be improved by utilizing treatment manuals for each treatment condition, additional efforts to maintain the integrity of each treatment (e.g., evaluating adherence, competence, and expectancies of therapists in both experimental and control conditions), measurement of multiple domains of outcome (i.e., structural and interpersonal change, as well as symptom reduction), long-term follow-up evaluations, and examination of moderating and mediating factors in treatment outcome. Multiple assessment points during treatment studies are especially important for evaluating trajectories and mechanisms of change in psychotherapy for BPD.

REFERENCES

Ablon, J. S., & Jones, E. E. (2002). Validity of controlled clinical trials of psychotherapy: Findings from the NIMH Treatment of Depression Collaborative Research Program. *American Journal of Psychiatry, 159*, 775–783.

American Psychiatric Association. (1980). *Diagnostic and statistical manual of mental disorders* (3rd ed.). Washington, DC: Author.

Appelbaum, A. (1981). Beyond interpretation: A response from beyond psychoanalysis. *Psychoanalytic Inquiry, 1*, 167–187.

Appelbaum, A. (2005). *Supportive Psychotherapy*. Arlington: American Psychiatric Publishing.

Araminta, T. (2000). Dialectical behavior therapy: A qualitative study of therapist and client experience (Doctoral dissertation, California School of Professional Psychology—San Diego, 2000). *Dissertation Abstracts International, 61*(1-B), 520.

Bateman, A., & Fonagy, P. (1999). Effectiveness of partial hospitalization in the treatment of borderline personality disorder: A randomized controlled trial. *American Journal of Psychiatry, 156*(10), 1563–1569.

Bateman, A., & Fonagy, P. (2001). Treatment of borderline personality disorder with psychoanalytically oriented partial hospitalization: An 18-month follow-up. *American Journal of Psychiatry, 158*(1), 36–42.

Bateman, A. W., & Fonagy, P. (2004). Mentalization-based treatment of BPD. *Journal of Personality Disorders, 18*(1), 36–51.

Binks, C. A., Fenton, M., McCarthy, L., Lee, T., Adams, C. E., & Duggan, C. (2006). Psychological therapies for people with borderline personality disorder (Cochrane Review). *The Cochrane Database of Systematic Reviews 2006*, Issue 1. Art. No.: CD005652. DOI:10.1002/14651858.CD005652.

Blatt, S. J., & Zuroff, D. C. (2005). Empirical evaluation of the assumptions in identifying evidence based treatments in mental health. *Clinical Psychology Review, 25*(4), 459–486.

Blum, N., Pfohl, B., St. John, D., Monahan, P., & Black, D. W. (2002). STEPPS: A cognitive-behavioral systems-based group treatment for outpatients with borderline personality disorder—a preliminary report. *Comprehensive Psychiatry, 43*(4), 301–310.

Bohus, M., Haaf, B., Stiglmayr, C., Pohl, U., Böhme, R., & Linehan, M. (2000). Evaluation of inpatient dialectical-behavioral therapy for borderline personality disorder—A prospective study. *Behaviour Research & Therapy, 38*(9), 875–887.

Borkovec, T. D., & Castonguay, L. G. (1998). What is the scientific meaning of empirically supported therapy? *Journal of Consulting and Clinical Psychology, 66*(1), 136–142.

Borkovec, T. D., & Nau, S. D. (1972). Credibility of analogue therapy rationales. *Journal of Behavior Therapy and Experimental Psychiatry, 3*, 257–260.

Brown, G. K., Newman, C. F., Charlesworth, S. E., Crits-Christoph, P., & Beck, A. T. (2004). An open clinical trial of cognitive therapy for borderline personality disorder. *Journal of Personality Disorders, 18*(3), 257–271.

Calhoun, K. S., Moras, K., Pilkonis, P. A., & Rehm, L. P. (1998). Empirically supported treatments: Implications for training. *Journal of Consulting and Clinical Psychology, 66*(1), 151–162.

Carroll, K. M., & Rounsaville, B. J. (2003). Bridging the gap: A hybrid model to link efficacy and effectiveness research in substance abuse treatment. *Psychiatric Services, 54*(3), 333–339.

Chambless, D. L., & Hollon, S. D. (1998). Defining empirically supported therapies. *Journal of Consulting & Clinical Psychology, 66*(1), 7–18.

Clarke, M., & Oxman, A. D. (1999). *Cochrane Reviewers' Handbook 4.0* [updated July 1999]. In: Review Manager (RevMan), Version 4.0. Oxford: The Cochrane Collaboration.

Clarkin, J. F. (1996). Treatment of personality disorders. *British Journal of Clinical Psychology, 35*, 641–642.

Clarkin, J. F., Foelsch, P. A., Levy, K. N., Hull, J. W., Delaney, J. C., & Kernberg, O. F. (2001). The development of a psychodynamic treatment for patients with borderline personality disorders: A preliminary study of behavioral change. *Journal of Personality Disorders, 16*(6), 487–495.

Clarkin, J. F., Koenigsberg, H., Yoemans, F., Selzer, M., Kernberg, P., Kernberg, O. F. (1992). Psychodynamic psychotherapy of the borderline patient. In J. F. Clarkin, E. Morziali, & H. Munroe-Blum (Eds.), *Borderline Personality Disorder: Clinical and Empirical Perspectives* (pp. 268–287). New York: Guilford.

Clarkin, J. F., & Levy, K. N. (2003). Influence of client variables on psychotherapy. In M. Lambert (Ed.), *Handbook of psychotherapy and behavior change* (5th ed., pp. 194–226). New York: Wiley.

Clarkin, J. F., & Levy, K. N. (2006). Introduction to a special issue on putative mechanisms of action in the psychotherapy treatment of borderline personality disorder. *Journal of Clinical Psychology, 62*, 405–410.

Clarkin, J. F., Levy, K. N., Lenzenweger, M. F., & Kernberg, O. F. (2004). The Personality Disorders Institute/Borderline Personality Disorder Research Foundation randomized control trial for borderline personality disorder: Rationale, methods, and patient characteristics. *Journal of Personality Disorders, 18*(1), 52–72.

Clarkin, J. F., Levy, K. N., Lenzenweger, M. F., & Kernberg, O. F. (2006). *Outcome of psychodynamic psychotherapy for borderline personality disorder: A multiwave study.* Manuscript submitted for publication.

Clarkin, J. F., Yeomans, F. E., & Kernberg, O. F. (1999). *Psychotherapy for borderline personality.* New York: Wiley.

Cookson, A., Espie, J., & Yates, K. (2001). The Edinburgh Project: A pilot study for the psychotherapeutic treatment of borderline and other severe personality disorders. *British Journal of Psychotherapy, 18*(1), 68–88.

Cohen, J. (1988). *Statistical power analysis for the behavioral sciences.* Mahwah, NJ: Erlbaum.

Corrigan, P. W. (2001). Getting ahead of the data: A threat to some behavior therapies. *Behavior Therapist, 24*(9), 189–193.

Cunningham, K., Wolbert, R., & Lillie, B. (2004). It's about me solving my problems: Clients' assessments of dialectical behavior therapy. *Cognitive and Behavioral Practice, 11*(2), 248–256.

Evans, K., Tyrer, P., Catalan, J., Schmidt, U., Davidson, K., Dent, J. et al. (1999). Manual-assisted cognitive-behaviour therapy (MACT): A randomized controlled trial of a brief intervention with bibliotherapy in the treatment of recurrent deliberate self-harm. *Psychological Medicine, 29,* 19–25.

Fonagy, P., Leigh, T., Steele, M., Steele, H., Kennedy, R., Mattoon, G., et al. (1996). The relation of attachment status, psychiatric classification and response to psychotherapy. *Journal of Consulting and Clinical Psychology, 64*, 22–31.

Gabbard, G. O., Gunderson, J. G., & Fonagy, P. (2002). The place of psychoanalytic treatments within psychiatry. *Archives of General Psychiatry, 59*(6), 505–510.

Garfield, S. L. (1990). Issues and methods in psychotherapy process research. *Journal of Consulting and Clinical Psychology, 58,* 273–280.

Giesen-Bloo, J., Van Dyck, R., Spinhoven, P., Van Tilburg, W., Dirksen, C., Van Asselt, et al. (2006). Outpatient psychotherapy for borderline personality disorder: A randomized trial of schema-focused therapy vs transference-focused psychotherapy. *Archives of General Psychiatry, 63,* 649–658.

Goldfried, M. R., & Wolfe, B. E. (1996). Psychotherapy practice and research: Repairing a strained alliance. *American Psychologist, 51*(10), 1007–1016.

Goldfried, M. R., & Wolfe, B. E. (1998). Toward a more clinically valid approach to therapy research. *Journal of Counseling and Clinical Psychology, 66*(1), 143–150.

Guthrie, E. (2000). Psychotherapy for patients with complex disorders and chronic symptoms: The need for a new research paradigm. *British Journal of Psychiatry, 177,* 131–137.

Guthrie, E., Kapur, N., Mackway-Jones, K., Chew-Graham, C., Moorey, J., Mendel, E., et al. (2001). Randomised controlled trial of brief psychological intervention after deliberate self poisoning. *British Medical Journal, 323*(7305), 135–138.

Howard, K. I., Orlinsky, D. E., & Lueger, R. J. (1995). The design of clinically relevant outcome research: Some considerations and an example. In M. Aveline & D. A. Shapiro (Eds.), *Research foundations for psychotherapy practice* (pp. 3–47). Chichester, UK: Wiley.

Humphreys, K., & Weisner, C. (2000). Use of exclusion criteria in selecting research subjects and its effect on the generalizability of alcohol treatment outcome studies. *American Journal of Psychiatry, 157,* 588–594.

Kazdin, A. E. (2003). *Research design in clinical psychology* (4th ed.). Needham Heights, MA: Allyn & Bacon.

Kernberg, O. F. (1984). *Severe personality disorders: Psychotherapeutic strategies.* New Haven, CT: Yale University Press.

Koerner, K. & Linehan, M. M. (2000). Research on dialectical behavior therapy for borderline personality disorder. *Psychiatric Clinics of North America, 23,* 151–167.

Koons, C. R., Robins, C. J., Tweed, J. L., Lynch, T. R., Gonzalez, A. M., Morse, J. Q., et al. (2001). Efficacy of dialectical behavior therapy in women veterans with borderline personality disorder. *Behavior Therapy, 32*(2), 371–390.

Kroll, J. (2000). Use of no-suicide contracts by psychiatrists in Minnesota. *American Journal of Psychiatry, 157,* 1684–1686.

Levy, K. N., Clarkin, J. F., Yeomans, F. E., Scott, L. N., Wasserman, R. H., & Kernberg, O. F. (2006). The mechanisms of change in the treatment of transference focused psychotherapy. *Journal of Clinical Psychology, 62,* 481–501.

Levy, K. N., Kelly, K. M., Meehan, K. B., Reynoso, J. S., Weber, M., Clarkin, J. F., & Kernberg, O. F. (in press). Change in attachment and reflective function in a randomized control trial of transference focused psychotherapy for borderline personality disorder. *Journal of Consulting and Clinical Psychology.*

Levy, K. N., Clarkin, J. F., Schiavi, J., Foelsch, P. A., & Kernberg, O. F. (2006). *Transference Focused Psychotherapy for patients diagnosed with borderline personality disorder: A comparison with a treatment-as-usual cohort.* Manuscript submitted for publication.

Levy-Mack, J. J., Jeglic, E. L., Wenzel, A., Brown, G. K., & Beck, A. T. (2005, August). *Effects of treatment attitude on therapy outcome in borderline patients.* Poster session presented at the annual meeting of the American Psychological Association, Washington, DC.

Liberman, R. P., & Eckman, T. (1981). Behavior therapy versus insight-oriented therapy for repeated suicide attempters. *Archives of General Psychiatry, 38*(10), 1126–1130.

Linehan, M. M. (1993). *Cognitive-behavioral treatment of borderline personality disorder.* New York: Guilford.

Linehan, M. M., Armstrong, H. E., Suarez, A., Allmon, D., & Heard, H. L. (1991). Cognitive-behavioral treatment of chronically parasuicidal borderline patients. *Archives of General Psychiatry, 48*(12), 1060–1064.

Linehan, M. M., Cochran, B. N., Mar, C. M., Levensky, E. R., & Comtois, K. A. (2000). Therapeutic burnout among borderline personality disordered clients and their therapists: Development and evaluation of two adaptations of the Maslach Burnout Inventory. *Cognitive and Behavioral Practice, 7,* 329–337.

Linehan, M. M., Comtois, K. A., Murray, A. M., Brown, M. Z., Gallop, R. J., Heard, H. L., et al. (2006). Two-year randomized control trial and follow-up of dialectical behavior therapy vs therapy by experts for suicidal behaviors and borderline personality disorder. *Archives of General Psychiatry, 63,* 757–766.

Linehan, M. M., Dimeff, L. A., Reynolds, S. K., Comtois, K. A., Welch, S. S., Heagerty, P., & Kivlahan, D. R. (2002). Dialectical behavior therapy versus comprehensive validation therapy plus 12-step for the treatment of opioid dependent women meeting criteria for borderline personality disorder. *Drug and Alcohol Dependence, 67,* 13–26.

Linehan, M. M., & Heard, H. L. (1993). Impact of treatment accessibility on clinical course of parasuicidal patients: Reply. *Archives of General Psychiatry, 50*(2), 157–158.

Linehan, M. M., Heard, H. L., & Armstrong, H. E. (1993). Naturalistic follow-up of a behavioral treatment for chronically suicidal borderline patients. *Archives of General Psychiatry, 50*(12), 971–974.

Linehan, M. M., Wagner, A. W., & Tutek, D. (1990). *DBT Expert Rating Scale.* Seattle, WA: University of Washington.

Linehan, M. M., Schmidt, H. I., Dimeff, L. A., Craft, J. C., Kanter, J., & Comtois, K. A. (1999). Dialectical behavior therapy for patients with borderline personality disorder and drug-dependence. *American Journal on Addictions, 8*(4), 279–292.

Little, L. B. (2000). Training in dialectical behavior therapy as a means of reducing therapist burnout (Doctoral dissertation, University of Hartford, 2000). *Dissertation Abstracts International, 61*(5-B), 2769.

Low, G. G., Jones, D., Duggan, C., Power, M., & MacLeod, A. (2001). The treatment of deliberate self-harm in borderline personality disorder using dialectical behaviour therapy: A pilot study in a high security hospital. *Behavioural and Cognitive Psychotherapy, 29*(1), 85–92.

Lynch, T. R., Chapman, A. L., Rosenthal, M. Z., Kuo, J. R., & Linehan, M. M. (2006). Mechanisms of change in dialectical behavior therapy: Theoretical and empirical observations. *Journal of Clinical Psychology, 62*(4), 459–480.

Markowitz, J., Skodol, A. E., Bleiberg, K., & Strasser-Vorus, T. (2004). IPT for borderline personality disorder. Paper presented to the NIMH International Think Tank for the More Effective Treatment of Borderline Personality Disorder, July 2004, Lincthinum, MD.

Maslach, C., & Jackson, S. E. (1986). *Maslach Burnout Inventory Manual, Second Edition.* Palo Alto: Consulting Psychologists Press.

Meares, R., Stevenson, J., & Comerford, A. (1999). Psychotherapy with borderline patients: I. A comparison between treated and untreated cohorts. *Australian and New Zealand Journal of Psychiatry, 33*(4), 467–472; discussion 478–481.

Mental Health Center of Greater Manchester, N. H. (1998). Integrating dialectical behavioral therapy into a community mental health program. *Psychiatric Services, 49*(10), 1338–1340.

Miller, G. A., Wyman, A. L., Huppert, J. D., Glassman, S. L., & Rathus, J. H. (2000). Analysis of behavioral skills utilized by suicidal adolescents receiving dialectical behavior therapy. *Cognitive and Behavioral Practice, 7*(2), 183–186.

Mitchell, J. E., Hoberman, H. N., Peterson, C. B., Mussell, M., & Pyle, R. L. (1996). Research on the psychotherapy of bulimia nervosa: Half empty or half full. *International Journal of Eating Disorders, 20*(3), 219–229.

Morrison, K. H., Bradley, R., & Westen, D. (2003). The external validity of controlled clinical trials of psychotherapy for depression and anxiety: A naturalistic study. *Psychology & Psychotherapy: Theory, Research & Practice, 76*(2), 109–132.

Munroe-Blum, H., & Marziali, E. (1995). A controlled trial of short-term group treatment for borderline personality disorder. *Journal of Personality Disorders, 9*(3), 190–198.

Nathan, P. E., Stuart, S. P., & Dolan, S. L. (2000). Research on psychotherapy efficacy and effectiveness: Between Scylla and Charybdis? *Psychological Bulletin, 126*(6), 964–981.

National Institute of Mental Health Workshop Summary. (2002, December 9–10). Psychotherapeutic interventions: How and why they work. Division of Services and Intervention Research, Rockville, MD. Retrieved April 1, 2003, from http://www.nimh.nih.gov/ scientific meetings/interventions.cfm.

Oldham, J. M., Gabbard, G. O., Goin, M. K., Gunderson, J., Soloff, P., Spiegel, D., et al. (2001). Practice guideline for the treatment of patients with borderline personality disorder. *American Journal of Psychiatry, 158*, 1–52.

Paris, J. (1999). Borderline personality disorder. In T. Millon, P. H. Blaney, & R. D. Davis (Eds.), *Oxford textbook of psychopathology* (pp. 625–652). New York: Oxford University Press.

Paul, G. L. (1967). Strategy of outcome research in psychotherapy. *Journal of Consulting and Clinical Psychology, 31*, 109–118.

Perry, J. C., Banon, E., & Ianni, F. (1999). Effectiveness of psychotherapy for personality disorders. *American Journal of Psychiatry, 156*(9), 1312–1321.

Perseius, K. I., Ojehagen, A., Ekdahl, S., Asberg, M., & Samuelsson, M. (2003). Treatment of suicidal and deliberate self-harming patients with borderline personality disorder using dialectical behavioral therapy: The patients' and the therapists' perceptions. *Archives of Psychiatric Nursing, 17*(5), 218–227.

Piper, W. E., Joyce, A. S., McCallum, M., & Azim, H. F. (1998). Interpretive and supportive forms of psychotherapy and patient personality variables. *Journal of Consulting and Clinical Psychology, 66*(3), 558–567.

Puerling, C. L. (2000). Effectiveness of DBT in an outpatient community mental health setting (Doctoral dissertation, Antioch University/New England Graduate School, 2000). *Dissertation Abstracts International, 61*(3-B), 1650.

Rathus, J. H., & Miller, A. L. (2002). Dialectical behavior therapy adapted for suicidal adolescents. *Suicide & Life-Threatening Behavior, 32*(2), 146–157.

Rosen, G. M., & Davison, G. R. (2003). Psychology should list empirically supported principles of change (ESPs) and not credential trademarked therapies or other treatment packages. *Behavior Modification, 27*, 300–312.

Rossi, J. S. (1990). Statistical power of psychological research: What have we gained in 20 years? *Journal of Consulting and Clinical Psychology, 58*(5), 646–656.

Ryle, A., & Golynkina, K. (2000). Effectiveness of time-limited cognitive analytic therapy of borderline personality disorder: Factors associated with outcome. *British Journal of Medical Psychology, 73* (Pt. 2), 197–210.

Salkovskis, P. M., Atha, C., & Storer, D. (1990). Cognitive-behavioural problem solving in the treatment of patients who repeatedly attempt suicide: A controlled trial. *British Journal of Psychiatry, 157,* 871–876.

Sanderson, C., Swenson, C., & Bohus, M. (2002). A critique of the American Psychiatric Practice Guideline for the Treatment of Patients with Borderline Personality Disorder. *Journal of Personality Disorders, 16,* 122–129.

Scheel, K. R. (2000). The empirical basis of dialectical behavior therapy: Summary, critique, and implications. *Clinical Psychology: Science and Practice, 7*(1), 68.

Seligman, M. E. P. (1995). The effectiveness of psychotherapy: The Consumer Reports study. *American Psychologist, 50*(12), 965–974.

Skodol, A. E., Gunderson, J. G., Pfohl, B., Widiger, T. A., Livesley, W. J., & Siever, L. J. (2002). The borderline diagnosis I: Psychopathology, comorbidity, and personality structure. *Biological Psychiatry, 51*(12), 936–950.

Smith, L. D., & Peck, P. L. (2004). Dialectical behavior therapy: A review and call to research. *Journal of Mental Health Counseling, 26,* 25–38.

Smith, T. E., Koenigsberg, H. W., Yeomans, F. E., Clarkin, J. F., & Selzer, M. A. (1995). Predictors of dropout in psychodynamic psychotherapy of borderline personality disorder. *Journal of Psychotherapy Practice & Research, 4,* 205–213.

Stevenson, J., & Meares, R. (1992). An outcome study of psychotherapy for patients with borderline personality disorder. *American Journal of Psychiatry, 149*(3), 358–362.

Telch, C. F., Agras, W. S., & Linehan, M. M. (2000). Group dialectical behavior therapy for binge-eating disorder: A preliminary, uncontrolled trial. *Behavior Therapy, 31*(3), 569–582.

Thompson-Brenner, H., Glass, S., & Westen, D. (2003). A multidimensional meta-analysis of psychotherapy for bulimia nervosa. *Clinical Psychology: Science and Practice, 10,* 269–287.

Torgersen, S., Kringlen, E., & Cramer, V. (2001). The prevalence of personality disorders in a community sample. *Archives of General Psychiatry, 58*(6), 590–596.

Trupin, E. W., Stewart, D. G., Beach, B., & Boesky, L. (2002). Effectiveness of dialectical behaviour therapy program for incarcerated female juvenile offenders. *Child & Adolescent Mental Health, 7*(3), 121–127.

Turner, R. M. (2000). Naturalistic evaluation of dialectical behavior therapy-oriented treatment for borderline personality disorder. *Cognitive and Behavioral Practice, 7,* 413–419.

Tyrer, P., Thompson, S., Schmidt, U., Jones, V., Knapp, M., Davidson, K., et al. (2003). Randomized controlled trial of brief cognitive behaviour therapy versus treatment as usual in recurrent deliberate self-harm: The POPMACT study. *Psychological Medicine, 33*(6), 969–976.

Verheul, R., van den Bosch, L. M., Koeter, M. W., De Ridder, M. A., Stijnen, T., & van den Brink, W. (2003). Dialectical behaviour therapy for women with borderline personality disorder: 12-month, randomised clinical trial in The Netherlands. *British Journal of Psychiatry, 182,* 135–140.

Weinberger, J. (1995). Common factors aren't so common: The common factors dilemma. *Clinical Psychology: Science and Practice, 2,* 45–69.

Weissman, M. M. (1993). The epidemiology of personality disorders: A 1990 update. *Journal of Personality Disorders, 7*(Suppl.), 44–62.

Weisz, J. R. (2003). *Psychotherapy for children and adolescents: Evidence-based treatments and case examples.* Cambridge: Cambridge University Press.

Westen, D. (2000). The efficacy of dialectical behavioral therapy for borderline personality disorder. *Clinical Psychology: Science and Practice, 7*, 92–94.

Westen, D., & Morrison, K. (2001). A multidimensional meta-analysis of treatments for depression, panic, and generalized anxiety disorder: An empirical examination of the status of empirically supported therapies. *Journal of Consulting & Clinical Psychology, 69*(6), 875–899.

Widiger, T. A., & Frances, A. J. (1989). Epidemiology, diagnosis, and comorbidity of borderline personality disorders. In A. Tasman, R. E. Hale, & J. Frances (Eds.), *Review of psychiatry* (Vol. 8, pp. 8–24). Washington, DC: American Psychiatric Press.

Widiger, T. A., & Weissman, M. M. (1991). Epidemiology of borderline personality disorder. *Hospital and Community Psychiatry, 42*(10), 1015–1021.

Wildgoose, A., Clarke, S., & Waller, G. (2001). Treating personality fragmentation and dissociation in borderline personality disorder: A pilot study of the impact of cognitive analytic therapy. *British Journal of Medical Psychology, 74* (Pt. 1), 47–55.

Yeomans, F. E., Gutfreund, J., Selzer, M. A., Clarkin, J. F., Hull, J. W., & Smith, T. E. (1994). Factors related to drop-outs by borderline patients: Treatment contract and therapeutic alliance. *Journal of Psychotherapy Practice & Research, 3*(1), 16–24.

Zanarini, M. C., Frankenburg, F. R., Dubo, E. D., Sickel, A. E., Trikha, A., & Levin, A. (1998). Axis I comorbidity of borderline personality disorder. *American Journal of Psychiatry, 155*(12), 1733–1739.

ENDNOTES

1. In the psychotherapy research literature, a distinction is made between efficacy and effectiveness research. Efficacy studies are those that maximize internal validity to evaluate the impact of treatment under strictly controlled conditions, usually in a research setting such as a university or medical school. Effectiveness studies typically evaluate the impact of a treatment in naturalistic settings and under conditions in which treatment is usually administered, and therefore, maximize external validity (Kazdin, 2003; Nathan, Stuart, & Dolan, 2000).

2. This sample size of 21 does not include 2 patients who were administratively discharged early in treatment because they did not agree to the study conditions (e.g., termination of other treatments and videotaping of sessions.)

3. Of the 30 TFP-treated patients in this study (Levy, Clarkin, Schiavi et al., 2006), 21 patients were the same as those treated in the pre-post study (Clarkin et al., 2001). Therefore, the 13.3% attrition rate includes dropouts from the pre-post study sample, from which four patients dropped out. None of the additional nine TFP patients in the Levy, Clarkin, Schiavi et al., (2006) study, and none of the seventeen TAU patients, dropped out.

4. Although Linehan et al. (1991) reported the results of a regression analysis to evaluate the relationship between number of therapist contact hours and parasuicidal behavior independent from treatment condition and found nonsignificant results, a regression analysis conducted in reverse order, with therapy hours entered into the equation first and treatment condition entered second, would have clarified the important question of whether or not treatment condition was significantly related to parasuicide over and above the contribution of therapist contact hours.

Conclusions
Let a Hundred Flowers Bloom; Let One Hundred Schools of Thought Contend

JOEL WEINBERGER AND STEFAN G. HOFMANN

So what can we conclude after reading 13 chapters on the art and science of psychotherapy? First, it seems that there is little doubt that the EST movement can be considered a revolution in psychotherapy research. Virtually no chapter failed to touch on it and, for most, it was a touchstone for the points made in the chapter. The authors differed, however, in their evaluations of the efficacy methodology underlying ESTs. All seemed to agree that there were some issues that needed to be addressed in this methodology. These ranged from thinking a little tweaking was in order to arguing that major flaws exist.

Litz and Salters-Pedneault are very favorably disposed toward efficacy studies. They believe that manuals need to be customized for patients seen in the real world. That is, they argue for flexibility. They provided examples from their work with PTSD and showed that manualized therapy can be sensitive to and respectful of individual differences. They addressed flexibility of therapist use of manuals and the combining of manualized treatments so as to obtain optimal results. Their chapter shows that manualized treatment is not without its art.

Nathan is also favorably disposed to efficacy studies. He discussed the apparent resistance to them and contrasted them with effectiveness studies. He presented a compelling case for efficacy research as well as an insightful analysis of resistance to it. He would supplement efficacy research with effectiveness studies. Specifically, he recommends using the results of efficacy studies to design effectiveness studies. Then, depending on results, he suggests alternating between the two "in bootstrap fashion." His model is the Onken/Hybrid Model of Behavioral Therapies Research.

Levy and Scott are a bit less favorably disposed to efficacy studies, seeing them as one tool in a multimethod toolbox. They discuss internal and external validity as the touchstones of the different methods available, with efficacy studies at one end (strong internal validity, relatively weak external validity) and case histories at the other (strong external validity, relatively weak internal validity). They provide an elegant review of different methodologies, describing the strengths and weaknesses of each and showing the values of each in a systematic research program. They apply their analysis to the study of Borderline Personality Disorder and show how each method can and has contributed to the understanding and treatment of this disorder.

Blaise and Hilsenroth are a bit further down the road concerning efficacy studies. They, like Levy and Scott, argue against its use as a gold standard for psychotherapy research and explicate their position in terms of internal and external validity. They review their own program of research, which uses what might be called, in Levy's terminology, naturalistic efficacy research. They study patients, as they appear in the clinic, without regard for particular diagnosis, in manualized short-term psychodynamic treatment. They describe their research program, which they term a "hybrid," in detail, as a more clinically real and externally valid alternative to efficacy research.

Westen is the most critical of efficacy research, detailing its weaknesses and offering alternative ways of studying psychotherapy. Contrary to Nathan, Westen would begin with effectiveness research and only when that yielded meaningful results would he design efficacy studies. Westen also argues that the correct control group for efficacy studies is the successfully practicing clinician, rather than a placebo or the overworked clinic that is now the modal "treatment as usual" (TAU). Even he, however, sees the value of efficacy research as part of an overall program of psychotherapy research.

Overall, the position on efficacy research as a generator of ESTs is that it has its place but ought not to be the exclusive mode of investigation of psychotherapy. All agreed on the value of empirical research; all agreed on efficacy research as a major player. The authors differed sharply in terms of how big a role it should play in the overall enterprise. For some (Litz & Salters-Pedneault; Nathan), it has pride of place, for others it is a flawed but useful research tool (Levy & Scott; Blaise & Hilsenroth; Westen) that needs to be supplemented by other methodologies (which are also flawed). Interestingly, no one advocated the exclusive use of ESTs or rigid adherence to manuals, although these positions were attributed to EST advocates. Either this volume did not include the individuals advocating these positions, the modal position in this area has changed, or this is not truly representative of the EST movement. We prefer to believe the latter. We believe that the debate more centers on the relative importance of the different methodologies and appropriate control groups than on a position of scientific exclusivity or rigid adherence. After all, methodological exclusivity and rigidity are not in the spirit of science.

A second major point was that the EST movement seems to suggest that each diagnostic entity must have its own unique EST. The alternative seems to be that efficacious interventions work for many if not all diagnostic categories and that all credible interventions seem to work about equally well. This outcome equivalence has been termed the "dodo verdict" and has led to the common factors movement (Weinberger & Rasco) and the advocacy of common principles of psychotherapy (Pachankis & Goldfried; Clinton, Gierlach, Zack, Beutler, & Castonguay). Clinton et al., Weinberger and Rasco, and Westen all pointed out that literally hundreds of ESTs would be required if separate, nonoverlapping ESTs were to be put into practice. No author argued for nonoverlapping treatment packages, however, and, although this might once have been the position of EST advocates, it seems no longer to be the case. On the other hand, it seems obvious that some unique aspects of a disorder might also require unique treatment strategies to target them. Unfortunately, however, there has been little cross-fertilization between nosology, psychopathology, and intervention. This is clearly an area of future research.

Ehrenreich, Buzella, and Barlow, advocates of the efficacy approach, argued persuasively for a common set of techniques applicable to all emotional disorders, which they termed a unified treatment approach. Their chapter was a scholarly tour de force first demonstrating that the emotional disorders have much in common and that certain treatment techniques (altering cognitive appraisals, preventing emotional avoidance, teaching new adaptive responses to emotions) can be applied to all emotional disorders. If this chapter represents the current state of the EST movement, the debate may not be over whether each disorder requires a separate treatment but, rather, over how overlapping or common therapeutic principles are. Common factor and common principle advocates argue that these principles or factors can be fruitfully applied to most psychological difficulties. Thus far, the EST advocates have only argued for common treatment techniques for the affective disorders. This does not mean that they oppose common treatment for other groups of disorders. It means that the position awaits further empirical scrutiny.

The chapters identified a variety of common principles or factors. Different authors emphasized different principles. Some emphasized patient factors (Cinton et al.; Levy & Scott), some treatment factors (Clinton et al.), some promoted patient belief that therapy will be beneficial and patient adoption of a reality-testing approach to problems (Pachankis & Goldfried). Arkowitz and Engle described working with resistance, a common experience in clinical work that is too often ignored by researchers. Weinberger and Rasco identified specific factors that seemed to cut across treatment like expectancy, exposure, and mastery. Some authors called these principles of change (Clinton et al.; Pachankis & Goldfried) whereas Weinberger and Rasco preferred the term common factors. A rose by any other name .... No author seemed to dispute the idea that there were therapeutic factors that cut across different diagnostic categories and treatment modalities.

One factor identified by many authors was the therapeutic relationship (Blais & Hilsenroth; Clinton et al.; Pachankis & Goldfried; Ruiz-Cordell & Safran; Weinberger & Rasco). This seems to be the common factor or principle of change par excellence. Ruiz-Cordell and Safran offer a detailed exposition of how the Safran group has studied this variable. They look at how therapeutic ruptures are created and mended and describe their critical clinical importance. Blaise and Hilsenroth also describe an empirical approach to studying this variable. Both chapters address teaching budding therapists the ins and outs of the therapeutic relationship and provide data that show that clinicians can learn how to effectively use the relationship and that therapeutic outcome is improved by such training.

Common factors or principles lead to another issue triggered by efficacy research. The efficacy approach is an outcome rather than a process approach. This is enormously important, but if we want to learn what makes a therapy effective, there seems to be no alternative to process research. Pachankis and Goldfried make this point most forcefully, although Weinberger and Rasco make it too.

Another issue concerns the place of practicing clinicians in the empirical testing of psychotherapy. Many chapters referred to the failure of clinicians to embrace empirical findings (Clinton et al.; Nathan; Pachankis & Goldfried; Westen). It is clear that research needs to be made more clinically relevant or at least explained better to practicing clinicians. Clinton et al. offer the Systematic Treatment Selection model of Beutler and his colleagues. This approach makes the principles of change practically available to practicing clinicians so that they can "tailor a treatment plan in order to maximize outcomes for a particular patient." Presumably, this user friendly way of disseminating research results would be seen as helpful to clinicians and would be used by them. Another way to bring clinicians into the empirical fold is to involve them in the research process that designs the treatment approaches they are then asked to use. Nathan, Pachankis, and Goldfried, Weinberger and Rasco, and Westen all advocate learning from clinicians and including them in the research enterprise. Nathan proposes a collaborative model, a Practice Research Network, based on the work of Borkovec and his colleagues. A network of clinics would be established in which researchers and practitioners would work together collaboratively "on clinically meaningful questions." Pachankis & Goldfried propose obtaining audiotapes from practicing clinicians to learn how they deal with alliance issues. These would then be examined empirically. Weinberger and Rasco as well as Westen propose designing treatments, in part, based on what successful clinicians do and say. The logic is that their experience is worth a great deal. Clinicians can tell researchers much, both explicitly and implicitly (through videos of their work and their comments about them). After all, they deal with important clinical issues on a daily basis. Westen provides a detailed plan for how this could be accomplished empirically. It would be central to the way he would study psychotherapy. His model of psychotherapy would begin by studying what clinicians do, seeing what works, and then testing it more rigorously in efficacy type studies. He would compare what practicing clinicians do with currently available ESTs and then modifying treatments based on the results.

Arkowitz and Engle provide a clinically rich and empirically informed treatise on how to work with resistance. Their conclusions could be fruitfully examined in more detail by clinical researchers. They, therefore, come from a more clinical perspective (albeit informed by empirical research). Shedler's chapter demonstrates that clinicians can provide highly useful data for researchers. Stricker advocates encouraging clinicians to engage in nonsystematic research of their own. He calls his model the "local clinical scientist." In this way, clinicians would know empirically what seems to work for them. This would make them better therapists and also better and more willing consumers of empirical research. Weinberger and Rasco endorsed this approach and suggested teaching it in graduate training. They also argued that researchers would do well to formally examine the findings of these local clinical scientists.

Shedler has written the only chapter that pertains to the clinical entities that researchers study. He and his colleague, Westen, developed an innovative way to identify and understand clinical entities. They have practicing clinicians Q-sort prototypical patients as well as patients that they currently treat. The Q-sort items are descriptive of patient characteristics and are written in jargon-free, experience near, language. Shedler reports reliable and valid results that hold across therapist theoretical orientation. These do not always (in fact, often do not) coincide with *DSM-IV* diagnostic categories. Thus far, the work has been restricted to Axis II disorders but could be expanded to Axis I as well. This work indicates that the diagnostic categories that researchers study may not represent nature carved at its joints. If the *DSM-IV* categories are at all artificial, it says much about the findings of outcome studies aimed at particular *DSM-IV* diagnostic categories. This work reinforces the notion that we should involve practicing clinicians more in our work and also argues for process research. Finally, it argues for the necessity of testing the validity of currently used diagnostic categories.

To summarize our major points: First, the chapters in this book indicate that efficacy research is a valuable, even revolutionary method for studying psychotherapy. It has led to much progress. It is not, however, the only method and it is not without its problems. The clinical as well as the scientific enterprise would benefit from a multitude of methods, all imperfect, that would, hopefully, triangulate on clinical "truth." Second, there are both specific and common factors or principles that underlie psychotherapeutic success. The field could benefit from a more detailed examination of these common factors or principles. We would then have a better idea of what principles hold generally and what is unique to a particular treatment or diagnostic entity. Process research would be of great benefit here. Third, we need to involve practicing clinicians more in the study of psychotherapy. At present, they do not make much use of empirical findings. Suggestions range from ways of making practicing clinicians better consumers, to collaboration between researchers and clinicians, to teaching clinicians to conduct informal research, to using clinician insights to design formal empirical research. Finally, researchers might want to revisit their conceptualizations of clinical entities. In order to study psychotherapy for a particular disorder, we need to be certain that it exists and that we understand its characteristics. Ideally, the knowledge gained by research on the psychopathology of a disorder could then be translated into clinically useful methods and therapeutic techniques (an approach that is in line with the current NIMH initiative of translational research).

The theme of this conclusion chapter is to "let a hundred flowers bloom, let one hundred schools of thought contend." By this we mean to argue for diversity of methodology, clinical, and theoretical orientation. Let the scientific enterprise sort it all out (without wasting energy by fighting unnecessary battles with one another). This quote was uttered by Mao Tse Dung in 1958. He was asking the intellectuals of China to constructively criticize the regime and suggest improvements. We chose this quote to indicate that openness to new and seemingly divergent ideas must be followed in practice as well as in word. No one would argue that openness and competition of ideas is in the interest of science and clinical success, just as no one would argue that constructive criticism of government combined with new ideas is in the interest of the body politic. But shortly after Mao uttered the above, he launched the Cultural Revolution, which had as its goal the exact opposite and resulted in horrific damage to the Chinese population.

Psychotherapy research is at a crossroads. There is conflict between practicing clinicians and researchers. There is conflict among researchers themselves. None of these conflicting groups (with small unimportant exceptions) would argue against empirical research or openness to ideas. We offer the Mao quote as an object lesson. We really should let all ideas contend in a scholarly, clinically useful, and open fashion. This should be carried out in practice, not just uttered as a maxim. We believe that this book is a fruitful step in this direction. Advocates of different points of view were contained amicably in one volume. We would hope that they will soon be amicably contained in journals, clinics, granting agencies, and the halls of academe. This will benefit science, psychotherapy, and the patients we all claim to serve and want to help.

Index

A

AAI, *see* Adult Attachment Interviews
Academia, capitalization of, 3
Acceptance, 177
Acceptance and Commitment Therapy (ACT), 200, 223
ACT, *see* Acceptance and Commitment Therapy
Active surgery, 110
Activities, variability of, 86
Adult Attachment Interviews (AAI), 251
Alcoholism, CBT for, 73
Alice in Wonderland, 105
Allegiance effect, 106
Alliance ruptures, 155–170, 175
    Brief Relational Psychotherapy, 166–167
    metacommunication, 163–165
    rupture resolution process and research, 159–163
    rupture resolution and therapeutic alliance, 156–159
    rupture resolution and therapist internal processes, 165–166
American Psychiatric Association, 32, 33, 73, 212
American Psychological Association (APA), 4, 31, 52, 108
    Division of Clinical Psychology, 73
    Presidential Task Force, 52, 89–91
    Society for Clinical Psychology, 57
    Task Force of Division 12, 132–133, 141, 142
    Task Force of Division 29, 133, 137, 142
    Task Force on Promotion and Dissemination of Psychological Procedure, xviii
AN, *see* Anorexia nervosa
Analysis of transference, 55
Anchoring heuristic, 94, 95
Anna Freud Center, 96
Anorexia nervosa (AN), 12
Antecedent cognitive reappraisal, 196–198, 200, 203
Antidepressant response, placebo response vs., 34
Antisocial personality disorder, 256, 259
Anxiety
    facing, 112

genetic influences on, 192
    triggers for, 203
Anxiety disorder(s), 58
    adolescent, 191, 194
    antecedent cognitive reappraisal and, 196
    borderline personality disorder and, 269
    CBT for, 73, 134, 179
    comorbid, 194
    future depression and, 193
    generalized, 197, 202
    manuals to treat, 194
    mood disorders and, 192
    motivational interviewing and, 177
    Task Force Focus, 142
Anxiety and Its Disorders, 7
Anxiety Disorders Interview Schedule, 192
APA, *see* American Psychological Association
Arkowitz, Hal, 171
Asch, Solomon, 91
Assessment-plus-treatment protocol, 71
Attachment style, 139
Attitudes, stability of, 86
Autistic children, 136
Automatic thoughts, 113
Avoidance, 161–162, 226, 260
Awareness-oriented role play, 167
Axis I disorders, 12, 20, 37, 245, *see also*
    Emotional disorders, treatment of;
    Trauma survivors, evidence-based treatment of
Axis II disorders, 37, 235–238, 245, 262, 305,
    see also Borderline personality
    disorder treatment, art and science
    of; Shedler-Westen Assessment
    Procedure, personality diagnosis with

B

Backward compatibility, 246
Barlow, David H., 7, 71, 191
Beck, Aaron T., 196
Behavior therapy, 10, 51, 71
Between session homework, 55
Beutler, Larry E., 131
Blais, Mark A., 31
BN, *see* Bulimia nervosa

Borderline personality disorder (BPD), 10, 21, 93, 104, 240
  characteristics of, 269
  composite description, 256–257
  outcome, patient variables predicting, 290
  patients, suicidality in, 281
  prevalence rates of, 269
  research, breakthrough for, 291
  transference-focused psychotherapy for, 286
Borderline Personality Disorders Research Foundation, 285
Borderline personality disorder treatment, art and science of, 269–299
  hierarchy of treatment evidence, 272–287
    comparison with alternative treatments, 285–287
    placebo, 283–285
    pre-post designs, 273–277
    quasi-experimental designs, 277–279
    randomized controlled trials, 279–280
    treatment-as-usual, 280–283
    wait-list control, 280
  pros and cons of RCTs, 271–272
  summary of RCTs, 287–292
    implications for mechanisms of change, 287–290
    integration of evidence, 291–292
Borderline personality pathology, 240–243
Borderline Psychotherapy Research Project, 275, 278
Bordin, Edward, 157
Boulder-model programs, 6
BPD, see Borderline personality disorder
Brief relational psychotherapy (BRT), 166–167
  central principles of, 166
  efficacy of, 167
  training in, 166–167
BRT, see Brief relational psychotherapy
Bulimia nervosa (BN), 8, 9, 19, 20
Buzzella, Brian A., 191

C

Castonguay, Louis G., 131
CAT, see Cognitive analytic therapy
Causation assumption, 12
CBT, see Cognitive behavior therapy
CCT, see Client-centered therapy
CDI, see Clinical Diagnostic Interview
Center for Anxiety and Related Disorders, 194

Change, see also Principles of change; Therapeutic change
  commonalities contributing to, 60
  higher-order principles of, 57
  process, debate about, 135
  resistance to, see Resistant ambivalence
  soft indices of, 70
Chinese Cultural Revolution, 306
Clarkin, John, 139, 275, 276
Clearing away the transference, 116
Client
  awareness, facilitation of, 56
  -centered therapy (CCT), 177, 180, 182, 183
  change, core ingredients necessary for, 50
  cognitive distortions, 61
  self-exploration, 149
  -therapist relationship, 57
Clinical Diagnostic Interview (CDI), 250
Clinical judgment, 17, 234, 235, 249
Clinically informed research, 4
Clinical psychology, 4
Clinical Severity Rating (CSR), 203
Clinical skills, therapist, 148–149
Clinical training programs, 5, 87
Clinical Trials and Translation Work Group, 74
Clinician–researcher partnership, 3–30
  developing complementary methodology, 16–22
    limits of ESTs, 18–20
    naturalistic studies, 20–22
  empirically supported complexity, 8–16
    causation assumption, 12–13
    control condition assumption, 13–14
    discreteness assumption, 11–12
    EBP–EST assumption, 14–15
    highly malleable psychological processes, 9–10
    hypothesis testing, 13
    implications, 15–16
    independence assumption, 10–11
Clinicism, effect of, 5
Clinton, David, 131
Cochrane Review, 291
Cognitive-affective processes, 165
Cognitive analytic therapy (CAT), 274
Cognitive-behavioral task, 157
Cognitive behavior therapy (CBT), 7, 134, 146, 167
  between-session homework in, 63
  bulimia nervosa and, 10
  depression and, 14
  duration of treatments, 20
  evidence-based, 212

group, 19
homework compliance, 179
manualized, 17, 212
models, 214
success rate, 14
training, 213, 214
treatment for emotional disorders using, 193
validity checks, 21
Cognitive heuristics, 87–88, 93, 94, 96
Cognitive myopia, 31
Cognitive processing therapy, 216
Cognitive therapy (CT), mastery experiences
	and, 115
Cognitive triad, 196
Common factors, *see* Empirically supported
	common factors
Comorbid disorders, 52, 194
Comparative Psychotherapy Process Scale
	(CPPS), 17–18, 21
Comparison/control treatments, 70
Compassion, 165–166
Complex PTSD, 214
Composite description, 252
Conditioned responses, 215
Conditioned stimuli, 215
Conflict splits, 180
Confrontation
	beneficial, 113
	problem, 107, 112
	rupture, 160
Consultation, 93
Consumer Reports, 72
Contact, 181
Control condition assumption, 13
Control experiences, 107
Control group, choice of, 14
Core psychological features, 252
Corrective emotional experiences, 56
Counter conditioning, 113
Counter-transference, management of, 137
CPPS, *see* Comparative Psychotherapy Process
	Scale
Criteria for Evaluating Treatment Guidelines, 52
Critical questions, interviewer's, 95
Cronbach, Lee, 31, 42
Cross-cultural skills, 95
CSR, *see* Clinical Severity Rating
CT, *see* Cognitive therapy
Culture-specific expertise, 95

D

Daubert trilogy of decisions, 91
DBT, *see* Dialectical behavior therapy
DBT Expert Rating Scale, 282
Dependent PD patients, composite description of,
	260–261
Depression
	borderline personality disorder and, 269
	genetic influences on, 192
	NIMH task force on, 194
	self-reported, 194
	studies of, 11, 105
Depressive core, 259
Depressive disorders, user friendly protocols
	to treat, 194
Diagnostic decisions, algorithm used for, 237
Diagnostic and Statistical Manual (DSM), 234,
	243
Dialectical behavior therapy (DBT), 10, 216,
	270, 274, 278
Dichotomous thinking, 243
Difficult-to-treat patients, 78
Directiveness, therapist, 138, 144
Disciplined inquiry, 88, 89
Discovery-oriented experiment, 180
Discrepancy, development of, 177
Discreteness assumption, 11
Distress-tolerance skills, 274
Doctoral training programs, 33
Dodo Bird Effect, 133
Dodo verdict, 105, 106, 118, 119, 302
Double approach–avoidance conflict, 174
Doubting, 202
Dream analysis, 112
Drug screens, 282
Drug trial research, 51, 64
DSM, see Diagnostic and Statistical Manual
DSM-IV, 11, 12
	criterion sets, criticism of, 259, 262
	diagnostic criteria, SWAP-200 PD scale
		scores vs., 250
	diagnostic threshold for bulimia nervosa, 19
	ED-NOS category, 17
	mood and anxiety disorders on axis I, 10–11
Dual diagnosis disorders, 104
Dynamic sizing, 95
Dysphoric core, 259
Dysphoric disorders, 58
Dysthymia, 195

E

Eating disorders (ED), 10, 269
Eating symptoms, remission of, 22
EBP, *see* Evidence-based practice
EBPSW, *see* Evidence-Based Practice in
     Social Work
Eclecticism, 60
ED, *see* Eating disorders
EDB, *see* Emotionally driven behaviors
Effectiveness
   distinction between efficacy and, 71
   models, 69
   -RCT model, 41
   research, 70
Efficacy
   model, 69
   principles predictive of, 144, 145
   research, 70, 71, 103
      criticism of, 302
      prototype for, 105
   studies, psychotherapy research and, 302
Efficacy/effectiveness models, 16, 69–71
   efforts to integrate, 73–77
   future prospects, 79–80
   meta-analysis of psychotherapy outcomes,
      77
EFT, *see* Emotion-Focused Therapy
Ehrenreich, Jill T., 191
Emotion(s)
   focused procedures, 149, 176, 180
   -provoking exercises, 203
   regulation strategies, 199
   untriggered, 198
Emotional avoidance, 197, 198–199
Emotional disorders
   problems characterizing, 117
   tripartite model of, 192
Emotional disorders, treatment of, 191–209
   application of unified approach, 200–204
   current treatments, 193–195
   new approach to treatment, 195
   shared factors, 191–193
   unified protocol, 196–200
      antecedent cognitive reappraisal,
         196–198
      emotional avoidance, 198–199
      modifying emotionally driven behaviors,
         200
Emotional engagement, maximizing, 223
Emotional expression, 181
Emotionally driven behaviors (EDB), 195, 196,
      200, 203

Emotional presence, 222–223
Emotional responses, 9, 15, 149
Emotion-Focused Therapy (EFT), 176, 180, 183
Empathy, 159, 162, 221
   accurate, 107
   lack of, 236, 259
   link between theory and, 95
   resistant ambivalence and, 176
   therapeutic change and, 108
Empirically derived treatments, 18
Empirically informed therapies, 78
Empirically supported common factors, 103–129
   common factors approach, 104–106
   different view of common factors, 106–119
      arguments against common factors
         approach, 118–119
      attributions of therapeutic outcome,
         116–117
      catching on of common factors approach,
         117–118
      confronting or facing problems, 112–114
      expectancies of treatment effectiveness,
         110–112
      factors, 106–107
      mastery, 114–116
      summarizing common factors, 117
      therapeutic relationship, 107–110
   EST approach, 103–104
   research, treatment, and training
      implications, 120–121
Empirically supported principles (ESPs), 272
Empirically supported therapies (ESTs), xvii,
      xviii, 5, 8, 31, 103, 270, *see also*
      Empirically supported common
      factors
   alternative approach to, 184
   assumptions, 9
   debates, influence on, 32
   diagnostic entity, 302
   efficacy designs used to identify, 9
   goal of, 37
   limits of, 18–20
   model, assumptions in, 104
   movement
      controversy surrounding, 134
      strongest reaction against, 137
   personality disorders and, 10
   researchers, 15
Empirically validated therapies (EVT), 32, 73
Empty chair technique, 113
Engle, David, 171
Equation modeling, 6, 10
Ersatz treatment, 104

ESPs, *see* Empirically supported principles
ESTs, *see* Empirically supported therapies
Evidence, weighing of, 97
Evidence-based practice (EBP), 4, 33, 211,
    212–214
  clinical utility of, 77–78
  definition of, 90
  dissemination of, 213, 214
  EBP–EST assumption, 14
  essential component of, 5
Evidence-Based Practice in Social Work
    (EBPSW), 71
Evidence-Based Practices for Social Workers,
    71
EVT, *see* Empirically validated therapies
Expectancies, 110, 216, 221
Expectancy, resistance to, 111
Experiment
  controls, 92
  discovery-oriented, 180
  limitations of, 92
Experimenter-generated treatments, 23
Exposure, 107, 112, 134, 136
  dissociation during, 225
  psychodynamic view of, 112
  therapy, 215
    dropout rates, 213
    questions asked during, 224
External validity, 90, 97
Extinction, 113
Eysenck, Hans J., 132

F

Facilitated communication, 136
FDA, *see* U.S. Food and Drug Administration
Fear(s)
  network, 223–224
  unconscious, 112
Feedback, patient, 93, 94
Fixed duration treatments, use of, 35, 36
Flashbacks, 225
Flexibility, maintaining, 216
Fragmentation, 49
Freud, 107, 116
Friedman, Lawrence, 156
Frustration tolerance, low, 217

G

GAD, *see* Generalized anxiety disorder

GAF, *see* Global Assessment of Functioning
    scale
Garbage in, garbage out, 118
Generalized anxiety disorder (GAD), 193, 197,
    202, 204
General neurotic syndrome, 193, 194
Gestalt therapy, 113, 179
Gierlach, Elaine, 131
Global Assessment of Functioning (GAF) scale,
    245
Goals of therapy, 157
Goldfried, Marvin R., 49
Goodness of treatment fit, 140
Graded task assignment, 115
Greenson, Ralph, 156
Grounding techniques, 225
Guide to Treatments that Work, A, 57

H

Hawaii Empirical Basis to Services Task Force,
    79
Healing setting, 105
Healthy functioning index, 245, 246
Heart disease, 3
Hilsenroth, Mark J., 31
Histrionic PD patients, composite description of,
    257–258
HIV-risk behaviors, 179
Hofmann, Stefan G., xvii, 301
Human error, 92
Humanistic treatments, 134
Hybrid model, 38–39, 40, 76
Hypertension, 173
Hypothesis
  confirmatory evidence and, 94
  testing
    assumption, 13, 95
    studies, group comparison and, 160

I

Identity disturbance, 240, 241
Ideological battles, 42
Idiographic data, nomothetic data vs., 87
IEPP, *see* Individual Expressive
    Psychodynamic Psychotherapy
IGP, *see* Interpersonal Group Psychotherapy
Illusory correlation, 93
Imaginal exposure, 225
Immune functioning, 112

Independence assumption, 10
Individual Expressive Psychodynamic
    Psychotherapy (IEPP), 284
In-session microprocesses, 60
Institute of Medicine, report of, 90
Insulin shock therapy, 136
Integration, nonspecific factors, 59
Internal validity, 90, 97
International Society for Traumatic Stress, 212
Interpersonal Group Psychotherapy (IGP), 284
Interpersonal-psychodynamic (IP)
    psychotherapy, 277
Interpersonal skills, 53, 148
Interpersonal therapy (IPT), 10
Intervention(s)
    causation assumption and, 12
    clinical variability in choice of, 9
    cognitive, 15
    courses, 63
    effects, Local Clinical Scientist and, 86
    factor, 21
    framework of, 149
    harmful, 136
    laboratory-derived, 17
    multi-observer assessment of, 41
    outcome and, 16
    -patient matching, 140
    principle-driven, 57–58
    psychodynamic, 22
    research centers, 73–74
    response to, 12
    strategies
        measurement of, 21
        testing of, 7
        theory-based systematization of, 213
    time elapsed between outcome
        measurement and, 271
    trauma survivors and, 219
    two-chair, 55
    universal adoption of, 94
Intrapsychic processes, 262
IP psychotherapy, see Interpersonal-
    psychodynamic psychotherapy
IPT, see Interpersonal therapy
Ironic processes, 175

J

Journal of Abnormal Psychology, 6
Journal of Consulting and Clinical
    Psychology, 6

K

Kernberg, Otto, 275, 276, 277, 284, 290
King, Rodney, 23

L

LCS, see Local Clinical Scientist
LEAD standard, see Longitudinal evaluation
    using all available data standard
Learning-based-behavioral approaches, 107
Learning theory, utility of, 59
Letting go, process of, 165
Levy, Kenneth N., 269
Litz, Brett T., 211
Local Clinical Scientist (LCS), 85–99, 121, 304
    action of, 94–97
    description of, 87
    difference between clinician and, 87
    lessons from social psychology, 91–92
    model, 85–88
    Presidential Task Force, 89–91
    similar approaches, 88–89
    word of caution, 92–94
Longitudinal evaluation using all available data
    (LEAD) standard, 251
Luborsky, Lester, 157

M

Major Depressive Disorder (MDD), 13, 183,
    195, 204
Maladaptive emotion regulation strategies, 199
Malleability assumption, 9
Managed health care, xviii, 3, 270
Manual(s)
    adherence to, 61
    -based treatments, 50
    flexibility offered by, 62, 301
    proliferation of, 51
Manualized therapy
    effectiveness of, 62
    NIMH-funded treatment research and, 51
    RCTs and, 5, 8, 35
    resolving ruptures using, 166
    strict conformity to, 62
Manuals-as-descriptive, manuals-as-
    prescriptive vs., 51
Mass trauma, 147–148
Mastery experiences, 107, 114
Mastery and pleasure technique, 115

Matching principles, 58
MBT, *see* Mentalization-based therapy
MDD, *see* Major Depressive Disorder
Measurement instrument, clinician as, 238
Medicaid programs, 52
Meniere's disease, 110
Mental health, cultural attitudes toward, 3
Mentalization-based therapy (MBT), 283, 287
Meta-analyses, 137, 139
Metacommunication, 160, 161, 163–165
Methodcentric reasoning, empirically
        supported treatment and, 31–47
    effectiveness-RCT model, 41
    hybrid model, 38–39
    limitations of RCT methodology, 33–34
    practice network model, 39
    RCT as method for studying psychotherapy,
        34–38
    role of RCT methodology, 33
MI, *see* Motivational Interviewing
Mindfulness in action, 167
Mindfulness training, 165, 224
Model(s)
    behavioral therapies research, 76
    Boulder, 6
    effectiveness-RCT, 41
    efficacy/effectiveness, 16, 69–71
    efforts to integrate, 73–77
    future prospects, 79–80
    meta-analysis of psychotherapy
        outcomes, 77
    EST, 104
    hybrid, 38–39, 40, 76
    Local Clinical Scientist, 85–88
    Onken/Hybrid Model of Behavioral
        Therapies Research, 79, 301
    practice network, 39
    public health, 74
    RCT, 35
    regulatory, 74
    resistant ambivalence, 172–176
    scientist-practitioner, 88
    therapeutic model of assessment, 109
    three-phase linear progression, 77
    tripartite, 192
Mood disorders
    anxiety disorders and, 192
    CBT for, 73
Motivational Interviewing (MI), 176
    anxiety disorders and, 177
    case illustration, 178–179
    efficacy of, 179
    goal of, 177

    principles of, 177
    resistance and, 226
    rolling with resistance in, 177
    self-efficacy and, 178
Mountain metaphor, 223
Multidimensional meta-analysis, 18

N

Narcissistic personality disorder, 234, 258
NASPR, *see* North American Society for
        Psychotherapy Research
Nathan, Peter E., 69
National Institute for Mental Health (NIMH),
        73, 194
    Clinical Trials and Translation Work Group,
        74
    -funded treatment research, 51
    initiative, 305
    Intervention research centers, 73–74
    process research grants awarded by, 55
    Treatment of Depression Collaborative
        Research Program, 51, 139
National professional organizations, 96
Natural disasters, response to, 147
Naturalistic designs, epitome of, 73
Naturalistic efficacy research, 302
Naturalistic studies
    data collected in, 15
    ESTs and, 270
    findings from, 36
    limitations of, 36
    multi-observer prospective studies, 20
    RCTs and, 73
    relapse and, 10
    therapeutic alliance and, 137
Need gratifying skills, 115
Negatively toned cognitions, 113
Negotiation process, 158
Networks of association, 15
NIMH, *see* National Institute for Mental Health
Nomothetic data, idiographic data vs., 87
Nonperfect behavior, 201
Nonspecific factors, xviii, 59
Nontreatment-related factors, 34
North American Society for Psychotherapy
        Research (NASPR), 57, 141
NOS conditions, *see* Not-otherwise specified
        conditions
No-suicide contracts, 289
Not-otherwise specified (NOS) conditions, 12

O

Obsessive-Compulsive Disorder (OCD), 195, 204, 261
OCD, *see* Obsessive-Compulsive Disorder
Oncologists, research-oriented, 233–234
Ongoing reality testing, 56, 63
Onken/Hybrid Model of Behavioral Therapies Research, 79, 301
Opposite action tendencies, 200
Outcome
  assessments, 70
  equivalence, 119
  measurements, time elapsed between interventions and, 271
  relationship factors and, 136
  research, 50–53, 120
  studies, patient characteristics and, 138

P

Pachankis, John E., 49
PAI, *see* Personality Assessment Inventory
Panic attack, 201
Panic Disorder with Agoraphobia (PDA), 194, 195
Paranoid patients
  characteristics of, 253
  composite description of, 254
  core psychological features shared by, 252
Paranoid personality disorder, 244
Parasuicidality, 283, 286
Parroting, 177
Participants variables, integration of technical interventions, relationship factors, and, 131–153
  integrative approach, 140–150
  applications of principle-based treatments to psychotherapy, 143–146
  framework of intervention, 149
  interpersonal/systemic versus intrapersonal/individual procedures, 149
  prescriptive psychotherapy, 146
  principle-based treatment for treating mass trauma, 147–148
  quality of therapeutic relationship, 148
  task force on empirically supported principles of therapeutic change, 141–143
  thematic/insight-oriented versus symptom/skill building procedures, 149–150
  therapeutic stance and general interpersonal style, 149
  therapist clinical skills, 148–149
  therapist interpersonal skills, 148
  participant factors that work, 137–139
  therapy outcome research, 132–137
  empirically supported treatments or equality of treatments, 132–135
  relationships that work, 137
  technique, relationship, and participant factors debate, 135
  treatments that work, 135–137
Patient(s)
  antisocial PD, composite description of, 256
  approach to, LCS model and, 94
  avoidant PD, composite description of, 260
  borderline PD, composite description of, 256–257
  characteristics, 8, 138
  dependent PD, composite description of, 260–261
  despair of, 163
  feedback, 93, 94
  -focused research, 72, 96, 97
  histrionic PD, composite description of, 257–258
  interventions tailored to, 150
  leap of faith of, 220
  narcissistic PD, composite description of, 258
  obsessive-compulsive PD, composite description of, 261
  paranoid
    characteristics of, 253
    composite description of, 254
    core psychological features shared by, 252
  people pleasing, 227
  prognostic factors, 140
  qualities, rating system, 143
  schizoid PD, composite description of, 254–255
  schizotypal PD, composite description of, 255
  self-disclosure, 211
  self-exploration, 165
  tension between therapist and, 155
  withdrawing, 165
Paul, Gordon, 75, 292
PD, *see* Personality disorder
PDA, *see* Panic Disorder with Agoraphobia
Pennsylvania Psychological Association, 96
People pleasing patients, 227

Perceived control, 197, 198
Personality
    aspects of, 10, 239
    pathology, 11, 237
    research on attributions, 117
    traits, 236
Personality assessment
    application of LCS model to, 85
    methods, structured, 235
Personality Assessment Inventory (PAI), 251
Personality diagnosis, *see also* Shedler-Westen
        Assessment Procedure, personality
        diagnosis with
    borderline personality pathology, 240–243
    case description, 238–240
    problems with clinical data, 238
    reliability and validity, 249–251
    treatment implications, 243–244
Personality disorder (PD), 58, 235
    antisocial, 256, 259
    avoidant, composite description of, 260
    borderline, 93, 104, 200, 214, 256–257, *see
        also* Borderline personality disorder
        treatment, art and science of
    classification of, 263
    conceptual definition of, 262
    dependent, composite description of,
        260–261
    diagnosis, 235, 245
    distinction between personality traits and,
        236
    histrionic, composite description of, 257–258
    identifying core features of, 252
    instruments used to assess, 237
    narcissistic, 234, 258
    obsessive-compulsive, composite
        description of, 261
    paranoid, 244, 253, 254
    personality traits vs., 236
    research, diagnostic gold standard in, 234
    schizoid, composite description of, 254–255
    schizotypal, composite description of, 255
    Score Profile, 246
    Task Force Principles and, 142, 147
    therapeutic change and, 149
Personality Disorders Institute at Cornell
        Medical Center, 271
Phase Model response, 35
Phobias, EDB and, 201
Physiological arousal, 192
Placebo, 110
    controls, 106
    surgery, 110

therapists, 13
treatment, 34, 283–285
Popper, Karl, 13
Positive affect, 192
Posttraumatic stress disorder (PTSD), 62,
        197, 198, 202, 204, 211, *see also*
        Trauma survivors, evidence-based
        treatment of
    borderline personality disorder and, 269
    CBT for, 212
    complex, 214
    DSM model of, 214
    public health costs associated with, 213
    treatment, 216–227
        options, 219
        studies of, 215
PPQ, *see* Psychotherapy Process Q-set
Practice clinics, 75
Practice network model, 39
Practice Research Network (PRN), 75, 96, 304
Pre-post designs, 273–277
Prescriptive psychotherapy, 146
Present-moment safety cues, 225
Presidential Task Force, 89–91, 92
Pretransference focused psychotherapy, 284
Principle-based approach to psychotherapy,
        49–68
    current approach to outcome research, 50–53
    increased interest in principles, 57–59
    principles of change, 55–56
    psychotherapy integration, 59–61
    psychotherapy process research, 53–55
    training, 61–64
Principles of change, 55–56, 117
    hypotheses of, 50
    identification of, 60, 118
    theoretical orientations, 55
    therapeutic relationship and, 303
Principles of Therapeutic Change That Work,
        150
PRN, *see* Practice Research Network
Problem
    confrontation, 107, 112
    -solving techniques, 115
    worst way to address, 23
Procedural knowledge, 15
Process-outcome research, goal of, 54
*Process of Psychotherapy: Empirical
        Foundations and Systems of
        Analysis, The*, 53
Process research, 50, 53–55
    clinical guidance emerging from, 55
    grants, 55

Professional education, 88
Projective identification, 240, 241
Prolonged exposure, 216
Prototype matching, 262
Psychiatric symptoms, evaluating, 39
Psychodynamic clinicians, 36, 94
Psychological First Aid, 147
Psychotherapy
    effectiveness of, 42
    empirical testing of, 304
    integration, 55, 59–61
    interpersonal-psychodynamic, 277
    outcomes, meta-analysis of, 77
    process research, 53
    unspecific and common factors in, xviii
Psychotherapy Process Q-set (PPQ), 12, 17
Psychotherapy Relationships that Work, 57
Psychotherapy research, see also Research,
        efficacy, effectiveness, and clinical
        utility of
    case formulation approach to, 71
    effectiveness-RCT model of, 41
    efficacy studies and, 302
    hybrid model of, 38, 40
    practice network model of, 39
PTSD, see Posttraumatic stress disorder
Public health model, 74
Pure cases, RCT studies and, 36

Q

Q-Sort method, SWAP based on, 239
Quasi-experimental designs, 277–279
Quintessential integrative psychotherapeutic
        factor, 107
Quintessential integrative variable, 156

R

Randomization, 76, 271, 272
Randomized clinical trials (RCTs), 5, 7, 8, 32,
        76, 270
    bulimia nervosa and, 10
    designs, within-cell variability of, 139
    extensively studied treatment in, 270
    funding of, 55
    gold standard of, 32, 33, 50
    impact of clinician effects in, 23
    manualized treatments and, 35
    methodology
        methodcentric reasoning and, 33
        role of, 33

model, appropriateness of for psychotherapy
        research, 41
Prescriptive Therapy, 146
    pros and cons of, 271–272
    research, lack of treatment comparison
        groups, 37
    study of psychotherapy using, 34–38
Rasco, Cristina, 103
Rational emotive therapy, 113, 115
RCTs, see Randomized clinical trials
Reactance phenomenon, 174
Reciprocal inhibition, 113
Regulatory model, 74
Relapse, likelihood of, 116
Relationship factors, see Participants variables,
        integration of technical interventions,
        relationship factors, and
Relationship ruptures, 109
Replication of findings, 70
Research
    clinically informed, 4
    evidence, sources of, 52
    grants, 3
    implications, 120–121
    -informed practices, 143
    judgment, errors in, 5
    outcome, 50–53
    paradigm, limitations of current, 50
    patient-focused, 72, 96, 97
    practice clinics, 75
    process, 50, 53–55
    psychotherapy, 4, 50
    quality of, 3–4
    two-chair approach, 176, 179–180, 182–183
Research, efficacy, effectiveness, and clinical
        utility of, 69–83
    efficacy and effectiveness models, 69–71
    efforts to integrate efficacy and
        effectiveness models, 73–77
    efficacy/effectiveness clinics, 74
    NIMH initiative, 73–74
    Practice Research Network, 74
    stage/hybrid model of behavioral
        therapies research, 76–77
    evidence-based practice, 77–78
    future prospects, 79–80
    history, 71–73
    meta-analyses of psychotherapy outcomes, 77
Researcher, see Partnership,
        clinician–researcher
Residual post-treatment symptomatology, 19
Resistance
    forms of, 226

motivational interviewing and, 226
overcoming, 225
theories of, 171–172
Resistant ambivalence, 171–188
strategies for working with, 176–183
Motivational Interviewing, 177–179
two-chair approach, 179–183
working model of, 172–176
Resolution processes, common themes in, 156
Revictimization experiences, 212
Ritualistic responses, 203
Rogers, Carl, 177
Role-play, 113
awareness-oriented, 167
exercises, 167
Rozin, Paul, 91
Ruiz-Cordell, Karyn D., 155
Rupture(s)
alliance, 175
confrontation, 160
withdrawal, 160, 161

S

Safety behaviors, 201
Safran, Jeremy D., 155
Salters-Pedneault, Kristalyn, 211
SASB, *see* Structural Analysis of Social
Behavior
Schema Focused Therapy, 287
Schizoid PD patients, composite description of,
254–255
Schizophrenia, 3, 136
Schizotypal PD patients, composite description
of, 255
SCID, *see* Structured Clinical Interview for
DSM-IV
Science, 6
Scientific method, 16
Scientific mindedness, 95
Scientist-practitioner model, 88
Scientist-practitioner recommendation, 87
Scott, Lori N., 269
Secondary traumatization, 221
Self-acceptance, 165, 166
Self-blame, 259, 262
Self-care, therapist, 221–222
Self-compassion, 163
Self-correction, 35
Self-critical directives, 175
Self-defeating verbalizations, 113
Self-destructive acts, 281

Self-destructive tendencies, 247
Self-disclosure, 222–223
Self-efficacy, 177, 178, 227
Self-esteem, 215
Self-exploration process, 161, 163, 165, 166
Self perception, 38
Self-reflection, capacity for, 139
Self-report questionnaires, 234, 237
Self-schemas, 173, 175
Seligman, Martin, 72
Selves Questionnaire, 173
Separation, 180
Separation anxiety disorder, 193–194
Sexual assault victims, 222
Shedler, Jonathan, 233
Shedler-Westen Assessment Procedure
(SWAP), personality diagnosis with,
233–268
borderline personality pathology, 240–243
case illustration, 244–249
assessing change in therapy, 248–249
narrative case description, 246–248
PD diagnosis, 245–246
integrating science and practice, 263
problem with clinical data, 238
reason for revising Axis II, 235–238
reliability and validity, 249–251
standard vocabulary for case description,
238–240
toward *DSM-V*, 252–262
antisocial PD, 259
anxious cluster, 259
discussion of empirical findings, 259–262
dramatic cluster, 253
identifying core features of PDs, 252
method, 252
odd cluster, 253
paranoid PD, 253
results, 252
treatment implications, 243–244
Short-term dynamic psychotherapy (STDP), 167
Shoulds, 174
Situational emotional exposure, 203
Slips, analysis of, 112
Social expectations, 94
Social perception, 38
Social phobia, 193–194
Social psychology, 91–92, 117
Social situations, 92
Society for Clinical Psychology, 57
Socratic Questioning, 95
Spider phobic, 117
Splitting, 240, 241, 243

SPT, *see* Supportive psychotherapy
State Medicaid programs, 52
STDP, *see* Short-term dynamic psychotherapy
STEPPS, *see* Systems Training for Emotional
    Predictability and Problem Solving
Sterba, Richard, 156
Stress-related paranoid ideation, 244
Structural Analysis of Social Behavior (SASB),
    54
Structured Clinical Interview for DSM-IV
    (SCID), 244
Structured interview, 234
STS, *see* Systematic Treatment Selection
Stuck-points, 225
Student readings, 63
Substance abuse, 212
    borderline personality disorder and, 269
    disorders, 58, 146, 177
Suicide completion rate, borderline personality
    disorder and, 269
Supportive psychotherapy (SPT), 285
SWAP, *see* Shedler-Westen Assessment
    Procedure, personality diagnosis with
Symptom change measures, 144
Systematic Treatment Selection (STS), 132, 143,
    145
Systems Training for Emotional Predictability
    and Problem Solving (STEPPS), 275

T

Task analysis, 160
Task Force of the Division of Clinical
    Psychology, 73
Task Force on Empirically Based Principles of
    Therapeutic Change, 132, 141, 147
Task Force on Therapeutic Principles that
    Work, 141
Tasks of therapy, 157
TAU, *see* Treatment as usual
Technical interventions, *see* Participants
    variables, integration of technical
    interventions, relationship factors, and
Temperamental risk factor, 192
Template for Developing Guidelines, 90
Terrorist-initiated disasters, response to, 147
Test-retest reliability, 237
Textbook of the future, 64
TFP, *see* Transference-Focused Psychotherapy
Theory-driven techniques, 131
Therapeutic alliance, 212
    anticipation of obstacles to, 219

bond component of, 157
capacity to build, 214
change and, 56, 60, 62, 63
conceptualization of, 158
development of, 139, 155
effectiveness of, 137
healing powers of, 148
identifying potential ruptures in, 54
importance of, 62, 156–157
need for stronger, 218
patient maladaptive beliefs and, 218
as process of negotiation, 158
quality of, 143, 155, 284
ruptures in, 155, 156, 158, *see also* Alliance
    ruptures
strength of, 140
therapist behaviors increasing, 135
variance in outcome and, 108
Therapeutic change, 145, 150
    agreed-upon principles of, 64
    applications of principle-based treatments,
        143
    best agents of, 57
    facilitation of, 149
    factors associated with, 58, 132, 141
    interest in identifying, 55
    model of, 195
    negative consequences on, 137
    patients' previous learning history and, 218
    personality disorder and, 149
    predictor of, 175
    process research and, 53–54
    technique vs. relationship dialogue and, 57
Therapeutic model of assessment (TMA), 109
Therapeutic outcome, attributions of, 107, 116
Therapeutic relationship(s), 15, 54, 106, 131,
        184, 303
    change and, 131
    collaborative exploration of, 164
    dynamics of, 218
    efficacy of, 108
    here-and-now of, 164, 166
    importance of, 176
    maintaining, 148, 215, 218
    negotiation and, 159
    power of, 137
    as principle of change, 303
    problems in, 175
    process observations in, 216
    quality of, 146, 148, 225
    resolving ruptures in, 109
    tension in, 160
    therapeutic change and, 175

therapist characteristics and, 217
Therapist
   behavior, 135
   burnout, 288
   characteristics, 217
   -client communications, 53
   clinical skills, 148–149
   disappointment in, 159
   frustration of beginning, 64
   internal processes, 165–166
   interpersonal skills, 148
   invited in, 178
   self-care, 221–222
   tension between patient and, 155
   thinking, fostering, 63
   training of, 61
Therapy(ies)
   assessing change in, 248
   client-centered, 177, 180, 182, 183
   cognitive analytic, 274
   cognitive processing, 216
   competition among types of, 184
   components of, 54
   dialectical behavior, 216
   empirically informed, 78
   exposure, 213, 215, 220, 224
   gestalt, 113, 179
   goals of, 157
   "how to" aspect of, xix
   manuals
      adherence to, 61
      flexibility offered by, 62
   principle essential to all approaches in, 55, 56
   response to, 58
   Schema Focused, 287
   tasks of, 157
   theories, reasons for not changing from
      different, 172
   trauma, 220, 222
   unstructured management of, 109
   validation, 285
   whole-package, 64
Third-party payers, 52, 64
Threatening issues, 112
Time of assessment, 192
Time-limited therapy, 149
TMA, see Therapeutic model of assessment
Training
   forms of, 63
   implications, 120–121
   LCS model and, 85
   mindfulness, 224
   principle-based, 61–64

Training in and Dissemination of Empirically-
      Validity Psychological Treatments:
      Report and Recommendations, 32
Trait optimism and pessimism, 111
Transference
   analysis of, 112
   -countertransference, 59
Transference-Focused Psychotherapy (TFP),
      275–276
Trauma
   bearing witness to, 221
   contextual factors, 218
   -related memories, 212
   stigmatizing, 227
   therapy, collaborative activities in, 220
Trauma survivors, evidence-based treatment of,
      211–230
   art in treatment of PTSD, 216–227
   bearing witness to trauma, 221
   caveats and cautions, 226–227
   choosing right intervention, 219–220
   imparting confidence and positive
      expectations, 220–221
   maintaining flexibility, 216–217
   maximizing emotional engagement,
      223–225
   overcoming resistance, 225–226
   self-disclosure and emotional presence,
      222–223
   therapist characteristics and therapeutic
      relationship, 217–219
   therapist self-care, 221–222
   complexity matters, 214–216
   evidence-based practices, 212–214
Treatment(s)
   clinically efficacious, 52
   conditions, replication of, 70
   contracts, 288
   credibility, 218, 271
   definition of, 135
   disparity between, 74
   effectiveness, expectancies of, 110, 106
   effects, maximization of, 292
   efficacy factors, 18–19, 106, 282
   empirically validated,73
   equality of, 132
   equivalency of, 136
   ersatz, 104
   fragmented approach to, 49
   humanistic, 134
   implications, 120–121
   inert, 283
   length, 42

manuals, 38, 50, 70, 103–104, 133
    comparison of, 136
    laboratory-derived, 41
    proliferation of, 51
    models, 134
    motivation for, 219
    outcome, patient characteristics and, 138
    packages, over-emphasis on, 136
    principle-based, 143
    qualities, unreliably rated variables, 144
    research, NIMH-funded, 51
    selection, basis of, 136
    stand-alone, 176, 179
    study design, drug-metaphor and, 272
    success, predictor of, 155
    theory-based, 61
    unified, 303
Treatment of choice, 16, 17, 18
Treatment of Depression Collaborative Research
    Program, 139
Treatment evidence, BPD, 272–287
    comparison with alternative treatments,
        285–287
    placebo, 283–285
    pre-post designs, 273–277
    quasi-experimental designs, 277–279
    randomized controlled trials, 279–280
    treatment-as-usual, 280–283
    wait-list control, 280
Treatment as usual (TAU), 13, 104, 111, 120,
        277, 280–283, 302
Tripartite model, 192
Trust, ability to build, 215
Two-chair approach, 55, 176, 179–180, 182–183
    case illustration, 181–182
    initial stage of, 180
    research on, 182
    resolving ambivalence using, 183
Two Disciplines of Scientific Psychology, The, 31
Type I error, 287
Type II error, 118, 287

U

UCS, see Unconditioned stimuli

Unconditioned stimuli (UCS), 215
Unconscious fears, 112
Unconscious processes, 114
Unified protocol (UP), 195, 196–200, 204
    antecedent cognitive reappraisal,
        196–198
    emotional avoidance, 198–199
    modifying emotionally driven behaviors,
        200
Unified treatment approach, 303
University of Michigan, 6
Unobjectionable positive transference, 156
UP, see Unified protocol
User friendliness, 194
U.S. Food and Drug Administration (FDA),
    34, 74
U.S. News and World Report, 5

V

Validation therapy, 285
Validity, proof of, 32
Vanderbilt II Study, 61, 156
Veterans Affairs and Defense, 212
Vicarious traumatization, 221
Victimization, 221, 222

W

Wait-list control, 280
Weinberger, Joel, xvii, 103, 301
Westen, Drew, 3
Whole-package therapies, 64
Wish/need, emergence of, 162
Withdrawal rupture, 160, 161
Working through, 114
Worry behaviors, 201

Z

Zack, Sanno E., 131
Zetzel, Elizabeth, 156